# DAVID HUME:
## PHILOSOPHICAL HISTORIAN

The Library of Liberal Arts

OSKAR PIEST, FOUNDER

# DAVID HUME:
# PHILOSOPHICAL HISTORIAN

Edited, with Introductory Essays, by
**DAVID FATE NORTON**
*Lecturer in Philosophy*
*University of California, San Diego*
and
**RICHARD H. POPKIN**
*Professor of Philosophy*
*University of California, San Diego*

The Library of Liberal Arts
*published by*
THE BOBBS-MERRILL COMPANY, INC.
A Subsidiary of Howard W. Sams & Co., Inc.
*Publishers* • Indianapolis • New York • Kansas City

David Hume: 1711–1776

# Acknowledgments

FIRST AND foremost we wish to thank Professor T. E. Jessop for assisting us in compiling Part II of the Bibliography found below, and for graciously allowing us to print (as Appendix A, p. 413) his compilation of the posthumous English and American editions of *The History of England*. We also wish to thank Mr. Lawrence Clark Powell, Director of the William Andrews Clark Memorial Library, for permission to print from the original proof sheets Hume's "Review of Robert Henry's *History of Great Britain*"; and The Clarendon Press, Oxford, for permission to reprint two letters from *The Letters of David Hume,* edited by J. Y. T. Greig (Oxford, 1932), and two letters from *New Letters of David Hume,* edited by Raymond Klibansky and Ernest Campbell Mossner (Oxford, 1954). Similarly, we gratefully acknowledge the permission granted us by the editors of *Texas Studies in Language and Literature* to reprint the letter of 8 June, 1756, from "New Hume Letters to Lord Elibank, 1748–1776," as it appeared in Volume IV, Number 3 (Autumn 1962) of that journal. We also wish to take this opportunity to thank Miss Betty Duimstra for her assistance in translating Latin phrases and titles, Mrs. Paula Hocks and Mr. Jack Ornstein for their help in preparing the manuscript, and M. Elaine Ross for preparing the Index.

D. F. N.
R. H. P.

# CONTENTS

# Skepticism and the Study of History

IN THE two centuries preceding the publication of David Hume's *History of England*, the attitude of the skeptical thinkers regarding history changed greatly. The skeptics of ancient Greece and the Renaissance found limited value or interest in compilations of historical data; by and large, they saw the achievements of the historians as fables, as poetry, or as lies, providing no serious contribution to the search for truth. However, from the late sixteenth century down to the eighteenth century, skeptics concerned themselves more and more with historical studies. Not only did they question the reliability of historical data and the reasoning processes involved in drawing conclusions about what had happened in the past, they also began to utilize historical studies as a basic form of skeptical argumentation. Some of the problems raised during this transition in skeptical concern, and some of the factors involved in bringing the transition about, were of major importance in developing the theory and methodology of what we now consider historical research. The enormous achievements of Pierre Bayle (1647–1706) and David Hume (1711–1776), both philosophical skeptics and important historians in their day, can, perhaps, be better appreciated when seen as the culminations of this phase of the history of modern skepticism. In this context, too, we may be able to appreciate better the prominence, among the most important writings of these major skeptics, of their major historical works—Bayle's *Historical and Critical Dictionary* and Hume's *History of England*.

At the outset of the Renaissance revival of skepticism, two attitudes toward historical study existed. The first was the evaluation of history as a minor form of knowledge, unworthy of attack. The skeptics treated many of the ancient historians as unreliable reporters of fabulous events. They regarded the type of data collected by these ancient scholars as relatively useless in describing the true or real nature of things. On the other hand, from Sextus Empiricus (*ca.* A.D. 200) to Michel de Montaigne (1533–1592), they employed historical data, often completely uncritically, to undermine confidence in the reliability of theories about any possible subject. Because human beings have disagreed about almost everything and because the theories accepted by the experts at various times have been rejected at later times, doubt could be cast on any given theory. Montaigne, for instance, brought up to date some types of historical materials to attack the achievements of Copernicus, Paracelsus, and others. In order to encourage distrust of certain theories, some skeptics introduced biographical data about the personal and social factors (vanity, fear, hope of reward or advancement, and so on) that led certain persons to espouse those theories. They used the Renaissance interest in the past in a type of skeptical genetic argument intended to dispel confidence in allegedly new discoveries. Pedants attempted to show how unoriginal Copernicus, Galileo, Descartes, and others actually were by pointing to the Greco-Roman and the Judeo-Islamic versions of their theories. Presumably, if these "new" theories had already been advanced in antiquity and in the Moslem Middle Ages, their status as new insights into the real nature of things was open to question.

Skeptical argumentation in one of the basic fields of controversy of the sixteenth and seventeenth centuries, that of religion, intensified and radically altered the use of historical data for skeptical purposes. Some of the fundamental issues in the religious and theological struggles of the Reformation and Counter Reformation involved detailed historical claims and counterclaims. Valla and Erasmus began the challenging of long-accepted historical documents and assertions about the origin and nature of Christianity. The revival of interest in Greek and Hebrew, and the impact of rabbinical and cabalistic literature in Europe in the sixteenth century, brought on further questions about the history and nature of the Christian religion. Radical attacks by Luther, Servetus, Calvin, and others cast doubt on some of the fundamental dogmas of Catholicism. The

Protestants, from the very beginning of their revolt, grounded their case, at least in part, on historical claims. They concerned themselves with the actual Biblical text, with its interpretation by the early Church and its distortion by the later Church, with the transformation of the Church from the Bride of Christ into a malevolent organization hiding crucial religious truths, and so on. Protestant scholars pushed aside the Scholastic method of analyzing and explaining theological points in order to engage in Biblical studies, grounded in philological examination of the texts; they issued historical diatribes about the development of the papacy, schisms, and heresies. Building on the achievements of humanistic savants such as Erasmus, Reuchlin, Colet, and other pre-Reformation reformers, the Protestants centered their arguments, in part, on historical claims, on textual researches, on revived studies of the early Fathers, on St. Augustine, on Jewish commentaries, on obscure medieval controversies, and like materials. In the ensuing battles, a type of skepticism developed that raised fundamental problems of the theory of knowledge with regard to historical materials and their evaluation. Further, a skepticism emerged concerning the very uniqueness and authenticity of the Judeo-Christian tradition and its conception of history. These two factors produced what was called *le pyrrhonisme historique,* historical Pyrrhonism, a doubt about the reliability of all information about the past, and about human ability to learn anything from history.

The Church itself had produced the first historical scholars: Erasmus, Cardinal Aleandro, the great Hebraist, Reuchlin, who introduced Hebrew into European Academia, and others. The Council of Trent tried to hold the line against the Reformation on quasi-historical grounds. It ruled in favor of the Vulgate, St. Jerome's Latin version of the Bible, as *the* authentic text, and argued, to some extent historically, against others. The Masoretic text (the one accepted in Hebrew by the Jews) was rejected as postdating the Vulgate because the Hebrew vowels were added later, and as unreliable because it was probably corrupted by the Jews. The Septuagint (the Greek Old Testament) was rejected because St. Jerome had found it needed correction.

The various Greek texts of the New Testament were rejected because St. Jerome had presumably studied them and, in the Vulgate, had corrected all the errors that had crept in. The Council considered the work of St. Jerome to be inspired, and it rejected all modern researches because dubious materials were employed as correctives to the one authentic text. The fact that all sorts of Chaldean, Syriac, Arabic, late Greek, and other sources had been found was disregarded, in favor of the uniquely privileged status of Jerome's efforts. On interpretative matters, the unanimous consensus of the Fathers and the Councils, rather than the findings of the Reformation scholars, was to be considered as authoritative on who believed what, and when.[1]

Following the Council's attempt to establish a historical position, a counterattack against Protestant historicism was mounted, using what the Catholics called "a new machine of war" to devastate the Reformers. Beginning with Juan Maldonado, the first Jesuit to teach at Paris, and his friend, Gentian Hervet, the secretary to the Cardinal of Lorraine, the Catholics developed a type of skeptical argumentation designed to show that the Protestants, resting their case on the Bible and their personal readings of it, would be reduced to complete doubt about truth in religion. Hervet, in the preface to his Latin translation (1569) of the classic of Greek skepticism, the writings of Sextus Empiricus, contended that the skeptical arguments would destroy Calvinism by showing that nothing could be known, and, therefore, that the claims of the Calvinists could not be established. Maldonado, in his Paris lectures and in his commentary on the Gospel according to St. Matthew, tried to show that the Calvinists, unaided by the Church's teachings and traditions, could not make sense of Scripture and would plunge them into doubt and irreligion, because they could not find its message with any certainty. Among those who used and applied this skeptical attack were St. François de Sales and the Cardinals Bellarmine and Du Perron. St. François de Sales attempted to show that the

[1] On the Reformation and Counter-Reformation controversies about the Bible, see Don Cameron Allen, *The Legend of Noah* (Urbana: University of Illinois Press, 1963), chaps. 1–3.

Calvinists could find no criterion of religious truth or evaluation of Scripture beyond unreliable subjective feelings, and that the Protestants were doomed to doubts about which Protestant was right—Calvin, Luther, Zwingli, etc. He denied that, in the light of this uncertainty, they could possibly find *the* road to salvation.

St. François, and, after him, the Jesuit Fathers Gontery and Veron (the latter was a teacher at La Flèche when Descartes was there), developed this kind of attack into the full-fashioned "new machine of war," blasting away at the historical core of the Reformation. If the Reformers based their case on the Bible, their argument ran: (a) how could one tell indubitably which book is in fact the *Bible;* (b) if that book could be located, how could one tell what it said; and (c) if what it said could be ascertained, how could one tell what to do about it? The traditional skeptical problems about the unreliability of human sense information were used to create difficulties about accepting as certain what is perceived. For example, we may think book X is the Bible, but is it really? What criteria can we appeal to? At each stage in the attack, these Counter Reformers used the skeptical arsenal to force the Protestants back to defending, as the fundamental standards of religious truth, either their subjective feelings about the matter or the questionable opinions of humans such as Calvin. Veron, an expert at this sort of warfare, argued that if one were to manage to locate the Bible, then one would be faced with the problem that all that such a book visibly contains is ink marks on paper. Because human eyesight is imperfect, he pointed out, we may err in our judgment as to what marks we think we see. Next we may err in interpreting the marks as words. We may err in what we judge these alleged words to mean. And then, as the words do not tell us how to interpret them, we may err in inferring conclusions from them. Logical standards are not revealed in Scripture but are human creations of pagans such as Zeno and Aristotle. How can we tell that their standards apply to Revelation, and if they do, that we have applied them correctly? If one appeals to the interpretations of the Fathers, then there are problems as to what the Fathers said, whether they meant what they appeared to have said, whether we interpreted them correctly, and so forth. Because all men are fallible, we may be mistaken at any point in the process of searching for religious truth. Therefore, Veron concludes from all this argumentation that we should accept an infallible judge, the Church, to settle religious questions, rather than rely on fallible man with his fallible faculties.

Some—Pierre Nicole and Pellison, for example—embellished the argument further, pointing out that if fallible man set out to find the truth in the Bible, he would be lost in an infinite process. To find the book in question and to interpret it, man would have to survey all likely books, would have to know all relevant languages, all possibly relevant historical data, and so forth. Without any ultimate or absolute standards, this examination would never stop, for one could never tell if one had, perchance, encountered the truth, and not just something that seemed true to a fallible man.

The embattled Protestants saw "the new machine of war" as a horrendous menace to all rational and scientific inquiry, and especially to all views that relied upon some documentary historical basis. Theologians such as Jean Daillé tried to show the far-reaching effects of this epistemological skepticism when applied to historical data. Developing what they took to be a *reductio ad absurdum* of Veron's kind of argumentation, they showed that the same problems applied to Catholicism. It too rested on documents and testimonies—what the Councils proclaimed, what the pope said, and so on. How could one tell what comprised an accurate report of a Council, what it said, or what it meant? How could one, in fact, tell what Veron said, and what he meant, and whether his views were those of his dotage, or just *juvenilia*? The ultimate in this kind of counterattack was, perhaps, the Calvinist Jean la Placette's work, *Of the Incurable Scepticism of the Church of Rome* (1688), in which he argued that, since all men are fallible save the pope, only the pope can tell who is the pope, and only the pope can tell when he makes an infallibly true pronouncement. Everyone else faces a historical problem: Information about who the pope is and what he has said rests on unreliable sense data and uncertain inferences, dubious reading of documents, and so on. Therefore, according to La Placette, the Catholic Church can have at most one member whose faith is not open to question.[2]

The polemics applying skepticism to the search for religious truth raged all through the seventeenth century, and all sides used the same kinds of arguments to show the unreliability and dubiousness of the religious claims of the others. The arguments laid bare the epistemological problems involved in determining the truth of any historical data, insofar as it, by nature, rested on documents and testimonies. Some of the participants could see the mass historical suicide taking place in this raising and pursuing of skeptical problems. The frenzy went so far that one strange figure, Father Jean Hardouin, challenged the authenticity of all historical writings (with the possible exception of Tacitus), calling them medieval forgeries. Others tried to find some data that could survive the skeptical probing; they sought to establish that monuments, coins, and inscriptions on coins and monuments had a stability and solidity that gave them more reliable status than documents, and that at least the weighty historical residue could be trusted. Others tried to work out "reasonable" standards against all-engulfing historical Pyrrhonism. From Hugo Grotius and William Chillingworth down to John Locke and the early theological leaders of the Royal Society, they tried to establish a kind of historical probabilism, employing the standards that "reasonable," "unprejudiced" men might accept in evaluating conflicting and questionable data. In concert with leading jurists, they tried to establish acceptable rules of evidence and of the reliability of documents and witnesses; and they formulated the now famous criterion of "reasonable doubt." Data and testimony would be acceptable if there was no "reasonable" cause for doubting them, even though there might be theoretical, metaphysical reasons for doubting. Skepticism with regard to historical data might, in theory, lead

[2] For further information about the "machine of war" and the Protestant and Catholic debate on this, see Richard H. Popkin, *The History of Scepticism from Erasmus to Descartes* (New York: The Humanities Press, 1964), chaps. 1 and 4.

to doubts about any alleged fact; but, in practice, by the adoption of "reasonable" criteria, many of these doubts could be set
aside, for no one in his right mind could or did actually take
them seriously.[3]

As scholars were looking for standards and data to fill the
requirements of theology, law, and other historically oriented
disciplines, another strand in the skeptical onslaught against
history was developing—an attack on the accepted historical
framework of the Judeo-Christian world. The attackers did not
challenge the data and, thus, the possible truth value of any
historical data. Rather, they challenged the interpretative assumptions underlying all data about man's past and thereby
transformed the role of historical researches. Throughout the
sixteenth and seventeenth centuries, historical investigation
resulted from religious struggles, as one side tried to show the
injustice of another side's contentions and to vindicate its own
claims. Some historical study was produced during political-
dynastic controversies, as a by-product of attempts to establish
the legitimacy of certain political developments and the illegiti-
macy of others. In the over-all interpretative framework then
accepted by the European intellectual world, the human drama,
as set forth in the historical record, is part of a theodicy. It is a
Providential history, the unfolding of man's relations with God.
In these terms, human history starts with the events in Genesis
and develops from there to its present diverse stages. Its most
crucial events are major experiences in the march from the
Creation to the Redemption and the Last Judgment. The turning points in human history are the Fall, starting the successive
drama, the Flood, the commencement of the particular development leading to contemporary man; the Exodus and the Covenant of Sinai, the beginning of Jewish history and the Mosaic
Dispensation; and the Incarnation, Crucifixion, and Resurrec-
tion, the end of man's developmental religious history. After
the coming of Jesus, human history should be a stage of watch-

[3] This tradition is discussed in Henry G. Van Leeuwen's *The Problem of
Certainty in English Thought, 1630–1690* ("International Archives of the
History of Ideas," Vol. III [The Hague: Martinus Nijhoff, 1963]).

ful waiting and preparation for the Second Coming and ultimate eternal salvation. In a sense, in the Christian theodicy,
historical occurrences from the Crucifixion until the Second
Coming are just the "Divine Comedy." Man can be saved or
damned in this interim world, but no major divine historical
event takes place. The human scene is ultimately meaningless
except for the possibility of salvation and for those happenings
that presage the Second Coming. Who is king of what does not
*really* matter unless this helps set the stage for the next level of
Providential history. Thus, wars against the infidels, conversion
of the Jews, or similar events can be important; but the rest is
essentially a chronicle of man's struggles with temptation.

For seventeenth-century Jews and millenarian Christians, history was still all Providential. Each event was still part of a
divine scheme, each a meaningful sign of God's relations with
man and a possible clue concerning the coming of the Messiah.
Some people of the period wrote court chronicles and annals,
notably of the events of the reign of François I or Charles V.
Jewish historians, however, were interpreting the dynastic struggles, the results of the voyages of exploration, or the economic
developments and crises of Europe, in much the same ways in
which the Biblical authors interpreted developments in ancient
Palestine—as the unfolding of God's relations with man, and as
the struggles of man to live within a divine economy. Renaissance Jewish historians, like their post-Biblical counterparts
up to the Talmudic rabbis, interpreted the dramatic events of
their day, such as the expulsion of the Jews from Spain (1492),
the flourishing of Jewish communities in France, Italy, and
Holland, or the downfall of their persecutors, as signs presaging
the commencement of the Messianic Age.[4] The Spanish medieval theologian, Judah ha-Levi, in his historical work, the *Kuzari*,
set forth the prevailing thesis that Jewish history was the heart
of world history. The last great work in this tradition of Providential history was Rabbi Manasseh ben Israel's *Hope of*

[4] See, for instance, Samuel Usque's sixteenth-century work, *Consolations
for the Tribulations of Israel*, trans. Martin A. Cohen (Philadelphia: Jewish
Publications Society of America, 1965).

*Israel* (1650). In his Preface, Manasseh ben Israel conceived of writing the continuation of Josephus, tracing the history of the Jews up to the mid-seventeenth century. He saw the dramatic developments of Spanish and Portuguese history as all part of the divine scheme. The collapse of Ferdinand's imperial designs, the conquest of Portugal by Spain, the debacle of the Spanish empire, were all parts of God's involvements with the Chosen People, Israel. Time's last great drama was at hand, the placing of the Jews in the four corners of the earth, presaging the millennium. The most famous, or infamous, part of Manasseh's work was his detailed discussion of the evidence that the American Indians are Jews, descendants from the lost tribes. For him, all of this constituted obvious signs that the Messianic Age was imminent in the seventeenth century. Other Jewish and Christian scholars were writing modern European histories showing that God was on their side. Millenarian Protestants joined Jewish writers in seeing the culmination of Judeo-Christian history as being just around the corner, and in preparing for the tragic Messianic drama played by Sabbetai Zevi in 1666.[5] As late as 1688, the Calvinist fanatic, Pierre Jurieu, was interpreting the Glorious Revolution in England as the accomplishment of divine prophecy. In a minor key, Archbishop Ussher, in the 1650's, was portraying all human history as developing from the same historical chronology, starting with the Creation described in Genesis, which he dated at 4004 B.C.

Despite the prevailing assumption that human history was the unfolding and continuation of the divine scheme portrayed in the Bible, Niccolò Machiavelli, without directly challenging the view, set forth a picture of the course of human events independent of divine Providence, showing that the dynamics of human

---

[5] Sabbetai Zevi (1626–1676), a Spanish Jew from Turkey, claimed to be the Messiah and announced the commencement of the Messianic Age in 1666. He had a stupendous effect on Jews and millenarian Christians all over the world at the time. His subsequent conversion to Islam completely demoralized his followers. The novel by Isaac Bashevis Singer, *Satan in Goray* (New York: Noonday Press, 1958), shows the tragic impact of Sabbetai Zevi's career on a small seventeenth-century Jewish community.

affairs could be discussed and analyzed in naturalistic terms. Machiavelli's revolutionary and starkly revealing presentation of man, although often deplored at the time as diabolical, began the interpretation of man's political and social behavior in terms of human forces and foibles alone. Even religious history, as some seventeenth-century theorists saw, could be interpreted apart from its alleged Providential character; it could be interpreted as a political means for keeping societies orderly and moral. Uriel da Costa (1591?–1647), a Jewish heretic in Amsterdam, went so far as to offer the theory that all extant religions were man-made and could and should be understood in terms of human developments, not divine ones.

More fundamental challenges to the Judeo-Christian historical assumptions were attacks on the uniqueness or authenticity of the Bible itself. Throughout the sixteenth and early seventeenth centuries, a wealth of data was found from the ancient world and from the newly discovered lands that did not seem to fit within the framework of Biblical history. While Manasseh ben Israel and Archbishop Ussher worked valiantly to make all of the pieces fit within the framework, a brilliant Frenchman, Isaac la Peyrère (Pereira) (1594–1676), offered the monumental hypothesis that was to shatter the initial assumption of Judeo-Christian history. Pereira, in 1655, published his pre-Adamite hypothesis, namely, that there were men before Adam, and that Biblical history is not the story of the origins of mankind, but only that of the Jews. Starting from internal evidence in Paul's Epistle to the Romans, and from the accounts in Genesis, Pereira burst out of the whole Judeo-Christian framework to introduce the evidence that was to overwhelm such attempts as Ussher's to preserve that framework. Pereira pointed to Chinese, Eskimo, Mexican, and other histories, showing that these cultures had begun many thousand years before 4004 B.C., and that they had developed independently of the events described in Genesis. The Flood, he insisted, must have been a crucial local event in Jewish history, but it was not an event in other independent histories. The Jews were descendants of Noah and his family. The rest of the world had separate and independent beginnings.

Pereira's monumental hypothesis, which was to become a commonplace within a century, was regarded in its day as a most dreadful and blasphemous view, to be repressed at all costs. The book was burned, the author imprisoned; he was released on condition that he apologize personally to the pope. In spite of recantations, and retirement to the pious Oratory, Pereira continued his accumulation of evidence—historical, anthropological, geographical, etc.—to show that Judeo-Christian history was not equivalent to world history. At the same time, he himself advanced a bizarre formulation of Providential history, namely, that the divine scheme involved two Messiahs: one for the Gentiles, who had already come; and one for the Jews, who was about to come. Therefore, he contended, the culmination of local Judeo-Christian history was at hand; it was time for Louis XIV to liberate Jerusalem, and for Jews and Christians to unite and to prepare for the Judeo-Christian Messianic Age and millennium, while the rest of the world went on its independent way.[6]

Almost immediately after Pereira's bombshell, Spinoza set forth his more far-reaching theory, that the Bible is not authentic history, and that all religion can and should be interpreted as an aberrant feature of human natural history. In his *Tractatus-Theologico-Politicus,* published in 1670, but written apparently as a rebuttal to the rabbis who had excommunicated him in 1656, Spinoza challenged many particular points, e.g., whether Moses wrote the Pentateuch. He also challenged the entire Providential picture of the world portrayed in the Bible. Insisting on reason as the sole judge of all matters, religious or scientific, Spinoza developed his theory of the world apart from the entire Judeo-Christian conception of God and his role. In-

6 On Pereira, see D. C. Allen's *Legend of Noah,* chaps. 4 and 6. Pereira's pre-Adamite theory was published in English in 1655, under the title *Men Before Adam.* His Messianic views appear in his early work, *Rappel aux Juifs* (1643). The British Museum has a copy of his suppressed translation and commentary on the Bible (1670) in which Pereira was still gathering evidence to support his pre-Adamite views. His friend and associate, Father Richard Simon, reported he was working on a new version of his *Rappel aux Juifs* at the time of his death.

stead, Spinoza set forth his universe, seen from the aspect of eternity, as a set of unchanging physical and psychological laws, in which human history was a somewhat illusory picture of an aspect of the essentially immutable God or Nature. In such a world, historical religion was to be understood as an effect of human fears and superstitions. In Spinoza's cosmology, religion did not provide the framework for interpreting human history; it was itself just one more item to be studied as part of natural history. It was to be a short step from this naturalistic analysis of religion to Hume's *Natural History of Religion*.

These two streams of skepticism about history—the epistemological attack on the data, and the attack on the Judeo-Christian historical framework—met in the work of Father Richard Simon (1638–1712), the founder of Biblical higher criticism, and that of Pierre Bayle. Simon was a friend and younger colleague of Pereira's at the Oratory. He was the foremost scholar of his day of all Near-Eastern languages, of the history of Judaism and early Christianity, and of the history of the various Biblical texts. After several provocative works on Judaism, on the Eastern Church, and on other similar subjects, Simon in 1678 prepared to publish his monumental effort, *The Critical History of the Old Testament,* a work that was suppressed while being printed. It was written, its author insisted, as the final blow in the skeptical war against Protestantism. If the Protestants were claiming to base their case on the text of the Bible, then Simon was prepared to drown them in a morass of scholarly quicksand. To ascertain what constituted an accurate text of the Bible, he contended, one would need not only to resolve the epistemological problems raised by Veron, but also to resolve a host of historical and philological questions. It would be necessary to examine the current texts, the ones they were based on, and so on, back to the oldest available sources. One would have to decide from among these which might be the most reliable. One would have to determine from these, as well as related historical materials, such as Biblical quotations appearing in the Church Fathers and the rabbinical writers, what might be the "best" texts. But, were these accurate? They were not the original ones, he emphasized, but copies, based on copies, which in turn were based on other copies, and so on, all of which might contain errors. The "best" texts were based upon the findings of critical scholarship, as well as the evaluations and judgments of Simon's contemporaries. Further, when deciding upon a "best" text, the critic would then have the problem of deciding what this text said or meant. Ascertaining this would involve studying languages and attempting to understand ancient usages and meanings. Nobody in the seventeenth century spoke Biblical Hebrew or Greek. They spoke the Hebrew and Greek of their own time, which might contain many variations from ancient versions. To turn back to an earlier literary context, Simon contended, one would have to look into all the background materials available and all the historical clues that might be helpful. Above all, human judgments would have to be made about some matters, such as what is metaphorical or symbolic, in the supposed "original" text; and these judgments might be wrong.[7]

Simon accepted and reinforced most of Spinoza's critical points about the authorship and development of Biblical texts. But he insisted that Spinoza drew the wrong conclusion. Seventeenth-century scholars faced the result of fifteen to thirty centuries of human beings' trying to record, preserve, and interpret the divine Revelation. They had documents that were the effects of various complex developments of various religious movements and social histories. These were not the words of Moses or Jesus, but copies of copies of copies, and so on, by human scribes attempting to record, within their individual fallible limits, what they thought constituted the Word of God. In his *Critical History of the New Testament,* Simon pointed out that the Gospel problem is even more complicated, as Jesus did not tell the Apostles to sit down and write, but rather to go out and

---

[7] On Simon, see Louis I. Bredvold, *The Intellectual Milieu of John Dryden* (Ann Arbor, Mich.: Ann Arbor Paperbacks, 1956), Chap. IV; Paul Hazard, *The European Mind, 1680–1715,* trans. J. Lewis May (Harmondsworth, England: Pelican Books, 1964), Pt. II, chap. 3; and Jean Steinmann, *Richard Simon et les origines de l'exégèse biblique* (Paris: Desclée de Brouiver, 1959).

preach. As a result, the written record developed later, in a language different from that actually spoken by Jesus or the Apostles.

Given this state of affairs, Simon argued that the Protestants were hardly in a position to stand very securely on *the* text of *the* Bible. In fact, he contended, it is doubtful that anyone of his day either possessed an accurate text of the Bible or was in a position to tell precisely what it meant in terms of its original statement when revealed by God. Because of this, fallible man had to have recourse to some infallible authority for guidance, and this was provided by the Church and its traditions.

Not only the Protestants, but also Catholic leaders like Bossuet, quickly denounced Simon's scholarly efforts as the most dangerous kind of historical Pyrrhonism. They pointed out that if men possess no guaranteed Biblical text, then what can revealed religious truth rest on? The type of historical investigation Simon introduced into every aspect of religion would yield only scholarly probabilities, not doctrinal certainties; and each tentative result would have to be further scrutinized and made subject to revision on the basis of further scholarship. Where or when would this scholarly investigation ever stop?

Bossuet, who quickly became Simon's archenemy, insisted that Christianity consisted of a series of dogmas proclaimed by the Church and was not some hypothesis about what early Christians might have said or meant. In addition, Bossuet announced, the textual problem was settled at the Council of Trent, when the Vulgate was declared *the* text. Simon immediately, and throughout the rest of his long scholarly life, pointed out that in order to establish what dogmas the Church holds, what they mean, and so forth, one has to rely on the records. In order to establish in what sense the Vulgate is the "best" text, one has to look at the data. St. Jerome did, Simon contended, exactly what Father Richard Simon was doing. He examined all the varying sources available in his time. He consulted rabbis; he looked into the Church Fathers; he studied the Hebrew text, the Greek text, the earlier Latin translations, as well as many others; and then he offered the Vulgate as the "best" text in terms of what he had found out. The Council of Trent, Simon contended, was not trying to prevent Bible scholarship, but to encourage it. Catholic scholars, from Erasmus to Cardinal Jiménez de Cisneros to Maldonado to Simon, had found difficulties in the Vulgate that could be explained or accounted for by further pious study of other texts and related materials. Catholic schools had given Simon the training in Hebrew, Arabic, Syriac, Greek, etc., and had encouraged his studies. He was only trying, to the best of his ability, to be helpful with an extremely difficult problem, that of ascertaining God's message from the morass of human documents. His studies on the New Testament, the Biblical commentators, the Bible editions and translations, the history of Church practices, and, finally, his own French translation of the New Testament, all pointed up more and more forcefully the problem of discovering past facts with exactitude, even despite the human predicament. The tasks always involved some interpretation and judgment. Because of this, humanistic scholars from Erasmus onward had stressed the need for critical evaluation. One had to judge the merits of sources and the meanings of documents. How could this be done by humans except by means of historical scholarship? The more one engaged in historical investigations, the more one found the problems rather than the answers. Simon's fantastic display of erudition and scholarly techniques revealed, on the historical, rather than the philosophical, plane, the endless character of the search for historical truth. He himself seems to have felt that he was constantly approaching a definite characterization of the "Spirit of the Message," expressed so diversely in so many sources and traditions. He was seeking the common core of Judeo-Christianity that appeared differently in each of the historical expressions. His opponents could see him only as driving them and himself into an infinite regress in the search for historical truth. They could see no way in which his method could end up in anything other than historical Pyrrhonism and a Spinozistic interpretation of the development of Judeo-Christianity; namely, that it was a human effort to discuss religion that can only be interpreted and evaluated in human terms. The connecting link between human historical events and God seemed to recede further and further away, the more Simon revealed the details of the human side of the story. (Two and a half centuries of Simon-like Bible scholarship do not seem to have helped in finding the link but only to have increased the problem while yielding more and more detail about human developments.)

The seventeeth-century culmination of the skeptical concern with history appears in the writings of the great skeptical historian, Pierre Bayle.[8] Bayle was raised on, and lived in, the religious controversies of the time. The son of a persecuted Huguenot minister, Bayle was confronted by the Catholic arguments against Calvinism when he studied at the Catholic University of Toulouse. He became a convert to Catholicism and then a *relaps* back to Calvinism. He fled to Geneva, where he finished his studies, and then taught at Sedan and, later, as a refugee, in Holland. From 1681 onward, when he began publishing, he fought against the Catholics who were denouncing Calvinism; against the fanatic orthodox Calvinists; against the liberal Protestants; and, finally, in his great *Historical and Critical Dictionary*, against almost everyone who had a theory on any theological, philosophical, scientific, or historical subject. Bayle had studied and mastered all of the skeptical techniques for showing the unreliability of human knowledge and claims in any and all intellectual areas. He absorbed the classical skeptical techniques and carried them still further. In his famous article "Pyrrho," Bayle challenged even the ultimate standard of truth

---

[8] On Bayle, see the two recent studies by Elisabeth Labrousse, *Pierre Bayle*, Vol. I, *Du pays de Foix à la cité d'Érasme* ("International Archives of the History of Ideas," Vol. I [The Hague: Martinus Nijhoff, 1963]), and *Pierre Bayle*, Vol. II, *Hétérodoxie et Rigorisme* ("International Archives," Vol. VI [The Hague: Martinus Nijhoff, 1964]); also the collective volume, *Pierre Bayle, le Philosophe de Rotterdam*, ed. Paul Dibon (Amsterdam: Elsevier, 1959); Pierre Bayle, *Historical and Critical Dictionary, Selections*, trans. and ed. Richard H. Popkin, "The Library of Liberal Arts," No. 175 (Indianapolis and New York: The Bobbs-Merrill Company, Inc., 1965). On Bayle's place in seventeenth-century skepticism, see Popkin's article in the Dibon volume, and his essay, "The High Road to Pyrrhonism," *American Philosophical Quarterly*, II (1965), 1–15.

of his time, self-evidence, arguing that a proposition could be self-evident and yet demonstratively false. Throughout the *Dictionary*, Bayle challenged all sorts of contentions, attempting to show that the most rational achievements of mankind always lead to doubts, perplexities, and paradoxes, until reason undermines itself, and man is left intellectually defenseless, unless he abandons reason completely and blindly accepts faith instead. On the theoretical level, Bayle was delighted to attack any proffered theory and to show that intellectual endeavor always constituted "the high road to Pyrrhonism."

In addition to skeptical analysis, Bayle wrote history. It is hard to tell which came first, but by his late twenties Bayle was both a devoted skeptical dialectician and a devoted historical pedant. His notebooks indicate that he had already decided to catalogue all the false and dubious information he found in historical studies and to try to correct it. In his earliest publications, he was impressed that the same data could be used to prove opposite religious theories; that each side could find or invent the documents to prove its case; and that witnesses, including living scholars, were so prejudiced that their testimony was more a tribute to their commitments than to what they had seen or heard. The participants in human history were also the partisans, and they could distort the data to fit their needs and ends. Bayle originally intended the *Dictionary* as a massive antidote to the misuses of historical data, a vast compilation of the errors and lies that abound in the *republic of letters*. He finally reduced the aim of his project to that of correcting and supplementing Louis Moréri's *Dictionary*. What emerged was an enormous but somewhat skewed compendium of man's moral and intellectual world, a document of seven to eight million words. An alleged biographical dictionary, it dealt with either the people misrepresented by Moréri or omitted by him. The heart of Bayle's work is found in the digressive footnotes, exhibiting both his historical and his dialectical sides. With a scholarly acumen worthy of Richard Simon, Bayle sifted through the data concerning Pope Joan's existence and vilified

his Protestant brethren for being so intellectually disreputable
as to have accepted such rubbish. With learned glee, he traced
the Catholic claim that Calvin had been guilty of sodomy. On
all sorts of points, Bayle patiently straightened out the historical
record. He traced back the sources, evaluated their merits,
pointed out misrepresentations and misunderstandings. At the
same time, and often in the same articles, he raised philosophical difficulties indicating that man is really incapable of being
sure about anything. His epistemological skepticism precluded
placing any reliance on human faculties or human conclusions.
He followed Veron, Simon, Nicole, and others in showing the
epistemological impossibility of knowing a past fact with certainty. He also persisted in trying to ascertain what, in fact, had
happened at various times, and in trying to determine how one
ought to go about discovering this. In the final article of the
*Dictionary,* "Zueris," Bayle devoted ten folio pages of notes to
the problems involved in deciding whether or not his opponent,
Pierre Jurieu, had said three days earlier that God commands
us to hate our enemies. Twelve hundred persons had heard him,
and still Jurieu denied he had made the statement. Bayle was
led into an examination of the whole problem of historical evidence and testimony, and of the means by which, in practice,
they can be sensibly evaluated. In the article "Grandier," he
tackled the problem of the evidence about the famous devils of
Loudon; long before Aldous Huxley, he decided that the data
had to be interpreted nonsupernaturally, and, in fact, as origi-
nating in *furor uterinus.* He rejected the "fact," reported in
somebody's annals, that George Buchanan, Montaigne's teacher,
had been arrested for taking part in a Passover seder in Bor-
deaux, on the grounds of the inherent implausibility of such an
event, and its incompatibility with Buchanan's later career.
He cast doubt on the "news" that Calvin had made a trip to
England, on the basis that this did not square with the over-
whelming mass of documentation about Calvin's life. He
showed the dubiousness of the purported fact that Spinoza had
once visited Paris. He analyzed and decimated several theories

about the killers of Henri III; and he offered his own solution
to the mystery of the parentage of Don Juan of Austria (namely,
that he was the son of Charles V and Charles's sister).

In all of these instances and many, many others, Bayle showed
how, in practice, one goes about deciding what is reliable data.
On the theoretical level, nonetheless, he insisted on casting all
in doubt—historical knowledge as well as any other. On this
level, he was the foremost exponent of historical Pyrrhonism.

In general, on the theoretical level, Bayle sought to show that
any attempt at understanding anything always seems to fail.
Even the most rational, and most comprehensive, theory, that
of Spinoza, he turned into a defense of superstition and into
rank irrationalism. But, if the theoretical world is basically unintelligible, to what can one turn? Bayle's answer appears to be,
to Revelation and the human comedy. Unfortunately, he continued, human reason encounters inordinate difficulties in lo-
cating, deciphering, and comprehending Revelation, as the
earlier polemicists had too well revealed. All that we humans
seem able to discover, he contended, all the skeptical difficulties
notwithstanding, is ourselves and our foibles.

Thus, he said, critical history ultimately reveals only the
human comedy. When the record is examined, and the best of
human acumen and ingenuity are applied to the study of man's
accounts of man's achievements, one finds man, naked and
alone. An intelligent, impartial examiner can tell when some-
one is lying or when the records are distorted. Practical standards, which may be theoretically indefensible, can yield the
"best" picture, by separating the lies, the rumors, the errors,
from the facts. Bayle, in practice, was a brilliant scholar for his
day. He lacked the complete erudition of a Simon, a Bishop
Huet, or a Leibniz, but he made up for it with his wit, insight,
and indefatigible search for data.

The human comedy Bayle revealed was man in a non-Provi-
dential world, man independent of a role in a divine scheme.
Spinoza may have presented the metaphysical structure of such
a world. Bayle portrayed it in flesh and blood. His many ob-

scene articles on such Old Testament heroes and heroines as Eve, Abimelech, Sarah, David, and Ham show this. Bayle portrayed the patriarchs and their ladies primarily in terms of their sex lives. As he loudly insisted, no matter how immoral and bawdy his discussions, he was not making it up. He cited chapter and verse (though in the article "Ham" he had to go into farfetched interpretations and commentaries). What he omitted that made his portraits so remarkable, and so shocking for his time, was the Providential dimension. These are not people seen in a divine drama. They are human, all too human; they are like later European royalty, all part of the human comedy.

If the Providential framework was missing, Bayle had substituted for it not chronicles and annals, but an interpretive framework based on human moral failings. History, he asserted (long before Gibbon also said it), is the miseries and misfortunes of mankind; and the fundamental causal factor influencing historical events is located between the navel and the knee.[9] Man, in Bayle's historical cosmos, makes no discernible moral or political progress. The historical study of man, from Biblical and classical times up to the seventeenth century, reveals what human nature is like. This picture is in some ways the final skeptical argument. Any confidence that one might have had in any human achievements was now completely undermined. All the theoretical trappings had been discarded, and scholars were left with man, fallible and failing to examine. The examiners were also fallible and failing, and they used methods that were theoretically indefensible. As they saw how the human race had milled around throughout history, any shred of con-

[9] A typical example of this appears at the beginning of Bayle's article "Henri IV," where he said, "Henri IV, King of France, was one of the greatest Princes recorded in history in recent centuries, and it can be said that if love of woman had allowed him to employ his good qualities to the utmost, he would have surpassed or equalled the heroes who are most admired. If the first time he debauched the daughter or wife of his neighbor, he had been punished in the style of Abelard, he would have become capable of conquering all of Europe, and would have been able to efface the glory of Alexander and the Caesars."

fidence they might have had in humanity was gone. As Bayle kept saying, all one can do is abandon reason and turn to unintelligible, and perhaps undiscoverable, faith.

After Bayle had woven together the various strands of skepticism regarding history and produced a critical historical skepticism, various learned professors tried valiantly to refute his position. But the combination of skepticism about human knowledge, including historical knowledge, and about the Judeo-Christian interpretive framework of human history was not to be easily overcome. Bayle provided what Voltaire called "The Arsenal of the Enlightenment." Part of this arsenal was the historical critique of human rational endeavors; part, the theoretical critique of man's faculties and achievements; and part, the historical presentation of man outside of Providential history.

The legacy of this seventeenth-century transition of skeptics against history to skeptics as historians fell to David Hume. He could take over Bayle's dialectic and use it to decimate rational philosophy. He could then propose to replace philosophy with the "science of man," in which history would serve as the laboratory study. In a thoroughly secularized world, shorn of Bayle's blind faith, the study of man in secular history could become the chief remaining means of evaluating and undermining man's pretensions and achievements. And, since Hume could see above the navel, he could introduce political and psychological factors to interpret the course of man's historical record, and to evaluate his alleged achievements. He could use the sort of practical tools and standards of historical research that Bayle had bequeathed him and the various facets of Bayle's historical Pyrrhonism with them. Hume was able, in a new age largely separated from the religious concerns of the past, to develop a philosophical and historical picture of secular man as the constructive issue of his fundamental skepticism. Bayle's historical world was essentially meaningless, unless one could find and accept faith. Hume's was an attempt, and one of the first, to portray human history as meaningful and comprehensible in its own secular terms, according to a complex of human and natural factors. Whether Hume or later philosophical historians succeeded is still, at least to this observer, open to serious question. Whether we have actually emerged from Bayle's world of doubt to a better understanding of ourselves is not so evident to me as it seems to be to some others. Possibly a re-examination of how we came to see ourselves as the products of natural and secular historical processes may throw much light on some of our present intellectual quandaries.

Richard H. Popkin

La Jolla, California
*July 1965*

# History and Philosophy in Hume's Thought

PERHAPS TO his misfortune, David Hume made important contributions to two fields that are regularly thought to be quite distinct, namely, national history and philosophy. Because these disciplines themselves appear so separate, it is often assumed that there are two distinct sides to Hume's work. As a matter of fact, one such "side" of his work, the historical, is at present greatly neglected—only Hume's devoted biographers and historians of history are sure to mention it. The historians of philosophy will also, sometimes, toward the conclusion of their studies of Hume, find space for a few pages on his monumental *History of England*. But, more often than not, they will interpret this work according to two of Hume's least trustworthy and shortest productions: "Of the Study of History"[1] and "My Own Life." But a study of Hume without a responsible study of Hume the historian must be considered somewhat cavalier if only because over one-half of his published work is to be found in the *History of England,* which was, for at least a hundred years, the standard history of the English nation.[2] Furthermore, it is

1 Reprinted below, pages 35–39.

2 Writing in 1846, Hume's nineteenth-century biographer, John Hill Burton, said that soon after the appearance of the initial volume in 1754, the *History of England* "took the place of a permanent marketable commodity— a sort of necessary of literary life . . . no author or speaker could launch into a defence of monarchical prerogative without triumphantly citing the opinion of Hume;—no friend of any popular cause . . . could appeal to history without condemning his plausible perversions. No season of a debating society has ever ended without the vexed questions he has started being discussed in conjunction with his name. Every newspaper has recorded the editor's opinion of the tendency of Hume's *History*. In reviews and magazines, and political pamphlets, the references laudatory or condemnatory, are still, notwithstanding all that has been done for British history in later times, unceasing; and some books, of no small bulk, have been written, solely against the *History,* as one pamphlet is written against another." (John Hill Burton, *The Life and Correspondence of David Hume* [2 vols.; Edinburgh, 1846], I, 399–400.) For further indications of the *History*'s popularity and importance, see below, Appendix A, p. 413.

not only because of the bulk of the *History* that such treatment is to be decried. Any number of Hume's other works are as much historical as philosophical; and there is a significant sense in which even his most "philosophical" work is historical.

Much effort has been expended in attempts to determine when Hume became interested in history. Was it, as his brief autobiography is thought to suggest, only when, despairing of literary success through other means, he began the *History of England?* The point of this effort is not merely the settling of a biographical question; it concerns rather the very question of the relation of history and philosophy in Hume's work. But the answer does not rest, fortunately, on the date of Hume's decision to write a history of England. It can be demonstrated that history and philosophy are inextricably connected in all of Hume's work. In the first place, both "An Historical Essay on Chivalry and Modern Honour" and what little remains of his notebooks, the earliest of his writings, are clearly concerned with historical matters. The *Treatise of Human Nature* (1739–1740) contains numerous references and allusions, of both a factual and a theoretical nature, to historical matters. The *Essays, Moral and Political* (1741–1742) are similarly marked. And such subsequent writings as the essay "Of Miracles," in the *Enquiry Concerning Human Understanding* (1748), and the *Political Discourses* (1752) make the appearance of the *History of England* (1754–1762) and the *Natural History of Religion* (1757) seem like predictable developments of a mind deeply involved with both history and philosophy.

Furthermore, this involvement does not stop with appending historical references and allusions to philosophical material to form a historical-philosophical mélange. There are logical ties between the historical and philosophical elements of Hume's thought. An obvious instance of such a tie is found in the area of political theory. It has been suggested many times that the claims and reasonings of the political and economic essays are illustrated, even verified, by the *History of England.* Hume himself suggests this line of thought when he says in the *Treatise* that "the study of history confirms the reasonings of true philosophy,"[3] and there is certainly something to be learned from looking to the *History* to confirm the *Treatise* and *Essays*.

For example, Hume had shown in the latter much interest in the contract theory of government—the view that individuals united under a covenant to form the state and then conveyed the power of the state on some governing institution. The view also receives Hume's attention in the *History*, where it is not only seen as a factor in the historical development of England, but also criticized on historical grounds. The Commons in the time of Charles I, Hume notes, established a noble and valuable principle, "that the people are the origin of all just power," and went on to pattern their actions accordingly, declaring that they themselves, "assembled in Parliament, being chosen by the people and representing them, are the supreme authority of the nation."[4] Thus the Commons were unified and strengthened in their resolve, upon finding such a clear basis on which to oppose the king and peers. Hume suggests that the ensuing developments, including the execution of Charles and the establishment of the Commonwealth, are scarcely explicable without the influence of this philosophical view.

But however influential the view, it is, as it happens, "belied by all history and experience." For those who maintain an original contract "between the magistrate and the people," Hume points out, "it happens unluckily" that there are revolutions of government and constitution which are carried on under such chaotic conditions, "with such violence, tumult, and disorder," that the "public voice can scarcely ever be heard"— in fact the opinions of the citizens are less attended to than normally. And although Hume is willing to admit that the Revolution of 1688 was exceptionally orderly, it is clear that he considered that of the 1640's to be far too tumultuous to rest, either in fact or principle, on the "public voice."[5]

---

[3] Bk. III, Pt. II, Sec. X. Because of the many different editions of them, all references to Hume's longer works will be of this form (i.e., to chapter or section). Page numbers in the present volume will also be given when the cited material is reprinted here.

[4] *History of England*, Chap. LIX.

[5] *History of England*, Chap. LXXI.

The *History* can be said, then, to supplement the *Essays*. Many of Hume's political essays, however, do not need supplementation from the *History*. "Of the Original Contract" makes its point without help from the *History* and makes it historically —the whole argument is historical and well documented by historical references. In it Hume allows the contract view the most charitable interpretation he can imagine, then goes on to argue that it is not justified by what we know of any government past or present, that it is not justified by "history or experience." Nearly every government that exists currently, or "of which there remains any record in story," has been "founded on usurpation or conquest or both, without any pretence of a fair consent or voluntary subjection of the people." The political structure of the world undergoes continual change—kingdoms increasing, empires decreasing, colonization, migration: "Is there anything discoverable in all these events but force and violence?"

This general historical argument Hume backs up with specific examples. The republic of Athens, he suggests, was the "most extensive democracy we read of in history," but if we note that women, aliens, and slaves were totally excluded from political affairs, "we shall find that that establishment was not at first made, nor any law ever voted, by a tenth part of those who were found to pay obedience to it." In addition, the Athenians claimed some foreign territories by right of dominion, depriving those peoples of their free choice of government. Finally, the government itself was often corrupt and disordered and failed to give even the few who were citizens a voice in affairs. Henry IV and Henry VII of England, he points out, had no title to the English throne other than that given by the supposed voice of the people, a parliamentary election. Yet they would never acknowledge this fact "lest they should thereby weaken their authority. Strange if the only real foundation of all authority be consent and promise."

Similarly, the Revolution of 1688 is cited. The "establishment" which took place then we must not allow to "deceive us or make us so much in love with a philosophical origin of government as to imagine all others monstrous and irregular"—

that is, even in this case the facts of history are far from corresponding to the detail of the contract theory. It was only a matter of the succession of monarchs, not the entire form of government, that was changed; and it was only a majority of seven hundred who made the decision for nearly ten million people, a majority of whom may have agreed with the decision. But "was the matter left the least to their choice? Was it not justly supposed to be from that moment decided and every man punished who refused to submit to the new sovereign?" Thus, throughout the whole essay, Hume's intention is not to show that the consent of the people is never "one just foundation of government," but to show, on the basis of historical evidence, "that it [i.e., consent] has very seldom had place in any degree, and never almost in its full extent, and that, therefore, some other foundation of government must also be admitted."[6]

In other essays, the procedure is much the same. Whatever view Hume puts forward, he turns to the data of history for evidence and support. In "That Politics may be Reduced to a Science,"[7] for example, it is on the basis of what "historians inform us" that certain maxims of political science may be deduced, while the entire essay "Of the Populousness of Ancient Nations"[8] is an attempt to shed light on an aspect of the ancient-modern controversy by means of careful reading and analysis of a host of ancient historians and other literary sources. Thus, whereas one can say that the *History of England* is tied to Hume's philosophy as an illustration of the political views to be found there, it is equally feasible to say that it was Hume's interest in history that led him to his political views, and that a thorough knowledge of history worked to shape his political views as much as his political views worked to shape his *History of England*.

There is another less obvious but more basic tie between

[6] "Of the Original Contract," in *David Hume's Political Essays*, ed. Charles W. Hendel, "The Library of Liberal Arts," No. 34 (New York: The Liberal Arts Press, Inc., 1953), pp. 43–63. See especially pp. 48–54.

[7] *David Hume's Political Essays*, pp. 12–23.

[8] Abriged version reprinted below, pp. 77–108.

history and philosophy in Hume: they are unified in his thought by means of his skepticism. What appear to be historical interests *and* philosophical interests are simply different aspects of the same over-all philosophical skepticism. In the first place, philosophical skepticism has been traditionally associated with a kind of history, a history on which the cogency of the skeptical claims about the weakness and fallibility of the human mind depend. Thus one finds many skeptics compiling a history of human opinion, a history that is something of a blend of comparative anthropology and the history of ideas. The point of such a history is to reveal the multiplicity of man's opinions as well as something about his nature—what his ideas are and how he comes to hold them and to hold them as true. In some ways, though he seems to have seen himself as undertaking an entirely new enterprise, the goal that Hume set for himself at the beginning of his career is an extension of this traditional skeptical enterprise. He introduces refinements along further skeptical lines, or, what is the same thing, along scientific lines according to Hume's understanding of science. For Hume, the method and nature of science were represented by Newton, and Newton's scientific work was widely seen, perhaps even by Newton himself, to be within the skeptical tradition and to be a form of skepticism.[9]

According to this kind of skepticism, complete certainty regarding the essential nature of reality seemed beyond the grasp of human faculties. It did seem, however, that an adequate level of certainty could be obtained with regard to appearances, or the phenomena of daily experience. Man's seemingly inherent inability to discover metaphysical truth was not to be taken as a reason for giving up all intellectual endeavor. One could fix one's attention upon the phenomena of experience in an effort to discover their relation to one another, and could also

[9] For a discussion of the relation of skepticism and the science of the Royal Society, including the work of Newton, see Henry G. Van Leeuwen, *The Problem of Certainty in English Thought, 1630–1690,* "International Archives of the History of Ideas," Vol. III (The Hague: Martinus Nijhoff, 1963).

try to express these relations in terms of rules or maxims that ranged from the merely probable to the morally certain. "Science" was apparently a term applied to any systematic attempt to achieve this kind of limited, probable truth. By the time Hume wrote the *Treatise,* some such constructive skepticism had been under discussion in England for over a century; and there is good reason to believe that it was this view of science that Hume had in mind when he undertook to establish on an experimental basis the "science of man."

The point of prime concern here, however, is not merely that Hume's science of man is skeptically based, but that, like other skeptics' inquiries into man's nature and opinions, it is also historically based. After pointing out in the Introduction of the *Treatise* that "reflection and premeditation would so disturb the operation of my natural principles, as must render it impossible to form any just conclusion from the phaenomeon," he goes on to say that:

> We must therefore glean up our experiments in this science from a cautious observation of human life, and take them as they appear in the common course of the world, by men's behaviour in company, in affairs, and in their pleasures. Where experiments of this kind are judiciously collected and compared, we may hope to establish on them a science, which will not be inferior in certainty, and will be much superior in utility to any other of human comprehension.

"A cautious observation of human life"—is there any way in which such observation might be carried out and yet not be historical? Granted, of course, the results need not necessarily take the form of a national history or a natural history of religion; but observation of human life, if the data of that observation are preserved, will result in what might be called a *Liber de gestis humanis,* a *Book of Human Deeds* or *Annals of the Human Race.* The body of Hume's work may be aptly considered a compendium of this sort. It begins with Book I of the *Treatise,* where the sources of our ideas and opinions are sought and where human "knowledge" is explained by what Locke called the "historical, plain method." Here what a man thinks and believes is explained in terms of his and his fellow man's experience, in terms of human history. From this starting point in the "history of ideas," so to speak, Hume went on, in the course of a life's work, to add to his "annals" many more chapters on many more subjects.

If, on the one hand, Hume set out to develop along the lines of constructive skepticism a historical science of man, then on the other he found himself involved in precisely the same skeptical problems that the new skeptical science was supposed to circumvent. He was faced with deciding what was appearance and what was reality, though now as concerned the past. To complete his science of man Hume needed a means of determining which statements about human experience were veridical. But in the science of man as much as in purely speculative metaphysics, a criterion of truth appears to be lacking, so that custom and education, one's personal experiences, play an overriding, though logically indefensible, part in the formation of the judgments and claims making up that science—just as the skeptics had claimed they did in the formation of man's speculative theories.

Hume was not unaware of this problem. There are scattered throughout his works a number of remarks that, if taken alone, would surely lead one to suppose that he was as skeptical about history as he was about metaphysics; that he was a historical skeptic who, contrary to fact, would expect very little from history and who would certainly not write it. In the first place, Hume points out that the study of the past is inherently difficult, for, when the object of thought is in the past, "the progression of the thought in passing to it from the present is contrary to nature, as proceeding from one point of time to that which is preceding, and from that to another preceding, in opposition to the natural course of succession."[10] And there are also further, more specific difficulties that Hume finds to be undermining the historian's quest for knowledge of the past. At least one of the objects of his study, human society, is a very

10 *Treatise*, Bk. II, Pt. III, Sec. VIII.

complex phenomenon that "admits not of any great accuracy," whereas, at the same time, the impact made upon the mind by past events is nothing like that of present ones.[11] This lightened quality makes them, one must assume, much more difficult to apprehend. It is equally troublesome that historical facts must somehow be passed down to the present. Such a fact, "while it passes by oral tradition from eyewitnesses, is disguised in every successive narration," until it comes to have very little, if any, resemblance to the "original truth on which it was founded." Men have frail memories, they love to elaborate and exaggerate, they are notably careless.[12] The advent of books and writings has improved the situation somewhat, but one cannot rely on them to any great extent. Ancient authors "are often improbable and never consistent,"[13] later documents are often forgeries or inaccurate for other reasons,[14] and even modern histories are little better: "I am convinced," Hume says, "that the History of England has never yet been written, not only for style, which is notorious to all the world, but also for matter; such is the ignorance and partiality of all our historians."[15] Finally, we have also a tendency to be overcredulous of the claims and accounts of our fellow men, "a remarkable propensity to believe whatever is reported," particularly concerning the unusual. The words used in these reports have an "intimate connection" with certain ideas in the mind, which have in turn a "connexion

[11] *Treatise*, Bk. III, Pt. II, Sec. III. "Any considerable space of time," Hume says, "sets objects at such a distance, that they seem, in a manner, to lose their reality, and have as little influence on the mind, as if they had never been in being. A man's title which is clear and certain at present, will seem obscure and doubtful fifty years hence, even tho' the facts, on which it is founded, shou'd be prov'd with the greatest evidence and certainty. The same facts have not the same influence after so long an interval of time."

[12] *The Natural History of Religion*, Sec. I.

[13] *History of England*, Chap. XII.

[14] See, for example, Hume's discussion of the Casket Letters (*History of England*, Chap. XXIX, pp. 184–192), and his remark about them cited just below p. xlii.

[15] Letter to James Oswald of Dunnikier, *The Letters of David Hume*, ed. J. Y. T. Greig, 2 vols. (Oxford: Clarendon Press, 1932), Letter 86, I, 179.

with the facts or objects, which they represent." It is because of this resemblance between ideas and facts that we give more assent to reports than is justified by our experience of their veracity; the "testimony of men" points out its causes, the facts (presumably) causing the ideas, directly. "No wonder, therefore, we are so rash in drawing our inferences from it."[16]

A working historian, particularly one who strives to convert his results into a science of man, would need to face these difficulties and to find some way of solving them. He would need some method that would enable him to determine just what the facts of history were. In this respect, Hume's historical skepticism seems to have had an effect on his positive historical contributions, namely, that of forcing him to see the need of a critical method in historical research. Hume does utilize such a method, and, though it cannot be said that he ever makes it fully explicit, it is possible to outline certain aspects of it in some detail. This we can do because Hume, when faced with making a decision on historical issues, particularly controversial ones, considers the issues in the light of several kinds of evidence that is evaluated according to more or less regular standards.

Even a hasty perusal of his work discloses that Hume reaches his conclusions by consideration of evidence offered by geographical fact, documents, laws, records, journals, secondary authorities, the present state of affairs, and even by silence.[17]

---

[16] *Treatise*, Bk. I, Pt. III, Sec. IX, p. 7. In the same place, Hume also says: "No weakness of human nature is more universal and conspicuous than what we commonly call Credulity, or a too easy faith in the testimony of others. . . ."

[17] These last two may need some explanation. The claim that Hume relies on the present state of affairs to determine past fact means simply that he counts as evidence of this or that past fact some present fact, as, for example, in Chapter I of the *History* he considers the present names of Scottish towns, lakes, etc., as an indication of the identity of the early inhabitants of Scotland. The claim that he relies on silence means that, e.g., he often takes as evidence that a practice was widely accepted, the fact that no one found the practice remarkable enough to note or object to, or as evidence that some very unusual event did not happen (as later claimed) the fact that no contemporary of the alleged event mentions it.

Most of these items offer evidence that falls under the general heading of "written testimony." In assessing the evidence offered by such testimony, Hume follows two lines of critical analysis. He knows that the very documents that offer the evidence must be put to a test, for such documents can be the source of error as well as of truth. With regard to the famous Casket Letters, for example, he says, "it is material to examine the Authenticity of the Letters; both, because, if genuine, they fix her Character [that of Mary Queen of Scots] beyond controversy, and if forg'd, they determine that of her Adversarys. . . . But unhappily, this Fact, which ought to end all Controversy, becomes the Source of fresh dispute." This means that first of all one must attempt to authenticate the documents from which evidence is to be drawn, a task that must be pursued with the same care and elaboration as that which is required for the subsequent determination of the facts to which the documents give evidence. Thus Hume approaches the documents of history with such critical questions as the following:

1. Is the handwriting or style that of the supposed writer?

2. Was the document considered to be by the alleged writer by his contemporaries, particularly by those who were relatively unbiased in the matters at hand?

3. If the documents are letters, are they natural, particular, and open to interpretation? Or do they appear to have been written merely for the sake of proving the point in question? If the latter, they may well be forgeries.

4. Are there any interested parties who might have forged the documents? If so, are their reasons for doing so greater than the risk they would run?

5. Can the possessor of the document give some credible account of how he obtained it; or, in the case of ancient materials, is there some credible account of how they survived at all? Are any other materials known to have survived in the same fashion?

6. Have the documents been made available to the public, or to some portion of it, for inspection?

7. Is the document chronologically consistent, or does it contain anachronisms? Does its style, character, and content corre-

spond to what we otherwise know of the period (or similar periods) of its supposed composition?[18]

Some documents will pass these critical tests, and, of course, some sorts of written testimony are not subject to them. But having satisfied oneself on the matter of the authenticity of the written material itself, one must still evaluate the testimony that it gives. Here again, Hume approaches the material with critical questions:

1. Is the testimony that is given a first-hand account?

2. Does the witness have any strong bias or interest that is likely to have influenced his opinion? "The wise," Hume says, "lend a very academic faith to every report which favours the passion of the reporter; whether it magnifies his country, his family, or himself, or in any other way strikes in with his natural inclinations and propensities."[19] At the same time, Hume gives particular weight to testimony that is contrary to the witness' interest.

3. Is the witness known to have been honest or dishonest in other cases, or to have a reputation for honesty or dishonesty?

4. Was the view of the witness accepted as correct by other eyewitnesses or contemporaries, or was it freely acknowledged correct by anyone who was cast in a bad light by it?

5. Is the testimony delivered in a manner that lends credibility to it? Is it offered in a straightforward discourse (rather than in a poetic or humorous one)? Is it given without undue hesitation or protestation? "We entertain a suspicion concerning any matter of fact, when the witnesses...deliver their testimony with hesitation, or, on the contrary, with too violent asseverations."[20]

6. Is the testimony credible? Are the events it allegedly reports reasonable and in conformity with nature?

Unfortunately, however helpful and systematic these critical

[18] For examples of questions like these and their answers, see the *History of England*, Chap. XXIX, notes 126 and 133, pp. 186–192, and "Of the Poems of Ossian," pp. 389–400.

[19] *An Enquiry Concerning Human Understanding*, Sec. X, "Of Miracles," pp. 71–72. This section is hereafter cited as "Of Miracles."

[20] "Of Miracles," p. 58.

xliv DAVID HUME: PHILOSOPHICAL HISTORIAN

questions appear, they do not, I believe, provide a satisfactory means for choosing between competing testimony and evidence. The difficulty lies in the fact that there is still no external or shared standard by which evidence can be evaluated. In brief, for Hume the assessment of evidence must necessarily remain, despite these apparent attempts to work by a general method, a matter of personal opinion and prior decision. This, I believe, is the proper interpretation of his most extended treatment of the problem of conflicting evidence, the essay "Of Miracles."

After some introductory remarks on the purpose of this essay, Hume begins his argument: "Though experience be our only guide in reasoning concerning matters of fact, it must be acknowledged that this guide is not altogether infallible, but in some cases is apt to lead us into errors." We are led by experience of our climate to expect any week in June to provide better weather than a week in December, but a contrary instance may very well take place—though if it does, we "would have no cause to complain of experience, because it commonly informs us beforehand of the uncertainty, by that contrariety of events which we may learn from a diligent observation." By this "diligent observation" we learn that from certain causes certain effects invariably follow, from other causes effects follow with varying degrees of reliability, "so that, in our reasonings concerning matter of fact, there are all imaginable degrees of assurance, from the highest certainty to the lowest species of moral [pragmatic] evidence." For this reason, Hume continues:

A wise man . . . proportions his belief to the evidence. In such conclusions as are founded on an infallible experience, he expects the event with the last degree of assurance and regards his past experience as a full *proof* of the future existence of that event. In other cases, he proceeds with more caution: He weighs the opposite experiments: He considers which side is supported by the greater number of experiments: To that side he inclines, with doubt and hesitation; and when at last he fixes his judgment, the evidence exceeds not what we properly call *probability*. All probability, then, supposes an opposition of experiments and observations, where the one side is found to overbalance the other, and to produce a degree of evidence, proportioned to the superiority. A hundred instances or experiments on one side, and fifty on another, afford a doubtful expectation of any event; though a hundred uniform experiments, with only one that is contradictory, reasonably beget a pretty strong degree of assurance. In all cases, we must balance the opposite experiments, where they are opposite, and deduct the smaller number from the greater, in order to know the exact force of the superior evidence.[21]

So far, however, Hume is only emphasizing the easy side of the matter, the computation of the relative strength of the evidence. He turns immediately, though, to the more difficult problem: what evidence is to count in the computation.[22] We not only generally rely on one species of evidence, "the testimony of men, and the reports of eye-witnesses and spectators," but it is "necessary to human life" that we do so. Nevertheless, it is to be pointed out that our reliance on this sort of evidence rests on no other foundation than our "observation of the veracity of human testimony, and of the usual conformity of facts to the reports of witnesses." The key word here is "usual," for we must not suppose that the conjunction of human testimony to the facts attested is perfect—our inference from testimony to facts is itself "founded merely on our experience of their constant and regular conjunction."[23] But whereas we may learn by experience that the human memory is to some degree reliable, and that man has both an "inclination to truth" and a sense of the shame involved in being detected in falsehood, such experience shows only that testimony is generally reliable. Furthermore, because we also learn by experience that there are in man a number of pernicious traits, a tendency to be biased and a

---

21 "Of Miracles," p. 56.

22 Later in the essay, Hume points out just how thorny this problem is: "I need not mention the difficulty of detecting a falsehood in any private or even public history. . . . Even a court of judicature, with all the authority, accuracy, and judgment, which they can employ, find themselves often at a loss to distinguish between truth and falsehood in the most recent actions." (p. 72.)

23 P. 57.

love of the marvelous, among others, we can only conclude that not all evidence or testimony can be taken at face value.

How then does one decide which testimony to accept? Hume's answer is this: "There are a number of circumstances to be taken into consideration in all judgments of this kind [i.e., of the connection between any testimony and the facts it attests]; and the ultimate standard, by which we determine all disputes, that may arise concerning them, is always derived from experience and observation."[24] But if this answer is not to be patently circular when historical questions are at issue—if it is not to be a claim that we settle disputing claims about the past by reference to the past—it must be that by "experience" Hume here means *personal* or *individual* experience, and that one evaluates evidence attesting to certain facts or events according to one's own observation and experience of similar facts or events. That he did mean only such limited, individual experience seems clear enough at the end of Part I of the essay:

> When any one tells me, that he saw [for example] a dead man restored to life, *I* immediately consider with *myself,* whether it be more probable, that this person should either deceive or be deceived, or that the fact, which he relates, should really have happened. *I* weigh the one miracle against the other; and according to the superiority, which *I* discover, *I* pronounce *my* decision, and always reject the greater miracle. If the falsehood of his testimony would be more miraculous, than the event which he relates; then, and not till then, can he pretend to command *my belief or opinion.*[25]

And if this passage leaves any room for doubting that Hume means that individual experience is our final standard, then the letter to Hugh Blair in which he discusses "Of Miracles" surely does not: "No man can have any other experience but his own. The experience of others becomes his only by the credit which he gives to their testimony; which proceeds from his own experience of human nature."[26]

24 P. 57.

25 P. 61. Italics added.

26 Part of this letter is reprinted below, pp. 402–404. See also *Enquiry,* Sec. VIII, "Of Liberty and Necessity," pp. 53–54, where "experience" seems to be used in just the way suggested here.

Seen in the present perspective (there are others—an analysis of Hume's religious views, for example), the remainder of the essay on miracles is, as Hume himself suggests, a case study in which these general conclusions are illustrated. The subject of miracles seems to have been chosen because it represents a clear instance of the necessity of deciding on the basis of one's own experience alone, and even before hearing it, what evidence to count and what to discount. Thus Hume suggests that:

> In order to encrease the probability against the testimony of witnesses, let us suppose, that the fact, which they affirm, instead of being only marvellous, is really miraculous; and suppose also, that the testimony, considered apart and in itself, amounts to an entire proof; in that case, there is proof against proof, of which the strongest must prevail, but still with a diminution of its force, in proportion to that of its antagonist.[27]

In Part II of the essay, Hume goes on to give the reasons for discounting the evidence of miracles that his experience and observation have taught him: the regularity of nature; man's love of the marvelous; the fact that far the greater number of miracles are reported from barbarous and ignorant nations; the opposition of miracles said to establish the truth of one religious view by those said to establish the truth of a contradictory view—these things and others are factors in Hume's conclusion "that the knavery and folly of men are such common phaenomena, that I should rather believe the most extraordinary events to arise from their concurrence" than admit even of any very remarkable natural phenomenon having occurred at some time in the past; they are also factors in his decision to "form a general resolution never to lend any attention to" the testimony for religious miracles.[28] Thus the crucial point seems to be a matter of prior decision. Our choice is between rejecting the evidence on the one hand, or taking it seriously on the other. Those who reject it will find there is "proof" against any miracle; those who accept it will find that there are miracles that are at least

27 P. 59.
28 Pp. 74–75.

probable, and some for which the evidence may amount to a full proof.[29] The fact is, however, at least in Hume's opinion, that such a choice must be made, and that it will be made according to our own experience.

Looking back, then, at the critical questions Hume utilized, we can see that even they are deeply impregnated with this personal element. True, they require a searching analysis of the document or testimony before us. All too often, however, words creep in whose use belies a prior commitment to a more or less fixed point of view—words such as "natural" or "credible," "reasonable" or "consistent"—words whose use reveals that even with his critical apparatus, Hume's evaluations of evidence were in the last analysis not scientific, but, to put it somewhat naïvely, subjective. They were not scientific because they rested solely, as Hume himself tells us they must, on his own personal experience, because his own unique background and biases, no more and no less, determined which direction these evaluations would take.

Hume's critical method, and with it, the science of man, failed, failed as he surely suggests all enterprises conceived after his model must fail. A science of man must "glean up" observations from a wide range of human experience. It must have information that only some form of historical knowledge can provide. But to his own credit as well as misfortune, Hume found that the very data on which he intended to rely were themselves problematic, and, more importantly, that the "science of history" by which one could separate good data from bad was in fact no science at all, but at best a mere reflection of each historian's personal experience, or, perhaps even more accurately, personal opinion. One needed to know facts about

---

[29] This seems to be the point of Hume's remark, also in the letter (Sec. IV) to Blair: "Does a man of sense run after every silly tale of witches or hobgoblins or fairies, and canvass particularly the evidence? I never knew any one, that examined and deliberated about nonsense who did not believe it before the end of his inquiries." That is to say, if one decides to attend to the evidence, one will end up believing it; Hume chose not to attend to it, and therefore ended up not believing it.

the past to find out "the springs and principles" of the human mind; but one had, at the same time, to decide what these springs and principles were in order to reach a decision, and even then only a strictly personal decision, as to what the facts were. The process is almost, but not quite, circular—it is insular; that is, it results in insularity and a failure to establish the common ground that we regularly take to be a necessary condition of a genuine science. Thus, though Hume never stopped trying to gather data and to produce a science of man, he did, as I think we have seen here, recognize and describe the most critical problem which that science faced. I do not believe that Hume found, or even thought that he had found, a satisfactory solution to this problem.

It may seem that we have come at last to the end of the line, that we have found at last where Hume's historical work becomes a *non sequitur* of his philosophical work. Hume himself, it has just been argued, shows that a science of man is not possible. Does not then his philosophy contradict, so to speak, his history? Does not his philosophy tell him that his historical efforts are doomed and to be abandoned because of the inevitable failure that awaits them? Doomed, perhaps, but not to be abandoned. Man must always, Hume goes on to say, act and choose. He not only thought, as apparently all skeptics have, that man must unavoidably believe in and participate in the world of appearances, but also that one who concerns himself with intellectual matters cannot refrain from forming and believing opinions about these matters. "Nature by an absolute and uncontroulable necessity has," he says, "determin'd us to judge as well as to breathe and feel."[30] If this, itself a historical-philosophical conclusion, is correct, then Hume was "determin'd," from the moment of his first interest, to make historical judgments and to continue doing so, even though these would always fall short of the judgments the hoped-for science of man demanded. Furthermore, from what has been said here, it appears that Hume "failed" as a philosopher because he failed as a

[30] *Treatise*, Bk. I, Pt. IV, Sec. I.

historian. Given his goal, an experimentally based science of man, it is just the failure to resolve in a satisfactory manner the problematic character of the data on which his science rested that leads to his philosophical failure—the first failure made the second inevitable. In other words, it may very well be that the most vexing problem Hume ever faced was that of finding out what the historical data were; because he failed to solve it, his philosophy collapsed into mere opinion. If this is the case, then it, too, indicates that history and philosophy are in Hume's thought inextricably bound together.

David Fate Norton

La Jolla, California
*July 1965*

# Selected Bibliography

## I. BACKGROUND STUDIES

ALLEN, DON CAMERON. *The Legend of Noah*. Urbana: University of Illinois Press, 1963.

BECKER, CARL L. *The Heavenly City of the Eighteenth-Century Philosophers*. New Haven: Yale Paperbacks, 1950.

BREDVOLD, LOUIS I. *The Intellectual Milieu of John Dryden*. Ann Arbor, Mich.: Ann Arbor Paperbacks, 1956.

CASSIRER, ERNST. *The Philosophy of the Enlightenment*. Translated by FRITZ C. A. KOELLN and JAMES P. PETTEGROVE. Boston: Beacon Paperback Series, 1955.

CROCKER, LESTER G. *An Age of Crisis: Man and World in Eighteenth Century French Thought*. Baltimore: The Johns Hopkins University Press, 1959.

HAZARD, PAUL. *The European Mind, 1680–1715*. Translated by J. LEWIS MAY. Harmondsworth, England: Pelican Books, 1964.

POPKIN, RICHARD H. *The History of Scepticism from Erasmus to Descartes*. Assen, the Netherlands: Van Gorcum & Co., 1960; New York: The Humanities Press, 1964.

STEPHEN, SIR LESLIE. *History of English Thought in the Eighteenth Century*. New York: Peter Smith, 1949.

THOMPSON, JAMES WESTFALL, with the collaboration of HOLM, BERNARD J. *A History of Historical Writing*. New York: The Macmillan Company, 1962.

VAN LEEUWEN, HENRY G. *The Problem of Certainty in English Thought, 1630–1690*. "International Archives of the History of Ideas," Vol. III. The Hague: Martinus Nijhoff, 1963.

## II. HUME'S WORKS AND LETTERS

*A Treatise of Human Nature,* Books I and II (1739) and Book III (1740).

*An Abstract of a Treatise of Human Nature* (1740).

*Essays, Moral and Political* (Vol. I: 1741; Vol. II: 1742; Vol. III: 1748).

*An Enquiry Concerning Human Understanding* (1748; originally published as *Philosophical Essays Concerning Human Understanding*).

*An Enquiry Concerning the Principles of Morals* (1751).

*Political Discourses* (1752).

*The History of Great Britain.* Vol. I, *Containing the Reigns of James I and Charles I* (1754; reprinted, 1755; second edition, 1759).

*The History of Great Britain.* Vol. II, *Containing the Commonwealth, and the Reigns of Charles II and James II* (1757; second edition, 1759).

*Four Dissertations:* "Natural History of Religion"; "Of the Passions"; "Of Tragedy"; "Of the Standard of Taste" (1757).

*The History of England, under the House of Tudor. Comprehending the Reigns of K. Henry VII, K. Henry VIII, K. Edward VI, Q. Mary, and Q. Elizabeth. . . .* In two volumes. (1759; reprinted, 1764).

*The History of England, from the Invasion of Julius Caesar to the Accession of Henry VII* (1762).

*The History of England, from the Invasion of Julius Caesar to the Revolution in 1688.* In six volumes. A new edition corrected (1762; new editions, 1763, 1778; reprints, 1767, 1770, 1772, 1773).

"My Own Life" (1777).

*Dialogues Concerning Natural Religion* (1779).

*The Letters of David Hume.* Edited by J. Y. T. GREIG. Oxford: Clarendon Press, 1932.

*New Letters of David Hume.* Edited by RAYMOND KLIBANSKY and ERNEST CAMPBELL MOSSNER. Oxford: Clarendon Press, 1954.

"New Hume Letters to Lord Elibank, 1748–1776," edited by ERNEST CAMPBELL MOSSNER, *Texas Studies in Literature and Language,* IV, No. 3 (1962), 431–460.

## III. WORKS ON HUME AS HISTORIAN[1]

BLACK, J. B. *The Art of History. A study of four great historians of the eighteenth century.* London: Methuen & Co., 1926.

BONGIE, LAURENCE L. "The Eighteenth-Century Marian Controversy and an Unpublished Letter by David Hume," *Studies in Scottish Literature,* I (1964) , 236–252.

BRODIE, GEORGE. *History of the British Empire . . . including a particular examination of Mr. Hume's statements. . . .* Edinburgh: Bell & Bradfute, 1822. A review of this work by J. S. Mill (*Westminster Review,* II [1824], 346–402) savagely attacks Hume's *History of England.*

BURTON, JOHN HILL. *Life and Correspondence of David Hume.* 2 vols. Edinburgh: W. Tait, 1846. (Chapters IX–XIV especially.)

CAMPBELL, GEORGE. *A Dissertation on Miracles: Containing an Examination of the Principles Advanced by David Hume, Esq.; in an Essay on Miracles.* Edinburgh, 1762.

DAVIS, GODFREY. "Hume's History of the Reign of James I" in *Elizabethan and Jacobean Studies Presented to Frank Percy Wilson.* Edited by H. J. DAVIS and H. L. GARDNER. Oxford: Clarendon Press, 1959.

FLEW, ANTHONY. *Hume's Philosophy of Belief. A Study of His First Inquiry.* New York: The Humanities Press, 1961. (Especially Chapter VIII, "Miracles and Methodology.")

GIARIZZO, GIUSEPPE. *David Hume Politico e Storico.* Turin, 1962. (Part II deals with Hume as historian.) Review by H. R. TREVOR-ROPER in *History and Theory,* III, No. 3 (1963) , 381–389.

GRENE, MARJORIE. "Hume: Sceptic and Tory?" *Journal of the History of Ideas,* IV (1943) , 333–348.

[1] For a more complete bibliography of works on Hume as historian see T. E. Jessop, *A Bibliography of David Hume and Scottish Philosophy.* A new and expanded version of this *Bibliography* is forthcoming in the series "International Archives of the History of Ideas" (The Hague: Martinus Nijhoff).

GREIG, J. Y. T. *David Hume*. London: J. Cape, 1931. (Chapter XX examines Hume as a historian.)

HUNT, WILLIAM. "Hume and Modern Historians," in *Cambridge History of English Literature*. Cambridge: Cambridge University Press, 1913. X, 279–296.

LAIRD, JOHN. *Hume's Philosophy of Human Nature*. London: Methuen & Co., 1932.

LEROY, ANDRÉ LOUIS. *David Hume*. Paris: Presses Universitaires de France, 1953. (Chapter XX examines Hume as a historian.)

MARSHALL, GEOFFREY. "David Hume and Political Scepticism," *Philosophical Quarterly*, IV (1954), 247–257.

MEYER, PAUL H. "Voltaire and Hume as Historians," *PMLA*, LXXIII (1958), 51–68.

MOSSNER, ERNEST CAMPBELL. "An Apology for David Hume, Historian," *PMLA*, LVI (1941), 657–690.

———. "David Hume's 'An Historical Essay on Chivalry and Modern Honour,'" *Modern Philology*, XLV (1947), 54–60.

———. *The Forgotten Hume: Le bon David*. New York: Columbia University Press, 1943. (See especially pp. 83–131.)

———. "Hume as Literary Patron: A Suppressed Review of Robert Henry's *History of Great Britain*, 1773," *Modern Philology*, XXXIX (1942), 361–382.

———. "Hume's Early Memoranda, 1729–40: The Complete Text," *Journal of the History of Ideas*, IX (1948), 492–518.

———. *The Life of David Hume*. Austin, Texas: University of Texas Press, 1954. (See especially Chapter 23.)

———. "Was Hume a Tory Historian? Facts and Reconsiderations," *Journal of the History of Ideas*, II (1941), 225–236.

——— and RANSOM, HARRY. "Hume and the 'Conspiracy of the Booksellers': The Publication and Early Fortunes of the *History of England*," *University of Texas Studies in English*, XXIX (1950), 162–182.

PALGRAVE, FRANCIS. "Hume and his Influence upon History," *Quarterly Review*, LXXIII (1844), 536–592.

SABINE, G. H. "Hume's Contribution to the Historical Method," *Philosophical Review*, XV (1906), 17–38.

TAYLOR, A. E. "David Hume and the Miraculous," in his *Philosophical Studies*. London: Macmillan & Co., 1934.

TREVOR-ROPER, HUGH R. "David Hume as a Historian," *The Listener*, LXV (Dec. 28, 1961), 1103–1104, 1119.

TYTLER, WILLIAM. *An Historical and Critical Enquiry into the Evidence produced . . . . against Mary Queen of Scots. With an Examination of the Rev. Dr. Robertson's Dissertation, and Mr. Hume's History with respect to that Evidence.* 3rd ed., Edinburgh: W. Drummond, 1772.

VOLTAIRE, F. M. A. DE. Notice of the *History of England* in *La Gazette Litteraire*, May 2, 1764. Reprinted in *Oeuvres complètes de Voltaire*, Paris, 1877–1885. XXV, 169–173.

# Note on the Text and Selections

THE TEXTS of the selections found in this volume are drawn from several sources. The excerpts from the *Treatise of Human Nature,* the essays "Of the Study of History," "Of National Characters," and "Of the Poems of Ossian," and "Of Miracles" (from *An Enquiry Concerning Human Understanding*) are reprinted from *The Philosophical Works of David Hume,* edited by T. H. Green and T. H. Grose (1874–1875). However, in cases of variant readings from edition to edition, only the latest and final choice of Hume has been reprinted here. The selections from the *History of England* have been taken from the edition of 1782, which contains all Hume's last corrections and additions; after the edition of 1778, which the editors were not able to consult, this must be considered the most authentic text available. The "Review of Robert Henry's *History of Great Britain*" is reprinted from the original proof sheets, corrected in Hume's own hand, which are now located in the William Andrews Clark Memorial Library, Los Angeles, California. And, finally, the letters here reprinted are based on the text established by their most recent editors (for complete details, see p. lii, above). However, all footnotes to the letters here reprinted were done by the editors of this volume.

In keeping with the style adopted by Liberal Arts Press, all footnotes within a given section or selection have been numbered consecutively, rather than page by page, the practice sometimes adopted by Hume. With the exception of the dates given in Chapters XLV to LIX of the *History of England,* all marginal headings have been deleted; the only other alterations of the text have been the modernization of some spellings and of the use of quotation marks; the substitution of roman for italicized versions of names; the modernization and clarification, where possible, of Hume's bibliographical footnotes; and the addition of notes and comments by the editors, which are enclosed in square brackets. The abbreviations HL and NHL have been used to refer, respectively, to *The Letters of David Hume,* edited by J. Y. T. Greig, and *New Letters of David Hume,* edited by Raymond Klibansky and Ernest Campbell Mossner.

So far as the selection of material for this volume is concerned, those familiar with Hume's work will appreciate the difficulty with which the editors were faced: by any standard, Hume's historical work constitutes well over half his total output as a writer, which means that it is no small amount. Unavoidably then, we have to omit some items and parts of other items that we would like to have included, most regrettably *The Natural History of Religion.* Also, a number of items that might have been included in this volume have already been included in other Liberal Arts Press editions of Hume; because this edition is to complement those other editions, only one item of any length, the essay "Of Miracles," has been repeated. It is hoped, however, that these limitations have not prevented us from presenting a volume that represents the nature and character of Hume's historical work, one that will reveal something of the relevance of that work for an adequate understanding of Hume.

D.F.N.
R. H. P.

# DAVID HUME:
# PHILOSOPHICAL HISTORIAN

# A TREATISE
# OF HUMAN NATURE

[A Treatise of Human Nature *(1739–1740) was the first and
most extensive statement of Hume's philosophical views. Although largely ignored in its day, it has come to be considered
the major presentation of Hume's theory of knowledge and of
his moral theories. The work is subtitled, "An Attempt to introduce the experimental Method of Reasoning into Moral Subjects," and, in part, develops Hume's "science of man." The
following extracts deal with the nature and problem of historical
knowledge.*]

From the *Introduction*

BUT IF this impossibility of explaining ultimate principles
should be esteemed a defect in the science of man, I will venture
to affirm, that 'tis a defect common to it with all the sciences,
and all the arts, in which we can employ ourselves, whether
they be such as are cultivated in the schools of the philosophers,
or practised in the shops of the meanest artisans. None of them
can go beyond experience, or establish any principles which are
not founded on that authority. Moral philosophy has, indeed,
this peculiar disadvantage, which is not found in natural, that
in collecting its experiments, it cannot make them purposely,
with premeditation, and after such a manner as to satisfy itself
concerning every particular difficulty which may arise. When I
am at a loss to know the effects of one body upon another in
any situation, I need only put them in that situation, and observe what results from it. But should I endeavour to clear up

3

after the same manner any doubt in moral philosophy, by placing myself in the same case with that which I consider, 'tis evident this reflection and premeditation would so disturb the
operation of my natural principles, as must render it impossible
to form any just conclusion from the phaenomenon. We must
therefore glean up our experiments in this science from a cautious observation of human life, and take them as they appear
in the common course of the world, by men's behaviour in company, in affairs, and in their pleasures. Where experiments of
this kind are judiciously collected and compared, we may hope
to establish on them a science which will not be inferior in
certainty, and will be much superior in utility to any other
of human comprehension.

# Book I. Of the Understanding

*From Part III, Section IV—Of the Component Parts of our Reasonings Concerning Cause and Effect*

THO' THE mind in its reasonings from causes or effects carries its view beyond those objects, which it sees or remembers, it must never lose sight of them entirely, nor reason merely upon its own ideas, without some mixture of impressions, or at least of ideas of the memory, which are equivalent to impressions. When we infer effects from causes, we must establish the existence of these causes; which we have only two ways of doing, either by an immediate perception of our memory or senses, or by an inference from other causes; which causes again we must ascertain in the same manner, either by a present impression, or by an inference from *their* causes, and so on, till we arrive at some object, which we see or remember. 'Tis impossible for us to carry on our inferences *in infinitum;* and the only thing, that can stop them, is an impression of the memory or senses, beyond which there is no room for doubt or inquiry.

To give an instance of this, we may choose any point of history, and consider for what reason we either believe or reject it. Thus we believe that Caesar was kill'd in the senate-house on the ides of March; and that because this fact is establish'd on the unanimous testimony of historians, who agree to assign this precise time and place to that event. Here are certain characters and letters present either to our memory or senses; which characters we likewise remember to have been us'd as the signs of certain ideas; and these ideas were either in the minds of such as were immediately present at that action, and receiv'd the ideas directly from its existence; or they were deriv'd from the testimony of others, and that again from another testimony, by a visible gradation, 'till we arrive at those who were eye-witnesses and spectators of the event. 'Tis obvious all this chain of argument or connexion of causes and effects, is at first founded on those characters or letters, which are seen or remember'd, and that without the authority either of the memory or senses our whole reasoning wou'd be chimerical and without foundation. Every link of the chain wou'd in that case hang upon another; there wou'd not be any thing fix'd to one end of it, capable of sustaining the whole; and consequently there wou'd be no belief nor evidence. And this actually is the case with all *hypothetical* arguments, or reasonings upon a supposition; there being in them, neither any present impression, nor belief of a real existence.

## From *Part III, Section IX—Of the Effects of Other Relations and Other Habits*

No WEAKNESS of human nature is more universal and conspicuous than what we commonly call Credulity, or a too easy faith in the testimony of others; and this weakness is also very naturally accounted for from the influence of resemblance. When we receive any matter of fact upon human testimony, our faith arises from the very same origin as our inferences from causes to effects, and from effects to causes; nor is there anything but our *experience* of the governing principles of human nature, which can give us any assurance of the veracity of men. But tho' experience be the true standard of this, as well as of all other judgments, we seldom regulate ourselves entirely by it; but have a remarkable propensity to believe whatever is reported, even concerning apparitions, enchantments, and prodigies, however contrary to daily experience and observation. The words or discourses of others have an intimate connexion with certain ideas in their mind; and these ideas have also a connexion with the facts or objects, which they represent. This latter connexion is generally much over-rated, and commands our assent beyond what experience will justify; which can proceed from nothing beside the resemblance betwixt the ideas and the facts. Other effects only point out their causes in an oblique manner; but the testimony of men does it directly, and is to be consider'd as an image as well as an effect. No wonder, therefore, we are so rash in drawing our inferences from it, and are less guided by experience in our judgments concerning it, than in those upon any other subject.

From *Part III, Section XIII—Of Unphilosophical Probability*

ALL THESE kinds of probability [i.e., types of probability based on causal reasoning] are receiv'd by philosophers, and allow'd to be reasonable foundations of belief and opinion. But there are others, that are deriv'd from the same principles, tho' they have not had the good fortune to obtain the same sanction.

. . . . . . . . . .

I add, as a *third* instance of this kind, that tho' our reasonings from proofs and from probabilities be considerably different from each other, yet the former species of reasoning often degenerates insensibly into the latter, by nothing but the multitude of connected arguments. 'Tis certain, that when an inference is drawn immediately from an object, without any intermediate cause or effect, the conviction is much stronger, and the persuasion more lively, than when the imagination is carry'd thro' a long chain of connected arguments, however infallible the connexion of each link may be esteem'd. 'Tis from the original impression, that the vivacity of all the ideas is deriv'd, by means of the customary transition of the imagination; and 'tis evident this vivacity must gradually decay in proportion to the distance, and must lose somewhat in each transition. Sometimes this distance has a greater influence than even contrary experiments wou'd have; and a man may receive a more lively conviction from a probable reasoning, which is close and immediate, than from a long chain of consequences, tho' just and conclusive in each part. Nay 'tis seldom such reasonings produce any conviction; and one must have a very strong and firm imagination to preserve the evidence to the end, where it passes thro' so many stages.

But here it may not be amiss to remark a very curious phae-nomenon, which the present subject suggests to us. 'Tis evident there is no point of ancient history, of which we can have any assurance, but by passing thro' many millions of causes and effects, and thro' a chain of arguments of almost an immeasur-able length. Before the knowledge of the fact cou'd come to the first historian, it must be convey'd thro' many mouths; and after it is committed to writing, each new copy is a new object, of which the connexion with the foregoing is known only by ex-perience and observation. Perhaps, therefore, it may be con-cluded from the precedent reasoning, that the evidence of all ancient history must now be lost; or at least, will be lost in time, as the chain of causes increases, and runs on to a greater length. But as it seems contrary to common sense to think, that if the republic of letters, and the art of printing continue on the same footing as at present, our posterity, even after a thousand ages, can ever doubt if there has been such a man as Julius Caesar; this may be consider'd as an objection to the present system. If belief consisted only in a certain vivacity, convey'd from an origi-nal impression, it wou'd decay by the length of the transition, and must at last be utterly extinguish'd: And *vice versa,* if belief on some occasions be not capable of such an extinction; it must be something different from that vivacity.

Before I answer this objection I shall observe, that from this topic there has been borrow'd a very celebrated argument against the *Christian Religion;*[1] but with this difference, that

---

1 [Green and Grose state that Hume is referring to John Craig's *Theo-logiae Christianae Principia Mathematica* (London, 1699). Bayle discussed this work and cited from it; cf. Pierre Bayle, *Historical and Critical Diction-ary,* "Third Clarification," trans. Richard H. Popkin, "The Library of Liberal Arts," No. 175 (Indianapolis and New York: The Bobbs-Merrill Co., Inc., 1965), p. 433; this may well be the source of Hume's knowledge of it since he does not seem to have known the particular form (geometrical) which the work took. A part of Craig's treatise has recently been reprinted with an English translation; cf. *Craig's Rules of Historical Evidence,* ed. and trans. George Nadel, in *History and Theory,* Supplement 4 (The Hague, 1964).]

the connexion betwixt each link of the chain in human testimony has been there suppos'd not to go beyond probability, and to be liable to a degree of doubt and uncertainty. And indeed it must be confest, that in this manner of considering the subject, (which however is not a true one) there is no history or tradition, but what must in the end lose all its force and evidence. Every new probability diminishes the original conviction; and however great that conviction may be suppos'd, 'tis impossible it can subsist under such re-iterated diminutions. This is true in general; tho' we shall find afterwards, that there is one very memorable exception, which is of vast consequence in the present subject of the understanding.

Mean while to give a solution of the preceding objection upon the supposition, that historical evidence amounts at first to an entire proof; let us consider, that tho' the links are innumerable, that connect any original fact with the present impression, which is the foundation of belief; yet they are all of the same kind, and depend on the fidelity of Printers and Copyists. One edition passes into another, and that into a third, and so on, till we come to that volume we peruse at present. There is no variation in the steps. After we know one, we know all of them; and after we have made one, we can have no scruple as to the rest. This circumstance alone preserves the evidence of history, and will perpetuate the memory of the present age to the latest posterity. If all the long chain of causes and effects, which connect any past event with any volume of history, were compos'd of parts different from each other, and which 'twere necessary for the mind distinctly to conceive, 'tis impossible we shou'd preserve to the end any belief or evidence. But as most of these proofs are perfectly resembling, the mind runs easily along them, jumps from one part to another with facility, and forms but a confus'd and general notion of each link. By this means a long chain of argument, has as little effect in diminishing the original vivacity, as a much shorter wou'd have, if compos'd of parts, which were different from each other, and of which each requir'd a distinct consideration.

A fourth unphilosophical species of probability is that deriv'd from *general rules,* which we rashly form to ourselves, and which are the source of what we properly call Prejudice. An Irishman cannot have wit, and a Frenchman cannot have solidity; for which reason, tho' the conversation of the former in any instance be visibly very agreeable, and of the latter very judicious, we have entertain'd such a prejudice against them, that they must be dunces or fops in spite of sense and reason. Human nature is very subject to errors of this kind; and perhaps this nation as much as any other.

# Book II. Of the Passions

From *Part III, Section I—Of Liberty and Necessity*

IT HAS been observ'd already, that in no single instance the ultimate connexion of any objects is discoverable, either by our senses or reason, and that we can never penetrate so far into the essence and construction of bodies, as to perceive the principle, on which their mutual influence depends. 'Tis their constant union alone, with which we are acquainted; and 'tis from the constant union the necessity arises. If objects had not an uniform and regular conjunction with each other, we shou'd never arrive at any idea of cause and effect; and even after all, the necessity, which enters into that idea, is nothing but a determination of the mind to pass from one object to its usual attendant, and infer the existence of one from that of the other. Here then are two particulars, which we are to consider as essential to necessity, viz. the constant *union* and the *inference* of the mind; and wherever we discover these we must acknowledge a necessity. As the actions of matter have no necessity, but what is deriv'd from these circumstances, and it is not by any insight into the essence of bodies we discover their connexion, the absence of this insight, while the union and inference remain, will never, in any case, remove the necessity. 'Tis the observation of the union, which produces the inference; for which reason it might be thought sufficient, if we prove a constant union in the actions of the mind, in order to establish the inference, along with the necessity of these actions. But that I may bestow a greater force on my reasoning, I shall examine these particulars apart, and shall first prove from experience, that our actions have a constant union with our motives, tempers, and circumstances, before I consider the inferences we draw from it.

To this end a very slight and general view of the common course of human affairs will be sufficient. There is no light, in

11

which we can take them, that does not confirm this principle.
Whether we consider mankind according to the difference of
sexes, ages, governments, conditions, or methods of education;
the same uniformity and regular operation of natural principles
are discernible. Like causes still produce like effects; in the
same manner as in the mutual action of the elements and powers
of nature.

There are different trees, which regularly produce fruit,
whose relish is different from each other; and this regularity will
be admitted as an instance of necessity and causes in external
bodies. But are the products of Guienne and of Champagne
more regularly different than the sentiments, actions, and passions of the two sexes, of which the one are distinguish'd by
their force and maturity, the other by their delicacy and softness?

Are the changes of our body from infancy to old age more
regular and certain than those of our mind and conduct? And
wou'd a man be more ridiculous, who wou'd expect that an
infant of four years old will raise a weight of three hundred
pound, than one, who from a person of the same age, wou'd
look for a philosophical reasoning, or a prudent and well-con-
certed action?

We must certainly allow, that the cohesion of the parts of
matter arises from natural and necessary principles, whatever
difficulty we may find in explaining them: And for a like reason
we must allow, that human society is founded on like principles;
and our reason in the latter case, is better than even that in the
former; because we not only observe, that men *always* seek society, but can also explain the principles, on which this universal propensity is founded. For is it more certain, that two flat
pieces of marble will unite together, than that two young savages
of different sexes will copulate? Do the children arise from this
copulation more uniformly, than does the parents' care for their
safety and preservation? And after they have arriv'd at years of
discretion by the care of their parents, are the inconveniencies
attending their separation more certain than their foresight of
these inconveniencies, and their care of avoiding them by a close
union and confederacy?

The skin, pores, muscles, and nerves of a day-labourer are different from those of a man of quality: So are his sentiments, actions and manners. The different stations of life influence the whole fabric, external and internal; and these different stations arise necessarily, because uniformly, from the necessary and uniform principles of human nature. Men cannot live without society, and cannot be associated without government. Government makes a distinction of property, and establishes the different ranks of men. This produces industry, traffic, manufactures, law-suits, war, leagues, alliances, voyages, travels, cities, fleets, ports, and all those other actions and objects, which cause such a diversity, and at the same time maintain such an uniformity in human life.

Shou'd a traveller, returning from a far country, tell us, that he had seen a climate in the fiftieth degree of northern latitude, where all the fruits ripen and come to perfection in the winter, and decay in the summer, after the same manner as in England they are produc'd and decay in the contrary seasons, he wou'd find few so credulous as to believe him. I am apt to think a traveller wou'd meet with as little credit, who shou'd inform us of people exactly of the same character with those in Plato's *Republic* on the one hand, or those in Hobbes's *Leviathan* on the other. There is a general course of nature in human actions, as well as in the operations of the sun and the climate. There are also characters peculiar to different nations and particular persons, as well as common to mankind. The knowledge of these characters is founded on the observation of an uniformity in the actions, that flow from them; and this uniformity forms the very essence of necessity.

I can imagine only one way of eluding this argument, which is by denying that uniformity of human actions, on which it is founded. As long as actions have a constant union and connexion with the situation and temper of the agent, however we may in words refuse to acknowledge the necessity, we really allow the thing. Now some may, perhaps, find a pretext to deny this regular union and connexion. For what is more capricious than human actions? What more inconstant than the desires of man?

And what creature departs more widely, not only from right reason, but from his own character and disposition? An hour, a moment is sufficient to make him change from one extreme to another, and overturn what cost the greatest pain and labour to establish. Necessity is regular and certain. Human conduct is irregular and uncertain. The one, therefore, proceeds not from the other.

To this I reply, that in judging of the actions of men we must proceed upon the same maxims, as when we reason concerning external objects. When any phaenomena are constantly and invariably conjoin'd together, they acquire such a connexion in the imagination, that it passes from one to the other, without any doubt or hesitation. But below this there are many inferior degrees of evidence and probability, nor does one single contrariety of experiment entirely destroy all our reasoning. The mind ballances the contrary experiments, and deducting the inferior from the superior, proceeds with that degree of assurance or evidence, which remains. Even when these contrary experiments are entirely equal, we remove not the notion of causes and necessity; but supposing that the usual contrariety proceeds from the operation of contrary and conceal'd causes, we conclude, that the chance or indifference lies only in our judgment on account of our imperfect knowledge, not in the things themselves, which are in every case equally necessary, tho' to appearance not equally constant or certain. No union can be more constant and certain, than that of some actions with some motives and characters; and if in other cases the union is uncertain, 'tis no more than what happens in the operations of body, nor can we conclude any thing from the one irregularity, which will not follow equally from the other.

'Tis commonly allow'd that mad-men have no liberty. But were we to judge by their actions, these have less regularity and constancy than the actions of wise-men, and consequently are farther remov'd from necessity. Our way of thinking in this particular is, therefore, absolutely inconsistent; but is a natural consequence of these confus'd ideas and undefin'd terms, which we so commonly make use of in our reasonings, especially on the present subject.

We must now show, that as the *union* betwixt motives and actions has the same constancy, as that in any natural operations, so its influence on the understanding is also the same, in *determining* us to infer the existence of one from that of another. If this shall appear, there is no known circumstance, that enters into the connexion and production of the actions of matter, that is not to be found in all the operations of the mind; and consequently we cannot, without a manifest absurdity, attribute necessity to the one, and refuse it to the other.

There is no philosopher, whose judgment is so riveted to this fantastical system of liberty, as not to acknowledge the force of *moral evidence,* and both in speculation and practice proceed upon it, as upon a reasonable foundation. Now moral evidence is nothing but a conclusion concerning the actions of men, deriv'd from the consideration of their motives, temper and situation. Thus when we see certain characters or figures describ'd upon paper, we infer that the person, who produc'd them, wou'd affirm such facts, the death of Caesar, the success of Augustus, the cruelty of Nero; and remembering many other concurrent testimonies we conclude, that those facts were once really existent, and that so many men, without any interest, wou'd never conspire to deceive us; especially since they must, in the attempt, expose themselves to the derision of all their contemporaries, when these facts were asserted to be recent and universally known. The same kind of reasoning runs thro' politics, war, commerce, oeconomy, and indeed mixes itself so entirely in human life, that 'tis impossible to act or subsist a moment without having recourse to it. A prince, who imposes a tax upon his subjects, expects their compliance. A general, who conducts an army, makes account of a certain degree of courage. A merchant looks for fidelity and skill in his factor or super-cargo. A man, who gives orders for his dinner, doubts not of the obedience of his servants. In short, as nothing more nearly interests us than our own actions and those of others, the greatest part of our reasonings is employ'd in judgments concerning them. Now I assert, that whoever reasons after this manner, does *ipso facto* believe the actions of the will to arise from necessity, and that he knows not what he means, when he denies it.

All those objects, of which we call the one *cause* and the other *effect*, consider'd in themselves, are as distinct and separate from each other, as any two things in nature, nor can we ever, by the most accurate survey of them, infer the existence of the one from that of the other. 'Tis only from experience and the observation of their constant union, that we are able to form this inference; and even after all, the inference is nothing but the effects of custom on the imagination. We must not here be content with saying, that the idea of cause and effect arises from objects constantly united; but must affirm, that 'tis the very same with the idea of these objects, and that the *necessary connexion* is not discover'd by a conclusion of the understanding, but is merely a perception of the mind. Wherever, therefore, we observe the same union, and wherever the union operates in the same manner upon the belief and opinion, we have the idea of causes and necessity, tho' perhaps we may avoid those expressions. Motion in one body in all past instances, that have fallen under our observation, is follow'd upon impulse by motion in another. 'Tis impossible for the mind to penetrate farther. From this constant union it *forms* the idea of cause and effect, and by its influence *feels* the necessity. As there is the same constancy, and the same influence in what we call moral evidence, I ask no more. What remains can only be a dispute of words.

And indeed, when we consider how aptly *natural* and *moral* evidence cement together, and form only one chain of argument betwixt them, we shall make no scruple to allow, that they are of the same nature, and deriv'd from the same principles. A prisoner, who has neither money nor interest, discovers the impossibility of his escape, as well from the obstinacy of the gaoler, as from the walls and bars with which he is surrounded; and in all attempts for his freedom chooses rather to work upon the stone and iron of the one, than upon the inflexible nature of the other. The same prisoner, when conducted to the scaffold, foresees his death as certainly from the constancy and fidelity of his guards as from the operation of the ax or wheel. His mind runs along a certain train of ideas: The refusal of the soldiers to consent to his escape, the action of the executioner; the separation of the head and body; bleeding, convulsive motions, and death. Here is a connected chain of natural causes and voluntary actions; but the mind feels no difference betwixt them in passing from one link to another; nor is less certain of the future event than if it were connected with the present impressions of the memory and senses by a train of causes cemented together by what we are pleas'd to call a *physical necessity*. The same experienc'd union has the same effect on the mind, whether the united objects be motives, volitions and actions; or figure and motion. We may change the names of things; but their nature and their operation on the understanding never change.

## From *Part III, Section VII—Of Contiguity, and Distance in Space and Time*

BUT FARTHER; tho' distance both in space and time has a considerable effect on the imagination, and by that means on the will and passions, yet the consequences of a removal in *space* are much inferior to those of a removal in *time*. Twenty years are certainly but a small distance of time in comparison of what history and even the memory of some may inform them of, and yet I doubt if a thousand leagues, or even the greatest distance of place this globe can admit of, will so remarkably weaken our ideas, and diminish our passions. A West-India merchant will tell you, that he is not without concern about what passes in Jamaica; tho' few extend their views so far into futurity, as to dread very remote accidents.

The cause of this phaenomenon must evidently lie in the different properties of space and time. Without having recourse to metaphysics, any one may easily observe, that space or extension consists of a number of co-existent parts dispos'd in a certain order, and capable of being at once present to the sight or feeling. On the contrary, time or succession, tho' it consists likewise of parts, never presents to us more than one at once; nor is it possible for any two of them ever to be co-existent. These qualities of the objects have a suitable effect on the imagination. The parts of extension being susceptible of an union to the senses, acquire an union in the fancy; and as the appearance of one part excludes not another, the transition or passage of the thought thro' the contiguous parts is by that means render'd more smooth and easy. On the other hand, the incompatibility of the parts of time in their real existence separates them in the imagination, and makes it more *difficult* for that faculty to trace any long succession or series of events. Every part must appear single and alone, nor can regularly have entrance into the fancy without banishing what is suppos'd to have been immediately precedent. By this means any distance in time causes a greater interruption in the thought than an equal distance in space, and consequently weakens more considerably the idea, and consequently the passions; which depend in a great measure, on the imagination, according to my system.

. . . . . . . . . . . .

Besides the propensity to a gradual progression thro' the points of space and time, we have another peculiarity in our method of thinking, which concurs in producing this phaenomenon. We always follow the succession of time in placing our ideas, and from the consideration of any object pass more easily to that, which follows immediately after it, than to that which went before it. We may learn this, among other instances, from the order, which is always observ'd in historical narrations. Nothing but an absolute necessity can oblige an historian to break the order of time, and in his *narration* give the precedence to an event, which was in *reality* posterior to another.

This will easily be apply'd to the question in hand, if we reflect on what I have before observ'd, that the present situation of the person is always that of the imagination, and that 'tis from thence we proceed to the conception of any distant object. When the object is past, the progression of the thought in passing to it from the present is contrary to nature, as proceeding from one point of time to that which is preceding, and from that to another preceding, in opposition to the natural course of the succession.

# Book III. Of Morals

*From Part II, Section IX—Of the Measures of Allegiance*

THERE IS a principle of human nature, which we have frequently taken notice of, that men are mightily addicted to *general rules,* and that we often carry our maxims beyond those reasons, which first induc'd us to establish them. Where cases are similar in many circumstances, we are apt to put them on the same footing, without considering, that they differ in the most material circumstances, and that the resemblance is more apparent than real. It may, therefore, be thought, that in the case of allegiance our moral obligation of duty will not cease, even tho' the natural obligation of interest, which is its cause, has ceas'd; and that men may be bound by *conscience* to submit to a tyrannical government against their own and the public interest. And indeed, to the force of this argument I so far submit, as to acknowledge, that general rules commonly extend beyond the principles, on which they are founded; and that we seldom make any exception to them, unless that exception have the qualities of a general rule, and be founded on very numerous and common instances. Now this I assert to be entirely the present case. When men submit to the authority of others, 'tis to procure themselves some security against the wickedness and injustice of men, who are perpetually carried, by their unruly passions, and by their present and immediate interest, to the violation of all the laws of society. But as this imperfection is inherent in human nature, we know that it must attend men in all their states and conditions; and that those, whom we choose for rulers, do not immediately become of a superior nature to the rest of mankind, upon account of their superior power and authority. What we expect from them depends not on a change of their nature but of their situation, when they acquire a more immediate interest in the preservation of order and the execution of justice. But besides that this interest is only more immediate in the execution of justice among their subjects; besides this, I say, we may often expect, from the irregularity of human nature, that they will neglect even this immediate interest, and be transported by their passions into all the excesses of cruelty and ambition. Our general knowledge of human nature, our observation of the past history of mankind, our experience of present times; all these causes must induce us to open the door to exceptions, and must make us conclude, that we may resist the more violent effects of supreme power, without any crime or injustice.

Accordingly we may observe, that this is both the general practice and principle of mankind, and that no nation, that cou'd find any remedy, ever yet suffer'd the cruel ravages of a tyrant, or were blam'd for their resistance. Those who took up arms against Dionysius or Nero, or Philip the second, have the favour of every reader in the perusal of their history; and nothing but the most violent perversion of common sense can ever lead us to condemn them. 'Tis certain, therefore, that in all our notions of morals we never entertain such an absurdity as that of passive obedience, but make allowances for resistance in the more flagrant instances of tyranny and oppression. The general opinion of mankind has some authority in all cases; but in this of morals 'tis perfectly infallible. Nor is it less infallible, because men cannot distinctly explain the principles, on which it is founded. Few persons can carry on this train of reasoning: "Government is a mere human invention for the interest of society. Where the tyranny of the governor removes this interest, it also removes the natural obligation to obedience. The moral obligation is founded on the natural, and therefore must cease where *that* ceases; especially where the subject is such as makes us foresee very many occasions wherein the natural obligation may cease, and causes us to form a kind of general rule for the regulation of our conduct in such occurrences." But tho' this train of reasoning be too subtile for the vulgar, 'tis certain, that all men have an implicit notion of it, and are sensible, that they owe obedience to government merely on account of the public interest; and at the same time, that human nature is so subject to frailties and passions, as may easily pervert this institution, and change their governors into tyrants and public enemies. If the sense of common interest were not our original motive to obedience, I wou'd fain ask, what other principle is there in human nature capable of subduing the natural ambition of men, and forcing them to such a submission? Imitation and custom are not sufficient. For the question still recurs, what motive first produces those instances of submission, which we imitate, and that train of actions, which produces the custom? There evidently is no other principle than common interest; and if interest first produces obedience to government, the obligation to obedience must cease, whenever the interest ceases, in any great degree, and in a considerable number of instances.

### Part II, Section X—Of the Objects of Allegiance

BUT THO', on some occasions, it may be justifiable, both in sound politics and morality, to resist supreme power, 'tis certain, that in the ordinary course of human affairs nothing can be more pernicious and criminal; and that besides the convulsions, which always attend revolutions, such a practice tends directly to the subversion of all government, and the causing an universal anarchy and confusion among mankind. As numerous and civiliz'd societies cannot subsist without government, so government is entirely useless without an exact obedience. We ought always to weigh the advantages, which we reap from authority, against the disadvantages; and by this means we shall become more scrupulous of putting in practice the doctrine of resistance. The common rule requires submission; and 'tis only in cases of grievous tyranny and oppression, that the exception can take place.

Since then such a blind submission is commonly due to magistracy, the next question is, *to whom it is due, and whom we are to regard as our lawful magistrates?* In order to answer this question, let us recollect what we have already establish'd concerning the origin of government and political society. When men have once experienc'd the impossibility of preserving any steady order in society, while every one is his own master, and violates or observes the laws of society, according to his present interest or pleasure, they naturally run into the invention of government, and put it out of their own power, as far as possible, to transgress the laws of society. Government, therefore, arises from the voluntary convention of men; and 'tis evident, that the same convention, which establishes government, will also determine the persons who are to govern, and will remove all doubt and ambiguity in this particular. And the voluntary consent of men must here have the greater efficacy, that the authority of the magistrates does *at first* stand upon the foundation of a promise of the subjects, by which they bind themselves to obedience; as in every other contract or engagement. The same promise, then, which binds them to obedience, ties them down to a particular person, and makes him the object of their allegiance.

But when government has been establish'd on this footing for some considerable time, and the separate interest, which we have in submission has produc'd a separate sentiment of morality, the case is entirely alter'd, and a promise is no longer able to determine the particular magistrate; since it is no longer consider'd as the foundation of government. We naturally suppose ourselves born to submission; and imagine, that such particular persons have a right to command, as we on our part are bound to obey. These notions of right and obligation are deriv'd from nothing but the *advantage* we reap from government, which gives us a repugnance to practise resistance ourselves, and makes us displeas'd with any instance of it in others. But here 'tis remarkable, that in this new state of affairs, the original sanction of government, which is *interest,* is not admitted to determine the persons whom we are to obey, as the original sanction did at first, when affairs were on the footing of a *promise.* A *promise* fixes and determines the persons, without any uncertainty: But 'tis evident, that if men were to regulate their conduct in this particular, by the view of a peculiar *interest,* either public or private, they wou'd involve themselves in endless confusion, and wou'd render all government, in a great measure, ineffectual. The private interest of every one is different; and tho' the public interest in itself be always one and the same, yet it becomes the source of as great dissentions, by reason of the different opinions of particular persons concerning it. The same interest, therefore, which causes us to submit to magistracy, makes us renounce itself in the choice of our magistrates, and binds us down to a certain form of government, and to particular persons, without allowing us to aspire to the utmost perfection in either. The case is here the same as in that law of nature concerning the stability of possession. 'Tis highly advantageous, and even absolutely necessary to society, that possession shou'd be stable; and this leads us to the establishment of such a rule: But we find, that were we to follow the same advantage, in assigning particular possessions to particular persons, we shou'd disappoint our end, and perpetuate the confusion, which that rule is intended to prevent. We must, therefore, proceed by general rules, and regulate ourselves by general interests, in modifying the law of nature concerning the stability of possession. Nor need we fear, that our attachment to this law will diminish upon account of the seeming frivolousness of those interests, by which it is determin'd. The impulse of the mind is deriv'd from a very strong interest; and those other more minute interests serve only to direct the motion, without adding anything to it, or diminishing from it. 'Tis the same case with government. Nothing is more advantageous to society than such an invention; and this interest is sufficient to make us embrace it with ardour and alacrity; tho' we are oblig'd afterwards to regulate and direct our devotion to government by several considerations, which are not of the same importance, and to choose our magistrates without having in view any particular advantage from the choice.

The *first* of those principles I shall take notice of, as a foundation of the right of magistracy, is that which gives authority to all the most establish'd governments of the world without exception: I mean, *long possession* in any one form of government, or succession of princes. 'Tis certain, that if we remount to the first origin of every nation, we shall find, that there scarce is any race of kings, or form of a commonwealth, that is not primarily founded on usurpation and rebellion, and whose title is not at first worse than doubtful and uncertain. Time alone gives solidity to their right; and operating gradually on the minds of men, reconciles them to any authority, and makes it seem just and reasonable. Nothing causes any sentiment to have a greater influence upon us than custom, or turns our imagination more strongly to any object. When we have been long accustom'd to obey any set of men, that general instinct or tendency, which we have to suppose a moral obligation attending loyalty, takes easily this direction, and chooses that set of men for its objects. 'Tis interest which gives the general instinct; but 'tis custom which gives the particular direction.

And here 'tis observable, that the same length of time has a different influence on our sentiments of morality, according to its different influence on the mind. We naturally judge of everything by comparison; and since in considering the fate of kingdoms and republics, we embrace a long extent of time, a small duration has not in this case a like influence on our sentiments, as when we consider any other object. One thinks he acquires a right to a horse, or a suit of cloths, in a very short time; but a century is scarce sufficient to establish any new government, or remove all scruples in the minds of the subjects concerning it. Add to this, that a shorter period of time will suffice to give a prince a title to any additional power he may usurp, than will serve to fix his right, where the whole is an usurpation. The kings of France have not been possess'd of absolute power for above two reigns; and yet nothing will appear more extravagant to Frenchmen than to talk of their liberties. If we consider what has been said concerning *accession*, we shall easily account for this phaenomenon.

When there is no form of government establish'd by *long* possession, the *present* possession is sufficient to supply its place, and may be regarded as the *second* source of all public authority. Right to authority is nothing but the constant possession of authority, maintain'd by the laws of society and the interests of mankind; and nothing can be more natural than to join this constant possession to the present one, according to the principles above-mention'd. If the same principles did not take place with regard to the property of private persons, 'twas because these principles were counter-ballanc'd by very strong considerations of interest; when we observ'd, that all restitution wou'd by that means be prevented, and every violence be authoriz'd and protected. And tho' the same motives may seem to have force, with regard to public authority, yet they are oppos'd by a contrary interest; which consists in the preservation of peace, and the avoiding of all changes, which, however they may be easily produc'd in private affairs, are unavoidably attended with bloodshed and confusion, where the public is interested.

Any one, who finding the impossibility of accounting for the right of the present possessor, by any receiv'd system of ethics, shou'd resolve to deny absolutely that right, and assert, that it is not authoriz'd by morality, wou'd be justly thought to maintain a very extravagant paradox, and to shock the common sense and judgment of mankind. No maxim is more conformable, both to prudence and morals, than to submit quietly to the government, which we find establish'd in the country where we happen to live, without enquiring too curiously into its origin and first establishment. Few governments will bear being examin'd so rigorously. How many kingdoms are there at present in the world, and how many more do we find in history, whose governors have no better foundation for their authority than that of present possession? To confine ourselves to the Roman and Grecian empire; is it not evident, that the long succession of emperors, from the dissolution of the Roman liberty, to the final extinction of that empire by the Turks, cou'd not so much as pretend to any other title to the empire? The election of the senate was a mere form, which always follow'd the choice of the legions; and these were almost always divided in the different provinces, and nothing but the sword was able to terminate the difference. 'Twas by the sword, therefore, that every emperor acquir'd, as well as defended his right; and we must either say, that all the known world, for so many ages, had no government, and ow'd no allegiance to any one, or must allow, that the right of the stronger, in public affairs, is to be receiv'd as legitimate, and authoriz'd by morality, when not oppos'd by any other title.

The right of *conquest* may be consider'd as a *third* source of the title of sovereigns. This right resembles very much that of present possession; but has rather a superior force, being seconded by the notions of glory and honour, which we ascribe to *conquerors,* instead of the sentiments of hatred and detestation, which attend *usurpers.* Men naturally favour those they love; and therefore are more apt to ascribe a right to successful violence, betwixt one sovereign and another, than to the successful rebellion of a subject against his sovereign.[1]

When neither long possession nor present possession, nor conquest take place, as when the first sovereign, who founded any monarchy, dies; in that case, the right of *succession* naturally prevails in their stead, and men are commonly induc'd to place the son of their late monarch on the throne, and suppose him to inherit his father's authority. The presum'd consent of the father; the imitation of the succession to private families, the interest, which the state has in choosing the person, who is most powerful, and has the most numerous followers; all these reasons lead men to prefer the son of their late monarch to any other person.[2]

These reasons have some weight; but I am persuaded, that to one, who considers impartially of the matter, 'twill appear, that there concur some principles of the imagination, along with those views of interest. The royal authority seems to be connected with the young prince even in his father's life-time, by

[1] It is not here asserted, that *present possession* or *conquest* are sufficient to give a title against *long possession* and *positive laws:* But only that they have some force, and will be able to cast the ballance where the titles are otherwise equal, and will even be sufficient *sometimes* to sanctify the weaker title. What degree of force they have is difficult to determine. I believe all moderate men will allow, that they have great force in all disputes concerning the rights of princes.

[2] To prevent mistakes I must observe, that this case of succession is not the same with that of hereditary monarchies, where custom has fix'd the right of succession. These depend upon the principle of long possession above explain'd.

the natural transition of the thought; and still more after his death: So that nothing is more natural than to complete this union by a new relation, and by putting him actually in possession of what seems so naturally to belong to him.

To confirm this we may weigh the following phaenomena, which are pretty curious in their kind. In elective monarchies the right of succession has no place by the laws and settled custom; and yet its influence is so natural, that 'tis impossible entirely to exclude it from the imagination, and render the subjects indifferent to the son of their deceas'd monarch. Hence in some governments of this kind, the choice commonly falls on one or other of the royal family, and in some governments they are all excluded. Those contrary phaenomena proceed from the same principle. Where the royal family is excluded, 'tis from a refinement in politics, which makes people sensible of their propensity to choose a sovereign in that family, and gives them a jealousy of their liberty, lest their new monarch, aided by this propensity, shou'd establish his family, and destroy the freedom of elections for the future.

The history of Artaxerxes, and the younger Cyrus, may furnish us with some reflections to the same purpose. Cyrus pretended a right to the throne above his elder brother, because he was born after his father's accession. I do not pretend, that this reason was valid. I wou'd only infer from it, that he wou'd never have made use of such a pretext, were it not for the qualities of the imagination above-mention'd, by which we are naturally inclin'd to unite by a new relation whatever objects we find already united. Artaxerxes had an advantage above his brother, as being the eldest son, and the first in succession: But Cyrus was more closely related to the royal authority, as being begot after his father was invested with it.

Shou'd it here be pretended, that the view of convenience may be the source of all the right of succession, and that men gladly take advantage of any rule, by which they can fix the successor of their late sovereign, and prevent that anarchy and confusion, which attends all new elections: To this I wou'd answer, that I readily allow, that this motive may contribute something to the

effect; but at the same time I assert, that without another principle, 'tis impossible such a motive shou'd take place. The interest
of a nation requires, that the succession to the crown shou'd be
fix'd one way or other; but 'tis the same thing to its interest in
what way it be fix'd: So that if the relation of blood had not an
effect independent of public interest, it would never have been
regarded, without a positive law; and 'twou'd have been impossible, that so many positive laws of different nations could ever
have concur'd precisely in the same views and intentions.

This leads us to consider the *fifth* source of authority, viz.,
*positive laws;* when the legislature establishes a certain form of
government and succession of princes. At first sight it may be
thought, that this must resolve into some of the preceding titles
of authority. The legislative power, whence the positive law is
deriv'd, must either be establish'd by original contract, long possession, present possession, conquest, or succession; and consequently the positive law must derive its force from some of
those principles. But here 'tis remarkable, that tho' a positive
law can only derive its force from these principles, yet it acquires
not all the force of the principle from whence it is deriv'd, but
loses considerably in the transition; as it is natural to imagine.
For instance; a government is establish'd for many centuries on
a certain system of laws, forms, and methods of succession. The
legislative power, established by this long succession, changes all
on a sudden the whole system of government, and introduces a
new constitution in its stead. I believe few of the subjects will
think themselves bound to comply with this alteration, unless it
have an evident tendency to the public good: But will think
themselves still at liberty to return to the ancient government.
Hence the notion of *fundamental laws;* which are suppos'd to be
inalterable by the will of the sovereign: And of this nature the
Salic law is understood to be in France. How far these fundamental laws extend is not determin'd in any government; nor is
it possible it ever shou'd. There is such an insensible gradation
from the most material laws to the most trivial, and from the
most ancient laws to the most modern, that 'twill be impossible
to set bounds to the legislative power, and determine how far it

may innovate in the principles of government. That is the work more of imagination and passion than of reason.

Whoever considers the history of the several nations of the world; their revolutions, conquests, increase, and diminution; the manner in which their particular governments are establish'd, and the successive right transmitted from one person to another, will soon learn to treat very lightly all disputes concerning the rights of princes, and will be convinc'd, that a strict adherence to any general rules, and the rigid loyalty to particular persons and families, on which some people set so high a value, are virtues that hold less of reason, than of bigotry and superstition. In this particular, the study of history confirms the reasonings of true philosophy; which, showing us the original qualities of human nature, teaches us to regard the controversies in politics as incapable of any decision in most cases, and as entirely subordinate to the interests of peace and liberty. Where the public good does not evidently demand a change; 'tis certain that the concurrence of all those titles, *original contract, long possession, present possession, succession,* and *positive laws,* forms the strongest title to sovereignty, and is justly regarded as sacred and inviolable. But when these titles are mingled and oppos'd in different degrees, they often occasion perplexity; and are less capable of solution from the arguments of lawyers and philosophers, than from the swords of the soldiery. Who shall tell me, for instance, whether Germanicus or Drusus, ought to have succeeded Tiberius, had he died while they were both alive, without naming any of them for his successor? Ought the right of adoption to be receiv'd as equivalent to that of blood in a nation, where it had the same effect in private families, and had already, in two instances, taken place in public? Ought Germanicus to be esteem'd the eldest son, because he was born before Drusus; or the younger, because he was adopted after the birth of his brother? Ought the right of the elder to be regarded in a nation, where the eldest brother had no advantage in the succession to private families? Ought the Roman empire at that time to be esteem'd hereditary, because of two examples; or ought it, even so early, to be regarded as belonging to the stronger, or the present possessor, as being founded on so recent an usurpation? Upon whatever principles we may pretend to answer these and such like questions, I am afraid we shall never be able to satisfy an impartial inquirer, who adopts no party in political controversies, and will be satisfied with nothing but sound reason and philosophy.

But here an English reader will be apt to enquire concerning that famous *revolution*, which has had such a happy influence on our constitution, and has been attended with such mighty consequences. We have already remark'd, that in the case of enormous tyranny and oppression, 'tis lawful to take arms even against supreme power; and that as government is a mere human invention for mutual advantage and security, it no longer imposes any obligation, either natural or moral, when once it ceases to have that tendency. But 'tho this *general* principle be authoriz'd by common sense, and the practice of all ages, 'tis certainly impossible for the laws, or even for philosophy, to establish any *particular* rules, by which we may know when resistance is lawful; and decide all controversies, which may arise on that subject. This may not only happen with regard to supreme power; but 'tis possible, even in some constitutions, where the legislative authority is not lodg'd in one person, that there may be a magistrate so eminent and powerful, as to oblige the laws to keep silence in this particular. Nor wou'd this silence be an effect only of their *respect*, but also of their *prudence;* since 'tis certain, that in the vast variety of circumstances, which occur in all governments, an exercise of power, in so great a magistrate, may at one time be beneficial to the public, which at another time wou'd be pernicious and tyrannical. But notwithstanding this silence of the laws in limited monarchies, 'tis certain, that the people still retain the right of resistance; since 'tis impossible, even in the most despotic governments, to deprive them of it. The same necessity of self-preservation, and the same motive of public good, give them the same liberty in the one case as in the other. And we may farther observe, that in such mix'd governments, the cases, wherein resistance is lawful, must occur much oftener, and greater indulgence be given to the subjects to defend themselves by force of arms, than in arbitrary governments. Not only where the chief magistrate enters into measures, in themselves, extremely pernicious to the public, but even when he wou'd encroach on the other parts of the constitution, and extend his power beyond the legal bounds, it is allowable to resist and dethrone him; tho' such resistance and violence may, in the general tenor of the laws, be deem'd unlawful and rebellious. For besides that nothing is more essential to public interest, than the preservation of public liberty; 'tis evident, that if such a mix'd government be once suppos'd to be establish'd, every part or member of the constitution must have a right of self-defence, and of maintaining its ancient bounds against the encroachment of every other authority. As matter wou'd have been created in vain, were it depriv'd of a power of resistance, without which no part of it cou'd preserve a distinct existence, and the whole might be crowded up into a single point: So 'tis a gross absurdity to suppose, in any government, a right without a remedy, or allow, that the supreme power is shar'd with the people, without allowing, that 'tis lawful for them to defend their share against every invader. Those, therefore, who wou'd seem to respect our free government, and yet deny the right of resistance, have renounc'd all pretensions to common sense, and do not merit a serious answer.

It does not belong to my present purpose to show, that these general principles are applicable to the late *revolution;* and that all the rights and privileges, which ought to be sacred to a free nation, were at that time threaten'd with the utmost danger. I am better pleas'd to leave this controverted subject, if it really admits of controversy; and to indulge myself in some philosophical reflections, which naturally arise from that important event.

*First,* We may observe, that shou'd the *lords* and *commons* in our constitution, without any reason from public interest, either depose the king in being, or after his death exclude the prince, who, by laws and settled custom, ought to succeed, no one wou'd esteem their proceedings legal, or think themselves bound to comply with them. But shou'd the king, by his unjust practices, or his attempts for a tyrannical and despotic power, justly forfeit his legal, it then not only becomes morally lawful and suitable to the nature of political society to dethrone him; but what is more, we are apt likewise to think, that the remaining members of the constitution acquire a right of excluding his next heir, and of choosing whom they please for his successor. This is founded on a very singular quality of our thought and imagination. When a king forfeits his authority, his heir ought naturally to remain in the same situation, as if the king were remov'd by death; unless by mixing himself in the tyranny, he forfeit it for himself. But tho' this may seem reasonable, we easily comply with the contrary opinion. The deposition of a king, in such a government as ours, is certainly an act beyond all common authority, and an illegal assuming a power for public good, which, in the ordinary course of government, can belong to no member of the constitution. When the public good is so great and so evident as to justify the action, the commendable use of this licence causes us naturally to attribute to the *parliament* a right of using farther licences; and the ancient bounds of the laws being once transgressed with approbation, we are not apt to be so strict in confining ourselves precisely within their limits. The mind naturally runs on with any train of action, which it has begun; nor do we commonly make any scruple concerning our duty, after the first action of any kind, which we perform. Thus at the *revolution,* no one who thought the deposition of the father justifiable, esteem'd themselves to be confin'd to his infant son; tho' had that unhappy monarch died innocent at that time, and had his son, by any accident, been convey'd beyond seas, there is no doubt but a regency wou'd have been appointed till he shou'd come to age, and cou'd be restor'd to his dominions. As the slightest properties of the imagination have an effect on the judgments of the people, it shows the wisdom of the laws and of the parliament to take advantage of such properties, and to choose the magistrates either in or out of a line, according as the vulgar will most naturally attribute authority and right to them.

*Secondly,* Tho' the accession of the Prince of Orange to the

throne might at first give occasion to many disputes, and his
title be contested, it ought not now to appear doubtful, but must
have acquir'd a sufficient authority from those three princes,
who have succeeded him upon the same title. Nothing is more
usual, tho' nothing may, at first sight, appear more unreasonable, than this way of thinking. Princes often *seem* to acquire a
right from their successors, as well as from their ancestors; and
a king, who during his life-time might justly be deem'd an
usurper, will be regarded by posterity as a lawful prince, because he has had the good fortune to settle his family on the
throne, and entirely change the ancient form of government.
Julius Caesar is regarded as the first Roman emperor; while
Sulla and Marius, whose titles were really the same as his, are
treated as tyrants and usurpers. Time and custom give authority
to all forms of government, and all successions of princes; and
that power, which at first was founded only on injustice and
violence, becomes in time legal and obligatory. Nor does the
mind rest there; but returning back upon its footsteps, transfers
to their predecessors and ancestors that right, which it naturally
ascribes to the posterity, as being related together, and united in
the imagination. The present king of France makes Hugh Capet
a more lawful prince than Cromwell; as the establish'd liberty of
the Dutch is no inconsiderable apology for their obstinate resistance to Philip the second.

# OF THE STUDY OF HISTORY

[*Although citations are often drawn from this essay in analyses of Hume's attitude toward history, it is seldom pointed out that he withdrew it from all editions of his* Essays *appearing after 1760, apparently on the grounds that it and certain others could "neither give Pleasure nor Instruction," and were merely "bad Immitations of the agreeable* Triffling *of Addison" (HL 468). In 1752 Hume wrote to Adam Smith: "In that edition [1748] I was engaged to act contrary to my Judgment in retaining the 6th & 7th Essays ["Of Love and Marriage" and "Of the Study of History"], which I had resolved to throw out, as too frivolous for the rest, and not very agreeable neither even in that trifling manner" (HL 78). But even if we must take the detail of the essay lightly, the early date of its first appearance, 1741, does serve as a further indication of Hume's lifelong interest in history.*]

THERE IS nothing which I would recommend more earnestly to my female readers than the study of history, as an occupation, of all others, the best suited both to their sex and education, much more instructive than their ordinary books of amusement, and more entertaining than those serious compositions, which are usually to be found in their closets. Among other important truths, which they may learn from history, they may be informed of two particulars, the knowledge of which may contribute very much to their quiet and repose; *That* our sex, as well as theirs, are far from being such perfect creatures as they are apt to imagine, and, *That* Love is not the only passion, which governs the male-world, but is often overcome by avarice, ambition, vanity, and a thousand other passions. Whether they be the false representations of mankind in those two particulars, which endear romances and novels so much to the fair sex, I know not; but must confess that I am sorry to see them have such an aversion to matter of fact, and such an appetite for falsehood. I remember I was once desired by a young beauty, for whom I had some passion, to send her some novels and romances for her amusement in the country; but was not so ungenerous as to take the advantage, which such a course of reading might have given me, being resolved not to make use of poisoned arms against her. I therefore sent her Plutarch's Lives, assuring her, at the same time, that there was not a word of truth in them from beginning to end. She perused them very attentively, 'till she came to the lives of Alexander and Caesar, whose names she had heard of by accident; and then returned me the book, with many reproaches for deceiving her.

I may indeed be told that the fair sex have no such aversion to history, as I have represented, provided it be *secret* history, and contain some memorable transaction proper to excite their curiosity. But as I do not find that truth, which is the basis of history, is at all regarded in those anecdotes, I cannot admit of this as a proof of their passion for that study. However this may be, I see not why the same curiosity might not receive a more proper direction, and lead them to desire accounts of those who lived in past ages, as well as of their contemporaries. What is it to Cleora, whether Fulvia entertains a secret commerce of *Love* with Philander or not? Has she not equal reason to be pleased, when she is informed (what is whispered about among historians) that Cato's sister had an intrigue with Caesar, and palmed her son, Marcus Brutus, upon her husband for his own, tho' in reality he was her gallant's? And are not the loves of Messalina or Julia as proper subjects of discourse as any intrigue that this city has produced of late years?

But I know not whence it comes, that I have been thus seduced into a kind of raillery against the ladies: Unless, perhaps, it proceed from the same cause, which makes the person, who is the favourite of the company, be often the object of their good-natured jests and pleasantries. We are pleased to address ourselves after any manner, to one who is agreeable to us; and, at the same time, presume that nothing will be taken amiss by a person, who is secure of the good opinion and affections of every one present. I shall now proceed to handle my subject more seriously, and shall point out the many advantages which flow from the study of history, and show how well suited it is to every one, but particularly to those who are debarred the severer studies, by the tenderness of their complexion, and the weakness of their education. The advantages found in history seem to be of three kinds, as it amuses the fancy, as it improves the understanding, and as it strengthens virtue.

In reality, what more agreeable entertainment to the mind, than to be transported into the remotest ages of the world, and to observe human society, in its infancy, making the first faint essays towards the arts and sciences: To see the policy of government, and the civility of conversation refining by degrees, and every thing which is ornamental to human life advancing towards its perfection. To remark the rise, progress, declension, and final extinction of the most flourishing empires: The virtues, which contributed to their greatness, and the vices, which drew on their ruin. In short, to see all human race, from the beginning of time, pass, as it were, in review before us; appearing in their true colours, without any of those disguises, which, during their life-time, so much perplexed the judgment of the beholders. What spectacle can be imagined, so magnificent, so various, so interesting? What amusement, either of the senses or imagination, can be compared with it? Shall those trifling pastimes, which engross so much of our time, be preferred as more satisfactory, and more fit to engage our attention? How perverse must that taste be, which is capable of so wrong a choice of pleasures?

But history is a most improving part of knowledge, as well as an agreeable amusement; and a great part of what we commonly call *Erudition,* and value so highly, is nothing but an acquaintance with historical facts. An extensive knowledge of this kind belongs to men of letters; but I must think it an unpardonable ignorance in persons of whatever sex or condition, not to be acquainted with the history of their own country, together with the histories of ancient Greece and Rome. A woman may behave herself with good manners, and have even some vivacity in her turn of wit; but where her mind is so unfurnished, 'tis impossible her conversation can afford any entertainment to men of sense and reflection.

I must add, that history is not only a valuable part of knowledge, but opens the door to many other parts, and affords materials to most of the sciences. And indeed, if we consider the shortness of human life, and our limited knowledge, even of what passes in our own time, we must be sensible that we should be for ever children in understanding, were it not for this invention, which extends our experience to all past ages, and to the most distant nations; making them contribute as much to our improvement in wisdom, as if they had actually lain under our observation. A man acquainted with history may, in some respect, be said to have lived from the beginning of the world, and to have been making continual additions to his stock of knowledge in every century.

There is also an advantage in that experience which is acquired by history, above what is learned by the practice of the world, that it brings us acquainted with human affairs, without diminishing in the least from the most delicate sentiments of virtue. And, to tell the truth, I know not any study or occupation so unexceptionable as history in this particular. Poets can paint virtue in the most charming colours; but, as they address themselves entirely to the passions, they often become advocates for vice. Even philosophers are apt to bewilder themselves in the subtility of their speculations; and we have seen some go as far as to deny the reality of all moral distinctions. But I think it a remark worthy the attention of the speculative, that the historians have been, almost without exception, the true friends of virtue, and have always represented it in its proper colours, however they may have erred in their judgments of particular persons. Machiavel himself discovers a true sentiment of virtue in his history of Florence. When he talks as a *Politician*, in his general reasonings, he considers poisoning, assassination and perjury, as lawful arts of power; but when he speaks as an *Historian*, in his particular narrations, he shows so keen an indignation against vice, and so warm an approbation of virtue, in many passages, that I could not forbear applying to him that remark of Horace, That if you chase away nature, tho' with ever so great indignity, she will always return upon you. Nor is this combination of historians in favour of virtue at all difficult to be accounted for. When a man of business enters into life and action, he is more apt to consider the characters of men, as they have relation to his interest, than as they stand in themselves; and has his judgment warped on every occasion by the violence of his passion. When a philosopher contemplates characters and manners in his closet, the general abstract view of the objects leaves the mind so cold and unmoved, that the sentiments of nature have no room to play, and he scarce feels the difference between vice and virtue. History keeps in a just medium betwixt these extremes, and places the objects in their true point of view. The writers of history, as well as the readers, are sufficiently interested in the characters and events, to have a lively sentiment of blame or praise; and, at the same time, have no particular interest or concern to pervert their judgment.

*Nam verae tum demum pectore ab imo Eliciuntur.*[1]

---

[1] Lucretius III. 57. ["For then, at last, a real cry is wrung from the bottom of his heart."]

# OF NATIONAL CHARACTERS

[*This essay, first published in 1748, contains Hume's clearest statement of his opinion on the relative importance of "physical" and "moral" causes as historical and sociological factors. Physical causes are "qualities of air and climate," which are supposed to affect the body, and shape thereby the character and manners of mankind, while moral causes are those circumstances which "render a peculiar set of manners habitual to us" by affecting the mind as "motives or reasons." Taking here as his subject matter the apparent differences between the inhabitants of various nations, Hume goes on to argue that these differences seem for the most part to be due to moral causes. Although Hume was a cosmopolitan citizen of the eighteenth century, the reader is certain to find that many of the views he espouses here are exceedingly biased and provincial. Approximately one-third of the essay has been omitted.*]

THE VULGAR are apt to carry all *national characters* to extremes; and having once established it as a principle, that any people are knavish, or cowardly, or ignorant, they will admit of no exception, but comprehend every individual under the same censure. Men of sense condemn these undistinguishing judgments: Though at the same time, they allow, that each nation has a peculiar set of manners, and that some particular qualities are more frequently to be met with among one people than among their neighbours. The common people in Switzerland have probably more honesty than those of the same rank in Ireland; and every prudent man will, from that circumstance alone, make a difference in the trust which he reposes in each. We have reason to expect greater wit and gaiety in a Frenchman than in a Spaniard; though Cervantes was born in Spain.

40

An Englishman will naturally be supposed to have more knowledge than a Dane; though Tycho Brahe was a native of Denmark.

Different reasons are assigned for these *national characters;* while some account for them from *moral,* others from *physical* causes. By *moral* causes, I mean all circumstances, which are fitted to work on the mind as motives or reasons, and which render a peculiar set of manners habitual to us. Of this kind are, the nature of the government, the revolutions of public affairs, the plenty or penury in which the people live, the situation of the nation with regard to its neighbours, and such like circumstances. By *physical* causes I mean those qualities of the air and climate, which are supposed to work insensibly on the temper, by altering the tone and habit of the body, and giving a particular complexion, which, though reflection and reason may sometimes overcome it, will yet prevail among the generality of mankind, and have an influence on their manners.

That the character of a nation will much depend on *moral* causes, must be evident to the most superficial observer; since a nation is nothing but a collection of individuals, and the manners of individuals are frequently determined by these causes. As poverty and hard labour debase the minds of the common people, and render them unfit for any science and ingenious profession; so where any government becomes very oppressive to all its subjects, it must have a proportional effect on their temper and genius, and must banish all the liberal arts from among them.

The same principle of moral causes fixes the character of different professions, and alters even that disposition, which the particular members receive from the hand of nature. A *soldier* and a *priest* are different characters, in all nations, and all ages; and this difference is founded on circumstances, whose operation is eternal and unalterable.

.    .    .    .    .    .    .    .    .    .    .

As to *physical* causes, I am inclined to doubt altogether of their operation in this particular; nor do I think, that men owe any thing of their temper or genius to the air, food, or climate.

I confess, that the contrary opinion may justly, at first sight, seem probable; since we find, that these circumstances have an influence over every other animal, and that even those creatures, which are fitted to live in all climates, such as dogs, horses, &c. do not attain the same perfection in all. The courage of bull-dogs and gamecocks seems peculiar to England. Flanders is re-markable for large and heavy horses: Spain for horses light, and of good mettle. And any breed of these creatures, transplanted from one country to another, will soon lose the qualities, which they derived from their native climate. It may be asked, why not the same with men?

There are few questions more curious than this, or which will oftener occur in our enquiries concerning human affairs; and therefore it may be proper to give it a full examination.

The human mind is of a very imitative nature; nor is it pos-sible for any set of men to converse often together, without acquiring a similitude of manners, and communicating to each other their vices as well as virtues. The propensity to company and society is strong in all rational creatures; and the same dis-position, which gives us this propensity, makes us enter deeply into each other's sentiments, and causes like passions and incli-nations to run, as it were by contagion, through the whole club or knot of companions. Where a number of men are united into one political body, the occasions of their intercourse must be so frequent, for defence, commerce, and government, that, to-gether with the same speech or language, they must acquire a resemblance in their manners, and have a common or national character, as well as a personal one, peculiar to each individual. Now though nature produces all kinds of temper and under-standing in great abundance, it does not follow, that she always produces them in like proportions, and that in every society the ingredients of industry and indolence, valour and cowardice, humanity and brutality, wisdom and folly, will be mixed after the same manner. In the infancy of society, if any of these dis-positions be found in greater abundance than the rest, it will naturally prevail in the composition, and give a tincture to the national character. Or should it be asserted, that no species of temper can reasonably be presumed to predominate, even in those contracted societies, and that the same proportions will always be preserved in the mixture; yet surely the persons in credit and authority, being still a more contracted body, cannot always be presumed to be of the same character; and their influence on the manners of the people, must, at all times, be very considerable. If on the first establishment of a republic, a Brutus should be placed in authority, and be transported with such an enthusiasm for liberty and public good, as to overlook all the ties of nature, as well as private interest, such an illustrious example will naturally have an effect on the whole society, and kindle the same passion in every bosom. Whatever it be that forms the manners of one generation, the next must imbibe a deeper tincture of the same dye; men being more susceptible of all impressions during infancy, and retaining these impressions as long as they remain in the world. I assert, then, that all national characters, where they depend not on fixed *moral* causes, proceed from such accidents as these, and that physical causes have no discernible operation on the human mind. It is a maxim in all philosophy, that causes which do not appear, are to be considered as not existing.

If we run over the globe, or revolve the annals of history, we shall discover every where signs of a sympathy or contagion of manners, none of the influence of air or climate.

*First.* We may observe, that, where a very extensive government has been established for many centuries, it spreads a national character over the whole empire, and communicates to every part a similarity of manners. Thus the Chinese have the greatest uniformity of character imaginable: though the air and climate in different parts of those vast dominions, admit of very considerable variations.

*Secondly.* In small governments, which are contiguous, the people have notwithstanding a different character, and are often as distinguishable in their manners as the most distant nations. Athens and Thebes were but a short day's journey from each other; though the Athenians were as remarkable for ingenuity, politeness, and gaiety, as the Thebans for dulness, rusticity, and a phlegmatic temper. Plutarch, discoursing of the effects of air on the minds of men, observes, that the inhabitants of the Piraeum possessed very different tempers from those of the higher town in Athens, which was distant about four miles from the former: But I believe no one attributes the difference of manners in Wapping[1] and St. James's, to a difference of air or climate.

*Thirdly.* The same national character commonly follows the authority of government to a precise boundary; and upon crossing a river or passing a mountain, one finds a new set of manners, with a new government. The Languedocians and Gascons are the gayest people in France; but whenever you pass the Pyrenees, you are among Spaniards. Is it conceivable, that the qualities of the air should change exactly with the limits of an empire, which depend so much on the accidents of battles, negotiations, and marriages?

*Fourthly.* When any set of men, scattered over distant nations, maintain a close society or communication together, they acquire a similitude of manners, and have but little in common with the nations amongst whom they live. Thus the Jews in Europe, and the Armenians in the east, have a peculiar character; and the former are as much noted for fraud, as the latter for probity.[2] The Jesuits, in all Roman-catholic countries, are also observed to have a character peculiar to themselves.

*Fifthly.* Where any accident, as a difference in language or religion, keeps two nations inhabiting the same country, from mixing with each other, they will preserve, during several centuries, a distinct and even opposite set of manners. The integ-

1 [A riverside dock district of Stepney metropolitan borough, London.]

2 A small sect or society amidst a greater are commonly most regular in their morals; because they are more remarked, and the faults of individuals draw dishonour on the whole. The only exception to this rule is, when the superstition and prejudices of the large society are so strong as to throw an infamy on the smaller society, independent of their morals. For in that case, having no character either to save or gain, they become careless of their behaviour, except among themselves.

rity, gravity, and bravery of the Turks, form an exact contrast to the deceit, levity, and cowardice of the modern Greeks.

*Sixthly.* The same set of manners will follow a nation, and adhere to them over the whole globe, as well as the same laws and language. The Spanish, English, French and Dutch colonies are all distinguishable even between the tropics.

*Seventhly.* The manners of a people change very considerably from one age to another, either by great alterations in their government, by the mixtures of new people, or by that inconstancy, to which all human affairs are subject. The ingenuity, industry, and activity of the ancient Greeks have nothing in common with the stupidity and indolence of the present inhabitants of those regions. Candour, bravery, and love of liberty formed the character of the ancient Romans; as subtilty, cowardice, and a slavish disposition do that of the modern. The old Spaniards were restless, turbulent, and so addicted to war, that many of them killed themselves, when deprived of their arms by the Romans.[3] One would find an equal difficulty at present, (at least one would have found it fifty years ago) to rouze up the modern Spaniards to arms. The Batavians were all soldiers of fortune, and hired themselves into the Roman armies. Their posterity make use of foreigners for the same purpose that the Romans did their ancestors. Though some few strokes of the French character be the same with that which Caesar has ascribed to the Gauls: yet what comparison between the civility, humanity, and knowledge of the modern inhabitants of that country, and the ignorance, barbarity, and grossness of the ancient? Not to insist upon the great difference between the present possessors of Britain, and those before the Roman conquest; we may observe that our ancestors, a few centuries ago, were sunk into the most abject superstition, last century they were inflamed with the most furious enthusiasm, and are now settled into the most cool indifference with regard to religious matters, that is to be found in any nation of the world.

*Eighthly.* Where several neighbouring nations have a very

[3] Livy, XXXIV. 17.

close communication together, either by policy, commerce, or travelling, they acquire a similitude of manners, proportioned to the communication. Thus all the Franks appear to have a uniform character to the eastern nations. The differences among them are like the peculiar accents of different provinces, which are not distinguishable, except by an ear accustomed to them, and which commonly escape a foreigner.

*Ninthly.* We may often remark a wonderful mixture of manners and characters in the same nation, speaking the same language, and subject to the same government: And in this particular the English are the most remarkable of any people, that perhaps ever were in the world. Nor is this to be ascribed to the mutability and uncertainty of their climate, or to any other *physical* causes; since all these causes take place in the neighbouring country of Scotland, without having the same effect. Where the government of a nation is altogether republican, it is apt to beget a peculiar set of manners. Where it is altogether monarchical, it is more apt to have the same effect; the imitation of superiors spreading the national manners faster among the people. If the governing part of a state consist altogether of merchants, as in Holland, their uniform way of life will fix their character. If it consists chiefly of nobles and landed gentry, like Germany, France, and Spain, the same effect follows. The genius of a particular sect or religion is also apt to mould the manners of a people. But the English government is a mixture of monarchy, aristocracy, and democracy. The people in authority are composed of gentry and merchants. All sects of religion are to be found among them. And the great liberty and independency, which every man enjoys, allows him to display the manners peculiar to him. Hence the English, of any people in the universe, have the least of a national character; unless this very singularity may pass for such.

If the characters of men depend on the air and climate, the degrees of heat and cold should naturally be expected to have a mighty influence; since nothing has a greater effect on all plants and irrational animals. And indeed there is some reason to think, that all nations, which live beyond the polar circles or between the tropics, are inferior to the rest of the species, and are incapable of all the higher attainments of the human mind. The poverty and misery of the northern inhabitants of the globe, and the indolence of the southern, from their few necessities, may, perhaps, account for this remarkable difference, without our having recourse to *physical* causes. This however is certain, that the characters of nations are very promiscuous in the temperate climates, and that almost all the general observations, which have been formed of the more southern or more northern people in these climates, are found to be uncertain and fallacious.[4]

. . . . . . . . . . .

The only observation, with regard to the difference of men in different climates, on which we can rest any weight, is the vulgar one, that people in the northern regions have a greater inclination to strong liquors, and those in the southern to love and women. One can assign a very probable *physical* cause for this difference. Wine and distilled waters warm the frozen blood in the colder climates, and fortify men against the injuries of the weather: As the genial heat of the sun, in the coun-

---

[4] I am apt to suspect the negroes, and in general all the other species of men (for there are four or five different kinds) to be naturally inferior to the whites. There never was a civilized nation of any other complexion than white, nor even any individual eminent either in action or speculation. No ingenious manufactures amongst them, no arts, no sciences. On the other hand, the most rude and barbarous of the whites, such as the ancient Germans, the present Tartars, have still something eminent about them, in their valour, form of government, or some other particular. Such a uniform and constant difference could not happen, in so many countries and ages, if nature had not made an original distinction betwixt these breeds of men. Not to mention our colonies, there are Negroe slaves dispersed all over Europe, of which none ever discovered any symptoms of ingenuity; tho' low people, without education, will start up amongst us, and distinguish themselves in every profession. In Jamaica indeed they talk of one negroe as a man of parts and learning; but 'tis likely he is admired for very slender accomplishments, like a parrot, who speaks a few words plainly.

tries exposed to his beams, inflames the blood, and exalts the passion between the sexes.[5]

Perhaps too, the matter may be accounted for by *moral* causes. All strong liquors are rarer in the north, and consequently are more coveted. Diodorus Siculus tells us, that the Gauls[6] in his time were great drunkards, and much addicted to wine; chiefly, I suppose, from its rarity and novelty. On the other hand, the heat in the southern climates, obliging men and women to go half naked, thereby renders their frequent commerce more dangerous, and inflames their mutual passion. This makes parents and husbands more jealous and reserved; which still further inflames the passion. Not to mention, that, as wom-

[5] [Bayle, in his article on "Daniel Ermita," Remarks F and I, discusses this phenomenon at great length, and this may be one of Hume's sources. Bayle stated: "It cannot be denied that the Christians of Europe are subject to two chief vices, drunkeness and lewdness. The first of these two vices reigns in the cold countries, the other in the warm ones. Bacchus and Venus have thus divided these nations. It so happens that, because the Reformation divided this part of Christendom in two, the part subject to Venus remained as it was, but the chief part of Bacchus' share renounced the papacy." In Remark I Bayle discusses the matter further, especially with reference to the question of whether Bacchus encroaches more on Venus than she does on Bacchus. In the course of this Remark Bayle elaborates on what the actual facts about northern drunkenness and southern lewdness are, whether there is not also northern lewdness, and what kinds of explanations—dietary, climatic, etc.—might account for the situation. Although Bayle holds that drinking and lewd behavior occur everywhere, excess, he feels, is a northern vice which tends to inhibit northern sexual activity.

Drunkenness, he points out, is really considered immoral in southern countries, while sexual promiscuity is not considered so wicked in either the north or the south. Hence, his considered final judgment is that "the empire of Venus ought not to be divided as the earth into five zones, one torrid, two temperate, and two cold: all its zones are torrid, with the sole difference being that they are more or less so. Never was a monarchy more universal than this one; no corner of the earth has avoided its yoke: there are some who aspire to independence, and who even undertake vows not to recognize its sovereignty, but they are often the most faithful subjects of this empire."]

[6] In V. 26. The same author ascribes taciturnity to that people; a new proof that national characters may alter very much. Taciturnity, as a national character, implies unsociableness. Aristotle in his *Politics* II. 9, says that the Gauls are the only warlike nation, who are negligent of women.

en ripen sooner in the southern regions, it is necessary to observe greater jealousy and care in their education; it being evident, that a girl of twelve cannot possess equal discretion to govern this passion, with one who feels not its violence till she be seventeen or eighteen. Nothing so much encourages the passion of love as ease and leisure, or is more destructive to it than industry and hard labour; and as the necessities of men are evidently fewer in the warm climates than in the cold ones, this circumstance alone may make a considerable difference between them.

But perhaps the fact is doubtful, that nature has, either from moral or physical causes, distributed these respective inclinations to the different climates. The ancient Greeks, though born in a warm climate, seem to have been much addicted to the bottle; nor were their parties of pleasure anything but matches of drinking among men, who passed their time altogether apart from the fair. Yet when Alexander led the Greeks into Persia, a still more southern climate, they multiplied their debauches of this kind, in imitation of the Persian manners.[7] So honourable was the character of a drunkard among the Persians, that Cyrus, the younger, soliciting the sober Lacedemonians for succour against his brother Artaxerxes, claims it chiefly on account of his superior endowments, as more valorous, more bountiful, and a better drinker.[8] Darius Hystaspes made it be inscribed on his tombstone, among his other virtues and princely qualities, that no one could bear a greater quantity of liquor. You may obtain any thing of the Negroes by offering them strong drink; and may easily prevail with them to sell, not only their children, but their wives and mistresses, for a cask of brandy. In France and Italy few drink pure wine, except in the greatest heats of summer; and indeed, it is then almost as necessary, in order to recruit the spirits, evaporated by heat, as it is in Sweden, during the winter, in order to warm the bodies congealed by the rigour of the season.

---

[7] *Babylonii maxime in vinum, & quae ebrietatem sequuntur, effusi sunt* ["The Babylonians particularly are lavishly addicted to wine and the concomitants of drunkenness"]. Quintus Curtius, V. 1. 37–38.

[8] Plutarch, *Symposium* I, quaest. 4.

If jealousy be regarded as a proof of an amorous disposition, no people were more jealous than the Muscovites, before their communication with Europe had somewhat altered their manners in this particular.

But supposing the fact true, that nature, by physical principles, has regularly distributed these two passions, the one to the northern, the other to the southern regions; we can only infer, that the climate may affect the grosser and more bodily organs of our frame; not that it can work upon those finer organs, on which the operations of the mind and understanding depend. And this is agreeable to the analogy of nature. The races of animals never degenerate when carefully tended; and horses, in particular, always show their blood in their shape, spirit, and swiftness: But a coxcomb may beget a philosopher; as a man of virtue may leave a worthless progeny.

I shall conclude this subject with observing, that though the passion for liquor be more brutal and debasing than love, which, when properly managed, is the source of all politeness and refinement; yet this gives not so great an advantage to the southern climates, as we may be apt, at first sight, to imagine. When love goes beyond a certain pitch, it renders men jealous, and cuts off the free intercourse between the sexes, on which the politeness of a nation will commonly much depend. And if we would subtilize and refine upon this point, we might observe, that the people, in very temperate climates, are the most likely to attain all sorts of improvement; their blood not being so inflamed as to render them jealous, and yet being warm enough to make them set a due value on the charms and endowments of the fair sex.

# AN ENQUIRY CONCERNING HUMAN UNDERSTANDING

[*Hume's* An Enquiry Concerning Human Understanding (*originally published in 1748 as the* Philosophical Essays concerning Human Understanding) *was the author's attempt to recast his views into a more popular and comprehensible form. The essay "Of Miracles," Section X of the* Enquiry, *immediately attracted the most attention, and many theologians tried to refute it. The essay was originally part of the* Treatise, *but it was apparently removed by Hume when he was trying to gain Bishop Butler's support and approbation. As Hume explained to Henry Home, "[I] accordingly inclose some* Reasonings concerning Miracles, *which I once thought of publishing with the rest, but which I am afraid will give too much offence, even as the world is disposed at present" (HL 6). The essay has continued to be one of Hume's most popular writings and contains one of the basic statements of his theory of historical knowledge.*]

# *From* Section VIII—Of Liberty and Necessity

As TO the first circumstance, the constant and regular conjunction of similar events; we may possibly satisfy ourselves by the following considerations. It is universally acknowledged, that there is a great uniformity among the actions of men, in all nations and ages, and that human nature remains still the same, in its principles and operations. The same motives always produce the same actions: The same events follow from the same causes. Ambition, avarice, self-love, vanity, friendship, generosity, public spirit; these passions, mixed in various degrees, and distributed through society, have been, from the beginning of the world, and still are, the source of all the actions and enterprizes, which have ever been observed among mankind. Would you know the sentiments, inclinations, and course of life of the Greeks and Romans? Study well the temper and actions of the French and English: You cannot be much mistaken in transferring to the former *most* of the observations, which you have made with regard to the latter. Mankind are so much the same, in all times and places, that history informs us of nothing new or strange in this particular. Its chief use is only to discover the constant and universal principles of human nature, by showing men in all varieties of circumstances and situations, and furnishing us with materials, from which we may form our observations, and become acquainted with the regular springs of human action and behaviour. These records of wars, intrigues, factions, and revolutions, are so many collections of experiments, by which the politician or moral philosopher fixes the principles of his science; in the same manner as the physician or the natural philosopher becomes acquainted with the nature of plants, minerals, and other external objects, by the experiments, which he forms concerning them. Nor are the earth, water, and other elements, examined by Aristotle, and Hippocrates, more like to those, which at present lie under our observation, than the men, described by Polybius and Tacitus, are to those, who now govern the world.

Should a traveller, returning from a far country, bring us an account of men, wholly different from any, with whom we were ever acquainted; men, who were entirely divested of avarice, ambition, or revenge; who knew no pleasure but friendship, generosity, and public spirit; we should immediately, from these circumstances, detect the falsehood, and prove him a liar, with the same certainty as if he had stuffed his narration with stories of centaurs and dragons, miracles and prodigies. And if we would explode any forgery in history, we cannot make use of a more convincing argument, than to prove, that the actions, ascribed to any person, are directly contrary to the course of nature, and that no human motives, in such circumstances, could ever induce him to such a conduct. The veracity of Quintus Curtius is as much to be suspected, when he describes the supernatural courage of Alexander, by which he was hurried on singly to attack multitudes, as when he describes his supernatural force and activity by which he was able to resist them. So readily and universally do we acknowledge a uniformity in human motives and actions as well as in the operations of body.

Hence likewise the benefit of that experience, acquired by long life and a variety of business and company, in order to instruct us in the principles of human nature, and regulate our future conduct, as well as speculation. By means of this guide, we mount up to the knowledge of men's inclinations and motives, from their actions, expressions, and even gestures; and again, descend to the interpretation of their actions from our knowledge of their motives and inclinations. The general observations, treasured up by a course of experience, give us the clue of human nature, and teach us to unravel all its intricacies. Pretexts and appearances no longer deceive us. Public declarations pass for the specious colouring of a cause. And though virtue and honour be allowed their proper weight and authority, that perfect disinterestedness, so often pretended to, is never expected in multitudes and parties; seldom in their leaders; and scarcely even in individuals of any rank or station. But were there no uniformity in human actions, and were every experiment, which we could form of this kind, irregular and anomalous, it were impossible to collect any general observations concerning mankind; and no experience, however accurately digested by reflection, would ever serve to any purpose. Why is the aged husbandman more skilful in his calling than the young beginner, but because there is a certain uniformity in the operation of the sun, rain, and earth, towards the production of vegetables; and experience teaches the old practitioner the rules, by which this operation is governed and directed?

We must not, however, expect, that this uniformity of human actions should be carried to such a length, as that all men, in the same circumstances, will always act precisely in the same manner, without making any allowance for the diversity of characters, prejudices, and opinions. Such a uniformity in every particular, is found in no part of nature. On the contrary, from observing the variety of conduct in different men, we are enabled to form a greater variety of maxims, which still suppose a degree of uniformity and regularity.

Are the manners of men different in different ages and countries? We learn thence the great force of custom and education, which mould the human mind from its infancy, and form it into a fixed and established character. Is the behaviour and conduct of the one sex very unlike that of the other? It is thence we become acquainted with the different characters, which nature has impressed upon the sexes, and which she preserves with constancy and regularity. Are the actions of the same person much diversified in the different periods of his life, from infancy to old age? This affords room for many general observations concerning the gradual change of our sentiments and inclinations, and the different maxims, which prevail in the different ages of human creatures. Even the characters, which are peculiar to each individual, have a uniformity in their influence; otherwise our acquaintance with the persons and our observation of their conduct, could never teach us their dispositions, or serve to direct our behaviour with regard to them.

# Section X—Of Miracles

## PART I

THERE IS, in Dr. Tillotson's writings, an argument against the *real presence,* which is as concise, and elegant, and strong as any argument can possibly be supposed against a doctrine, so little worthy of a serious refutation. It is acknowledged on all hands, says that learned prelate, that the authority, either of the scripture or of tradition, is founded merely in the testimony of the apostles, who were eye-witnesses to those miracles of our Saviour, by which he proved his divine mission. Our evidence, then, for the truth of the *Christian* religion is less than the evidence for the truth of our senses; because, even in the first authors of our religion, it was no greater; and it is evident it must diminish in passing from them to their disciples; nor can any one rest such confidence in their testimony, as in the immediate object of his senses. But a weaker evidence can never destroy a stronger; and therefore, were the doctrine of the real presence ever so clearly revealed in scripture, it were directly contrary to the rules of just reasoning to give our assent to it. It contradicts sense, though both the scripture and tradition, on which it is supposed to be built, carry not such evidence with them as sense; when they are considered merely as external evidences, and are not brought home to every one's breast, by the immediate operation of the Holy Spirit.

Nothing is so convenient as a decisive argument of this kind, which must at least *silence* the most arrogant bigotry and superstition, and free us from their impertinent solicitations. I flatter myself, that I have discovered an argument of a like nature, which, if just, will, with the wise and learned, be an everlasting check to all kinds of superstitious delusion, and consequently, will be useful as long as the world endures. For so long, I presume, will the accounts of miracles and prodigies be found in all history, sacred and profane.

Though experience be our only guide in reasoning concerning matters of fact; it must be acknowledged, that this guide is
not altogether infallible, but in some cases is apt to lead us into
errors. One, who in our climate, should expect better weather
in any week of June than in one of December, would reason
justly, and comformably to experience; but it is certain, that
he may happen, in the event, to find himself mistaken. However,
we may observe, that, in such a case, he would have no cause
to complain of experience; because it commonly informs us
beforehand of the uncertainty, by that contrariety of events,
which we may learn from a diligent observation. All effects follow not with like certainty from their supposed causes. Some
events are found, in all countries and all ages, to have been constantly conjoined together: Others are found to have been more
variable, and sometimes to disappoint our expectations; so that,
in our reasonings concerning matter of fact, there are all imaginable degrees of assurance, from the highest certainty to the
lowest species of moral evidence.

A wise man, therefore, proportions his belief to the evidence.
In such conclusions as are founded on an infallible experience,
he expects the event with the last degree of assurance, and regards his past experience as a full *proof* of the future existence
of that event. In other cases, he proceeds with more caution:
He weighs the opposite experiments: He considers which side
is supported by the greater number of experiments: To that
side he inclines, with doubt and hesitation; and when at last
he fixes his judgment, the evidence exceeds not what we properly call *probability*. All probability, then, supposes an opposition of experiments and observations, where the one side is
found to overbalance the other, and to produce a degree of
evidence, proportioned to the superiority. A hundred instances
or experiments on one side, and fifty on another, afford a doubtful expectation of any event; though a hundred uniform experiments, with only one that is contradictory, reasonably beget a
pretty strong degree of assurance. In all cases, we must balance
the opposite experiments, where they are opposite, and deduct
the smaller number from the greater, in order to know the
exact force of the superior evidence.

To apply these principles to a particular instance; we may observe, that there is no species of reasoning more common, more useful, and even necessary to human life, than that which is derived from the testimony of men, and the reports of eyewitnesses and spectators. This species of reasoning, perhaps, one may deny to be founded on the relation of cause and effect. I shall not dispute about a word. It will be sufficient to observe, that our assurance in any argument of this kind is derived from no other principle than our observation of the veracity of human testimony, and of the usual conformity of facts to the reports of witnesses. It being a general maxim, that no objects have any discoverable connexion together, and that all the inferences, which we can draw from one to another, are founded merely on our experience of their constant and regular conjunction; it is evident, that we ought not to make an exception to this maxim in favour of human testimony, whose connexion with any event seems, in itself, as little necessary as any other. Were not the memory tenacious to a certain degree; had not men commonly an inclination to truth and a principle of probity; were they not sensible to shame, when detected in a falsehood: Were not these, I say, discovered by *experience* to be qualities, inherent in human nature, we should never repose the least confidence in human testimony. A man delirious, or noted for falsehood and villainy, has no manner of authority with us.

And as the evidence, derived from witnesses and human testimony, is founded on past experience, so it varies with the experience, and is regarded either as a *proof* or a *probability,* according as the conjunction between any particular kind of report and any kind of object has been found to be constant or variable. There are a number of circumstances to be taken into consideration in all judgments of this kind; and the ultimate standard, by which we determine all disputes, that may arise concerning them, is always derived from experience and observation. Where this experience is not entirely uniform on any side, it is attended with an unavoidable contrariety in our judgments, and with the same opposition and mutual destruction of argument as in every other kind of evidence. We frequently hesitate concerning the reports of others. We balance the opposite circumstances, which cause any doubt or uncertainty; and when we discover a superiority on any side, we incline to it; but still with a diminution of assurance, in proportion to the force of its antagonist.

This contrariety of evidence, in the present case, may be derived from several different causes; from the opposition of contrary testimony; from the character or number of the witnesses; from the manner of their delivering their testimony; or from the union of all these circumstances. We entertain a suspicion concerning any matter of fact, when the witnesses contradict each other; when they are but few, or of a doubtful character; when they have an interest in what they affirm; when they deliver their testimony with hesitation, or on the contrary, with too violent asseverations. There are many other particulars of the same kind, which may diminish or destroy the force of any argument, derived from human testimony.

Suppose, for instance, that the fact, which the testimony endeavours to establish, partakes of the extraordinary and the marvellous; in that case, the evidence, resulting from the testimony, admits of a diminution, greater or less, in proportion as the fact is more or less unusual. The reason, why we place any credit in witnesses and historians, is not derived from any *connexion*, which we perceive *à priori*, between testimony and reality, but because we are accustomed to find a conformity between them. But when the fact attested is such a one as has seldom fallen under our observation, here is a contest of two opposite experiences; of which the one destroys the other, as far as its force goes, and the superior can only operate on the mind by the force, which remains. The very same principle of experience, which gives us a certain degree of assurance in the testimony of witnesses, gives us also, in this case, another degree of assurance against the fact, which they endeavour to establish; from which contradiction there necessarily arises a counterpoise, and mutual destruction of belief and authority.

*I should not believe such a story were it told me by Cato;* was a proverbial saying in Rome, even during the lifetime of that philosophical patriot.[1] The incredibility of a fact, it was allowed, might invalidate so great an authority.

The Indian prince, who refused to believe the first relations concerning the effects of frost, reasoned justly; and it naturally required very strong testimony to engage his assent to facts, that arose from a state of nature, with which he was unacquainted, and which bore so little analogy to those events, of which he had constant and uniform experience. Though they were not contrary to his experience, they were not conformable to it.[2]

But in order to increase the probability against the testimony of witnesses, let us suppose, that the fact, which they affirm, instead of being only marvellous, is really miraculous; and suppose also, that the testimony, considered apart and in itself, amounts to an entire proof; in that case, there is proof against proof, of which the strongest must prevail, but still with a diminution of its force, in proportion to that of its antagonist.

A miracle is a violation of the laws of nature; and as a firm and unalterable experience has established these laws, the proof against a miracle, from the very nature of the fact, is as entire as any argument from experience can possibly be imagined. Why

---

[1] Plutarch, *Lives,* "Cato the Younger" XIX.

[2] No Indian, it is evident, could have experience that water did not freeze in cold climates. This is placing nature in a situation quite unknown to him; and it is impossible for him to tell *à priori* what will result from it. It is making a new experiment, the consequence of which is always uncertain. One may sometimes conjecture from analogy what will follow; but still this is but conjecture. And it must be confessed, that, in the present case of freezing, the event follows contrary to the rules of analogy, and is such as a rational Indian would not look for. The operations of cold upon water are not gradual, according to the degrees of cold; but whenever it comes to the freezing point, the water passes in a moment, from the utmost liquidity to perfect hardness. Such an event, therefore, may be denominated *extraordinary,* and requires a pretty strong testimony, to render it credible to people in a warm climate: But still it is not *miraculous,* nor contrary to uniform experience of the course of nature in cases where all the circumstances are the same. The inhabitants of Sumatra have always seen water fluid in their own climate, and the freezing of their rivers ought to be deemed a prodigy: But they never saw water in Muscovy during the winter; and therefore they cannot reasonably be positive what would there be the consequence.

is it more than probable, that all men must die; that lead cannot, of itself, remain suspended in the air; that fire consumes wood, and is extinguished by water; unless it be, that these events are found agreeable to the laws of nature, and there is required a violation of these laws, or in other words, a miracle to prevent them? Nothing is esteemed a miracle, if it ever happen in the common course of nature. It is no miracle that a man, seemingly in good health, should die on a sudden: because such a kind of death, though more unusual than any other, has yet been frequently observed to happen. But it is a miracle, that a dead man should come to life; because that has never been observed, in any age or country. There must, therefore, be a uniform experience against every miraculous event, otherwise the event would not merit that appellation. And as an uniform experience amounts to a proof, there is here a direct and full *proof*, from the nature of the fact, against the existence of any miracle; nor can such a proof be destroyed, or the miracle rendered credible, but by an opposite proof, which is superior.[3]

The plain consequence is (and it is a general maxim worthy of our attention), "That no testimony is sufficient to establish a

[3] Sometimes an event may not, *in itself, seem* to be contrary to the laws of nature, and yet, if it were real, it might, by reason of some circumstances, be denominated a miracle; because, in *fact*, it is contrary to these laws. Thus if a person, claiming a divine authority, should command a sick person to be well, a healthful man to fall down dead, the clouds to pour rain, the winds to blow, in short, should order many natural events, which immediately follow upon his command; these might justly be esteemed miracles, because they are really, in this case, contrary to the laws of nature. For if any suspicion remain, that the event and command concurred by accident, there is no miracle and no transgression of the laws of nature. If this suspicion be removed, there is evidently a miracle, and a transgression of these laws; because nothing can be more contrary to nature than that the voice or command of a man should have such an influence. A miracle may be accurately defined, *a transgression of a law of nature by a particular volition of the Deity, or by the interposition of some invisible agent.* A miracle may either be discoverable by men or not. This alters not its nature and essence. The raising of a house or ship into the air is a visible miracle. The raising of a feather, when the wind wants ever so little of a force requisite for that purpose, is as real a miracle, though not so sensible with regard to us.

miracle, unless the testimony be of such a kind, that its falsehood would be more miraculous, than the fact, which it endeavours to establish: And even in that case there is a mutual destruction of arguments, and the superior only gives us an assurance suitable to that degree of force, which remains, after deducting the inferior." When any one tells me, that he saw a dead man restored to life, I immediately consider with myself, whether it be more probable, that this person should either deceive or be deceived, or that the fact, which he relates, should really have happened. I weigh the one miracle against the other; and according to the superiority, which I discover, I pronounce my decision, and always reject the greater miracle. If the falsehood of his testimony would be more miraculous, than the event which he relates; then, and not till then, can he pretend to command my belief or opinion.

## PART II

In the foregoing reasoning we have supposed, that the testimony, upon which a miracle is founded, may possibly amount to an entire proof, and that the falsehood of that testimony would be a real prodigy; But it is easy to show, that we have been a great deal too liberal in our concession, and that there never was a miraculous event established on so full an evidence.

For *first*, there is not to be found in all history, any miracle attested by a sufficient number of men, of such unquestioned good-sense, education, and learning, as to secure us against all delusion in themselves; of such undoubted integrity, as to place them beyond all suspicion of any design to deceive others; of such credit and reputation in the eyes of mankind, as to have a great deal to lose in case of their being detected in any falsehood; and at the same time, attesting facts, performed in such a public manner, and in so celebrated a part of the world, as to render the detection unavoidable: All which circumstances are requisite to give us a full assurance in the testimony of men.

*Secondly*. We may observe in human nature a principle, which, if strictly examined, will be found to diminish extremely the assurance, which we might, from human testimony, have, in any kind of prodigy. The maxim, by which we commonly conduct ourselves in our reasonings, is, that the objects, of which we have no experience, resemble those, of which we have; that what we have found to be most usual is always most probable; and that where there is an opposition of arguments, we ought to give the preference to such as are founded on the greatest number of past observations. But though, in proceeding by this rule, we readily reject any fact which is unusual and incredible in an ordinary degree; yet in advancing farther, the mind observes not always the same rule; but when anything is affirmed utterly absurd and miraculous, it rather the more readily admits of such a fact, upon account of that very circumstance, which ought to destroy all its authority. The passion of *surprize* and *wonder*, arising from miracles, being an agreeable emotion, gives a sensible tendency towards the belief of those events, from which it is derived. And this goes so far, that even those who cannot enjoy this pleasure immediately, nor can believe those miraculous events, of which they are informed, yet love to partake of the satisfaction at second-hand or by rebound, and place a pride and delight in exciting the admiration of others.

With what greediness are the miraculous accounts of travellers received, their descriptions of sea and land monsters, their relations of wonderful adventures, strange men, and uncouth manners? But if the spirit of religion join itself to the love of wonder, there is an end of common sense; and human testimony, in these circumstances, loses all pretensions to authority. A religionist may be an enthusiast, and imagine he sees what has no reality: He may know his narrative to be false, and yet persevere in it, with the best intentions in the world, for the sake of promoting so holy a cause: Or even where this delusion has not place, vanity, excited by so strong a temptation, operates on him more powerfully than on the rest of mankind in any other circumstances; and self-interest with equal force. His auditors may not have, and commonly have not, sufficient judgment to canvass his evidence: What judgment they have, they renounce by principle, in these sublime and mysterious subjects: Or if they were ever so willing to employ it, passion and a heated imagination disturb the regularity of its operations. Their credulity increases his impudence: And his impudence overpowers their credulity.

Eloquence, when at its highest pitch, leaves little room for reason or reflection; but addressing itself entirely to the fancy or the affections, captivates the willing hearers, and subdues their understanding. Happily, this pitch it seldom attains. But what a Tully or a Demosthenes could scarcely effect over a Roman or Athenian audience, every Capuchin, every itinerant or stationary teacher can perform over the generality of mankind, and in a higher degree, by touching such gross and vulgar passions.

The many instances of forged miracles, and prophecies, and supernatural events, which, in all ages, have either been detected by contrary evidence, or which detect themselves by their absurdity, prove sufficiently the strong propensity of mankind to the extraordinary and the marvellous, and ought reasonably to beget a suspicion against all relations of this kind. This is our natural way of thinking, even with regard to the most common and most credible events. For instance: There is no kind of report, which rises so easily, and spreads so quickly, especially in country places and provincial towns, as those concerning marriages; insomuch that two young persons of equal condition never see each other twice, but the whole neighbourhood immediately join them together. The pleasure of telling a piece of news so interesting, of propagating it, and of being the first reporters of it, spreads the intelligence. And this is so well known, that no man of sense gives attention to these reports, till he find them confirmed by some greater evidence. Do not the same passions, and others still stronger, incline the generality of mankind to believe and report, with the greatest vehemence and assurance, all religious miracles?

*Thirdly.* It forms a strong presumption against all supernatural and miraculous relations, that they are observed chiefly to abound among ignorant and barbarous nations; or if a civilized people has ever given admission to any of them, that people will be found to have received them from ignorant and barbarous ancestors, who transmitted them with that inviolable sanction and authority, which always attend received opinions. When we peruse the first histories of all nations, we are apt to imagine ourselves transported into some new world; where the whole frame of nature is disjointed, and every element performs its operations in a different manner, from what it does at present. Battles, revolutions, pestilence, famine, and death, are never the effect of those natural causes, which we experience. Prodigies, omens, oracles, judgments, quite obscure the few natural events, that are intermingled with them. But as the former grow thinner every page, in proportion as we advance nearer the enlightened ages, we soon learn, that there is nothing mysterious or supernatural in the case, but that all proceeds from the usual propensity of mankind towards the marvelous, and that, though this inclination may at intervals receive a check from sense and learning, it can never be thoroughly extirpated from human nature.

"It is strange," a judicious reader is apt to say, upon the perusal of these wonderful historians, "that such prodigious events never happen in our days." But it is nothing strange, I hope, that men should lie in all ages. You must surely have seen instances enow of that frailty. You have yourself heard many such marvellous relations started, which, being treated with scorn by all the wise and judicious, have at last been abandoned even by the vulgar. Be assured, that those renowned lies, which have spread and flourished to such a monstrous height, arose from like beginnings; but being sown in a more proper soil, shot up at last into prodigies almost equal to those which they relate.

It was a wise policy in that false prophet, Alexander, who, though now forgotten, was once so famous, to lay the first scene of his impostures in Paphlagonia, where, as Lucian tells us, the people were extremely ignorant and stupid, and ready to swallow even the grossest delusion. People at a distance, who are weak enough to think the matter at all worth inquiry, have no opportunity of receiving better information. The stories come magnified to them by a hundred circumstances. Fools are industrious in propagating the imposture; while the wise and learned are contented, in general, to deride its absurdity, without informing themselves of the particular facts, by which it may be distinctly refuted. And thus the impostor above-mentioned was enabled to proceed, from his ignorant Paphlagonians, to the enlisting of votaries, even among the Grecian philosophers, and men of the most eminent rank and distinction in Rome: Nay, could engage the attention of the sage emperor Marcus Aurelius; so far as to make him trust the success of a military expedition to his delusive prophecies.

The advantages are so great, of starting an imposture among an ignorant people, that, even though the delusion should be too gross to impose on the generality of them (*which, though seldom, is sometimes the case*) it has a much better chance for succeeding in remote countries, than if the first scene has been laid in a city renowned for arts and knowledge. The most ignorant and barbarous of these barbarians carry the report abroad. None of their countrymen have a large correspondence, or sufficient credit and authority to contradict and beat down the delusion. Men's inclination to the marvellous has full opportunity to display itself. And thus a story, which is universally exploded in the place where it was first started, shall pass for certain at a thousand miles distance. But had Alexander fixed his residence at Athens, the philosophers of that renowned mart of learning had immediately spread, throughout the whole Roman empire, their sense of the matter; which, being supported by so great authority, and displayed by all the force of reason and eloquence, had entirely opened the eyes of mankind. It is true; Lucian, passing by chance through Paphlagonia, had an opportunity of performing this good office. But, though much to be wished, it does not always happen, that every Alexander meets with a Lucian, ready to expose and detect his impostures.

I may add as a *fourth* reason, which diminishes the authority of prodigies, that there is no testimony for any, even those which have not been expressly detected, that is not opposed by an infinite number of witnesses; so that not only the miracle destroys the credit of testimony, but the testimony destroys itself. To make this the better understood, let us consider, that, in matters of religion, whatever is different is contrary; and that it is impossible the religions of ancient Rome, of Turkey, of Siam, and of China should, all of them, be established on any solid foundation. Every miracle, therefore, pretended to have been wrought in any of these religions (and all of them abound in miracles), as its direct scope is to establish the particular system to which it is attributed; so has it the same force, though more indirectly, to overthrow every other system. In destroying a rival system, it likewise destroys the credit of those miracles, on which that system was established; so that all the prodigies of different religions are to be regarded as contrary facts, and the evidences of these prodigies, whether weak or strong, as opposite to each other. According to this method of reasoning, when we believe any miracle of Mahomet or his successors, we have for our warrant the testimony of a few barbarous Arabians: And on the other hand, we are to regard the authority of Titus Livius, Plutarch, Tacitus, and, in short, of all the authors and witnesses, Grecian, Chinese, and Roman Catholic who have related any miracle in their particular religion; I say we are to regard their testimony in the same light as if they had mentioned that Mahometan miracle, and had in express terms contradicted it, with the same certainty as they have for the miracle they relate. This argument may appear over subtile and refined; but is not in reality different from the reasoning of a judge, who supposes, that the credit of two witnesses, maintaining a crime against any one, is destroyed by the testimony of two others, who affirm him to have been two hundred leagues distant, at the same instant when the crime is said to have been committed.

One of the best attested miracles in all profane history, is that which Tacitus reports of Vespasian, who cured a blind man in Alexandria, by means of his spittle, and a lame man by the mere touch of his foot; in obedience to a vision of the god Serapis, who had enjoined them to have recourse to the Emperor, for these miraculous cures. The story may be seen in that fine historian;[4] where every circumstance seems to add weight to the testimony, and might be displayed at large with all the force of argument and eloquence, if any one were now concerned to enforce the evidence of that exploded and idolatrous superstition. The gravity, solidity, age, and probity of so great an emperor, who, through the whole course of his life, conversed in a familiar manner with his friends and courtiers, and never affected those extraordinary airs of divinity assumed by Alexander and Demetrius. The historian, a cotemporary writer, noted for candour and veracity, and withal, the greatest and most penetrating genius, perhaps, of all antiquity; and so free from any tendency to credulity, that he even lies under the contrary imputation, of atheism and profaneness: The persons, from whose authority he related the miracle, of established character for judgment and veracity, as we may well presume; eye-witnesses of the fact, and confirming their testimony, after the Flavian family was despoiled of the empire, and could no longer give any reward, as the price of a lie. *Utrumque, qui interfuere, nunc quoque memorant, postquam nullum mendacio pretium.*[5] To which if we add the public nature of the facts, as related, it will appear, that no evidence can well be supposed stronger for so gross and so palpable a falsehood.

There is also a memorable story related by Cardinal de Retz, which may well deserve our consideration. When that intriguing politician fled into Spain, to avoid the persecution of his enemies, he passed through Saragossa, the capital of Arragon, where he was shown, in the cathedral, a man, who had served seven years as a door-keeper, and was well known to every body in town, that had ever paid his devotions at that church. He had been seen, for so long a time, wanting a leg; but recovered that

---

[4] *The Histories* IV. 81. Suetonius gives nearly the same account in *Lives of the Caesars* VIII. 7.

[5] ["Those who were present mention both incidents even now when there is no longer any reward for telling a lie."]

limb by the rubbing of holy oil upon the stump; and the cardinal assures us that he saw him with two legs. This miracle was vouched by all the canons of the church; and the whole company in town were appealed to for a confirmation of the fact; whom the cardinal found, by their zealous devotion, to be thorough believers of the miracle. Here the relater was also cotemporary to the supposed prodigy, of an incredulous and libertine character, as well as of great genius; the miracle of so *singular* a nature as could scarcely admit of a counterfeit, and the witnesses very numerous, and all of them, in a manner, spectators of the fact, to which they gave their testimony. And what adds mightily to the force of the evidence, and may double our surprize on this occasion, is, that the cardinal himself, who relates the story, seems not to give any credit to it, and consequently cannot be suspected of any concurrence in the holy fraud. He considered justly, that it was not requisite, in order to reject a fact of this nature, to be able accurately to disprove the testimony, and to trace its falsehood, through all the circumstances of knavery and credulity which produced it. He knew, that, as this was commonly altogether impossible at any small distance of time and place; so was it extremely difficult, even where one was immediately present, by reason of the bigotry, ignorance, cunning, and roguery of a great part of mankind. He therefore concluded, like a just reasoner, that such an evidence carried falsehood upon the very face of it, and that a miracle supported by any human testimony, was more properly a subject of derision than of argument.

There surely never was a greater number of miracles ascribed to one person, than those, which were lately said to have been wrought in France upon the tomb of Abbé Paris, the famous Jansenist, with whose sanctity the people were so long deluded. The curing of the sick, giving hearing to the deaf, and sight to the blind, were every where talked of as the usual effects of that holy sepulchre. But what is more extraordinary; many of the miracles were immediately proved upon the spot, before judges of unquestioned integrity, attested by witnesses of credit and distinction, in a learned age, and on the most eminent theatre that is now in the world. Nor is this all: A relation of them was published and dispersed every where; nor were the Jesuits, though a learned body, supported by the civil magistrate, and determined enemies to those opinions, in whose favour the miracles were said to have been wrought, ever able distinctly to refute or detect them.⁶ Where shall we find such a number of

⁶ This book was writ by Mons. Montgeron, counsellor or judge of the parliament of Paris, a man of figure and character, who was also a martyr to the cause, and is now said to be somewhere in a dungeon on account of his book.

There is another book in three volumes (called *Recueil des Miracles de l'Abbé Paris*) giving an account of many of these miracles, and accompanied with prefatory discourses, which are very well written. There runs, however, through the whole of these a ridiculous comparison between the miracles of our Saviour and those of the Abbé; wherein it is asserted, that the evidence for the latter is equal to that for the former: As if the testimony of men could ever be put in the balance with that of God himself, who conducted the pen of the inspired writers. If these writers, indeed, were to be considered merely as human testimony, the French author is very moderate in his comparison: since he might, with some appearance of reason, pretend, that the Jansenist miracles much surpass the other in evidence and authority. The following circumstances are drawn from authentic papers, inserted in the above-mentioned book.

Many of the miracles of Abbé Paris were proved immediately by witnesses before the officiality or bishop's court at Paris, under the eye of Cardinal Noailles, whose character for integrity and capacity was never contested even by his enemies.

His successor in the archbishopric was an enemy to the Jansenists, and for that reason promoted to the see by the court. Yet 22 rectors or *curés* of Paris, with infinite earnestness, press him to examine those miracles, which they assert to be known to the whole world, and undisputably certain: But he wisely forbore.

The Molinist party had tried to discredit these miracles in one instance, that of Madamoiselle le Franc. But, besides that their proceedings were in many respects the most irregular in the world, particularly in citing only a few of the Jansenist witnesses, whom they tampered with: Besides this, I say, they soon found themselves overwhelmed by a cloud of new witnesses, one hundred and twenty in number, most of them persons of credit and substance in Paris, who gave oath for the miracle. This was accompanied with a solemn and earnest appeal to the parliament. But the parliament were forbidden by authority to meddle in the affair. It was at last observed, that where men are heated by zeal and enthusiasm, there is no degree of human testimony so strong as may not be procured for the greatest absurdity: And

circumstances, agreeing to the corroboration of one fact? And what have we to oppose to such a cloud of witnesses, but the absolute impossibility or miraculous nature of the events, which they relate? And this surely, in the eyes of all reasonable people, will alone be regarded as a sufficient refutation.

Is the consequence just, because some human testimony has

---

those who will be so silly as to examine the affair by that medium, and seek particular flaws in the testimony, are almost sure to be confounded. It must be a miserable imposture, indeed, that does not prevail in that contest.

All who have been in France about that time have heard of the reputation of Mons. Heraut, the *lieutenant de Police,* whose vigilance, penetration, activity, and extensive intelligence have been much talked of. This magistrate, who by the nature of his office is almost absolute, was invested with full powers, on purpose to suppress or discredit these miracles; and he frequently seized immediately, and examined the witnesses and subjects of them: But never could reach any thing satisfactory against them.

In the case of Madamoiselle Thibaut he sent the famous De Sylva to examine her; whose evidence is very curious. The physician declares, that it was impossible she could have been so ill as was proved by witnesses; because it was impossible she could, in so short a time, have recovered so perfectly as he found her. He reasoned, like a man of sense, from natural causes; but the opposite party told him, that the whole was a miracle, and that his evidence was the very best proof of it.

The Molinists were in a sad dilemma. They durst not assert the absolute insufficiency of human evidence, to prove a miracle. They were obliged to say, that these miracles were wrought by witchcraft and the devil. But they were told, that this was the resource of the Jews of old.

No Jansenist was ever embarrassed to account for the cessation of the miracles, when the church-yard was shut up by the king's edict. It was the touch of the tomb, which produced these extraordinary effects; and when no one could approach the tomb, no effects could be expected. God, indeed, could have thrown down the walls in a moment; but he is master of his own graces and works, and it belongs not to us to account for them. He did not throw down the walls of every city like those of Jericho, on the sounding of the rams' horns, nor break up the prison of every apostle, like that of St. Paul.

No less a man, than the Duc de Chatillon, a duke and peer of France, of the highest rank and family, gives evidence of a miraculous cure, performed upon a servant of his, who had lived several years in his house with a visible and palpable infirmity.

I shall conclude with observing, that no clergy are more celebrated for

the utmost force and authority in some cases, when it relates
the battle of Philippi or Pharsalia for instance; that therefore
all kinds of testimony must, in all cases, have equal force and
authority? Suppose that the Caesarean and Pompeian factions
had, each of them, claimed the victory in these battles, and that
the historians of each party had uniformly ascribed the advantage to their own side; how could mankind, at this distance,
have been able to determine between them? The contrariety is
equally strong between the miracles related by Herodotus or
Plutarch, and those delivered by Mariana, Bede, or any monkish
historian.

The wise lend a very academic faith to every report which
favours the passion of the reporter; whether it magnifies his
country, his family, or himself, or in any other way strikes in

---

strictness of life and manners than the secular clergy of France, particularly
the rectors or curés of Paris, who bear testimony to these impostures.

The learning, genius, and probity of the gentlemen, and the austerity of
the nuns of Port-Royal, have been much celebrated all over Europe. Yet
they all give evidence for a miracle, wrought on the niece of the famous
Pascal, whose sanctity of life, as well as extraordinary capacity, is well known.
The famous Racine gives an account of this miracle in his famous history
of Port-Royal, and fortifies it with all the proofs, which a multitude of nuns,
priests, physicians, and men of the world, all of them of undoubted credit,
could bestow upon it. Several men of letters, particularly the bishop of
Tournay, thought this miracle so certain, as to employ it in the refutation of
atheists and free-thinkers. The queen-regent of France, who was extremely
prejudiced against the Port-Royal, sent her own physician to examine the
miracle, who returned an absolute convert. In short, the supernatural cure
was so uncontestable, that it saved, for a time, that famous monastery from
the ruin with which it was threatened by the Jesuits. Had it been a cheat, it
had certainly been detected by such sagacious and powerful antagonists, and
must have hastened the ruin of the contrivers. Our divines, who can build
up a formidable castle from such despicable materials; what a prodigious
fabric could they have reared from these and many other circumstances,
which I have not mentioned! How often would the great names of Pascal,
Racine, Arnaud, Nicole, have resounded in our ears? But if they be wise,
they had better adopt the miracle, as being more worth, a thousand times,
than all the rest of their collection. Besides, it may serve very much to their
purpose. For that miracle was really performed by the touch of an authentic
holy prickle of the holy thorn, which composed the holy crown, which, etc.

with his natural inclinations and propensities. But what greater temptation than to appear a missionary, a prophet, an ambassador from heaven? Who would not encounter many dangers and difficulties, in order to attain so sublime a character? Or if, by the help of vanity and a heated imagination, a man has first made a convert of himself, and entered seriously into the delusion; who ever scruples to make use of pious frauds, in support of so holy and meritorious a cause?

The smallest spark may here kindle into the greatest flame; because the materials are always prepared for it. The *avidum genus auricularum*,[7] the gazing [gaping?] populace, receive greedily, without examination, whatever sooths superstition, and promotes wonder.

How many stories of this nature, have, in all ages, been detected and exploded in their infancy? How many more have been celebrated for a time, and have afterwards sunk into neglect and oblivion? Where such reports, therefore, fly about, the solution of the phaenomenon is obvious; and we judge in conformity to regular experience and observation, when we account for it by the known and natural principles of credulity and delusion. And shall we, rather than have a recourse to so natural a solution, allow of a miraculous violation of the most established laws of nature?

I need not mention the difficulty of detecting a falsehood in any private or even public history, at the place, where it is said to happen; much more when the scene is removed to ever so small a distance. Even a court of judicature, with all the authority, accuracy, and judgment, which they can employ, find themselves often at a loss to distinguish between truth and falsehood in the most recent actions. But the matter never comes to any issue, if trusted to the common method of altercation and debate and flying rumours; especially when men's passions have taken part on either side.

In the infancy of new religions, the wise and learned commonly esteem the matter too inconsiderable to deserve their

---

[7] Lucretius, IV. 594. [*Ut omne humanum genus est avidum nimis auricularum.* "The whole human race is too greedy for ears to twitch."]

attention or regard. And when afterwards they would willingly detect the cheat, in order to undeceive the deluded multitude, the season is now past, and the records and witnesses, which might clear up the matter, have perished beyond recovery.

No means of detection remain, but those which must be drawn from the very testimony itself of the reporters: And these, though always sufficient with the judicious and knowing, are commonly too fine to fall under the comprehension of the vulgar.

Upon the whole, then, it appears, that no testimony for any kind of miracle has ever amounted to a probability, much less to a proof; and that, even supposing it amounted to a proof, it would be opposed by another proof; derived from the very nature of the fact, which it would endeavour to establish. It is experience only, which gives authority to human testimony; and it is the same experience, which assures us of the laws of nature. When, therefore, these two kinds of experience are contrary, we have nothing to do but substract the one from the other, and embrace an opinion, either on one side or the other, with that assurance which arises from the remainder. But according to the principle here explained, this substraction, with regard to all popular religions, amounts to an entire annihilation; and therefore we may establish it as a maxim, that no human testimony can have such force as to prove a miracle, and make it a just foundation for any such system of religion.

I beg the limitations here made may be remarked, when I say, that a miracle can never be proved, so as to be the foundation of a system of religion. For I own, that otherwise, there may possibly be miracles, or violations of the usual course of nature, of such a kind as to admit of proof from human testimony; though, perhaps, it will be impossible to find any such in all the records of history. Thus, suppose, all authors, in all languages, agree, that, from the first of January 1600 there was a total darkness over the whole earth for eight days: Suppose that the tradition of this extraordinary event is still strong and lively among the people: That all travellers, who return from foreign countries, bring us accounts of the same tradition, without the least varia-

tion or contradiction: It is evident, that our present philosophers, instead of doubting the fact, ought to receive it as certain,
and ought to search for the causes whence it might be derived.
The decay, corruption, and dissolution of nature, is an event
rendered probable by so many analogies, that any phaenomenon, which seems to have a tendency towards that catastrophe,
comes within the reach of human testimony, if that testimony be
very extensive and uniform.

But suppose, that all the historians who treat of England,
should agree, that, on the first of January 1600, Queen Elizabeth
died; that both before and after her death she was seen by her
physicians and the whole court, as is usual with persons of her
rank; that her successor was acknowledged and proclaimed by
the parliament; and that, after being interred a month, she
again appeared, resumed the throne, and governed England for
three years: I must confess that I should be surprized at the oc-
currence of so many odd circumstances, but should not have the
least inclination to believe so miraculous an event. I should not
doubt of her pretended death, and of those other public circumstances that followed it: I should only assert it to have been pretended, and that it neither was, nor possibly could be real. You
would in vain object to me the difficulty, and almost impossibility of deceiving the world in an affair of such consequence;
the wisdom and solid judgment of that renowned queen; with
the little or no advantage which she could reap from so poor an
artifice: All this might astonish me; but I would still reply, that
the knavery and folly of men are such common phaenomena,
that I should rather believe the most extraordinary events to
arise from their concurrence, than admit of so signal a violation
of the laws of nature.

But should this miracle be ascribed to any new system of
religion; men, in all ages, have been so much imposed on by
ridiculous stories of that kind, that this very circumstance would
be a full proof of a cheat, and sufficient, with all men of sense,
not only to make them reject the fact, but reject it without
farther examination. Though the Being to whom the miracle is
ascribed, be, in this case, Almighty, it does not, upon that ac-

count, become a whit more probable; since it is impossible for us to know the attributes or actions of such a Being, otherwise than from the experience which we have of his productions, in the usual course of nature. This still reduces us to past observation, and obliges us to compare the instances of the violation of truth in the testimony of men, with those of the violation of the laws of nature by miracles, in order to judge which of them is most likely and probable. As the violations of truth are more common in the testimony concerning religious miracles, than in that concerning any other matter of fact; this must diminish very much the authority of the former testimony, and make us form a general resolution, never to lend any attention to it, with whatever specious pretence it may be covered.

Lord Bacon seems to have embraced the same principles of reasoning. "We ought," says he, "to make a collection of particular history of all monsters and prodigious births or productions, and in a word of every thing new, rare, and extraordinary in nature. But this must be done with the most severe scrutiny, lest we depart from truth. Above all, every relation must be considered as suspicious, which depends in any degree upon religion, as the prodigies of Livy: And no less so, every thing that is to be found in the writers of natural magic or alchimy, or such authors, who seem, all of them, to have an unconquerable appetite for falsehood and fable."[8]

I am the better pleased with the method of reasoning here delivered, as I think it may serve to confound those dangerous friends or disguised enemies to the *Christian Religion,* who have undertaken to defend it by the principles of human reason. Our most holy religion is founded on *Faith,* not on reason; and it is a sure method of exposing it to put it to such a trial as it is, by no means, fitted to endure. To make this more evident, let us examine those miracles, related in scripture; and not to lose ourselves in too wide a field, let us confine ourselves to such as we find in the *Pentateuch,* which we shall examine, according to the principles of those pretended Christians, not as the word or

8 *Novum Organum,* Bk. II, aph. 29.

testimony of God himself, but as the production of a mere human writer and historian. Here then we are first to consider a book, presented to us by a barbarous and ignorant people, written in an age when they were still more barbarous, and in all probability long after the facts which it relates, corroborated by no concurring testimony, and resembling those fabulous accounts, which every nation gives of its origin. Upon reading this book, we find it full of prodigies and miracles. It gives an account of a state of the world and of human nature entirely different from the present: Of our fall from that state: Of the age of man, extended to near a thousand years: Of the destruction of the world by a deluge: Of the arbitrary choice of one people, as the favourites of heaven; and that people the countrymen of the author: Of their deliverance from bondage by prodigies the most astonishing imaginable: I desire any one to lay his hand upon his heart, and after a serious consideration declare, whether he thinks that the falsehood of such a book, supported by such a testimony, would be more extraordinary and miraculous than all the miracles it relates; which is, however, necessary to make it be received, according to the measures of probability above established.

What we have said of miracles may be applied, without any variation, to prophecies; and indeed, all prophecies are real miracles, and as such only, can be admitted as proofs of any revelation. If it did not exceed the capacity of human nature to foretel future events, it would be absurd to employ any prophecy as an argument for a divine mission or authority from heaven. So that, upon the whole, we may conclude, that the *Christian Religion* not only was at first attended with miracles, but even at this day cannot be believed by any reasonable person without one. Mere reason is insufficient to convince us of its veracity: And whoever is moved by *Faith* to assent to it, is conscious of a continued miracle in his own person, which subverts all the principles of his understanding, and gives him a determination to believe what is most contrary to custom and experience.

# OF THE POPULOUSNESS OF
# ANCIENT NATIONS

[*This essay in demography Hume first published in 1752 as one
of the* Political Discourses. *The question that it considers, the
relative size of the populations of the ancient and modern world,
Hume thought "the most curious and important of all Questions
of Erudition" (NHL 11). What he meant by saying that the
problem was one of "Erudition" is readily apparent to one who
reads over the footnotes with an eye to the authors cited (though
many notes have been omitted here, sometimes without indication, because the essay is abridged to less than half its original
length). Hume gives the banner of superior numbers to the
modern world, though only tentatively. Writing to John
Clephane on April 18, 1750 (HL 66), he remarks that "The last
thing I took my hand from was a very learned, elaborate discourse, concerning the populousness of antiquity; although
not altogether in opposition to Vossius and Montesquieu, who
exaggerate the affair infinitely; but, starting some doubts, and
scruples, and difficulties, sufficient to make us suspend our judgment on that head."*

*For the many interesting biographical details surrounding
this essay and the Rev. Robert Wallace's countering production,*
A Dissertation on the Numbers of Mankind in Ancient and
Modern Times, *see E. C. Mossner,* The Forgotten Hume. Le
Bon David *(New York: Columbia University Press, 1943), pp.
105–131.*]

THERE IS very little ground, either from reason or observation,
to conclude the world eternal or incorruptible. The continual
and rapid motion of matter, the violent revolutions with which

77

every part is agitated, the changes remarked in the heavens, the plain traces as well as tradition of an universal deluge, or general convulsion of the elements; all these prove strongly the mortality of this fabric of the world, and its passage, by corruption or dissolution, from one state or order to another. It must therefore, as well as each individual form which it contains, have its infancy, youth, manhood, and old age; and it is probable, that, in all these variations, man, equally with every animal and vegetable will partake. In the flourishing age of the world, it may be expected, that the human species should possess greater vigour both of mind and body, more prosperous health, higher spirits, longer life, and a stronger inclination and power of generation. But if the general system of things, and human society of course, have any such gradual revolutions, they are too slow to be discernible in that short period which is comprehended by history and tradition. Stature and force of body, length of life, even courage and extent of genius, seem hitherto to have been naturally, in all ages, pretty much the same. The arts and sciences, indeed, have flourished in one period, and have decayed in another: But we may observe, that, at the time when they rose to greatest perfection among one people, they were perhaps totally unknown to all the neighbouring nations; and though they universally decayed in one age, yet in a succeeding generation they again revived, and diffused themselves over the world. As far, therefore, as observation reaches, there is no universal difference discernible in the human species; and though it were allowed, that the universe, like an animal body, had a natural progress from infancy to old age; yet as it must still be uncertain, whether, at present, it be advancing to its point of perfection, or declining from it, we cannot thence presuppose any decay in human nature.[1] To prove, therefore, or account for that superior popu-

[1] Columella says (III. 8) that in Egypt and Africa the bearing of twins was frequent, and even customary; *gemini partus familiares, ac poene solennes sunt.* If this was true, there is a physical difference both in countries and ages. For travellers make no such remarks on these countries at present. On the contrary, we are apt to suppose the northern nations more prolific. As those two countries were provinces of the Roman empire, it is difficult, though not altogether absurd, to suppose that such a man as Columella might be mistaken with regard to them.

lousness of antiquity, which is commonly supposed, by the imaginary youth or vigour of the world, will scarcely be admitted by any just reasoner. These *general physical* causes ought entirely to be excluded from this question.

There are indeed some more *particular physical* causes of importance. Diseases are mentioned in antiquity, which are almost unknown to modern medicine; and new diseases have arisen and propagated themselves, of which there are no traces in ancient history. In this particular we may observe, upon comparison, that the disadvantage is much on the side of the moderns. Not to mention some others of less moment; the small-pox commits such ravages, as would almost alone account for the great superiority ascribed to ancient times. The tenth or the twelfth part of mankind, destroyed every generation, should make a vast difference, it may be thought, in the numbers of the people; and when joined to venereal distempers, a new plague diffused every where, this disease is perhaps equivalent, by its constant operation, to the three great scourges of mankind, war, pestilence, and famine. Were it certain, therefore, that ancient times were more populous than the present, and could no moral causes be assigned for so great a change; these physical causes alone, in the opinion of many, would be sufficient to give us satisfaction on that head.

But is it certain, that antiquity was so much more populous, as is pretended? The extravagancies of Vossius, with regard to this subject, are well known. But an author of much greater genius and discernment has ventured to affirm, that, according to the best computations which these subjects will admit of, there are not now, on the face of the earth, the fiftieth part of mankind, which existed in the time of Julius Caesar.[2] It may easily be observed, that the comparison, in this case, must be imperfect, even though we confine ourselves to the scene of ancient history; Europe, and the nations round the Mediterranean. We know not exactly the numbers of any European kingdom, or even city, at present: How can we pretend to calculate those of ancient cities and states, where historians have

2 *Lettres Persanes.* See also *L'Esprit des Loix,* Bk. XXIII, chaps. 17, 18, 19. [Montesquieu is the author of these works.]

left us such imperfect traces? For my part, the matter appears to me so uncertain, that, as I intend to throw together some reflections on that head, I shall intermingle the enquiry concerning *causes* with that concerning *facts;* which ought never to be admitted, where the facts can be ascertained with any tolerable assurance. We shall, *first,* consider whether it be probable, from what we know of the situation of society in both periods, that antiquity must have been more populous; *secondly,* whether in reality it was so. If I can make it appear, that the conclusion is not so certain as is pretended, in favour of antiquity, it is all I aspire to.

In general, we may observe, that the question, with regard to the comparative populousness of ages or kingdoms, implies important consequences, and commonly determines concerning the preference of their whole police, their manners, and the constitution of their government. For as there is in all men, both male and female, a desire and power of generation, more active than is ever universally exerted, the restraints, which they lie under, must proceed from some difficulties in their situation, which it belongs to a wise legislature carefully to observe and remove. Almost every man who thinks he can maintain a family will have one; and the human species, at this rate of propagation, would more than double every generation. How fast do mankind multiply in every colony or new settlement; where it is an easy matter to provide for a family; and where men are nowise straitened or confined, as in long established governments? History tells us frequently of plagues, which have swept away the third or fourth part of a people: Yet in a generation or two, the destruction was not perceived; and the society had again acquired their former number. The lands which were cultivated, the houses built, the commodities raised, the riches acquired, enabled the people, who escaped, immediately to marry, and to rear families, which supplied the place of those who had perished. And for a like reason, every wise, just, and mild government, by rendering the condition of its subjects easy and secure, will always abound most in people, as well as in commodities and riches. A country, indeed, whose climate and soil are fitted for vines, will naturally be more populous than one which produces corn only, and that more populous than one which is only fitted for pasturage. In general, warm climates, as the necessities of the inhabitants are there fewer, and vegetation more powerful, are likely to be most populous: But if everything else be equal, it seems natural to expect, that, wherever there are most happiness and virtue, and the wisest institutions, there will also be most people.

The question, therefore, concerning the populousness of ancient and modern times, being allowed of great importance, it will be requisite, if we would bring it to some determination, to compare both the *domestic* and *political* situation of these two periods, in order to judge of the facts by their moral causes; which is the *first* view in which we proposed to consider them.

The chief difference between the *domestic* oeconomy of the ancients and that of the moderns consists in the practice of slavery, which prevailed among the former, and which has been abolished for some centuries throughout the greater part of Europe. Some passionate admirers of the ancients, and zealous partizans of civil liberty, (for these sentiments, as they are, both of them, in the main, extremely just, are found to be almost inseparable) cannot forbear regretting the loss of this institution; and whilst they brand all submission to the government of a single person with the harsh denomination of slavery, they would gladly reduce the greater part of mankind to real slavery and subjection. But to one who considers coolly on the subject it will appear, that human nature, in general, really enjoys more liberty at present, in the most arbitary government of Europe, than it ever did during the most flourishing period of ancient times. As much as submission to a petty prince, whose dominions extend not beyond a single city, is more grievous than obedience to a great monarch; so much is domestic slavery more cruel and oppressive than any civil subjection whatsoever. The more the master is removed from us in place and rank, the greater liberty we enjoy; the less are our actions inspected and controled; and the fainter that cruel comparison becomes between our own subjection, and the freedom, and even dominion of another. The remains which are found of domestic slavery, in the American colonies, and among some European nations, would never surely create a desire of rendering it more universal. The little humanity, commonly observed in persons, accustomed, from their infancy, to exercise so great authority over their fellow-creatures, and to trample upon human nature, were sufficient alone to disgust us with that unbounded dominion. Nor can a more probable reason be assigned for the severe, I might say, barbarous manners of ancient times, than the practice of domestic slavery; by which every man of rank was rendered a petty tyrant, and educated amidst the flattery, submission, and low debasement of his slaves.

According to ancient practice, all checks were on the inferior, to restrain him to the duty of submission; none on the superior, to engage him to the reciprocal duties of gentleness and humanity. In modern times, a bad servant finds not easily a good master, nor a bad master a good servant; and the checks are mutual, suitably to the inviolable and eternal laws of reason and equity.

.    .    .    .    .    .    .    .    .    .

But our present business is only to consider the influence of slavery on the populousness of a state. It is pretended, that, in this particular, the ancient practice had infinitely the advantage, and was the chief cause of that extreme populousness, which is supposed in those times. At present, all masters discourage the marrying of their male servants, and admit not by any means the marriage of the female, who are then supposed altogether incapacitated for their service. But where the property of the servants is lodged in the master, their marriage forms his riches, and brings him a succession of slaves that supply the place of those whom age and infirmity have disabled. He encourages, therefore, their propagation as much as that of his cattle; rears the young with the same care; and educates them to some art or calling, which may render them more useful or valuable to him. The opulent are, by this policy, interested in the being at least, though not in the well-being of the poor; and enrich themselves,

by increasing the number and industry of those who are subjected to them. Each man, being a sovereign in his own family,
has the same interest with regard to it, as the prince with regard
to the state; and has not, like the prince, any opposite motives
of ambition or vainglory, which may lead him to depopulate his
little sovereignty. All of it is, at all times, under his eye; and he
has leisure to inspect the most minute detail of the marriage and
education of his subjects.[3]

Such are the consequences of domestic slavery, according to
the first aspect and appearance of things: But if we enter more
deeply into the subject, we shall perhaps find reason to retract
our hasty determinations. The comparison is shocking between
the management of human creatures and that of cattle; but
being extremely just, when applied to the present subject, it
may be proper to trace the consequences of it. At the capital,
near all great cities, in all populous, rich, industrious provinces,
few cattle are bred. Provisions, lodging, attendance, labour are
there dear; and men find their account better in buying the cattle after they come to a certain age, from the remoter and
cheaper countries. These are consequently the only breeding
countries for cattle; and by a parity of reason, for men too, when
the latter are put on the same footing with the former. To rear
a child in London, till he could be serviceable, would cost much
dearer, than to buy one of the same age from Scotland or Ireland; where he had been bred in a cottage, covered with rags,
and fed on oatmeal or potatoes. Those who had slaves, therefore, in all the richer and more populous countries, would discourage the pregnancy of the females, and either prevent or
destroy the birth. The human species would perish in those
places where it ought to encrease the fastest; and a perpetual

---

[3] We may here observe, that if domestic slavery really increased populousness, it would be an exception to the general rule, that the happiness of
any society and its populousness are necessary attendants. A master, from
humour or interest, may make his slaves very unhappy, yet be careful, from
interest, to increase their number. Their marriage is not a matter of choice
with them, more than any other action of their life.

recruit be wanted from the poorer and more desert provinces. Such a continued drain would tend mightily to depopulate the state, and render great cities ten times more destructive than with us; where every man is master of himself, and provides for his children from the powerful instinct of nature, not the calculations of sordid interest. If London, at present, without much increasing, needs a yearly recruit from the country, of 5,000 people, as is usually computed, what must it require, if the greater part of the tradesmen and common people were slaves, and were hindered from breeding by their avaricious masters?

.    .    .    .    .    .    .    .    .    .    .

Consider this passage of Plutarch,[4] speaking of the Elder Cato. "He had a great number of slaves, whom he took care to buy at the sales of prisoners of war; and he chose them young, that they might easily be accustomed to any diet or manner of life, and be instructed in any business or labour, as men teach any thing to young dogs or horses.—And esteeming love the chief source of all disorders, he allowed the male slaves to have a commerce with the female in his family, upon paying a certain sum for this privilege: But he strictly prohibited all intrigues out of his family." Are there any symptoms in this narration of that care which is supposed in the ancients, of the marriage and propagation of their slaves? If that was a common practice, founded on general interest, it would surely have been embraced by Cato, who was a great oeconomist, and lived in times when the ancient frugality and simplicity of manners were still in credit and reputation.

It is expressly remarked by the writers of the Roman law, that scarcely any ever purchase slaves with a view of breeding from them.

.    .    .    .    .    .    .    .    .    .    .

Our lackeys and house-maids, I own, do not serve much to multiply their species: But the ancients, besides those who attended on their person, had almost all their labour performed,

4 *Lives*, "Cato the Elder" XXI.

and even manufactures executed, by slaves, who lived, many of them, in their family; and some great men possessed to the number of 10,000. If there be any suspicion, therefore, that this institution was unfavourable to propagation, (and the same reason, at least in part, holds with regard to ancient slaves as modern servants) how destructive must slavery have proved?

.   .   .   .   .   .   .   .   .   .   .

The ancients talk so frequently of a fixed, stated portion of provisions assigned to each slave,[5] that we are naturally led to conclude, that slaves lived almost all single, and received that portion as a kind of board-wages.

The practice, indeed, of marrying slaves seems not to have been very common, even among the country-labourers, where it is more naturally to be expected.

.   .   .   .   .   .   .   .   .   .   .

It is indeed recommended by Varro,[6] to propagate young shepherds in the family from the old ones. For as grasing farms were commonly in remote and cheap places, and each shepherd lived in a cottage apart, his marriage and encrease were not liable to the same inconveniencies as in dearer places, and where many servants lived in the family; which was universally the case in such of the Roman farms as produced wine or corn. If we consider this exception with regard to shepherds, and weigh the reasons of it, it will serve for a strong confirmation of all our foregoing suspicions.[7]

Columella,[8] I own, advises the master to give a reward, and even liberty to a female slave, that had reared him above three children: A proof that sometimes the ancients propagated from their slaves; which, indeed, cannot be denied. Were it otherwise, the practice of slavery, being so common in antiquity, must have

[5] See Cato, *De re rustica* LVI; Terence, *Phormio* 43; Seneca, *Epistulae morales* LXXX. 7.

[6] II. 10.

[7] *Pastoris duri est hic filius, ille bubulci* ["This is the son of a rude shepherd, that of a ploughman"]; Juvenal, *Satires* XI. 151.

[8] *De re rustica* I. 8. 19.

been destructive to a degree which no expedient could repair. All I pretend to infer from these reasonings is, that slavery is in general disadvantageous both to the happiness and populousness of mankind, and that its place is much better supplied by the practice of hired servants.

. . . . . . . . . . .

Our modern convents are, no doubt, bad institutions: But there is reason to suspect, that anciently every great family in Italy, and probably in other parts of the world, was a species of convent. And though we have reason to condemn all those popish institutions, as nurseries of superstition, burthensome to the public, and oppressive to the poor prisoners, male as well as female; yet may it be questioned whether they be so destructive to the populousness of a state, as is commonly imagined. Were the land, which belongs to a convent, bestowed on a nobleman, he would spend its revenue on dogs, horses, grooms, footmen, cooks, and house-maids; and his family would not furnish many more citizens than the convent.

The common reason, why any parent thrusts his daughters into nunneries, is, that he may not be overburthened with too numerous a family; but the ancients had a method almost as innocent, and more effectual to that purpose, to wit, exposing their children in early infancy. This practice was very common; and is not spoken of by any author of those times with the horror it deserves, or scarcely[9] even with disapprobation. Plutarch, the humane, good-natured Plutarch,[10] mentions it as a merit in Attalus, king of Pergamus, that he murdered, or, if you will, exposed all his own children, in order to leave his crown to the son of his brother, Eumenes; signalizing in this manner his gratitude and affection to Eumenes, who had left him his heir preferably to that son. It was Solon, the most celebrated of the sages of Greece, that gave parents permission by law to kill their children.[11]

9 Tacitus blames it (*Germania* XIX).

10 *Moralia* "De fraterno amore." Seneca also approves of the exposing of sickly infirm children (*De ira* I. 15.).

11 Sextus Empiricus, *Pyrrhoniarum hypotoposeon* III. 211.

Shall we then allow these two circumstances to compensate each other, to wit, monastic vows, and the exposing of children, and to be unfavourable, in equal degrees, to the propagation of mankind? I doubt the advantage is here on the side of antiquity. Perhaps, by an odd connexion of causes, the barbarous practice of the ancients might rather render those times more populous. By removing the terrors of too numerous a family it would engage many people in marriage; and such is the force of natural affection, that very few, in comparison, would have resolution enough, when it came to the push, to carry into execution their former intentions.

. . . . . . . . .

Of all sciences there is none, where first appearances are more deceitful than in politics. Hospitals for foundlings seem favourable to the increase of numbers; and perhaps, may be so, when kept under proper restrictions. But when they open the door to every one, without distinction, they have probably a contrary effect, and are pernicious to the state. It is computed, that every ninth child born at Paris, is sent to the hospital; though it seems certain, according to the common course of human affairs, that it is not a hundredth child whose parents are altogether incapacitated to rear and educate him. The great difference, for health, industry, and morals, between an education in an hospital and that in a private family, should induce us not to make the entrance into the former too easy and engaging. To kill one's own child is shocking to nature, and must therefore be somewhat unusual; but to turn over the care of him upon others, is very tempting to the natural indolence of mankind.

Having considered the domestic life and manners of the ancients, compared to those of the moderns; where, in the main, we seem rather superior, so far as the present question is concerned; we shall now examine the *political* customs and institutions of both ages, and weigh their influence in retarding or forwarding the propagation of mankind.

Before the increase of the Roman power, or rather till its full establishment, almost all the nations, which are the scene of ancient history, were divided into small territories or petty com-

monwealths, where of course a great equality of fortune prevailed, and the center of the government was always very near
its frontiers.

This was the situation of affairs not only in Greece and Italy,
but also in Spain, Gaul, Germany, Afric, and a great part of the
Lesser Asia: And it must be owned, that no institution could be
more favourable to the propagation of mankind. For, though a
man of an overgrown fortune, not being able to consume more
than another, must share it with those who serve and attend
him; yet their possession being precarious, they have not the same
encouragement to marry, as if each had a small fortune, secure
and independent. Enormous cities are, besides, destructive to
society, beget vice and disorder of all kinds, starve the remoter
provinces, and even starve themselves, by the prices to which
they raise all provisions. Where each man had his little house
and field to himself, and each county had its capital, free and
independent; what a happy situation of mankind! How favourable to industry and agriculture; to marriage and propagation!
The prolific virtue of men, were it to act in its full extent, without that restraint which poverty and necessity imposes on it,
would double the number every generation: And nothing surely
can give it more liberty, than such small commonwealths, and
such an equality of fortune among the citizens. All small states
naturally produce equality of fortune, because they afford no
opportunities of great increase; but small commonwealths
much more, by that division of power and authority which is
essential to them.

.    .    .    .    .    .    .    .    .    .

It must be owned, that the situation of affairs in modern
times, with regard to civil liberty, as well as equality of fortune,
is not near so favourable, either to the propagation or happiness
of mankind. Europe is shared out mostly into great monarchies;
and such parts of it as are divided into small territories, are
commonly governed by absolute princes, who ruin their people
by a mimicry of the greater monarchs, in the splendor of their
court and number of their forces. Switzerland alone and Holland resemble the ancient republics; and though the former is

far from possessing any advantage either of soil, climate, or commerce, yet the numbers of people, with which it abounds, notwithstanding their enlisting themselves into every service in Europe, prove sufficiently the advantages of their political institutions.

The ancient republics derived their chief or only security from the numbers of their citizens. The Trachinians having lost great numbers of their people, the remainder, instead of enriching themselves by the inheritance of their fellow-citizens, applied to Sparta, their metropolis, for a new stock of inhabitants. The Spartans immediately collected ten thousand men; among whom the old citizens divided the lands of which the former proprietors had perished.[12]

After Timoleon had banished Dionysius from Syracuse, and had settled the affairs of Sicily, finding the cities of Syracuse and Sellinuntium extremely depopulated by tyranny, war, and faction, he invited over from Greece some new inhabitants to repeople them.[13] Immediately forty thousand men (Plutarch[14] says sixty thousand) offered themselves; and he distributed so many lots of land among them, to the great satisfaction of the ancient inhabitants: A proof at once of the maxims of ancient policy, which affected populousness more than riches; and of the good effects of these maxims, in the extreme populousness of that small country, Greece, which could at once supply so great a colony. The case was not much different with the Romans in early times. He is a pernicious citizen, said M. Curius, who cannot be content with seven acres.[15] Such ideas of equality could not fail of producing great numbers of people.

We must now consider what disadvantages the ancients lay under with regard to populousness, and what checks they received from their political maxims and institutions. There are commonly compensations in every human condition: and though these compensations be not always perfectly equal, yet

12 Diodorus Siculus, XII. 59. Thucydides, III. 92.
13 Diodorus Siculus, XVI. 82. 4–5.
14 *Lives*, "Timoleon" XXIII. 4.
15 Pliny, XVIII. 4. 18.

they serve, at least, to restrain the prevailing principle. To compare them and estimate their influence, is indeed difficult, even where they take place in the same age, and in neighbouring countries: But where several ages have intervened, and only scattered lights are afforded us by ancient authors; what can we do but amuse ourselves by talking *pro* and *con,* on an interesting subject, and thereby correcting all hasty and violent determinations?

*First,* We may observe, that the ancient republics were almost in perpetual war, a natural effect of their martial spirit, their love of liberty, their mutual emulation, and that hatred which generally prevails among nations that live in close neighbourhood. Now, war in a small state is much more destructive than in a great one; both because all the inhabitants, in the former case, must serve in the armies; and because the whole state is frontier, and is all exposed to the inroads of the enemy.

The maxims of ancient war were much more destructive than those of modern; chiefly by that distribution of plunder, in which the soldiers were indulged. The private men in our armies are such a low set of people, that we find any abundance, beyond their simple pay, breeds confusion and disorder among them, and a total dissolution of discipline. The very wretchedness and meanness of those, who fill the modern armies, render them less destructive to the countries which they invade: One instance, among many, of the deceitfulness of first appearances in all political reasonings.[16]

Ancient battles were much more bloody, by the very nature of the weapons employed in them. The ancients drew up their men 16 or 20, sometimes 50 men deep, which made a narrow front; and it was not difficult to find a field, in which both armies might be marshalled, and might engage with each other. Even where any body of the troops was kept off by hedges, hil-

---

16 The ancient soldiers, being free citizens, above the lowest rank, were all married. Our modern soldiers are either forced to live unmarried, or their marriages turn to small account towards the increase of mankind. A circumstance which ought, perhaps, to be taken into consideration, as of some consequence in favour of the ancients.

locks, woods, or hollow ways, the battle was not so soon decided between the contending parties, but that the others had time to overcome the difficulties which opposed them, and take part in the engagement. And as the whole army was thus engaged, and each man closely buckled to his antagonist, the battles were commonly very bloody, and great slaughter was made on both sides, especially on the vanquished. The long thin lines, required by fire-arms, and the quick decision of the fray, render our modern engagements but partial rencounters, and enable the general, who is foiled in the beginning of the day, to draw off the greater part of his army, sound and entire.

The battles of antiquity, both by their duration, and their resemblance to single combats, were wrought up to a degree of fury quite unknown to later ages. Nothing could then engage the combatants to give quarter, but the hopes of profit, by making slaves of their prisoners. In civil wars, as we learn from Tacitus,[17] the battles were the most bloody, because the prisoners were not slaves.

What a stout resistance must be made, where the vanquished expected so hard a fate! How inveterate the rage, where the maxims of war were, in every respect, so bloody and severe!

.   .   .   .   .   .   .   .   .   .   .

But, *secondly*, it appears that ancient manners were more unfavourable than the modern, not only in times of war, but also in those of peace; and that too in every respect, except the love of civil liberty and of equality, which is, I own, of considerable importance. To exclude faction from a free government, is very difficult, if not altogether impracticable; but such inveterate rage between the factions, and such bloody maxims, are found, in modern times amongst religious parties alone. In ancient history, we may always observe, where one party prevailed, whether the nobles or people (for I can observe no difference in this respect) that they immediately butchered all of the opposite party who fell into their hands, and banished such as had been so fortunate as to escape their fury. No form of process, no law,

17 *The Histories* II. 44.

no trial, no pardon. A fourth, a third, perhaps near half of the city was slaughtered, or expelled, every revolution; and the exiles always joined foreign enemies, and did all the mischief possible to their fellow-citizens; till fortune put it in their power to take full revenge by a new revolution. And as these were frequent in such violent governments, the disorder, diffidence, jealousy, enmity, which must prevail, are not easy for us to imagine in this age of the world.

There are only two revolutions I can recollect in ancient history, which passed without great severity, and great effusion of blood in massacres and assassinations, namely, the restoration of the Athenian Democracy by Thrasybulus, and the subduing of the Roman republic by Caesar.

.    .    .    .    .    .    .    .    .    .    .

At Athens, the thirty tyrants and the nobles, in a twelve-month, murdered, without trial, about 1,200 of the people, and banished above the half of the citizens that remained.[18] In Argos, near the same time, the people killed 1,200 of the nobles; and afterwards their own demagogues, because they had refused to carry their prosecutions farther.[19] The people also in Corcyra killed 1,500 of the nobles, and banished a thousand.[20] These numbers will appear the more surprising, if we consider the extreme smallness of these states. But all ancient history is full of such instances.

.    .    .    .    .    .    .    .    .    .    .

If such was the disposition of men's minds among that refined people, what may be expected in the commonwealths of Italy, Afric, Spain, and Gaul, which were denominated barbarous? Why otherwise did the Greeks so much value themselves on their humanity, gentleness, and moderation, above all other nations? This reasoning seems very natural. But unluckily the

18 Diodorus Siculus, XIV. 5. Isocrates says there were only 5,000 banished. He makes the number of those killed amount to 1,500 (*Areopagiticus* 153). Aeschines (*Contra Ctesiphon* 455) assigns precisely the same number. Seneca (*De tranquillitate animi* V) says 1,300.

19 Diodorus Siculus, XV. 58.

20 *Ibid.*, XIII. 48.

history of the Roman commonwealth, in its earlier times, if we give credit to the received accounts, presents an opposite conclusion. No blood was ever shed in any sedition at Rome, till the murder of the Gracchi. Dionysius Halicarnassaeus,[21] observing the singular humanity of the Roman people in this particular, makes use of it as an argument that they were orginally of Grecian extraction: Whence we may conclude, that the factions and revolutions in the barbarous republics were usually more violent than even those of Greece above-mentioned.

If the Romans were so late in coming to blows, they made ample compensation, after they had once entered upon the bloody scene; and Appian's history of their civil wars contains the most frightful picture of massacres, proscriptions, and forfeitures, that ever was presented to the world. What pleases most, in that historian, is that he seems to feel a proper resentment of these barbarous proceedings; and talks not with that provoking coolness and indifference, which custom had produced in many of the Greek historians.[22]

The maxims of ancient politics contain, in general, so little humanity and moderation, that it seems superfluous to give any

21 I. 89.

22 The authorities cited above, are all historians, orators, and philosophers, whose testimony is unquestioned. 'Tis dangerous to rely upon writers who deal in ridicule and satyr. What will posterity, for instance, infer from this passage of Dr. Swift? "I told him, that in the kingdom of Tribnia (Britain) by the natives called Langdon (London) where I had sojourned some time in my travels, the bulk of the people consist, in a manner, wholly of discoverers, witnesses, informers, accusers, prosecutors, evidences, swearers, together with their several subservient and subaltern instruments, all under the colours, the conduct, and pay of ministers of state and their deputies. The plots in that kingdom are usually the workmanship of those persons," &c. Gulliver's Travels. Such a representation might suit the government of Athens; but not that of England, which is a prodigy even in modern times, for humanity, justice, and liberty. Yet the Doctor's satyr, tho' carried to extremes, as is usual with him, even beyond other satyrical writers, did not altogether want an object. The Bishop of Rochester, who was his friend, and of the same party, had been banished a little before by a bill of attainder, with great justice, but without such a proof as was legal, or according to the strict forms of common law,

particular reason for the acts of violence committed at any particular period.

. . . . . . . . . . . .

In those days there was no medium between a severe, jealous Aristocracy, ruling over discontented subjects; and a turbulent, factious, tyrannical Democracy. At present, there is not one republic in Europe, from one extremity of it to the other, that is not remarkable for justice, lenity, and stability, equal to, or even beyond Marseilles, Rhodes, or the most celebrated in antiquity. Almost all of them are well-tempered Aristocracies.

But *thirdly*, there are many other circumstances, in which ancient nations seem inferior to the modern, both for the happiness and increase of mankind. Trade, manufactures, industry, were no where, in former ages, so flourishing as they are at present in Europe. The only garb of the ancients, both for males and females, seems to have been a kind of flannel, which they wore commonly white or grey, and which they scoured as often as it became dirty. Tyre, which carried on, after Carthage, the greatest commerce of any city in the Mediterranean, before it was destroyed by Alexander, was no mighty city, if we credit Arrian's account of its inhabitants.[23] Athens is commonly supposed to have been a trading city: But it was as populous before the Median war as at any time after it, according to Herodotus;[24] yet its commerce, at that time, was so inconsiderable, that, as the same historian observes,[25] even the neighbouring coasts of Asia were as little frequented by the Greek as the pillars of Hercules: For beyond these he conceived nothing.

Great interest of money, and great profits of trade, are an infallible indication, that industry and commerce are but in their infancy. We read in Lysias[26] of 100 *per cent.* profit made

---

[23] II. 24. There were 8,000 killed during the seige; and the captives amounted to 30,000. Diodorus Siculus (XVII. 46) says only 13,000: But he accounts for this small number, by saying that the Tyrians had sent away before-hand part of their wives and children to Carthage.

[24] V. 97; he makes the number of the citizens amount to 30,000.

[25] *Ibid.,* VIII. 132.

[26] Oration XXXII, *Against Diogeiton* 25.

on a cargo of two talents, sent to no greater distance than from Athens to the Adriatic: Nor is this mentioned as an instance of extraordinary profit.

.    .    .    .    .    .    .    .    .    .

The barbarity of the ancient tyrants, together with the extreme love of liberty, which animated those ages, must have banished every merchant and manufacturer, and have quite depopulated the state, had it subsisted upon industry and commerce. While the cruel and suspicious Dionysius was carrying on his butcheries, who, that was not detained by his landed property, and could have carried with him any art or skill to procure a subsistence in other countries, would have remained exposed to such implacable barbarity? The persecutions of Philip II. and Lewis XIV. filled all Europe with the manufacturers of Flanders and of France.

I grant, that agriculture is the species of industry chiefly requisite to the subsistence of multitudes; and it is possible, that this industry may flourish, even when manufactures and other arts are unknown and neglected. Switzerland is at present a remarkable instance where, we find, at once, the most skilful husbandmen, and the most bungling tradesmen, that are to be met with in Europe. That agriculture flourished in Greece and Italy, at least in some parts of them, and at some periods, we have reason to presume; And whether the mechanical arts had reached the same degree of perfection, may not be esteemed so material; especially, if we consider the great equality of riches in the ancient republics, where each family was obliged to cultivate, with the greatest care and industry, its own little field, in order to its subsistence.

.    .    .    .    .    .    .    .    .    .

All our later improvements and refinements, have they done nothing towards the easy subsistence of men, and consequently towards their propagation and increase? Our superior skill in mechanics; the discovery of new worlds, by which commerce has been so much enlarged; the establishment of posts; and the use of bills of exchange: These seem all extremely useful to the encouragement of art, industry, and populousness. Were we to strike off these, what a check should we give to every kind of business and labour, and what multitudes of families would immediately perish from want and hunger? And it seems not probable, that we could supply the place of these new inventions by any other regulation or institution.

Have we reason to think, that the police of ancient states was any wise comparable to that of modern, or that men had then equal security, either at home, or in their journies by land or water? I question not, but every impartial examiner would give us the preference in this particular.

Thus, upon comparing the whole, it seems impossible to assign any just reason, why the world should have been more populous in ancient than in modern times. The equality of property among the ancients, liberty, and the small divisions of their states, were indeed circumstances favourable to the propagation of mankind: But their wars were more bloody and destructive, their governments more factious and unsettled, commerce and manufactures more feeble and languishing, and the general police more loose and irregular. These latter disadvantages seem to form a sufficient counterbalance to the former advantages; and rather favour the opposite opinion to that which commonly prevails with regard to this subject.

But there is no reasoning, it may be said, against matter of fact. If it appear that the world was then more populous than at present, we may be assured that our conjectures are false, and that we have overlooked some material circumstance in the comparison. This I readily own: All our preceding reasonings, I acknowledge to be mere trifling, or, at least, small skirmishes and frivolous rencounters, which decide nothing. But unluckily the main combat, where we compare facts, cannot be rendered much more decisive. The facts, delivered by ancient authors, are either so uncertain or so imperfect as to afford us nothing positive in this matter. How indeed could it be otherwise? The very facts, which we must oppose to them, in computing the populousness of modern states, are far from being either certain or complete. Many grounds of calculation proceeded on by celebrated writers, are little better than those of the Emperor Heliogabalus, who formed an estimate of the immense greatness of Rome, from ten thousand pound weight of cobwebs which had been found in that city.[27]

It is to be remarked, that all kinds of numbers are uncertain in ancient manuscripts, and have been subject to much greater corruptions than any other part of the text; and that for an obvious reason. Any alteration, in other places, commonly affects the sense or grammar, and is more readily perceived by the reader and transcriber.

Few enumerations of inhabitants have been made of any tract of country by any ancient author of good authority, so as to afford us a large enough view for comparison.

It is probable, that there was formerly a good foundation for the number of citizens assigned to any free city; because they entered for a share in the government, and there were exact registers kept of them. But as the number of slaves is seldom mentioned, this leaves us in as great uncertainty as ever, with regard to the populousness even of single cities.

The first page of Thucydides is, in my opinion, the commencement of real history. All preceding narrations are so intermixed with fable, that philosophers ought to abandon them, in a great measure, to the embellishment of poets and orators.[28]

With regard to remote times, the numbers of people assigned are often ridiculous, and lose all credit and authority. The free citizens of Sybaris, able to bear arms, and actually drawn out in battle, were 300,000. They encountered at Siagra with 100,000 citizens of Crotona, another Greek city contiguous to them; and

[27] Aelius Lampridius, *Life of Heliogabalus*. XXVI.

[28] In general, there is more candour and sincerity in ancient historians, but less exactness and care, than in the moderns. Our speculative factions, especially those of religion, throw such an illusion over our minds, that men seem to regard impartiality to their adversaries and to heretics, as a vice or weakness: But the commonness of books, by means of printing, has obliged modern historians to be more careful in avoiding contradictions and incongruities. Diodorus Siculus is a good writer, but it is with pain I see his narration contradict, in so many particulars, the two most authentic pieces of all Greek history, to wit, Xenophon's expedition, and Demosthenes's orations. Plutarch and Appian seem scarce ever to have read Cicero's epistles.

were defeated. This is Diodorus Siculus's[29] account; and is very seriously insisted on by that historian.[30] Strabo also mentions the same number of Sybarites.

Diodorus Siculus,[31] enumerating the inhabitants of Agrigentum, when it was destroyed by the Carthaginians, says, that they amounted to 20,000 citizens, 200,000 strangers besides slaves, who, in so opulent a city as he represents it, would probably be, at least, as numerous. We must remark, that the women and the children are not included; and that, therefore, upon the whole, this city must have contained near two millions of inhabitants.[32] And what was the reason of so immense an increase! They were industrious in cultivating the neighbouring fields, not exceeding a small English county; and they traded with their wine and oil to Africa, which, at that time, produced none of these commodities.

.   .   .   .   .   .   .   .   .   .   .

It is a usual fallacy, to consider all the ages of antiquity as one period, and to compute the numbers contained in the great cities mentioned by ancient authors, as if these cities had been all contemporary. The Greek colonies flourished extremely in Sicily during the age of Alexander: But in Augustus's time they were so decayed, that almost all the produce of that fertile island was consumed in Italy.[33]

Let us now examine the numbers of inhabitants assigned to particular cities in antiquity; and omitting the numbers of Nineveh, Babylon, and the Egyptian Thebes, let us confine ourselves to the sphere of real history, to the Grecian and Roman states. I must own, the more I consider this subject, the more am I inclined to scepticism, with regard to the great populousness ascribed to ancient times.

Athens is said by Plato[34] to be a very great city; and it was

29 XII. 9.
30 VI. 26.
31 XIII. 90.
32 Diogenes Laertius (VIII. 63, "Empedocles") says that Agrigentum contained only 800,000 inhabitants.
33 Strabo, VI. 273.
34 *Apology* 29D.

surely the greatest of all the Greek[35] cities, except Syracuse, which was nearly about the same size in Thucydides's[36] time, and afterwards increased beyond it. For Cicero[37] mentions it as the greatest of all the Greek cities in his time; not comprehending, I suppose, either Antioch or Alexandria under that denomination. Athenaeus[38] says, that, by the enumeration of Demetrius Phalereus, there were in Athens 21,000 citizens, 10,000 strangers, and 400,000 slaves. This number is much insisted on by those whose opinion I call in question, and is esteemed a fundamental fact to their purpose: But, in my opinion, there is no point of criticism more certain, than that Athenaeus and Ctesicles, whom he quotes, are here mistaken, and that the number of slaves is, at least, augmented by a whole cypher, and ought not to be regarded as more than 40,000.

*First,* When the number of citizens is said to be 21,000 by Athenaeus,[39] men of full age are only understood. For, (1.) Herodotus says,[40] that Aristagoras, ambassador from the Ionians, found it harder to deceive one Spartan than 30,000 Athenians; meaning, in a loose way, the whole state, supposed to be met in one popular assembly, excluding the women and children. (2.) Thucydides[41] says, that, making allowance for all the absentees in the fleet, army, garrisons, and for people employed in their private affairs, the Athenian assembly never rose to five thousand. (3.) The forces, enumerated by the same historian,[42] being all citizens, and amounting to 13,000 heavy-armed infantry, prove the same method of calculation; as also the whole tenor of the Greek historians, who always understand men of full age

---

[35] Argos seems also to have been a great city; for Lysias contents himself with saying that it did not exceed Athens (Oration XXXIX, *Against the Subversion of the Ancestral Constitution of Athens* 8).

[36] VI. See also Plutarch, *Lives,* "Nicias" XVII.

[37] *In Verrem* IV. 52. Strabo (VI. 270) says, it was twenty-two miles in compass. But then we are to consider, that it contained two harbours within it; one of which was a very large one, and might be regarded as a kind of bay.

[38] VI. 20.

[39] Demosthenes assigns 20,000; *Against Aristogeiton* 785.

[40] V. 99.

[41] VIII. 72.

[42] II. 13. Diodorus Siculus's account (XII. 40) perfectly agrees.

when they assign the number of citizens in any republic. Now, these being but the fourth of the inhabitants, the free Athenians were by this account 84,000; the strangers 40,000; and the slaves, calculating by the smaller number, and allowing that they married and propagated at the same rate with freemen, were 160,000; and the whole of the inhabitants 284,000: A number surely large enough. The other number, 1,720,000, makes Athens larger than London and Paris united.

*Secondly,* There were but 10,000 houses in Athens.[43]

*Thirdly,* Though the extent of the walls, as given us by Thucydides,[44] be great (to wit, eighteen miles, beside the seacoast): Yet Xenophon[45] says, there was much waste ground within the walls. They seem indeed to have joined four distinct and separate cities.

*Fourthly,* No insurrection of the slaves, or suspicion of insurrection, is ever mentioned by historians; except one commotion of the miners.[46]

*Fifthly,* The treatment of slaves by the Athenians is said by Xenophon,[47] and Demosthenes,[48] and Plautus,[49] to have been extremely gentle and indulgent: Which could never have been the case, had the disproportion been twenty to one. The disproportion is not so great in any of our colonies; yet are we obliged to exercise a rigorous military government over the negroes.

*Sixthly,* No man is ever esteemed rich for possessing what may be reckoned as equal distribution of property in any country, or even triple or quadruple that wealth. Thus every person in England is computed by some to spend sixpence a day: Yet is he esteemed but poor who has five times that sum. Now Timarchus is said by Aeschines[50] to have been left in easy circumstances; but he was master only of ten slaves employed in manufactures. Lysias and his brother, two strangers, were pro-

[43] Xenophon, *Memorabilia* III. 6. 14.
[44] II. 13.
[45] *Ways and Means* II. 6.
[46] Athenaeus, *Banquet of the Learned* VI. 104.
[47] *The Polity of the Athenians* I.
[48] *Third Philippic* 31.
[49] *Stichus* 430–434.
[50] *Against Timarchus* 42.

scribed by the thirty for their great riches; though they had but sixty a-piece.[51] Demosthenes was left very rich by his father; yet he had no more than fifty-two slaves.[52] His work-house, of twenty cabinet-makers, is said to be a very considerable manufactory.[53]

.    .    .    .    .    .    .    .    .    .    .

Besides, we are to consider, that the number assigned by Athenaeus,[54] whatever it is, comprehends all the inhabitants of Attica, as well as those of Athens. The Athenians affected much a country life, as we learn from Thucydides;[55] and when they were all chased into town, by the invasion of their territory during the Peloponnesian war, the city was not able to contain them; and they were obliged to lie in the porticoes, temples, and even streets, for want of lodging.[56]

The same remark is to be extended to all the other Greek cities; and when the number of citizens is assigned, we must always understand it to comprehend the inhabitants of the neighbouring country, as well as of the city. Yet, even with this allowance, it must be confessed, that Greece was a populous country, and exceeded what we could imagine concerning so narrow a territory, naturally not very fertile, and which drew no supplies of corn from other places. For, excepting Athens, which traded to Pontus for that commodity, the other cities seem to have subsisted chiefly from their neighbouring territory.[57]

.    .    .    .    .    .    .    .    .    .    .

Allowing, therefore, this remark to be just, that Europe is become warmer than formerly; how can we account for it? Plainly, by no other method, than by supposing that the land is

51 Oration XII, *Against Eratosthenes.*

52 *Against Aphobus* 816.

53 *Ibid.*

54 The same author affirms, that Corinth had once 460,000 slaves, Aegina 470,000. But the foregoing arguments hold stronger against these facts, which are indeed entirely absurd and impossible. It is however remarkable, that Athenaeus cites so great an authority, as Aristotle for this last fact: And the scholiast on Pindar mentions the same number of slaves in Aegina.

55 II. 14.

56 *Ibid.,* II. 17.

57 Demosthenes, *Against Leptines* 466.

at present much better cultivated, and that the woods are cleared, which formerly threw a shade upon the earth, and kept the rays of the sun from penetrating to it. Our northern colonies in America become more temperate, in proportion as the woods are felled;[58] but in general, every one may remark that cold is still much more severely felt, both in North and South America, than in places under the same latitude in Europe.

Saserna, quoted by Columella,[59] affirmed that the disposition of the heavens was altered before his time, and that the air had become much milder and warmer; as appears hence, says he, that many places now abound with vineyards and olive planta-tions, which formerly, by reason of the rigour of the climate, could raise none of these productions. Such a change, if real, will be allowed an evident sign of the better cultivation and peopling of countries before the age of Saserna;[60] and if it be continued to the present times, is a proof, that these advantages have been continually increasing throughout this part of the world.

Let us now cast our eye over all the countries which are the scene of ancient and modern history, and compare their past and present situation: We shall not, perhaps, find such founda-tion for the complaint of the present emptiness and desolation of the world. Aegypt is represented by Maillet, to whom we owe the best account of it, as extremely populous; though he esteems the number of its inhabitants to be diminished. Syria, and the Lesser Asia, as well as the coast of Barbary, I can readily own, to be desert in comparison of their ancient condition. The de-population of Greece is also obvious. But whether the country now called Turkey in Europe may not, in general, contain more

[58] The warm southern colonies also become more healthful: And it is remarkable, that in the Spanish histories of the first discovery and conquest of these countries, they appear to have been very healthful; being then well peopled and cultivated. No account [is given] of the sickness or decay of Cortes's or Pizarro's small armies.

[59] De re rustica I. 1.

[60] He seems to have lived about the time of the younger Africanus; Columella, De re rustica I. 1. 5.

inhabitants than during the flourishing period of Greece, may be a little doubtful. The Thracians seem then to have lived like the Tartars at present, by pasturage and plunder:[61] The Getes were still more uncivilized:[62] And the Illyrians were no better.[63] These occupy nine-tenths of that country: And though the government of the Turks be not very favourable to industry and propagation; yet it preserves at least peace and order among the inhabitants; and is preferable to that barbarous, unsettled condition, in which they anciently lived.

Poland and Muscovy in Europe are not populous; but are certainly much more so than the ancient Sarmatia and Scythia; where no husbandry or tillage was ever heard of, and pasturage was the sole art by which the people were maintained. The like observation may be extended to Denmark and Sweden. No one ought to esteem the immense swarms of people, which formerly came from the North, and over-ran all Europe, to be any objection to this opinion. When a whole nation, or even half of it remove their seat, it is easy to imagine, what a prodigious multitude they must form; with what desperate valour they must make their attacks; and how the terror they strike into the invaded nations will make these magnify, in their imagination, both the courage and multitude of the invaders. Scotland is neither extensive nor populous; but were the half of its inhabitants to seek new seats, they would form a colony as numerous as the Teutons and Cimbri; and would shake all Europe, supposing it in no better condition for defence than formerly.

Germany has surely at present twenty times more inhabitants than in ancient times, when they cultivated no ground, and each tribe valued itself on the extensive desolation which it spread around; as we learn from Caesar,[64] and Tacitus,[65] and Strabo.[66] A proof, that the division into small republics will not

[61] Xenophon, *Anabasis* VII; Polybius, IV. 45.
[62] Ovid, *passim;* Strabo VII.
[63] Polybius, II. 12.
[64] *De Bello Gallico* VI. 23.
[65] *Germania.*
[66] VII.

alone render a nation populous, unless attended with the spirit of peace, order, and industry.

The barbarous condition of Britain in former times is well known, and the thinness of its inhabitants may easily be conjectured, both from their barbarity, and from a circumstance mentioned by Herodian,[67] that all Britain was marshy, even in Severus's time, after the Romans had been fully settled in it above a century.

It is not easily imagined, that the Gauls were anciently much more advanced in the arts of life than their northern neighbours; since they travelled to this island for their education in the mysteries of the religion and philosophy of the Druids.[68] I cannot, therefore, think, that Gaul was then near so populous as France is at present.

Were we to believe, indeed, and join together the testimony of Appian, and that of Diodorus Siculus, we must admit of an incredible populousness in Gaul. The former historian[69] says, that there were 400 nations in that country; the latter[70] affirms, that the largest of the Gallic nations consisted of 200,000 men, besides women and children, and the least of 50,000. Calculating, therefore, at a medium, we must admit of near 200 millions of people, in a country, which we esteem populous at present, though supposed to contain little more than twenty.[71] Such calculations, therefore, by their extravagance, lose all manner of authority.

.    .    .    .    .    .    .    .    .    .    .

Spain is, perhaps, decayed from what it was three centuries ago; but if we step backward two thousand years, and consider the restless, turbulent, unsettled condition of its inhabitants, we may probably be inclined to think that it is now much more populous. Many Spaniards killed themselves, when deprived of

[67] III. 47.

[68] Caesar, *De Bello Gallico* VI. 13. Strabo (VII. 290) says, the Gauls were not much more improved than the Germans.

[69] *Celt.* Pt. I, Bk. IV. 2.

[70] V. 25.

[71] Ancient Gaul was more extensive than modern France.

their arms by the Romans.[72] It appears from Plutarch[73] that robbery and plunder were esteemed honourable among the Spaniards. Hirtius[74] represents in the same light the situation of that country in Caesar's time; and he says, that every man was obliged to live in castles and walled towns for his security. It was not till its final conquest under Augustus, that these disorders were repressed.[75] The account which Strabo[76] and Justin[77] give of Spain, corresponds exactly with those above mentioned. How much, therefore, must it diminish from our idea of the populousness of antiquity, when we find that Tully, comparing Italy, Afric, Gaul, Greece, and Spain, mentions the great number of inhabitants, as the peculiar circumstance, which rendered this latter country formidable?

Italy however, it is probable, has decayed: But how many great cities does it still contain? Venice, Genoa, Pavia, Turin, Milan, Naples, Florence, Leghorn, which either subsisted not in ancient times, or were then very inconsiderable? If we reflect on this, we shall not be apt to carry matters to so great an extreme as is usual, with regard to this subject.

.    .    .    .    .    .    .    .    .

Polybius supposes, that Greece had become more prosperous and flourishing after the establishment of the Roman yoke;[78] and though that historian wrote before these conquerors had degenerated, from being the patrons, to be the plunderers of

[72] Livy XXXIV. 17.

[73] *Lives*, "Caius Marius" VI.

[74] *The Spanish Wars* VIII.

[75] Velleius Parterculus II. 90. 4.

[76] III.

[77] XLIV.

[78] II. 62. It may perhaps be imagined, that Polybius, being dependent on Rome, would naturally extol the Roman dominion. But, in the *first* place, Polybius, though one sees sometimes instances of his caution, discovers no symptoms of flattery. *Secondly,* This opinion is only delivered in a single stroke, by the by, while he is intent upon another subject; and it is allowed, if there be any suspicion of an author's insincerity, that these oblique propositions discover his real opinion better than his more formal and direct assertions.

mankind; yet, as we find from Tacitus,[79] that the severity of the emperors afterwards corrected the licence of the governors, we have no reason to think that extensive monarchy so destructive as it is often represented.

We learn from Strabo,[80] that the Romans, from their regard to the Greeks, maintained, to his time, most of the privileges and liberties of that celebrated nation; and Nero afterwards rather increased them.[81] How therefore can we imagine, that the Roman yoke was so burdensome over that part of the world? The oppression of the proconsuls was checked; and the magistracies in Greece being all bestowed, in the several cities, by the free votes of the people, there was no necessity for the competitors to attend the emperor's court. If great numbers went to seek their fortunes in Rome, and advance themselves by learning or eloquence, the commodities of their native country, many of them would return with the fortunes which they had acquired, and thereby enrich the Grecian commonwealths.

But Plutarch says, that the general depopulation had been more sensibly felt in Greece than in any other country. How is this reconcileable to its superior privileges and advantages?

Besides, this passage, by proving too much, really proves nothing. *Only three thousand men able to bear arms in all Greece!* Who can admit so strange a proposition, especially if we consider the great number of Greek cities, whose names still remain in history, and which are mentioned by writers long after the age of Plutarch? There are there surely ten times more people at present, when there scarcely remains a city in all the bounds of ancient Greece. That country is still tolerably cultivated, and furnishes a sure supply of corn, in case of any scarcity in Spain, Italy, or the south of France.

We may observe, that the ancient frugality of the Greeks, and their equality of property, still subsisted during the age of Plutarch; as appears from Lucian.[82] Nor is there any ground to

[79] *Annals* I. 2.
[80] VIII and IX.
[81] Plutarch, *De his qui sero a Numine puniuntur.*
[82] *De Mercede conductis potentium familiaribus.*

imagine, that that country was possessed by a few masters, and a great number of slaves.

It is probable, indeed, that military discipline, being entirely useless, was extremely neglected in Greece after the establishment of the Roman empire; and if these commonwealths, formerly so warlike and ambitious, maintained each of them a small city-guard, to prevent mobbish disorders, it is all they had occasion for: And these, perhaps, did not amount to 3,000 men, throughout all Greece. I own, that, if Plutarch had this fact in his eye, he is here guilty of a gross paralogism, and assigns causes no wise proportioned to the effects. But is it so great a prodigy, that an author should fall into a mistake of this nature?[83]

But whatever force may remain in this passage of Plutarch, we shall endeavour to counterbalance it by as remarkable a pas-

[83] I must confess that that discourse of Plutarch, concerning the silence of the oracles, is in general of so odd a texture, and so unlike his other productions, that one is at a loss what judgment to form of it. 'Tis wrote in dialogue, which is a method of composition that Plutarch commonly little affects. The personages he introduces advance very wild, absurd, and contradictory opinions, more like the visionary systems or ravings of Plato than the solid sense of Plutarch. There runs also thro' the whole an air of superstition and credulity, which resembles very little the spirit that appears in other philosophical compositions of that author. For 'tis remarkable, that tho' Plutarch be an historian as superstitious as Herodotus or Livy, yet there is scarcely, in all antiquity, a philosopher less superstitious, excepting Cicero and Lucian. I must therefore confess, that a passage of Plutarch, cited from this discourse, has much less authority with me, than if it had been found in most of his other compositions.

There is only one other discourse of Plutarch liable to like objections, viz., that *concerning those whose punishment is delayed by the Deity*. It is also wrote in dialogue, contains like superstitious, wild visions, and seems to have been chiefly composed in rivalship to Plato, particularly his last book *de republica*.

And here I cannot but observe, that Mons. Fontenelle, a writer eminent for candor, seems to have departed a little from his usual character, when he endeavours to throw a ridicule upon Plutarch on account of passages to be met with in this dialogue concerning oracles. The absurdities here put into the mouths of the several personages are not to be ascribed to Plutarch. He makes them refute each other; and, in general, he seems to intend the ridiculing of those very opinions, which Fontenelle would ridicule him for maintaining. See *Histoire des oracles*.

sage in Diodorus Siculus, where the historian, after mentioning Ninus's army of 1,700,000 foot and 200,000 horse, endeavours to support the credibility of this account by some posterior facts; and adds, that we must not form a notion of the ancient populousness of mankind from the present emptiness and depopulation which is spread over the world.[84] Thus an author, who lived at that very period of antiquity which is represented as most populous,[85] complains of the desolation which then prevailed, gives the preference to former times, and has recourse to ancient fables as a foundation for his opinion. The humour of blaming the present, and admiring the past, is strongly rooted in human nature, and has an influence even on persons endued with the profoundest judgment and most extensive learning.

[84] II. 5.
[85] He was cotemporary with Caesar and Augustus.

# THE HISTORY OF ENGLAND

[The History of England, from the Invasion of Julius Caesar to the Revolution in 1688 *was first published during the years 1754–1762. The initial volume, containing the reigns of James I and Charles I (1603–1649), appeared in 1754; the second, containing the Commonwealth and the reigns of Charles II and James II (1649–1688) in 1756 (imprinted "1757," however). Thereafter, Hume published four volumes, two in 1759 under the title* The History of England, under the House of Tudor *(1485–1603), and another two in 1762 entitled* The History of England, from the Invasion of Julius Caesar to the Accession of Henry VII. *The first collected edition was also published in 1762; subsequent collected editions during Hume's lifetime appeared in 1763, 1770, 1772 (Dublin), 1773, 1778 (corrected and improved, but not seen, by Hume).*

*Hume was disappointed by the early reception of the first volume, but sales soon increased, and* The History *became a best-seller within his lifetime, as is attested by the number of editions published. After Hume's death the popularity of the work grew to great proportions—though only recently H. R. Trevor-Roper (see Bibliography, p. liii) has suggested that Macaulay set out to dethrone Hume, and succeeded: "At all events," Trevor-Roper says, "in Victorian England, Macaulay's advocacy prevailed. Hume went out of fashion . . . pushed off the bookstalls" by Macaulay. But if this is true, it is not the whole story, as the patient labors of Professor Jessop show. Not only did Hume retain his popularity during Macaulay's lifetime, but it was not until Victorian England was largely a thing of the past that his popularity and fashionableness waned. The total number of complete posthumous editions of* The History *so far discovered is approximately 125; and in addition there were several abridgments, one of which alone was circulated in*

*well over 100,000 copies (see Appendix A, p. 413). Macaulay's
influence was at least, then, slow in taking effect on the bookstalls.*

*The selections here are all more or less self-explanatory, with
the exception of the material taken from Chapters XLV–LV.
Here the excerpts have been chosen to illustrate Hume's view
of the struggle between Crown and Commons which led, finally,
to civil war, the execution of Charles I, and the establishment
of the Commonwealth. The marginal dates in this section are
all Hume's, though some of them have been relocated because
of the abridgments. Footnotes followed by an asterisk were,
because of their length, originally printed at the end of those
volumes in which they appeared.]*

## *From* Chapter I

THE CURIOSITY, entertained by all civilised nations, of enquiring into the exploits and adventures of their ancestors, commonly excites a regret that the history of remote ages should always be so much involved in obscurity, uncertainty, and contradiction. Ingenious men, possessed of leisure, are apt to push their researches beyond the period in which literary monuments are framed or preserved; without reflecting, that the history of past events is immediately lost or disfigured when entrusted to memory and oral tradition, and that the adventures of barbarous nations, even if they were recorded, could afford little or no entertainment to men born in a more cultivated age. The convulsions of a civilised state usually compose the most instructive and most interesting part of its history; but the sudden, violent, and unprepared revolutions incident to Barbarians, are so much guided by caprice, and terminate so often in cruelty, that they disgust us by the uniformity of their appearance; and it is rather fortunate for letters that they are buried in silence and oblivion. The only certain means by which nations can indulge their curiosity in researches concerning their remote origin, is to consider the language, manners, and customs of their ancestors, and to compare them with those of the neighbouring nations. The fables, which are commonly employed to supply the place of true history, ought entirely to be disregarded; or if any exception be admitted to this general rule, it can only be in favour of the ancient Grecian fictions, which are so celebrated and so agreeable that they will ever be the objects of the attention of mankind. Neglecting, therefore, all traditions, or rather tales, concerning the more early history of Britain, we shall only consider the state of the inhabitants as it appeared to the Romans on their invasion of this country: we shall briefly run over the events which attended the conquest made by that empire, as belonging more to Roman than British story: we

111

shall hasten through the obscure and uninteresting period of Saxon annals: and shall reserve a more full narration for those times when the truth is both so well ascertained and so complete as to promise entertainment and instruction to the reader.

All ancient writers agree in representing the first inhabitants of Britain as a tribe of the Gauls or Celtae, who peopled that island from the neighbouring continent. Their language was the same, their manners, their government, their superstition; varied only by those small differences, which time or a communication with the bordering nations must necessarily introduce. The inhabitants of Gaul, especially in those parts which lie contiguous to Italy, had acquired, from a commerce with their southern neighbours, some refinement in the arts, which gradually diffused themselves northwards, and spread but a very faint light over this island. The Greek and Roman navigators or merchants (for there were scarcely any other travellers in those ages) brought back the most shocking accounts of the ferocity of the people, which they magnified, as usual, in order to excite the admiration of their countrymen. The south-east parts, however, of Britain, had already, before the age of Caesar, made the first and most requisite step towards a civil settlement; and the Britons, by tillage and agriculture, had there increased to a great multitude.[1] The other inhabitants of the island still maintained themselves by pasture: they were clothed with skins of beasts: they dwelt in huts, which they reared in the forests and marshes, with which the country was covered: they shifted easily their habitation, when actuated either by the hopes of plunder, or the fear of an enemy: the convenience of feeding their cattle was even a sufficient motive for removing their seats: and as they were ignorant of all the refinements of life, their wants and their possessions were equally scanty and limited.

The Britons were divided into many small nations or tribes; and being a military people, whose sole property was their arms and their cattle, it was impossible, after they had acquired a relish of liberty, for their princes or chieftains to establish any

[1] Caesar, *De Bello Gallico* IV.

despotic authority over them. Their governments, though monarchical,[2] were free, as well as those of all the Celtic nations;
and the common people seem even to have enjoyed more liberty among them,[3] than among the nations of Gaul,[4] from
whom they were descended. Each state was divided into factions
within itself:[5] it was agitated with jealousy or animosity against
the neighbouring states: and while the arts of peace were yet
unknown, wars were the chief occupation, and formed the chief
object of ambition, among the people.

The religion of the Britons was one of the most considerable
parts of their government; and the Druids, who were their
priests, possessed great authority among them. Besides minis-
tering at the altar, and directing all religious duties, they pre-
sided over the education of youth; they enjoyed an immunity
from wars and taxes; they possessed both the civil and criminal
jurisdiction; they decided all controversies among states as well
as among private persons, and whoever refused to submit to
their decree was exposed to the most severe penalties. The
sentence of excommunication was pronounced against him: he
was forbidden access to the sacrifices or public worship: he was
debarred all intercourse with his fellow-citizens, even in the
common affairs of life: his company was universally shunned,
as profane and dangerous: he was refused the protection of
law:[6] and death itself became an acceptable relief from the
misery and infamy to which he was exposed. Thus, the bands
of government, which were naturally loose among that rude
and turbulent people, were happily corroborated by the terrors
of their superstition.

No species of superstition was ever more terrible than that of
the Druids. Besides the severe penalties, which it was in the
power of the ecclesiastics to inflict in this world, they inculcated
the eternal transmigration of souls; and thereby extended their

[2] Diodorus Siculus, IV. Pomponius Mela, III. 6. Strabo, IV.

[3] Cassius Dionysius, LXXV.

[4] Caesar, *De Bello Gallico* VI.

[5] Tacitus, *Agricola.*

[6] Caesar, *De Bello Gallico* VI. Strabo, IV.

authority as far as the fears of their timorous votaries. They
practised their rites in dark groves or other secret recesses;[7] and
in order to throw a greater mystery over their religion, they
communicated their doctrines only to the initiated, and strictly
forbad the committing of them to writing; lest they should at
any time be exposed to the examination of the profane vulgar.
Human sacrifices were practised among them: the spoils of war
were often devoted to their divinities; and they punished with
the severest tortures whoever dared to secrete any part of the
consecrated offering: these treasures they kept in woods and
forests, secured by no other guard than the terrors of their religion;[8] and this steddy conquest over human avidity may be
regarded as more signal than their prompting men to the most
extraordinary and most violent efforts. No idolatrous worship
ever attained such an ascendant over mankind as that of the
ancient Gauls and Britons; and the Romans, after their conquest, finding it impossible to reconcile those nations to the
laws and institutions of their masters, while it maintained its
authority, were at last obliged to abolish it by penal statutes;
a violence which had never, in any other instance, been practised by those tolerating conquerors.[9]

.    .    .    .    .    .    .    .    .    .    .    .

But the period was now come, when that enormous fabric of
the Roman empire, which had diffused slavery and oppression,
together with peace and civility, over so considerable a part
of the globe, was approaching towards its final dissolution. Italy,
and the centre of the empire, removed, during so many ages,
from all concern in the wars, had entirely lost the military
spirit, and were peopled by an enervated race, equally disposed
to submit to a foreign yoke, or to the tyranny of their own rulers.
The emperors found themselves obliged to recruit their legions
from the frontier provinces, where the genius of war, though
languishing, was not totally extinct; and these mercenary forces,
careless of laws and civil institutions, established a military gov-

---

7 Pliny, XII. 1.
8 Caesar, *De Bello Gallico* VI.
9 Suetonius, *Lives of the Caesars,* "The Deified Claudius."

ernment, no less dangerous to the sovereign than to the people. The farther progress of the same disorders introduced the bordering barbarians into the service of the Romans; and those fierce nations, having now added discipline to their native bravery, could no longer be restrained by the impotent policy of the emperors, who were accustomed to employ one in the destruction of the others. Sensible of their own force, and allured by the prospect of so rich a prize, the northern barbarians, in the reign of Arcadius and Honorius, assailed at once all the frontiers of the Roman empire; and having first satiated their avidity by plunder, began to think of fixing a settlement in the wasted provinces. The more distant barbarians, who occupied the deserted habitations of the former, advanced in their acquisitions, and pressed with their incumbent weight the Roman state, already unequal to the load which it sustained. Instead of arming the people in their own defence, the emperors recalled all the distant legions, in whom alone they could repose confidence; and collected the whole military force for the defence of the capital and centre of the empire. The necessity of self-preservation had superseded the ambition of power; and the ancient point of honour, never to contract the limits of the empire, could no longer be attended to in this desperate extremity.

Britain by its situation was removed from the fury of these barbarous incursions; and being also a remote province, not much valued by the Romans, the legions which defended it were carried over to the protection of Italy and Gaul. But that province, though secured by the sea against the inroads of the greater tribes of barbarians, found enemies on its frontiers, who took advantage of its present defenceless situation. The Picts and Scots, who dwelt in the northern parts, beyond the wall of Antonihus, made incursions upon their peaceable and effeminate neighbours; and besides the temporary depredations which they committed, these combined nations threatened the whole province with subjection, or, what the inhabitants more dreaded, with plunder and devastation. The Picts seem to have been a tribe of the native British race, who, having been chased into the northern parts by the conquests of Agricola, had there intermingled with the ancient inhabitants: the Scots were derived from the same Celtic origin, had first been established in Ireland, had migrated to the north-west coasts of this island, and had long been accustomed, as well from their old as their new seats, to infest the Roman province by piracy and rapine.[10]

10* This question has been disputed with as great zeal and even acrimony between the Scotch and Irish antiquaries, as if the honour of their respective countries were the most deeply concerned in the decision. We shall not enter into any detail on so uninteresting a subject; but shall propose our opinion in a few words. It appears more than probable, from the similitude of language and manners, that Britain either was originally peopled, or was subdued, by the migration of inhabitants from Gaul, and Ireland from Britain: the position of the several countries, is an additional reason that favours this conclusion. It appears also probable, that the migrations of that colony of Gauls or Celts, who peopled or subdued Ireland, was originally made from the north-west parts of Britain; and this conjecture (if it do not merit a higher name) is founded both on the Irish language, which is a very different dialect from the Welsh and from the language anciently spoken in South Britain, and on the vicinity of Lancashire, Cumberland, Galloway, and Argyleshire, to that island. These events, as they passed long before the age of history and records, must be known by reasoning alone, which in this case seems to be pretty satisfactory: Caesar and Tacitus, not to mention a multitude of other Greek and Roman authors, were guided by like inferences. But besides these primitive facts, which lie in a very remote antiquity, it is a matter of positive and undoubted testimony, that the Roman province of Britain, during the time of the lower empire, was much infested by bands of robbers or pyrates, whom the provincial Britons called Scots or Scuits; a name which was probably used as a term of reproach, and which these banditti themselves did not acknowledge or assume. We may infer from two passages in Claudian, and from one in Orosius and another in Isidore, that the chief seat of these Scots was in Ireland. That some part of the Irish freebooters migrated back to the north-west parts of Britain, whence their ancestors had probably been derived in a more remote age, is positively asserted by Bede, and implied in Gildas; though neither of these authors explain whether the Irish Scots made their settlements by force or consent, or by a mixture of both. I grant, that neither Bede nor Gildas are Caesars or Tacituses; but such as they are, they remain the sole testimony on the subject, and therefore must be relied on for want of better: happily, the frivolousness of the question corresponds to the weakness of the authorities. Not to mention, that, if any part of the traditional history of a barbarous people can be relied on, it is the genealogy of nations, and even

These tribes, finding their more opulent neighbours exposed to invasion, soon broke over the Roman wall, no longer defended by the Roman arms; and though a contemptible enemy in themselves, met with no resistance from the unwarlike inhabitants. The Britons, accustomed to have recourse to the emperors for defence as well as government, made supplications to Rome; and one legion was sent over for their protection. This force was an over-match for the barbarians, repelled their invasion, routed them in every engagement, and having chased them into their ancient limits, returned in triumph to the defence of the southern provinces of the empire.[11] Their retreat brought on a new invasion of the enemy. The Britons made again an application to Rome, and again obtained the assistance of a legion, which proved effectual for their relief: But the Romans, reduced

sometimes that of families. It is in vain to argue against these facts from the supposed warlike disposition of the Highlanders, and unwarlike of the ancient Irish. Those arguments are still much weaker than the authorities. Nations change very quickly in these particulars. The Britons were unable to resist the Picts and Scots, and invited over the Saxons for their defence, who repelled those invaders: yet the same Britons valiantly resisted for a hundred and fifty years not only this victorious band of Saxons, but infinite numbers more, who poured in upon them from all quarters. Robert Bruce in 1322 made a peace, in which England, after many defeats, was constrained to acknowledge the independence of his country: yet in no more distant period than ten years after, Scotland was totally subdued by a small handful of English, led by a few private noblemen. All history is full of such events. The Irish Scots, in the course of two or three centuries, might find time and opportunities sufficient to settle in North Britain, though we can neither assign the period nor causes of that revolution. Their barbarous manner of life rendered them much fitter than the Romans for subduing these mountaineers. And in a word, it is clear, from the language of the two countries, that the Highlanders and the Irish are the same people, and that the one are a colony from the other. We have positive evidence, which, though from neutral persons, is not perhaps the best that may be wished for, that the former sprang from the latter: we have no evidence at all that the latter sprang from the former. I shall add, that the name of Erse or Irish, given by the low country Scots to the language of the Scotch Highlanders, is a certain proof of the traditional opinion, delivered from father to son, that the latter people came originally from Ireland.

[11] Gildas, *The Fall of Britain*. Bede, *The Ecclesiastical History of the English Nation*, Bk. I, chap. 12. Paulus Diaconus, *History of the Lombards*.

to extremities at home, and fatigued with those distant expeditions, informed the Britons that they must no longer look to them for succour, exhorted them to arm in their own defence, and urged, that as they were now their own masters, it became them to protect by their valour that independence which their ancient lords had conferred upon them.[12] That they might leave the island with the better grace, the Romans assisted them in erecting anew the wall of Severus, which was built entirely of stone, and which the Britons had not at that time artificers skilful enough to repair.[13] And having done this last good office to the inhabitants, they bid a final adieu to Britain, about the year 448; after being masters of the more considerable part of it during the course of near four centuries.

12 Bede, Bk. I, chap. 12.
13 *Ibid.*

# *From* Chapter X, Appendix II, Chapter XII, and Chapter XIII

## [THE JEWS IN MEDIEVAL ENGLAND]

[*These excerpts relating to medieval persecutions of the Jews are quite unusual for their day. Hume, in presenting these facts, and in discussing Jewish usury, places the onus for the grim events primarily on the hypocritical and mercenary attitudes of the so-called Christians of the time. In a letter of 1764 (HL 229), Hume stated: "Manifold have been the persecutions, dear Sir, which the unhappy Jews, in several ages, have suffered from the misguided zeal of the Christians. . . ." Unlike many eighteenth-century writers, such as Montesquieu, Hume did not attempt to excuse the persecutions or make the Jews at least partly culpable because of their anti-Christian attitudes, their rapacious instincts, or (as the Enlightenment saw it) their superstitious beliefs. Hume's non-anti-Semitic attitude is surprising not only because it was unusual at the time, but also because of the strong agitation dating from 1753 against allowing Jews to have the rights of English citizens. However Hume, unlike Boswell, does not seem to have known or associated with the upper-class Sephardic Jews in Britain.*

*Charles Dickens' philo-Semitic portrayal of the medieval persecutions, in his* A Child's History of England, *carries Hume's judgment of the situation even further, stressing the villanies of the Christians and the innocence of the Jews. See, for instance, Chapters XIII (on Richard the Lion-Hearted) and XVI (on Edward I).*]

## *From* Chapter X—Richard I

THE KING, impelled more by the love of military glory than by superstition, acted, from the beginning of his reign, as if the sole purpose of his government had been the relief of the Holy Land, and the recovery of Jerusalem from the Saracens. This zeal against infidels, being communicated to his subjects, broke out in London on the day of his coronation, and made them find a crusade less dangerous and attended with more immediate profit. The prejudices of the age had made the lending of money on interest pass by the invidious name of usury: yet the necessity of the practice had still continued it, and the greater part of that kind of dealing fell every where into the hands of the Jews, who, being already infamous on account of their religion, had no honor to lose, and were apt to exercise a profession, odious in itself, by every kind of rigor, and even sometimes by rapine and extortion. The industry and frugality of this people had put them in possession of all the ready money which the idleness and profusion common to the English with other European nations, enabled them to lend at exorbitant and unequal interest. The monkish writers represent it as a great stain on the wise and equitable government of Henry, that he had carefully protected this infidel race from all injuries and insults; but the zeal of Richard afforded the populace a pretence for venting their animosity against them. The king had issued an edict, prohibiting their appearance at his coronation; but some of them, bringing him large presents from their nation, presumed, in confidence of that merit, to approach the hall in which he dined: being discovered, they were exposed to the insults of the bystanders; they took to flight; the people pursued them; the rumor was spread that the king had issued orders to massacre all the Jews; a command so agreeable was executed in an instant on such as fell into the hands of the populace; those who had kept at home were exposed to equal danger; the people, moved by rapacity and zeal, broke into their houses, which they plundered, after having murdered the owners; where the Jews barricaded their doors, and defended themselves with vigor, the rabble set fire to their houses and made way through the flames to exercise the pillage and violence; the usual licentiousness of London, which the sovereign power with difficulty restrained, broke out with fury, and continued these outrages; the houses of the richest citizens, though Christians, were next attacked and plundered; and weariness and satiety at last put an end to the disorder: yet when the king empowered Glanville, the justiciary, to inquire into the authors of these crimes, the guilt was found to involve so many of the most considerable citizens, that it was deemed more prudent to drop the prosecution; and very few suffered the punishment due to this enormity. But the disorder stopped not at London. The inhabitants of the other cities of England, hearing of this slaughter of the Jews, imitated the example: in York, five hundred of that nation, who had retired into the castle for safety, and found themselves unable to defend the place, murdered their own wives and children, threw the dead bodies over the walls upon the populace, and then setting fire to the houses, perished in the flames. The gentry of the neighborhood, who were all indebted to the Jews, ran to the cathedral, where their bonds were kept, and made a solemn bonfire of the papers before the altar. The compiler of the Annals of Waverley, in relating these events, blesses the Almighty for thus delivering over this impious race to destruction.[1]

## From Appendix II—The Feudal and Anglo-Norman Government and Manners

BUT THE most barefaced acts of tyranny and oppression were practised against the Jews, who were entirely out of the protection of law, were extremely odious from the bigotry of the people, and were abandoned to the immeasurable rapacity of the king and his ministers. Besides many other indignities to which they were continually exposed, it appears that they were once all thrown into prison, and the sum of sixty-six thousand marks exacted for their liberty:[2] at another time, Isaac the Jew paid,

[1] *Gale's Collect.* III, 165.

[2] Thomas Madox, *The History and Antiquities of the Exchequer of the Kings of England,* p. 151. This happened in the reign of King John.

alone, five thousand one hundred marks;[3] Brun, three thousand marks;[4] Jurnet, two thousand; Bennet, five hundred: at another, Licorica, widow of David the Jew, of Oxford, was required to pay six thousand marks; and she was delivered over to six of the richest and discreetest Jews in England, who were to answer for the sum.[5] Henry III. borrowed five thousand marks from the earl of Cornwall; and for his repayment consigned over to him all the Jews in England.[6] The revenue arising from exactions upon this nation was so considerable, that there was a particular court of exchequer set apart for managing it.[7]

## *From* Chapter XII—Henry III

INTEREST HAD in that age mounted to an enormous height, as might be expected from the barbarism of the times and men's ignorance of commerce. Instances occur of fifty *per cent.* paid for money.[8] There is an edict of Philip Augustus, near this period, limiting the Jews in France to forty-eight per cent.[9] Such profits tempted the Jews to remain in the kingdom, notwithstanding the grievous oppressions to which, from the prevalent bigotry and rapine of the age, they were continually exposed. It is easy to imagine how precarious their state must have been under an indigent prince, somewhat restrained in his tyranny over his native subjects, but who possessed an unlimited authority over the Jews, the sole proprietors of money in the kingdom, and hated on account of their riches, their religion, and their

[3] *Ibid.*
[4] *Ibid.*, p. 153.
[5] *Ibid.*, p. 168.
[6] *Ibid.*, p. 156.
[7] *Ibid.*, p. 156, chap. vii.
[8] Matthew Paris, *Chronica Majora*, p. 586.
[9] Nicolas Brussel, *Nouvel Examen de l'usage géneral des fiefs en France* . . . , I, 576.

usury; yet will our ideas scarcely come up to the extortions which in fact we find to have been practised upon them. In the year 1241, twenty thousand marks were exacted from them,[10] two years after, money was again extorted; and one Jew alone, Aaron of York, was obliged to pay above four thousand marks:[11] in 1250, Henry renewed his oppressions; and the same Aaron was condemned to pay him thirty thousand marks upon an accusation of forgery:[12] the high penalty imposed upon him, and which, it seems, he was thought able to pay, is rather a presumption of his innocence than of his guilt. In 1255, the king demanded eight thousand marks from the Jews, and threatened to hang them if they refused compliance. They now lost all patience, and desired leave to retire with their effects out of the kingdom. But the king replied, "How can I remedy the oppressions you complain of? I am myself a beggar. I am spoiled, I am stripped of all my revenues; I owe above two hundred thousand marks; and if I had said three hundred thousand, I should not exceed the truth; I am obliged to pay my son, Prince Edward, fifteen thousand marks a year; I have not a farthing; and I must have money, from any hand, from any quarter, or by any means." He then delivered over the Jews to the earl of Cornwall, that those whom the one brother had flayed, the other might embowel, to make use of the words of the historian.[13] King John, his father, once demanded ten thousand marks from a Jew of Bristol; and on his refusal, ordered one of his teeth to be drawn every day till he should comply. The Jew lost seven teeth, and then paid the sum required of him.[14] One talliage laid upon the Jews, in 1243, amounted to sixty thousand marks;[15] a sum equal to the whole yearly revenue of the crown.

To give a better pretence for extortions, the improbable and absurd accusation, which has been at different times advanced

10 Paris, p. 372.
11 *Ibid.*, p. 410.
12 *Ibid.*, p. 525.
13 *Ibid.*, p. 606.
14 *Ibid.*, p. 160.
15 Madox, p. 152.

against that nation, was revived in England, that they had crucified a child in derision of the sufferings of Christ. Eighteen of them were hanged at once for this crime;[16] though it is no-wise credible that even the antipathy borne them by the Christians, and the oppressions under which they labored, would ever have pushed them to be guilty of that dangerous enormity. But it is natural to imagine, that a race exposed to such insults and indignities, both from king and people, and who had so uncertain an enjoyment of their riches, would carry usury to the utmost extremity, and by their great profits make themselves some compensation for their continual perils.

Though these acts of violence against the Jews proceeded much from bigotry, they were still more derived from avidity and rapine. So far from desiring in that age to convert them, it was enacted by law in France, that if any Jew embraced Christianity, he forfeited all his goods, without exception, to the king or his superior lord. These plunderers were careful lest the profits accruing from their dominion over that unhappy race should be diminished by their conversion.[17]

### From Chapter XIII—Edward I

AMONG THE various disorders to which the kingdom was subject, no one was more universally complained of than the adulteration of the coin; and as this crime required more art than the English of that age, who chiefly employed force and violence in their iniquities, were possessed of, the imputation fell upon the Jews.[18] Edward also seems to have indulged a strong preposses-

---

16 Paris, p. 613.

17 Brussel, I, 622. Charles du Cange, *Glossarium mediae . . . latinitatis,* article *"Judaei."*

18 Thomas Walsingham, *Historia Anglicana,* p. 48. Walter de Hemmingford, *Chronicle of English Affairs,* I, 6.

sion against that nation; and this ill-judged zeal for Christianity being naturally augmented by an expedition to the Holy Land, he let loose the whole rigor of his justice against that unhappy people. Two hundred and eighty of them were hanged at once for this crime in London alone, besides those who suffered in other parts of the kingdom.[19] The houses and lands, (for the Jews had of late ventured to make purchases of that kind) as well as the goods of great multitudes, were sold and confiscated; and the king, lest it should be suspected that the riches of the sufferers were the chief part of their guilt, ordered a moiety of the money raised by these confiscations to be set apart, and bestowed upon such as were willing to be converted to Christianity. But resentment was more prevalent with them than any temptation from their poverty; and very few of them could be induced by interest to embrace the religion of their persecutors. The miseries of this people did not here terminate. Though the arbitrary talliages and exactions levied upon them had yielded a constant and a considerable revenue to the crown, Edward, prompted by his zeal and his rapacity, resolved some time after[20] to purge the kingdom entirely of that hated race, and to seize to himself at once their whole property as the reward of his labor.[21] He left them only money sufficient to bear their charges into foreign countries, where new persecutions and extortions awaited them: but the inhabitants of the cinque ports, imitating the bigotry and avidity of their sovereign, despoiled most of them of this small pittance, and even threw many of them into the sea; a crime for which the king, who was determined to be the sole plunderer in his dominions, inflicted a capital punishment upon them. No less than fifteen thousand Jews were at this time robbed of their effects, and banished the kingdom: very few of that nation have since lived in England: and as it is impossible for a nation to subsist without lenders of money, and none will lend without a compensation, the practice of usury, as

[19] Thomas de Wykes, *Chronicle,* p. 107.
[20] In the year 1290.
[21] Walsingham, p. 54. Hemmingford, I, 20. Nicolas Trivet, *Annales sex Regum Angliae* . . . , p. 266.

it was then called, was thenceforth exercised by the English themselves upon their fellow-citizens, or by Lombards and other foreigners. It is very much to be questioned, whether the dealings of these new usurers were equally open and unexceptionable with those of the old. By a law of Richard, it was enacted, that three copies should be made of every bond given to a Jew; one to be put into the hands of a public magistrate, another into those of a man of credit, and a third to remain with the Jew himself.[22] But as the canon law, seconded by the municipal, permitted no Christian to take interest, all transactions of this kind must, after the banishment of the Jews, have become more secret and clandestine, and the lender, of consequence, be paid both for the use of his money, and for the infamy and danger which he incurred by lending it.

[22] Trivet, p. 128.

## *From* Chapter XX—Henry VI

### [JOAN OF ARC]

IN THE village of Domremi near Vaucouleurs, on the borders of Lorraine, there lived a country girl of twenty-seven years of age, called Joan d'Arc, who was servant in a small inn, and who in that station had been accustomed to tend the horses of the guests, to ride them without a saddle to the watering-place, and to perform other offices, which, in well-frequented inns, commonly fall to the share of the men servants.[1] This girl was of an irreproachable life, and had not hitherto been remarked for any singularity; whether that she had met with no occasion to excite her genius, or that the unskilful eyes of those who conversed with her, had not been able to discern her uncommon merit. It is easy to imagine, that the present situation of France was an interesting object even to persons of the lowest rank, and would become the frequent subject of conversation: A young prince, expelled his throne by the sedition of native subjects, and by the arms of strangers, could not fail to move the compassion of all his people, whose hearts were uncorrupted by faction; and the peculiar character of Charles,[2] so strongly inclined to friendship and the tender passions, naturally rendered him the hero of that sex, whose generous minds know no bounds in their affections. The siege of Orleans, the progress of the English before that place, the great distress of the garrison and inhabitants, the importance of saving this city and its brave defenders, had turned thither the public eye; and Joan, inflamed by the general sentiment, was seized with a wild desire

1 Edward Hall, *The Union of the Noble and Illustre Families of Lancastre and York,* fol. 107. Engrerrand de Monstrelet, *Chronique,* II, 42. Richard Grafton, *A Chronicle at Large and meere Historye of the Affayres of England,* p. 534.

2 [Charles VII (1403–1461), King of France from 1422 to 1461, though crowned in Rheims only in 1429.]

of bringing relief to her sovereign in his present distresses. Her unexperienced mind, working day and night on this favourite object, mistook the impulses of passion for heavenly inspirations; and she fancied, that she saw visions, and heard voices, exhorting her to re-establish the throne of France, and to expel the foreign invaders. An uncommon intrepidity of temper made her overlook all the dangers which might attend her in such a path; and thinking herself destined by heaven to this office, she threw aside all that bashfulness and timidity, so natural to her sex, her years, and her low station. She went to Vaucouleurs; procured admission to Baudricourt, the governor; informed him of her inspirations and intentions; and conjured him not to neglect the voice of God, who spoke through her, but to second those heavenly revelations, which impelled her to this glorious enterprise. Baudricourt treated her at first with some neglect; but on her frequent returns to him, and importunate solicitations, he began to remark something extraordinary in the maid, and was inclined, at all hazards, to make so easy an experiment. It is uncertain, whether this gentleman had discernment enough to perceive, that great use might be made with the vulgar of so uncommon an engine; or, what is more likely, in that credulous age, was himself a convert to this visionary: But he adopted at last the schemes of Joan; and he gave her some attendants, who conducted her to the French court, which at that time resided at Chinon.

It is the business of history to distinguish between the *miraculous* and the *marvellous;* to reject the first in all narrations merely profane and human; to doubt the second; and when obliged by unquestionable testimony, as in the present case, to admit of something extraordinary, to receive as little of it as is consistent with the known facts and circumstances. It is pretended, that Joan, immediately on her admission, knew the king, though she had never seen his face before, and though he purposely kept himself in the crowd of courtiers, and had laid aside every thing in his dress and apparel which might distinguish him: That she offered him, in the name of the supreme Creator, to raise the siege of Orleans, and conduct him to Rheims

to be there crowned and anointed; and on his expressing doubts
of her mission, revealed to him, before some sworn confidents, a
secret, which was unknown to all the world beside himself, and
which nothing but a heavenly inspiration could have discovered
to her: And that she demanded, as the instrument of her future
victories, a particular sword which was kept in the church of St.
Catherine of Fierbois, and which, though she had never seen it,
she described by all its marks, and by the place in which it had
long lain neglected.[3] This is certain, that all these miraculous
stories were spread abroad, in order to captivate the vulgar. The
more the king and his ministers were determined to give in to the
illusion, the more scrupulous they pretended. An assembly of
grave doctors and theologians cautiously examined Joan's mission, and pronounced it undoubted and supernatural. She was
sent to the parliament, then residing at Poictiers; and was inter-
rogated before that assembly: The presidents, the counsellors,
who came persuaded of her imposture, went away convinced of
her inspiration. A ray of hope began to break through that
despair, in which the minds of all men were before enveloped.
Heaven had now declared itself in favour of France, and had
laid bare its out-stretched arm to take vengeance on her invaders. Few could distinguish between the impulse of inclination and the force of conviction; and none would submit to the
trouble of so disagreeable a scrutiny.

After these artificial precautions and preparations had been
for some time employed, Joan's requests were at last complied
with: She was armed cap-a-pee, mounted on horseback, and
shown in that martial habiliment before the whole people. Her
dexterity in managing her steed, though acquired in her former
occupation, was regarded as a fresh proof of her mission; and she
was received with the loudest acclamations by the spectators.
Her former occupation was even denied: She was no longer the
servant of an inn: She was converted into a shepherdess, an
employment much more agreeable to the imagination. To
render her still more interesting, near ten years were subtracted

[3] Hall, fol. 107. Raphael Holinshed, *Chronicles,* p. 600.

from her age; and all the sentiments of love and of chivalry were thus united to those of enthusiasm, in order to inflame the fond fancy of the people with prepossessions in her favour.

When the engine was thus dressed up in full splendour, it was determined to essay its force against the enemy. Joan was sent to Blois, where a large convoy was prepared for the supply of Orleans, and an army of ten thousand men, under the command of St. Severe, assembled to escort it. She ordered all the soldiers to confess themselves before they set out on the enterprise: She banished from the camp all women of bad fame: She displayed in her hands a consecrated banner; where the Supreme Being was represented grasping the globe of earth, and surrounded with flower de luces: And she insisted, in right of her prophetic mission, that the convoy should enter Orleans by the direct road from the side of Beausse: But the count of Dunois,[4] unwilling to submit the rules of the military art to her inspirations, ordered it to approach by the other side of the river, where, he knew, the weakest part of the English army was stationed.

Previous to this attempt, the maid had written to the regent, and to the English generals before Orleans, commanding them, in the name of the omnipotent Creator, by whom she was commissioned, immediately to raise the siege, and to evacuate France; and menacing them with divine vengeance in case of their disobedience. All the English affected to speak with derision of the maid, and of her heavenly commission; and said, that the French king was now indeed reduced to a sorry pass, when he had recourse to such ridiculous expedients: But they felt their imagination secretly struck with the vehement persuasion which prevailed in all around them; and they waited with anxious expectation, not unmixed with horror, for the issue of these extraordinary preparations.

As the convoy approached the river, a sally was made by the garrison on the side of Beausse, to prevent the English general from sending any detachment to the other side: The provisions

4 [Jean, Comte de Dunois (*ca.* 1403–1468), commander of the French forces.]

were peaceably embarked in boats, which the inhabitants of Orleans had sent to receive them: The maid covered with her troops the embarkation: Suffolk[5] did not venture to attack her: And the French general carried back the army in safety to Blois; an alteration of affairs which was already visible to all the world, and which had a proportional effect on the minds of both parties.

The maid entered the city of Orleans arrayed in her military garb, and displaying her consecrated standard; and was received as a celestial deliverer by all the inhabitants. They now believed themselves invincible under her influence; and Dunois himself, perceiving such a mighty alteration both in friends and foes, consented that the next convoy, which was expected in a few days, should enter by the side of Beausse. The convoy approached: No sign of resistance appeared in the besiegers: The waggons and troops passed without interruption between the redoubts of the English: A dead silence and astonishment reigned among those troops, formerly so elated with victory, and so fierce for the combat.

The earl of Suffolk was in a situation very unusual and extraordinary, and which might well confound the man of the greatest capacity and firmest temper. He saw his troops overawed, and strongly impressed with the idea of a divine influence accompanying the maid. Instead of banishing these vain terrors by hurry, and action, and war, he waited till the soldiers should recover from the panic; and he thereby gave leisure for those prepossessions to sink still deeper into their minds. The military maxims, which are prudent in common cases, deceived him in these unaccountable events. The English felt their courage daunted and overwhelmed; and thence inferred a divine vengeance hanging over them. The French drew the same inference from an inactivity so new and unexpected. Every circumstance was now reversed in the opinions of men, on which all depends: The spirit resulting from a long course of uninter-

5 [William de la Pole, fourth Earl and first Duke of Suffolk (1396–1450), commander of the English forces at Orléans from November 1428 until captured the following summer.]

rupted success was on a sudden transferred from the victors to the vanquished.

The maid called aloud, that the garrison should remain no longer on the defensive; and she promised her followers the assistance of Heaven in attacking those redoubts of the enemy which had so long kept them in awe, and which they had never hitherto dared to insult. The generals seconded her ardour: An attack was made on one redoubt, and it proved successful:[6] All the English who defended the entrenchments were put to the sword, or taken prisoners; And Sir John Talbot himself, who had drawn together, from the other redoubts, some troops to bring them relief, durst not appear in the open field against so formidable an enemy.

Nothing, after this success, seemed impossible to the maid and her enthusiastic votaries. She urged the generals to attack the main body of the English in their entrenchments: But Dunois, still unwilling to hazard the fate of France by too great temerity, and sensible that the least reverse of fortune would make all the present visions evaporate, and restore every thing to its former condition, checked her vehemence, and proposed to her first to expel the enemy from their forts on the other side of the river, and thus lay the communication with the country entirely open, before she attempted any more hazardous enterprise. Joan was persuaded, and these forts were vigourously assailed. In one attack the French were repulsed; the maid was left almost alone; she was obliged to retreat, and join the runaways; but displaying her sacred standard, and animating them with her countenance, her gestures, her exhortations, she led them back to the charge, and overpowered the English in their entrenchments. In the attack of another fort, she was wounded in the neck with an arrow; she retreated a moment behind the assailants; she pulled out the arrow with her own hands; she had the wound quickly dressed; and she hastened back to head the troops, and to plant her victorious banner on the ramparts of the enemy.

[6] Monstrelet, II, 45.

By all these successes, the English were entirely chased from their fortifications on that side: They had lost above six thousand men in these different actions; and, what was still more important, their wonted courage and confidence was wholly gone, and had given place to amazement and despair. The maid returned triumphant over the bridge, and was again received as the guardian angel of the city. After performing such miracles, she convinced the most obdurate incredulity of her divine mission: Men felt themselves animated as by a superior energy, and thought nothing impossible to that divine hand which so visibly conducted them. It was in vain even for the English generals to oppose with their soldiers the prevailing opinion of supernatural influence: They themselves were probably moved by the same belief: The utmost they dared to advance was, that Joan was not an instrument of God; she was only the implement of the Devil: But as the English had felt, to their sad experience, that the Devil might be allowed sometimes to prevail, they derived not much consolation from the enforcing of this opinion.

It might prove extremely dangerous for Suffolk, with such intimidated troops, to remain any longer in the presence of so courageous and victorious an enemy; he therefore raised the siege, and retreated with all the precaution imaginable. The French resolved to push their conquests, and to allow the English no leisure to recover from their consternation. Charles formed a body of six thousand men, and sent them to attack Jergeau, whither Suffolk had retired with a detachment of his army. The siege lasted ten days; and the place was obstinately defended. Joan displayed her wonted intrepidity on the occasion. She descended into the fossee in leading the attack; and she there received a blow on the head with a stone, by which she was confounded, and beaten to the ground: But she soon recovered herself; and in the end rendered the assault successful: Suffolk was obliged to yield himself prisoner to a Frenchman called Renaud; but, before he submitted, he asked his adversary, whether he were a gentleman? On receiving a satisfactory answer, he demanded, whether he were a knight? Renaud replied, that he had not yet attained that honour. "Then I make you one," replied Suffolk: Upon which he gave him the blow with his sword, which dubbed him into that fraternity; and he immediately surrendered himself his prisoner.

The remainder of the English army was commanded by Fastolffe, Scales, and Talbot, who thought of nothing but of making their retreat, as soon as possible, into a place of safety; while the French esteemed the overtaking them equivalent to a victory. So much had the events which passed before Orleans altered every thing between the two nations! The vanguard of the French, under Richemont and Xaintrailles, attacked the rear of the enemy at the village of Patay. The battle lasted not a moment: The English were discomfited, and fled: The brave Fastolffe himself showed the example of flight to his troops; and the order of the garter was taken from him, as a punishment for this instance of cowardice.[7] Two thousand men were killed in this action, and both Talbot and Scales taken prisoners.

In the account of all these successes, the French writers, to magnify the wonder, represent the maid (who was now known by the appellation of "the Maid of Orleans") as not only active in combat, but as performing the office of general; directing the troops, conducting the military operations, and swaying the deliberations in all councils of war. It is certain that the policy of the French court endeavoured to maintain this appearance with the public: But it is much more probable, that Dunois and the wiser commanders prompted her in all her measures, than that a country girl, without experience or education, could, on a sudden, become expert in a profession which requires more genius and capacity than any other active scene of life. It is sufficient praise that she could distinguish the persons on whose judgment she might rely: that she could seize their hints and suggestions, and, on a sudden, deliver their opinions as her own; and that she could curb, on occasion, that visionary and enthusiastic spirit with which she was actuated, and could temper it with prudence and discretion.

The raising of the siege of Orleans was one part of the maid's promise to Charles: The crowning of him at Rheims was the

[7] Monstrelet, II, 46.

other: And she now vehemently insisted that he should forth-with set out on that enterprise. A few weeks before, such a pro-posal would have appeared the most extravagant in the world. Rheims lay in a distant quarter of the kingdom; was then in the hands of a victorious enemy; the whole road which led to it was occupied by their garrisons; and no man could be so sanguine as to imagine that such an attempt could so soon come within the bounds of possibility. But as it was extremely the interest of Charles to maintain the belief of something extraordinary and divine in these events, and to avail himself of the present con-sternation of the English, he resolved to follow the exhortations of his warlike prophetess, and to lead his army upon this promis-ing adventure. Hitherto he had kept remote from the scene of war: As the safety of thestate depended upon his person, he had been persuaded to restrain his military ardour: But observing this prosperous turn of affairs, he now determined to appear at the head of his armies, and to set the example of valour to all his soldiers. And the French nobility saw at once their young sovereign assuming a new and more brilliant character, sec-onded by fortune, and conducted by the hand of heaven; and, they caught fresh zeal to exert themselves in replacing him on the throne of his ancestors.

Charles set out for Rheims at the head of twelve thousand men: He passed by Troye, which opened its gates to him: Chalons imitated the example: Rheims sent him a deputation with its keys, before his approach to it: And he scarcely per-ceived, as he passed along, that he was marching through an enemy's country. The ceremony of his coronation was here per-formed[8] with the holy oil, which a pigeon had brought to king Clovis from heaven on the first establishment of the French monarchy: The maid of Orleans stood by his side in complete armour, and displayed her sacred banner, which had so often dissipated and confounded his fiercest enemies: And the people shouted with the most unfeigned joy on viewing such a com-plication of wonders. After the completion of the ceremony, the maid threw herself at the king's feet, embraced his knees, and

8 Monstrelet, II, 48.

with a flood of tears, which pleasure and tenderness extorted from her, she congratulated him on this singular and marvellous event.

Charles, thus crowned and anointed, become more respectable in the eyes of all his subjects, and seemed, in a manner, to receive anew, from a heavenly commission, his title to their allegiance. The inclinations of men swaying their belief, no one doubted of the inspirations and prophetic spirit of the maid: So many incidents, which passed all human comprehension, left little room to question a superior influence: And the real and undoubted facts brought credit to every exaggeration, which could scarcely be rendered more wonderful. Laon, Soissons, Chateau-Thierri, Provins, and many other towns and fortresses in that neighbourhood, immediately after Charles's coronation, submitted to him on the first summons; and the whole nation was disposed to give him the most zealous testimonies of their duty and affection.

Nothing can impress us with a higher idea of the wisdom, address, and resolution of the duke of Bedford,[9] than his being able to maintain himself in so perilous a situation, and to preserve some footing in France, after the defection of so many places, and amidst the universal inclination of the rest to imitate that contagious example. This prince seemed present every where by his vigilance and foresight: He employed every resource which fortune had yet left him: He put all the English garrisons in a posture of defence: He kept a watchful eye over every attempt among the French towards an insurrection: He retained the Parisians in obedience, by alternately employing caresses and severity: And knowing that the duke of Burgundy was already wavering in his fidelity, he acted with so much skill and prudence, as to renew in this dangerous crisis, his alliance with that prince; an alliance of the utmost importance to the credit and support of the English government.

The small supplies which he received from England set the talents of this great man in a still stronger light. The ardour of

9 [John of Lancaster, Duke of Bedford (1389–1435), third son of Henry IV, and regent after the death of his brother, Henry V, in 1422.]

the English for foreign conquests was now extremely abated by time and reflection: The parliament seems even to have become sensible of the danger which might attend their farther progress: No supply of money could be obtained by the regent during his greatest distresses: And men enlisted slowly under his standard, or soon deserted, by reason of the wonderful accounts which had reached England, of the magic, and sorcery, and diabolical power of the maid of Orleans.[10] It happened fortunately, in this emergency, that the bishop of Winchester, now created a cardinal, landed at Calais with a body of five thousand men, which he was conducting into Bohemia, on a crusade against the Hussites. He was persuaded to lend these troops to his nephew during the present difficulties;[11] and the regent was thereby enabled to take the field, and to oppose the French king, who was advancing with his army to the gates of Paris.

The extraordinary capacity of the duke of Bedford appeared also in his military operations. He attempted to restore the courage of his troops by boldly advancing to the face of the enemy; but he chose his posts with so much caution, as always to decline a combat, and to render it impossible for Charles to attack him. He still attended that prince in all his movements; covered his own towns and garrisons; and kept himself in a posture to reap advantage from every imprudence or false step of the enemy. The French army, which consisted mostly of volunteers, who served at their own expence, soon after retired, and was disbanded: Charles went to Bourges, the ordinary place of his residence; but not till he had made himself master of Compiegne, Beauvais, Senlis, Sens, Laval, Lagni, St. Denis, and of many places in the neighbourhood of Paris, which the affections of the people had put into his hands.

The regent endeavoured to revive the declining state of his affairs by bringing over the young king of England, and having him crowned and anointed at Paris.[12] All the vassals of the crown who lived within the provinces possessed by the English,

10 Thomas Rymer, *Foedera*, X, 459, 472.
11 *Ibid.*, p. 421.
12 *Ibid.*, p. 432.

swore a new allegiance, and did homage to him. But this ceremony was cold and insipid, compared with the lustre which had
attended the coronation of Charles at Rheims; and the duke of
Bedford expected more effect from an accident, which put into
his hands the person that had been the author of all his calamities.

The maid of Orleans, after the coronation of Charles, declared to the count of Dunois, that her wishes were now fully
gratified, and that she had no farther desire than to return to her
former condition, and to the occupation and course of life which
became her sex: But that nobleman, sensible of the great advantages which might still be reaped from her presence in the
army, exhorted her to persevere, till, by the final expulsion of
the English, she had brought all her prophecies to their full
completion. In pursuance of this advice, she threw herself into
the town of Compiegne, which was at that time besieged by the
duke of Burgundy, assisted by the earls of Arundel and Suffolk;
and the garrison, on her appearance, believed themselves thenceforth invincible. But their joy was of short duration. The maid,
next day, after her arrival, headed a sally upon the quarters of
John of Luxembourg; she twice drove the enemy from their
entrenchments; finding their numbers to increase every moment,
she ordered a retreat; when hard pressed by the pursuers, she
turned upon them, and made them again recoil; but being
here deserted by her friends, and surrounded by the enemy, she
was at last, after exerting the utmost valour, taken prisoner by
the Burgundians.[13] The common opinion was, that the French
officers, finding the merit of every victory ascribed to her, had,
in envy to her renown, by which they themselves were so much
eclipsed, willingly exposed her to this fatal accident.

The envy of her friends, on this occasion, was not a greater
proof of her merit than the triumph of her enemies. A complete victory would not have given more joy to the English and
their partisans. The service of *Te Deum,* which has so often
been profaned by princes, was publicly celebrated, on this for-

---

[13] John Stowe [either *Annals* or *Chronicles of England*], p. 371.

tunate event, at Paris. The duke of Bedford fancied, that, by the captivity of that extraordinary woman, who had blasted all his successes, he should again recover his former ascendant over France; and, to push farther the present advantage, he purchased the captive from John of Luxemburg, and formed a prosecution against her, which, whether it proceeded from vengeance or policy, was equally barbarous and dishonourable.

There was no possible reason, why Joan should not be regarded as a prisoner of war, and be entitled to all the courtesy and good usage, which civilised nations practise towards enemies on these occasions. She had never, in her military capacity, forfeited, by any act of treachery or cruelty, her claim to that treatment: She was unstained by any civil crime: Even the virtues and the very decorums of her sex had ever been rigidly observed by her: And though her appearing in war, and leading armies to battle, may seem an exception, she had thereby performed such signal service to her prince, that she had abundantly compensated for this irregularity; and was, on that very account, the more an object of praise and admiration. It was necessary, therefore, for the duke of Bedford to interest religion some way in the prosecution; and to cover, under that cloak, the violation of justice and humanity.

The bishop of Beauvais, a man wholly devoted to the English interests, presented a petition against Joan, on pretence that she was taken within the bounds of his diocese; and he desired to have her tried by an ecclesiastical court for sorcery, impiety, idolatry, and magic: The university of Paris was so mean as to join in the same request: Several prelates, among whom the cardinal of Winchester was the only Englishman, were appointed her judges: They held their court in Roüen, where the young king of England then resided: And the maid, clothed in her former military apparel, but loaded with irons, was produced before this tribunal.

She first desired to be eased of her chains: Her judges answered, that she had once already attempted an escape, by throwing herself from a tower: She confessed the fact, maintained the justice of her intention, and owned that, if she could, she would still execute that purpose. All her other speeches showed the same firmness and intrepidity: Though harassed with interrogatories during the course of near four months, she never betrayed any weakness or womanish submission; and no advantage was gained over her. The point, which her judges pushed most vehemently, was her visions and revelations and intercourse with departed saints; and they asked her, whether she would submit to the church the truth of these inspirations: She replied, that she would submit them to God, the fountain of truth. They then exclaimed, that she was a heretic, and denied the authority of the church. She appealed to the pope: They rejected her appeal.

They asked her, why she put trust in her standard, which had been consecrated by magical incantations: She replied, that she put trust in the Supreme Being alone, whose image was impressed upon it. They demanded, why she carried in her hand that standard at the anointment and coronation of Charles at Rheims: She answered, that the person who had shared the danger, was entitled to share the glory. When accused of going to war, contrary to the decorums of her sex, and of assuming government and command over men; she scrupled not to reply, that her sole purpose was to defeat the English, and to expel them the kingdom. In the issue, she was condemned for all the crimes of which she had been accused, aggravated by heresy; her revelations were declared to be inventions of the devil to delude the people; and she was sentenced to be delivered over to the secular arm.

Joan, so long surrounded by inveterate enemies, who treated her with every mark of contumely; brow-beaten and overawed by men of superior rank, and men invested with the ensigns of a sacred character, which she had been accustomed to revere, felt her spirit at last subdued; and those visionary dreams of inspiration, in which she had been buoyed up by the triumphs of success, and the applauses of her own party, gave way to the terrors of that punishment to which she was sentenced. She publicly declared herself willing to recant; she acknowledged the illusion of those revelations which the church had rejected;

and she promised never more to maintain them. Her sentence was then mitigated: She was condemned to perpetual imprisonment, and to be fed during life on bread and water.

Enough was now done to fulfil all political views, and to convince both the French and the English, that the opinion of divine influence, which had so much encouraged the one, and daunted the other, was entirely without foundation. But the barbarous vengeance of Joan's enemies was not satisfied with this victory. Suspecting, that the female dress, which she had now consented to wear, was disagreeable to her, they purposely placed in her apartment a suit of men's apparel; and watched for the effects of that temptation upon her. On the sight of a dress in which she had acquired so much renown, and which, she once believed, she wore by the particular appointment of heaven, all her former ideas and passions revived; and she ventured in her solitude to clothe herself again in the forbidden garment. Her insidious enemies caught her in that situation: Her fault was interpreted to be no less than a relapse into heresy: No recantation would now suffice, and no pardon could be granted her. She was condemned to be burned in the marketplace of Roüen; and the infamous sentence was accordingly executed. This admirable heroine, to whom the more generous superstition of the ancients would have erected altars, was, on pretence of heresy and magic, delivered over alive to the flames, and expiated, by that dreadful punishment, the signal services which she had rendered to her prince and to her native country.

# *From* Chapter XXIII—Edward V and Richard III

THUS HAVE we pursued the history of England through a series of many barbarous ages; till we have at last reached the dawn of civility and science, and have the prospect, both of greater certainty in our historical narrations, and of being able to present to the reader a spectacle more worthy of his attention. The want of certainty, however, and of circumstances, is not alike to be complained of throughout every period of this long narration. This island possess many ancient historians of good credit; as well as many historical monuments; and it is rare, that the annals of so uncultivated a people, as were the English as well as the other European nations, after the decline of Roman learning, have been transmited to posterity so complete, and with so little mixture of falsehood and of fable. This advantage we owe entirely to the clergy of the church of Rome; who, founding their authority on their superior knowledge, preserved the precious literature of antiquity from a total extinction;[1] and, under shelter of their numerous privileges and immunities, acquired a security, by means of the superstition, which they would in

[1]* Every one that has perused the ancient monkish writers knows, that however barbarous their own style, they are full of allusions to the Latin classics, especially the poets. There seems also, in those middle ages, to have remained many ancient books that are now lost. Malmesbury, who flourished in the reign of Henry I. and king Stephen, quotes Livy's description of Caesar's passage over the Rubicon. Fitz-Stephen, who lived in the reign of Henry II. alludes to a passage in the larger history of Sallust. In the collection of letters, which passes under the name of Thomas a Becket, we see how familiar all the ancient history and ancient books were to the more ingenious and more dignified churchmen of that time, and consequently how much that order of men must have surpassed all the other members of the society. That prelate and his friends call each other philosophers in all the course of their correspondence, and consider the rest of the world as sunk in total ignorance and barbarism.

vain have claimed, from the justice and humanity of those turbulent and licentious ages. Nor is the spectacle altogether un-
entertaining and uninstructive which the history of those times
presents to us. The view of human manners, in all their variety
of appearances, is both profitable and agreeable; and if the
aspect in some periods seem horrid and deformed, we may
thence learn to cherish with the greater anxiety that science and
civility which has so close a connexion with virtue and humanity, and which, as it is a sovereign antidote against superstition,
is also the most effectual remedy against vice and disorders of
every kind.

The rise, progress, perfection, and decline of art and science,
are curious objects of contemplation, and intimately connected
with a narration of civil transactions. The events of no particular period can be fully accounted for, but by considering the
degrees of advancement which men have reached in those particulars.

Those who cast their eye on the general revolutions of society
will find, that, as almost all improvements of the human mind
had reached nearly to their state of perfection about the age of
Augustus, there was a sensible decline from that point or period;
and men thenceforth relapsed gradually into ignorance and barbarism. The unlimited extent of the Roman empire, and the
consequent despotism of its monarchs, extinguished all emulation, debased the generous spirits of men, and depressed that
noble flame by which all the refined arts must be cherished and
enlivened. The military government which soon succeeded,
rendered even the lives and properties of men insecure and precarious; and proved destructive to those vulgar and more necessary arts of agriculture, manufactures, and commerce; and, in
the end, to the military art and genius itself, by which alone the
immense fabric of the empire could be supported. The irruption
of the barbarous nations which soon followed, overwhelmed all
human knowledge, which was already far in its decline; and men
sunk every age deeper into ignorance, stupidity, and superstition; till the light of ancient science and history had very nearly
suffered a total extinction in all the European nations.

But there is a point of depression, as well as of exaltation, from which human affairs naturally return in a contrary direction, and beyond which they seldom pass either in their advancement or decline. The period in which the people of Christendom were the lowest sunk in ignorance, and consequently in disorders of every kind, may justly be fixed at the eleventh century, about the age of William the Conqueror; and from that aera, the sun of science beginning to re-ascend, threw out many gleams of light, which preceded the full morning, when letters were revived in the fifteenth century. The Danes, and other northern people, who had so long infested all the coasts, and even the inland parts of Europe, by their depredations, having now learned the arts of tillage and agriculture, found a certain subsistence at home, and were no longer tempted to desert their industry, in order to seek a precarious livelihood by rapine, and by the plunder of their neighbours. The feudal governments also, among the more southern nations, were reduced to a kind of system; and though that strange species of civil polity was ill fitted to insure either liberty or tranquillity, it was preferable to the universal licence and disorder which had every where preceded it. But perhaps there was no event which tended farther to the improvement of the age, than one which has not been much remarked, the accidental finding of a copy of Justinian's Pandects, about the year 1130, in the town of Amalfi in Italy.

The ecclesiastics, who had leisure, and some inclination to study, immediately adopted with zeal this excellent system of jurisprudence, and spread the knowledge of it throughout every part of Europe. Besides the intrinsic merit of the performance, it was recommended to them by its original connexion with the imperial city of Rome, which being the seat of their religion, seemed to acquire a new lustre and authority by the diffusion of its laws over the western world. In less than ten years after the discovery of the Pandects, Vacarius, under the protection of Theobald, archbishop of Canterbury, read public lectures of civil law in the university of Oxford; and the clergy every where, by their example as well as exhortation, were the means of diffusing the highest esteem for this new science. That order of

men having large possessions to defend, was, in a manner, neces-
sitated to turn their studies towards the law; and their properties
being often endangered by the violence of the princes and
barons, it became their interest to enforce the observance of
general and equitable rules, from which alone they could receive protection. As they possessed all the knowledge of the age,
and were alone acquainted with the habits of thinking, the
practice as well as science of the law fell mostly into their hands:
and though the close connexion which, without any necessity,
they formed between the canon and civil law, begat a jealousy
in the laity of England, and prevented the Roman jurisprudence
from becoming the municipal law of the country, as was the case
in many states of Europe, a great part of it was secretly transferred into the practice of the courts of justice, and the imitation
of their neighbours made the English gradually endeavour to
raise their own law from its original state of rudeness and imperfection.

It is easy to see what advantages Europe must have reaped by
its inheriting at once from the ancients so complete an art, which
was also so necessary for giving security to all other arts, and
which, by refining, and still more by bestowing, solidity on the
judgment, served as a model to farther improvements. The sensible utility of the Roman law, both to public and private interest,
recommended the study of it, at a time when the more exalted
and speculative sciences carried no charms with them; and thus
the last branch of ancient literature which remained uncorrupted, was happily the first transmitted to the modern world:
for it is remarkable, that in the decline of Roman learning, when
the philosophers were universally infected with superstition
and sophistry, and the poets and historians with barbarism, the
lawyers, who in other countries are seldom models of science
or politeness, were yet able, by the constant study and close
imitation of their predecessors, to maintain the same good sense
in their decisions and reasonings, and the same purity in their
language and expression.

What bestowed an additional merit on the civil law, was the
extreme imperfection of that jurisprudence which preceded it

among all the European nations, especially among the Saxons or ancient English. The absurdities which prevailed at that time in the administration of justice, may be conceived from the authentic monuments which remain of the ancient Saxon law; where a pecuniary commutation was received for every crime, where stated prices were fixed for men's lives and members, where private revenges were authorised for all injuries, where the use of the ordeal, corsnet,[2] and afterwards of the duel, was the received method of proof, and where the judges were rustic freeholders, assembled of a sudden, and deciding a cause from one debate or altercation of the parties. Such a state of society was very little advanced beyond the rude state of nature: violence universally prevailed, instead of general and equitable maxims: the pretended liberty of the times was only an incapacity of submitting to government: and men, not protected by law in their lives and properties, sought shelter by their personal servitude and attachments under some powerful chieftain, or by voluntary combinations.

The gradual progress of improvement raised the Europeans somewhat above this uncultivated state; and affairs, in this island particularly, took early a turn which was more favourable to justice and to liberty. Civil employments and occupations soon became honourable among the English: the situation of that people rendered not the perpetual attention to wars so necessary as among their neighbours, and all regard was not confined to the military profession: the gentry, and even the nobility, began to deem an acquaintance with the law a necessary part of education: they were less diverted, than afterwards, from studies of this kind by other sciences; and in the age of Henry VI. as we are told by Fortescue, there were in the inns of court about two thousand students, most of them men of honourable birth, who gave application to this branch of civil knowledge: a circumstance which proves that a considerable progress was already made in the science of government, and which prognosticated a still greater.

One chief advantage which resulted from the introduction

2 [Or "corsned," a piece of consecrated bread used in determining the guilt of an accused person.]

and progress of the arts, was the introduction and progress of freedom; and this consequence affected men both in their *personal* and *civil* capacities.

If we consider the ancient state of Europe, we shall find that the far greater part of the society were every where bereaved of their *personal* liberty, and lived entirely at the will of their masters. Every one that was not noble was a slave: the peasants were sold along with the land: the few inhabitants of cities were not in a better condition: even the gentry themselves were subjected to a long train of subordination under the greater barons or chief vassals of the crown; who, though seemingly placed in a high state of splendour, yet, having but a slender protection from law, were exposed to every tempest of the state, and, by the precarious condition in which they lived, paid dearly for the power of oppressing and tyrannizing over their inferiors. The first incident which broke in upon this violent system of government was the practice, begun in Italy, and imitated in France, of erecting communities and corporations, endowed with privileges and a separate municipal government, which gave them protection against the tyranny of the barons, and which the prince himself deemed it prudent to respect.[3] The relaxation of the feudal tenures, and an execution somewhat stricter, of the public law, bestowed an independence on vassals, which was unknown to their forefathers. And even the peasants themselves, though later than other orders of the state, made their escape from those bonds of villenage or slavery in which they had formerly been retained.

It may appear strange, that the progress of the arts, which

---

[3] There appear early symptoms of the jealousy entertained by the barons against the progress of the arts, as destructive of their licentious power. A law was enacted, 7 Henry IV. chap. 17. prohibiting any one who did not possess twenty shillings a year in land from binding his sons apprentices to any trade. They found already that the cities began to drain the country of the labourers and husbandmen; and did not foresee how much the increase of commerce would increase the value of their estates. See farther, Bartholomew de Cotton, *Historia Anglicana*, p. 179. The kings, to encourage the boroughs, granted them this privilege, that any villain who had lived a twelvemonth in any corporation, and had been of the guild, should be thenceforth regarded as free.

seems, among the Greeks and Romans, to have daily encreased the number of slaves, should, in later times, have proved so general a source of liberty; but this difference in the events proceeded from a great difference in the circumstances which attended those institutions. The ancient barons, obliged to maintain themselves continually in a military posture, and little emulous of elegance or splendor, employed not their villains as domestic servants, much less as manufacturers; but composed their retinue of freemen, whose military spirit rendered the chieftain formidable to his neighbours, and who were ready to attend him in every warlike enterprise. The villains were entirely occupied in the cultivation of their master's land, and paid their rents either in corn and cattle and other produce of the farm, or in servile offices, which they performed about the baron's family, and upon the farms which he retained in his own possession. In proportion as agriculture improved and money increased, it was found that these services, though extremely burdensome to the villain, were of little advantage to the master; and that the produce of a large estate could be much more conveniently disposed of by the peasants themselves who raised it, than by the landlord or his bailiff, who were formerly accustomed to receive it. A commutation was therefore made of rents for services, and of money-rents for those in kind; and as men in a subsequent age discovered that farms were better cultivated where the farmer enjoyed a security in his possession, the practice of granting leases to the peasant began to prevail, which entirely broke the bonds of servitude, already much relaxed from the former practices. After this manner, villenage went gradually into disuse throughout the more civilized parts of Europe: the interest of the master, as well as that of the slave, concurred in this alteration. The latest laws, which we find in England for enforcing or regulating this species of servitude, were enacted in the reign of Henry VII. And though the ancient statutes on this subject remain still unrepealed by parliament, it appears that, before the end of Elizabeth, the distinction of villain and freeman was totally, though insensibly, abolished, and that no person remained in the state to whom the former laws could be applied.

Thus *personal* freedom became almost general in Europe; an advantage which paved the way for the increase of *political* or *civil* liberty, and which, even where it was not attended with this salutary effect, served to give the members of the community some of the most considerable advantages of it.

The constitution of the English government, ever since the invasion of this island by the Saxons, may boast of this pre-eminence, that in no age the will of the monarch was ever entirely absolute and uncontroulled: but in other respects the balance of power has extremely shifted among the several orders of the state; and this fabric has experienced the same mutability that has attended all human institutions.

The ancient Saxons, like the other German nations, where each individual was enured to arms, and where the independence of men was secured by a great equality of possessions, seem to have admitted a considerable mixture of democracy into their form of government, and to have been one of the freest nations of which there remains any account in the records of history. After this tribe was settled in England, especially after the dissolution of the Heptarchy, the great extent of the kingdom produced a great inequality in property; and the balance seems to have inclined to the side of aristocracy. The Norman conquest threw more authority into the hands of the sovereign, which, however, admitted of great controul; though derived less from the general forms of the constitution, which were inaccurate and irregular, than from the independent power enjoyed by each baron in his particular district or province. The establishment of the great charter exalted still higher the aristocracy, imposed regular limits on royal power, and gradually introduced some mixture of Democracy into the constitution. But even during this period, from the accession of Edward I. to the death of Richard III. the condition of the commons was nowise eligible; a kind of Polish aristocracy prevailed; and though the kings were limited, the people were as yet far from being free. It required the authority almost absolute of the sovereigns, which took place in the subsequent period, to pull down those disorderly and licentious tyrants, who were equally averse from peace and from freedom, and to establish that regular execution of the laws, which, in a following age, enabled the people to erect a regular and equitable plan of liberty.

In each of these successive alterations, the only rule of government which is intelligible or carries any authority with it, is the established practice of the age, and the maxims of administration which are at that time prevalent and universally assented to. Those who, from a pretended respect to antiquity, appeal, at every turn, to an original plan of the constitution, only cover their turbulent spirit and their private ambition under the appearance of venerable forms; and, whatever period they pitch on for their model, they may still be carried back to a more ancient period, where they will find the measures of power entirely different, and where every circumstance, by reason of the greater barbarity of the times, will appear still less worthy of imitation. Above all, a civilized nation, like the English, who have happily established the most perfect and most accurate system of liberty that was ever found compatible with government, ought to be cautious in appealing to the practice of their ancestors, or regarding the maxims of uncultivated ages as certain rules for their present conduct. An acquaintance with the ancient periods of their government is chiefly *useful*, by instructing them to cherish their present constitution, from a comparison or contrast with the condition of those distant times. And it is also *curious*, by showing them the remote, and commonly faint and disfigured originals of the most finished and most noble institutions, and by instructing them in the great mixture of accident, which commonly concurs with a small ingredient of *wisdom* and foresight in erecting the complicated fabric of the most perfect government.

# *From* Chapter XXXIX—Elizabeth
## [MARY QUEEN OF SCOTS]

THE EARL of Bothwel[1] was of a considerable family and power in Scotland; and though not distinguished by any talents either of a civil or military nature, he had made a figure in that party, which opposed the greatness of the earl of Murray,[2] and the more rigid reformers. He was a man of profligate manners; had involved his opulent fortune in great debts; and even reduced himself to beggary, by his profuse expences;[3] and seemed to have no resource but in desperate councils and enterprises. He had been accused more than once of an attempt to assassinate Murray; and though the frequency of these accusations on all sides diminish somewhat the credit due to any particular imputation, they prove sufficiently the prevalence of that detestable practice in Scotland, and may in that view serve to render such rumours the more credible. This man had of late acquired the favour and entire confidence of Mary;[4] and all her measures were directed by his advice and authority. Reports were spread of more particular intimacies between them; and these reports gained ground from the continuance or rather increase of her hatred towards her husband.[5] That young prince was reduced to such a state of desperation, by the neglects which he underwent from his queen and the courtiers, that he had once re-

1 [James Hepburn, fourth Earl of Bothwell (1536?–1578), lord high admiral of Scotland.]

2 [James Stewart, Earl of Mar and afterwards Earl of Moray (1531?–1570), Regent of Scotland; often identified as "Regent Murray." He was the natural son of James V of Scotland, and hence half-brother of Mary Queen of Scots.]

3 Robert Keith, *The History of the Affairs of the Church and State of Scotland. . . , p. 240.*

4 [Mary Stuart, Queen of Scotland (1542–1587); married in 1558 to the French dauphin, she became Queen of France when he became Francis II in 1559. Francis died the next year.]

5 Sir James Melville, *Memoirs*, pp. 66, 77.

solved to fly secretly into France or Spain, and had even provided a vessel for that purpose.[6] Some of the most considerable
nobility, on the other hand, observing her rooted aversion to
him, had proposed some expedients for a divorce; and though
Mary is said to have spoken honourably on the occasion, and to
have embraced the proposal no farther than it should be found
consistent with her own honour and her son's legitimacy,[7] men
were inclined to believe, that the difficulty of finding proper
means for effecting that purpose, was the real cause of laying
aside all farther thoughts of it. So far were the suspicions against
her carried, that when Henry,[8] discouraged with the continued
proofs of her hatred, left the court and retired to Glasgow, an
illness of an extraordinary nature, with which he was seized
immediately on his arrival in that place, was universally
ascribed by her enemies to a dose of poison, which, it was pretended, she had administered to him.

While affairs were in this situation, all those who wished
well to her character or to public tranquillity, were extremely
pleased, and somewhat surprised, to hear, that a friendship
was again conciliated between them, that she had taken a journey to Glasgow on purpose to visit him during his sickness, that
she behaved towards him with great tenderness, that she had
brought him along with her, and that she appeared thenceforth determined to live with him on a footing more suitable
to the connections between them. Henry, naturally uxorious,
and not distrusting this sudden reconciliation, put himself implicitly into her hands, and attended her to Edinburgh. She
lived in the palace of Holy-rood-house; but as the situation of
the place was low, and the concourse of people about the court
was necessarily attended with noise, which might disturb him

---

[6] Keith, pp. 845–848.

[7] William Camden, *Annales rerum Anglicarum . . . regnante Elizabetha*,
p. 404. Walter Goodall, *Examination of the Letters Said to be Written by
Mary Queen of Scots to James, Earl of Bothwell*, II, 317.

[8] [Henry Stewart or Stuart, Lord Darnley (1545–1567), to whom Mary was
married in 1565.]

in his present infirm state of health, these reasons were assigned for fitting up an apartment for him in a solitary house, at some distance, called the Kirk of Field. Mary here gave him marks of kindness and attachment; she conversed cordially with him; and she lay some nights in a room below his; but on the ninth of February, she told him, that she would pass that night in the palace, because the marriage of one of her servants was there to be celebrated in her presence. About two o'clock in the morning the whole town was much alarmed at hearing a great noise; and was still more astonished, when it was discovered that the noise came from the King's house, which was blown up by gunpowder; that his dead body was found at some distance in a neighbouring field; and that no marks either of fire, contusion, or violence appeared upon it.[9]

No doubt could be entertained but Henry was murdered; and general conjecture soon pointed towards the earl of Bothwel as the author of the crime.[10] But as his favour with Mary was visible, and his power great, no one ventured to declare openly his sentiments; and all men remained in silence and mute astonishment. Voices, however, were heard in the streets, during the darkness of the night, proclaiming Bothwel, and even Mary herself, to be murderers of the king; bills were secretly affixed on the walls to the same purpose; offers were made, that, upon giving proper securities, his guilt should be openly proved. But after one proclamation from the court, offering a reward and indemnity to any one that would discover the author of that villany, greater vigilance was employed in searching out the spreaders of the libels and reports against Bothwel and the

[9] It was imagined that Henry had been strangled before the house was blown up. But this supposition is contradicted by the confession of the criminals; and there is no necessity to admit it in order to account for the condition of his body. There are many instances that men's lives have been saved who had been blown up in ships. Had Henry fallen on water he had not probably been killed.

[10] Melville, p. 78. *Cabala . . . Mysteries of State and Government . . .* , p. 136.

queen, than in tracing the contrivers of the king's assassination, or detecting the regicides.[11]

The earl of Lenox,[12] who lived at a distance from court, in poverty and contempt, was roused by the report of his son's murder, and wrote to the queen imploring speedy justice against the assassins; among whom he named the earl of Bothwel, Sir James Balfour, and Gilbert Balfour his brother, David Chalmers,[13] and four others of the queen's household; all of them persons who had been mentioned in the bills affixed to the walls at Edinburgh.[14] Mary took his demand of speedy justice in a very literal sense; and allowing only fifteen days for the examination of this important affair, she sent a citation to Lenox, requiring him to appear in court, and prove his charge against Bothwel.[15] This nobleman, meanwhile, and all the other persons, accused by Lenox, enjoyed their full liberty;[16] Bothwel himself was continually surrounded with armed men;[17] took his place in council;[18] lived during some time in the house with Mary;[19] and seemed to possess all his wonted confidence and familiarity with her. Even the castle of Edinburgh, a place of great consequence in this critical time, was entrusted to him, and under him, to his creature, Sir James Balfour, who had himself been publicly charged as an accomplice in the king's murder.[20] Lenox, who had come as far as Stirling, with a view of appearing at the trial, was informed of all these cir-

---

11 James Anderson, *Collections Relating to the History of Mary Queen of Scotland*, II, 38; IV, 167, 168. Spotswood, *History of the Church and State of Scotland from the Year of Our Lord 203 to the End of the Reign of King James VI, 1625*, p. 200. Keith, p. 374.

12 [Matthew Stewart, fourth or twelfth Earl of Lennox (1516–1571).]

13 [James Balfour, Lord Pittendreich (d. 1583), Scottish judge; Gilbert Balfour, his brother; and David Chalmers, Lord Ormond, Scottish historian and judge.]

14 Keith, p. 372. Anderson, II, 3.

15 Keith, p. 373.

16 *Ibid.*, pp. 374, 375.

17 *Ibid.*, p. 405.

18 Anderson, I, 38, 40, 50, 52.

19 *Ibid.*, II, 274.

20 Spotswood, p. 201.

cumstances; and reflecting on the small train which attended him, he began to entertain very just apprehensions from the power, insolence, and temerity of his enemy. He wrote to Mary, desiring that the day of trial might be prorogued; and conjured her, by all the regard which she bore to her own honour, to employ more leisure and deliberation in determining a question of such extreme moment.[21] No regard was paid to his application: the jury was enclosed, of which the earl of Caithness[22] was chancellor; and though Lenox, foreseeing this precipitation, had ordered Cunningham,[23] one of his retinue, to appear in court, and protest in his name, against the acquittal of the criminal, the jury proceeded to a verdict.[24] The verdict was such as it behoved them to give, where neither accuser nor witness appeared; and Bothwel was absolved from the king's murder. The jury, however, apprehensive that their verdict would give great scandal, and perhaps expose them afterwards to some danger, entered a protest, in which they represented the necessity of their proceedings.[25] It is remarkable, that the indictment was laid against Bothwel for committing the crime on the ninth of February, not the tenth, the real day on which Henry was assassinated.[26] The interpretation generally put upon this error, too gross, it was thought, to have proceeded from mistake, was, that the secret council, by whom Mary was governed, not trusting entirely to precipitation, violence, and authority, had provided this plea by which they ensured, at all adventures, a plausible pretence for acquitting Bothwel.

Two days after this extraordinary transaction, a parliament was held; and though the verdict in favour of Bothwel was attended with such circumstances as strongly confirmed, rather than diminished, the general opinion of his guilt, he was the

21 Keith, p. 375. Anderson, I, 52.
22 [George Sinclair, fourth Earl of Caithness (d. 1582).]
23 [Alexander Cunningham, fifth Earl of Glencairn (d. 1574), member of the Scottish privy council.]
24 Keith, p. 376. Anderson, II, 106. Spotswood, p. 201.
25 Spotswood, p. 201. Anderson, I, 113.
26 Keith, p. 374. Anderson, II, 93. Spotswood, p. 201,

person chosen to carry the royal sceptre on the first meeting of the national assembly.[27] In this parliament, a rigorous act was made against those who set up defamatory bills; but no notice was taken of the king's murder.[28] The favour, which Mary openly bore to Bothwel, kept every one in awe; and the effects of this terror appeared more plainly in another transaction, which ensued immediately upon the dissolution of the parliament. A bond or association was framed; in which the subscribers, after relating the acquittal of Bothwel by a legal trial, and mentioning a farther offer, which he had made, to prove his innocence by single combat, oblige themselves, in case any person should afterwards impute to him the king's murder, to defend him with their whole power against such calumniators. After this promise, which implied no great assurance in Bothwel of his own innocence, the subscribers mentioned the necessity of their queen's marriage, in order to support the government; and they recommended Bothwel to her as a husband.[29] This paper was subscribed by all the considerable nobility there present. In a country, divided by violent factions, such a concurrence in favour of one nobleman, nowise distinguished above the rest, except by his flagitious conduct, could never have been obtained, had not every one been certain, at least firmly persuaded, that Mary was fully determined on this measure.[30] Nor would such a motive have sufficed to influence men, commonly so stubborn and intractable, had they not been taken by surprise, been ignorant of each other's sentiments, and overawed

[27] Keith, p. 78. David Crawford, *Memoirs of the Affairs of Scotland*, p. 14.

[28] Keith, p. 380.

[29] *Ibid.*, p. 381.

[30]* Mary herself confessed, in her instructions to the ambassadors whom she sent to France, that Bothwel persuaded all the noblemen, that their application in favour of his marriage was agreeable to her. Keith, p. 389. Anderson, I, 94. Murray afterwards produced to queen Elizabeth's commissioners, a paper signed by Mary, by which she permitted them to make this application to her. This permission was a sufficient declaration of her intentions, and was esteemed equivalent to a command. Anderson, IV, 59. They even asserted, that the house in which they met, was surrounded with armed men. Goodall, II, 141.

by the present power of the court, and by the apprehensions of farther violence, from persons so little governed by any principles of honour and humanity. Even with all these circumstances, the subscription to this paper may justly be regarded as a reproach to the nation.

The subsequent measures of Bothwel were equally precipitate and audacious. Mary having gone to Stirling to pay a visit to her son, he assembled a body of eight hundred horse, on pretence of pursuing some robbers on the borders; and having waylaid her on her return, he seized her person near Edinburgh, and carried her to Dunbar, with an avowed design of forcing her to yield to his purpose. Sir James Melvil,[31] one of her retinue, was carried along with her, and says not, that he saw any signs of reluctance or constraint: he was even informed, as he tells us, by Bothwel's officers, that the whole transaction was managed in concert with her.[32] A woman, indeed, of that spirit and resolution, which is acknowledged to belong to Mary, does not usually, on these occasions, give such marks of opposition to *real* violence, as can appear anywise doubtful or ambiguous. Some of the nobility, however, in order to put matters to farther trial, sent her a private message; in which they told her, that if, in reality, she lay under force, they would use all their efforts to rescue her. Her answer was, that she had indeed been carried to Dunbar by violence, but ever since her arrival had been so well treated, that she willingly remained with Bothwel.[33] No one gave himself thenceforth any concern to relieve her from a captivity, which was believed to proceed entirely from her own approbation and connivance.

This unusual conduct was at first ascribed to Mary's sense of the infamy attending her purposed marriage; and her desire of finding some colour to gloss over the irregularity of her conduct. But a pardon, given to Bothwel a few days after, made the public carry their conjectures somewhat farther. In this deed,

[31] [Sir James Melville (1535–1617), member of the Scottish privy council, appointed gentleman of the bedchamber by Mary.]
[32] Melville, p. 80.
[33] Spotswood, p. 202.

Bothwel received a pardon for the violence committed on the queen's person; and for *all other crimes:* a clause, by which the murder of the king was indirectly forgiven. The rape was then conjectured to have been only a contrivance, in order to afford a pretence for indirectly remitting a crime, of which it would have appeared scandalous to make openly any mention.[34]

These events passed with such rapidity, that men had no leisure to admire sufficiently one incident, when they were surprised with a new one equally rare and uncommon. There still, however, remained one difficulty, which it was not easy to foresee how the queen and Bothwel, determined as they were to execute their shameful purpose, could find expedients to overcome. The man who had procured the subscription of the nobility, recommending him as a husband to the queen, and who had acted this seeming violence on her person, in order to force her consent, had been married two years before to another woman; to a woman of merit, of a noble family, sister to the earl of Huntley. But persons blinded by passion, and infatuated with crimes, soon shake off all appearances of decency. A suit was commenced for a divorce between Bothwel and his wife; and this suit was opened at the same instant in two different, or rather opposite, courts; in the court of the archbishop of St. Andrews, which was popish, and governed itself by the canon law; and in the new consistorial or commissariot court, which was protestant, and was regulated by the principles of the reformed teachers. The plea, advanced in each court, was so calculated as to suit the principles which there prevailed: in the archbishop's court, the pretence of consanguinity was employed, because Bothwel was related to his wife in the fourth degree; in the commissariot court, the accusation of adultery was made use of against him. The parties too, who applied for the divorce, were different in different courts: Bothwel was the person who sued in the former; his wife in the latter. And the suit in both courts was opened, pleaded, examined, and decided with the utmost precipitation; and a sentence of divorce was pronounced in four days.[35]

34 Anderson, Vol. IV, pt. ii. p. 61.
35 Anderson, II, 280.

The divorce being thus obtained, it was thought proper that Mary should be conducted to Edinburgh, and should there appear before the courts of judicature, and should acknowledge herself restored to entire freedom. This was understood to be contrived in a view of obviating all doubts with regard to the validity of her marriage. Orders were then given to publish in the church the banns between the queen and the duke of Orkney;[36] for that was the title which he now bore; and Craig,[37] a minister of Edinburgh, was applied to for that purpose. This clergyman, not content with having refused compliance, publicly in his sermons condemned the marriage, and exhorted all who had access to the queen, to give her their advice against so scandalous an alliance. Being called before the council, to answer for this liberty, he showed a courage which might cover all the nobles with shame, on account of their tameness and servility. He said, that, by the rules of the church, the earl of Bothwel, being convicted of adultery, could not be permitted to marry; that the divorce between him and his former wife was plainly procured by collusion, as appeared by the precipitation of the sentence, and the sudden conclusion of his marriage with the queen; and that all the suspicions which prevailed, with regard to the king's murder, and the queen's concurrence in the former rape, which thence receive undoubted confirmation. He therefore exhorted Bothwel, who was present, no longer to persevere in his present criminal enterprises; and turning his discourse to the other counsellors, he charged them to employ all their influence with the queen, in order to divert her from a measure, which would load her with eternal infamy and dishonour. Not satisfied even with this admonition, he took the first opportunity of informing the public, from the pulpit, of the whole transaction, and expressed to them his fears, that, notwithstanding all remonstrances, their sovereign was still obstinately bent on her fatal purpose. "For himself," he said, "he had already discharged his conscience, and yet again would taken heaven and earth to witness, that he ab-

36 [Bothwell was created Duke of Orkney and Shetland after the marriage on May 15, 1567.]

37 [John Craig (1512?–1600).]

horred and detested that marriage, as scandalous and hateful in the sight of mankind: but since the Great, as he perceived, either by their flattery or silence, gave countenance to the measure, he besought the Faithful to pray fervently to the Almighty, that a resolution, taken contrary to all law, reason, and good conscience, might, by the divine blessing, be turned to the comfort and benefit of the church and kingdom." These speeches offended the court extremely; and Craig was anew summoned before the council, to answer for his temerity in thus passing the bounds of his commission. But he told them, that the bounds of his commission were the word of God, good laws, and natural reason; and were the queen's marriage tried by any of these standards, it would appear infamous and dishonourable, and would be so esteemed by the whole world. The council were so overawed by this heroic behaviour in a private clergyman, that they dismissed him without farther censure or punishment.[38]

But though this transaction might have recalled Bothwel and the queen of Scots from their infatuation, and might have instructed them in the dispositions of the people, as well as in their own inability to oppose them; they were still resolute to rush forward to their own manifest destruction. The marriage was solemnized by the bishop of Orkney,[39] a protestant, who was afterwards deposed by the church for this scandalous compliance. Few of the nobility appeared at the ceremony: they had most of them, either from shame or fear, retired to their own houses. The French ambassador, Le Croc, an aged gentleman of honour and character, could not be prevailed on, though a dependent of the house of Guise, to countenance the marriage by his presence.[40] Elizabeth remonstrated, by friendly letters and messages, against the marriage:[41] the court of France made like opposition; but Mary, though on all other occasions she was extremely obsequious to the advice of her relations in that country, was here determined to pay no regard to their opinion.

---

[38] Spotswood, p. 203. Anderson, II, 280.
[39] [Not identified by the editors.]
[40] Spotswood, p. 203. Melville, p. 82.
[41] Keith, p. 392. Sir Dudley Digges, *The Compleat Ambassador*, p. 14.

The news of these transactions, being carried to foreign countries, filled Europe with amazement, and threw infamy, not only
on the principal actors in them, but also on the whole nation,
who seemed, by their submission and silence, and even by their
declared approbation, to give their sanction to these scandalous
practices.[42] The Scots, who resided abroad, met with such reproaches, that they durst no where appear in public; and they
earnestly exhorted their countrymen at home, to free them from
the public odium, by bringing to condign punishment the
authors of such atrocious crimes. This intelligence, with a little
more leisure for reflection, roused men from their lethargy; and
the rumours which, from the very beginning,[43] had been spread
against Mary, as if she had concurred in the king's murder,
seemed now, by the subsequent transactions, to have received
a strong confirmation and authority. It was every where said,
that even though no particular and direct proofs had as yet been
produced of the queen's guilt, the whole tenor of her late
conduct was sufficient, not only to beget suspicion, but to produce entire conviction against her: that her sudden resolution
of being reconciled to her husband, whom before she had long
and justly hated; her bringing him to court, from which she
had banished him by neglects and rigours; her fitting up separate apartments for him; were all of them circumstances which,
though trivial in themselves, yet, being compared with the subsequent events, bore a very unfavourable aspect for her: that
the least which, after the king's murder, might have been expected in her situation, was a more than usual caution in her
measures, and an extreme anxiety to punish the real assassins,
in order to free herself from all reproach and suspicion: that
no woman, who had any regard to her character, would allow
a man, publicly accused of her husband's murder, so much as
to approach her presence, far less give him a share in her councils, and endow him with favour and authority: that an acquittal, merely in the absence of accusers, was very ill fitted to
satisfy the public; especially if that absence proceeded from a

[42] Melville, p. 82. Keith, p. 402. Anderson, I, 128, 134.
[43] Crawford, p. 11. Keith, Preface, p. 9.

designed precipitation of the sentence, and from the terror which her known friendship for the criminal had infused into every one: that the very mention of her marriage to such a person, in such circumstances, was horrible; and the contrivances of extorting a consent from the nobility, and of concerting a rape, were gross artifices, more proper to discover her guilt than prove her innocence: that where a woman thus shows a consciousness of merited reproach, and, instead of correcting, provides only thin glosses to cover her exceptionable conduct, she betrays a neglect of fame, which must either be the effect or the cause of the most shameful enormities: that to espouse a man, who had, a few days before, been so scandalously divorced from his wife; who, to say the least, was believed to have, a few months before, assassinated her husband; was so contrary to the plainest rules of behaviour, that no pretence of indiscretion or imprudence could account for such a conduct: that a woman, who, so soon after her husband's death, though not attended with any extraordinary circumstances, contracts a marriage, which might, in itself be the most blameless, cannot escape severe censure; but one who overlooks, for her pleasure, so many other weighty considerations, was equally capable, in gratifying her appetites, to neglect every regard to honour and humanity: that Mary was not ignorant of the prevailing opinion of the public, with regard to her own guilt, and of the inferences which would every where be drawn from her conduct; and therefore, if she still continued to pursue measures which gave such just offence, she ratified, by her actions, as much as she could by the most formal confession, all the surmises and imputations of her enemies: that a prince was here murdered in the face of the world; Bothwel alone was suspected and accused; if he were innocent, nothing could absolve him, either in Mary's eyes or those of the public, but the detection and conviction of the real assassin; yet no inquiry was made to that purpose, though a parliament had been assembled; the sovereign and wife was here plainly silent from guilt, the people from terror: that the only circumstance which opposed all these presumptions, or rather proofs, was the benignity and goodness of her preceding behaviour, which seemed to remove her from all suspicions of such atrocious inhumanity; but that the characters of men were extremely variable, and persons, guilty of the worst actions, were not naturally of the worst and most criminal dispositions: that a woman who, in a critical and dangerous moment, had sacrificed her honour to a man of abandoned principle, might thenceforth be led blindfold by him to the commission of the most enormous crimes, and was in reality no longer at her own disposal: and that, though one supposition was still left to alleviate her blame, namely, that Bothwel, presuming on her affection towards him, had of himself committed the crime, and had never communicated it to her, yet such a sudden and passionate love to a man, whom she had long known, could not easily be accounted for, without supposing some degree of preceding guilt; and as it appeared, that she was not afterwards restrained, either by shame or prudence, from incurring the highest reproach and danger, it was not likely that a sense of duty or humanity would have a more powerful influence over her.

These were the sentiments which prevailed throughout Scotland; and as the protestant teachers, who had great authority, had long borne an animosity to Mary, the opinion of her guilt was, by that means, the more widely diffused, and made the deeper impression on the people. Some attempts made by Bothwel, and, as is pretended, with her consent, to get the young prince into his power, excited the most serious attention; and the principal nobility, even many of those who had formerly been constrained to sign the application in favour of Bothwel's marriage, met at Stirling, and formed an association for protecting the prince, and punishing the king's murderers.[44] The earl of Athole[45] himself, a known catholic, was the first author of this confederacy: the earls of Argyle, Morton, Marre, Glencarne, the lords Boyd, Lindesey, Hume, Semple, Kirkaldy of Grange, Tulibardine, and secretary Lidington, entered zeal-

[44] Keith, p. 394.
[45] [John Stewart, fourth Earl of Atholl (d. 1579), member of the Scottish privy council.]

ously into it. The earl of Murray, foreseeing such turbulent times, and being desirous to keep free of these dangerous factions, had, some time before, desired and obtained Mary's permission to retire into France.

Lord Hume[46] was first in arms; and, leading a body of eight hundred horse, suddenly environed the queen of Scots and Bothwel in the castle of Borthwic. They found means of making their escape to Dunbar; while the confederate lords were assembling their troops at Edinburgh, and taking measures to effect their purpose. Had Bothwel been so prudent as to keep within the fortress of Dunbar, his enemies must have dispersed for want of pay and subsistence; but hearing that the associated lords were fallen into distress, he was so rash as to take the field, and advance towards them. The armies met at Carberry Hill, about six miles from Edinburgh; and Mary soon became sensible that her own troops disapproved of her cause, and were averse to spill their blood in the quarrel.[47] After some bravadoes of Bothwel, where he discovered very little courage, she saw no resource but that of holding a conference with Kirkaldy of Grange,[48] and of putting herself, upon some general promises, into the hands of the confederates. She was conducted to Edinburgh, amidst the insults of the populace; who reproached her with her crimes, and even held before her eyes, which way soever she turned, a banner, on which were painted the murder of her husband, and the distresses of her infant son.[49] Mary, overwhelmed with her calamities, had recourse to tears and lamentations. Meanwhile, Bothwel, during her conference with Grange, fled unattended to Dunbar; and fitting out a few small ships, set sail for the Orkneys, where he subsisted during some time by piracy. He was pursued thither by Grange, and his ship was taken, with several of his servants, who afterwards discovered all the circumstances of the king's murder, and were pun-

---

46 [Alexander Home, fifth Baron Home (d. 1575).]
47 Keith, p. 402. Spotswood, p. 207.
48 [Sir William Kirkcally of Grange (d. 1573).]
49 Melville, pp. 83, 84.

ished for the crime.[50] Bothwel himself escaped in a boat, and found means to get a passage to Denmark, where he was thrown into prison, lost his senses, and died miserably about ten years after: an end worthy of his flagitious conduct and behaviour.

The queen of Scots, now in the hands of an enraged faction, met with such treatment as a sovereign may naturally expect from subjects, who have their future security to provide for, as well as their present animosity to gratify. It is pretended, that she behaved with a spirit very little suitable to her condition, avowed her inviolable attachment to Bothwel,[51] and even wrote him a letter, which the lords intercepted, where she declared, that she would endure any extremity, nay resign her dignity and crown itself, rather than relinquish his affections.[52] The malcontents, finding the danger to which they were exposed, in case Mary should finally prevail, thought themselves obliged to proceed with rigour against her; and they sent her next day under a guard to the castle of Lochlevin, situated in a lake of that name. The mistress of the house was mother to the earl of Murray; and as she pretended to have been lawfully married to the late king of Scots, she naturally bore an animosity to Mary, and treated her with the utmost harshness and severity.

Elizabeth, who was fully informed of all these incidents, seemed touched with compassion towards the unfortunate queen; and all her fears and jealousies being now laid asleep, by the consideration of that ruin and infamy in which Mary's conduct had involved her, she began to reflect on the instability of human affairs, the precarious state of royal grandeur, the danger of encouraging rebellious subjects; and she resolved to employ her authority for alleviating the calamities of her unhappy kinswoman. She sent Sir Nicholas Throgmorton[53] am-

50 Anderson, II, 165, 166ff.

51 Keith, p. 419.

52 Melville, p. 84. The reality of this letter appears somewhat disputable; chiefly because Murray and his associates never mentioned it in their accusation of her before queen Elizabeth's commissioners.

53 [Sir Nicolas Throckmorton (1515–1571), also ambassador to France, 1559–1563.]

bassador to Scotland, in order to remonstrate both with Mary and the associated lords; and she gave him instructions, which, though mixed with some lofty pretensions, were full of that good sense which were so natural to her, and of that generosity which the present interesting conjuncture had called forth. She empowered him to declare in her name to Mary, that the late conduct of that princess, so enormous, and in every respect so unjustifiable, had given her the highest offence; and though she felt the movements of pity towards her, she had once determined never to interpose in her affairs, either by advice or assistance, but to abandon her entirely, as a person whose condition was totally desperate, and honour irretrievable: that she was well assured, that other foreign princes, Mary's near relations, had embraced the same resolution; but, for her part, the later events had touched her heart with more tender sympathy, and had made her adopt measures more favourable to the liberty and interests of the unhappy queen: that she was determined not to see her oppressed by her rebellious subjects, but would employ all her good offices, and even her power, to redeem her from captivity, and place her in such a condition as would at once be compatible with her dignity, and the safety of her subjects: that she conjured her to lay aside all thoughts of revenge, except against the murderers of her husband; and as she herself was his near relation, she was better entitled than the subjects of Mary, to interpose her authority on that head; and she therefore besought that princess, if she had any regard to her own honour and safety, not to oppose so just and reasonable a demand: that after those two points were provided for, her own liberty, and the punishment of her husband's assassins, the safety of her infant son was next to be considered; and there seemed no expedient more proper for that purpose, than sending him to be educated in England: and that, besides the security which would attend his removal from a scene of faction and convulsions, there were many other beneficial consequences, which it was easy to foresee as the result of his education in that country.[54]

[54] Keith, pp. 411, 412ff.

The remonstrances, which Throgmorton was instructed to make to the associated lords, were entirely conformable to these sentiments, which Elizabeth entertained in Mary's favour. She empowered him to tell them, that, whatever blame she might throw on Mary's conduct, any opposition to their sovereign was totally unjustifiable, and incompatible with all order and good government: that it belonged not to them to reform, much less to punish, the mal-administration of their prince; and the only arms which subjects could in any case lawfully employ against the supreme authority, were entreaties, counsels, and representations: that if these expedients failed, they were next to appeal by their prayers to Heaven; and to wait with patience till the Almighty, in whose hands are the hearts of princes, should be pleased to turn them to justice and to mercy: that she inculcated not this doctrine, because she herself was interested in its observance; but because it was universally received in all well-governed states, and was essential to the preservation of civil society: that she required them to restore their queen to liberty; and promised, in that case, to concur with them in all proper expedients for regulating the government, for punishing the king's murderers, and for guarding the life and liberty of the infant prince: and that if the services, which she had lately rendered the Scottish nation, in protecting them from foreign usurpation, were duly considered by them, they would repose confidence in her good offices, and would esteem themselves blameworthy in having hitherto made no application to her.[55]

Elizabeth, besides these remonstrances, sent, by Throgmorton, some articles of accommodation, which he was to propose to both parties, as expedients for the settlement of public affairs; and though these articles contained some important restraints on the sovereign power, they were in the main calculated for Mary's advantage, and were sufficiently indulgent to her.[56] The associated lords, who determined to proceed with greater severity, were apprehensive of Elizabeth's partiality; and

55 *Ibid.*, pp. 414, 415, 429.
56 *Ibid.*, p. 416.

being sensible that Mary would take courage from the protection of that powerful princess,[57] they thought proper, after several affected delays, to refuse the English ambassador all access to her. There were four different schemes proposed in Scotland, for the treatment of the captive queen: one, that she should be restored to her authority under very strict limitations: the second, that she should be obliged to resign her crown to the prince, be banished the kingdom, and be confined either to France or England; with assurances from the sovereign, in whose dominions she should reside, that she should make no attempts to the disturbance of the established government: the third, that she should be publicly tried for her crimes, of which her enemies pretended to have undoubted proof, and be sentenced to perpetual imprisonment: the fourth was still more severe, and required, that, after her trial and condemnation, capital punishment should be inflicted upon her.[58] Throgmorton supported the mildest proposal; but though he promised his mistress's guarantee for the performance of articles, threatened the ruling party with immediate vengeance in case of refusal,[59] and warned them not to draw on themselves, by their violence, the public reproach, which now lay upon their queen; he found that, excepting secretary Lidington, he had not the good fortune to convince any of the leaders. All counsels seemed to tend towards the more severe expedients; and the preachers, in particular, drawing their examples from the rigorous maxims of the Old Testament, which can only be warranted by particular revelations, inflamed the minds of the people against their unhappy sovereign.[60]

There were several pretenders to the regency of the young prince, after the intended deposition of Mary. The earl of Lenox claimed that authority as grandfather to the prince: the duke of Chatelrault,[61] who was absent in France, had pretentions as

---

[57] *Ibid.*, p. 427.

[58] *Ibid.*, p. 420.

[59] *Ibid.*, p. 428.

[60] *Ibid.*, pp. 422, 426.

[61] [James Hamilton, second Earl of Arran and Duke of Châtelheraut (d. 1575).]

next heir to the crown: but the greatest number of the associated lords inclined to the earl of Murray, in whose capacity
they had entire trust, and who possessed the confidence of the
preachers and more zealous reformers. All measures being therefore concerted, three instruments were sent to Mary, by the
hands of lord Lindesey,[62] and Sir Robert Melvil;[63] by one of
which she was to resign the crown in favour of her son, by another to appoint Murray regent, by the third to name a council
which should administer the government till his arrival in
Scotland. The queen of Scots, seeing no prospect of relief, lying
justly under apprehensions for her life, and believing that no
deed, which she executed during her captivity, could be valid,
was prevailed on, after a plentiful effusion of tears, to sign
these three instruments; and she took not the trouble of in-
specting any one of them.[64] In consequence of this forced resignation, the young prince was proclaimed king, by the name of
James VI.[65] He was soon after crowned at Stirling, and the earl
of Morton[66] took in his name the coronation-oath; in which a
promise to extirpate heresy was not forgotten. Some republican
pretensions, in favour of the people's power, were countenanced
in this ceremony;[67] and a coin was soon after struck, on which
the famous saying of Trajan was inscribed, *Pro me; si merear,
in me:* for me; if I deserve it, against me.[68] Throgmorton had
orders from his mistress not to assist the coronation of the king
of Scots.[69]

The council of regency had not long occasion to exercise
their authority. The earl of Murray arrived from France, and
took possession of his high office. He paid a visit to the captive
queen; and spoke to her in a manner which better suited her
past conduct than her present condition. This harsh treatment
quite extinguished in her breast any remains of affection to-

[62] [David Lindsay, tenth Earl of Crawford (d. 1574).]
[63] [Robert Melville, first Baron of Melville (1527–1621).]
[64] Melville, p. 85. Spotswood, p. 211. Anderson, III, 19.
[65] [Afterwards James I of England.]
[66] [James Douglas, fourth Earl of Morton (d. 1581).]
[67] Keith, pp. 439, 440.
[68] *Ibid.*, p. 440; Appendix, p. 150.
[69] Keith, p. 430.

wards him.[70] Murray proceeded afterwards to break, in a more public manner, all terms of decency with her. He summoned a parliament; and that assembly, after voting that she was undoubtedly an accomplice in her husband's murder, condemned her to imprisonment, ratified her demission of the crown, and acknowledged her son for king and Murray for regent.[71] The regent, a man of vigour and abilities, employed himself successful in reducing the kingdom. He bribed Sir James Balfour to surrender the castle of Edinburgh: he constrained the garrison of Dunbar to open their gates: and he demolished that fortress.

But though every thing thus bore a favourable aspect to the new government, and all men seemed to acquiesce in Murray's authority; a violent revolution, however necessary, can never be effected without great discontents; and it was not likely that, in a country where the government, in its most settled state, possessed a very disjointed authority, a new establishment should meet with no interruption or disturbance. Few considerable men of the nation seemed willing to support Mary, so long as Bothwel was present; but the removal of that obnoxious nobleman had altered the sentiments of many. The duke of Chatelrault, being disappointed of the regency, bore no goodwill to Murray; and the same sentiments were embraced by all his numerous retainers: several of the nobility, finding that others had taken the lead among the associators, formed a faction apart, and opposed the prevailing power: and besides their being moved by some remains of duty and affection towards Mary, the malcontent lords, observing every thing carried to extremity against her, were naturally led to embrace her cause, and shelter themselves under her authority. All who retained any propensity to the catholic religion, were induced to join this party; and even the people in general, though they had formerly either detested Mary's crimes, or blamed her imprudence, were now inclined to compassionate her present situation, and lamented that a person, possessed of so many ami-

70 Melville, p. 87. Keith, p. 445.
71 Anderson, II, 206ff.

able accomplishments, joined to such high dignity, should be treated with such extreme severity.[72] Animated by all these motives, many of the principal nobility, now adherents to the queen of Scots, met at Hamilton, and concerted measures for supporting the cause of that princess.

While these humours were in fermentation, Mary was employed in contrivances for effecting her escape; and she engaged, by her charms and caresses, a young gentleman, George Douglas, brother to the laird of Lochlevin,[73] to assist her in that enterprise. She even went so far as to give him hopes of espousing her, after her marriage with Bothwel should be dissolved on the plea of force; and she proposed this expedient to the regent, who rejected it. Douglas, however, perservered in his endeavours to free her from captivity; and having all opportunities of access to the house, he was at last successful in the undertaking. He conveyed her in disguise into a small boat, and himself rowed her ashore. She hastened to Hamilton; and the news of her arrival in that place being immediately spread abroad, many of the nobility flocked to her with their forces. A bond of association for her defence was signed by the earls of Argyle, Huntley, Eglington, Crawford, Cassilis, Rothes, Montrose, Sutherland, Errol, nine bishops, and nine barons, besides many of the most considerable gentry.[74] And in a few days an army to the number of six thousand men, was assembled under her standard.

Elizabeth was no sooner informed of Mary's escape, than she discovered her resolution of persevering in the same generous and friendly measures which she had hitherto pursued. If she had not employed force against the regent, during the imprisonment of that princess, she had been chiefly withheld by the fear of pushing him to greater extremities against her;[75] but

[72] George Buchanan, *Rerum Scoticarum Historia*, Bk XVIII, chap. 53. [See footnote 98, p. 178.]

[73] [Sir William Douglas of Lochleven, sixth or seventh Earl of Morton (d. 1606); William did not approve of his younger brother's efforts on behalf of Mary.]

[74] Keith, p. 475.

[75] *Ibid.*, p. 463. *Cabala*, p. 141.

she had proposed to the court of France an expedient, which, though less violent, would have been no less effectual for her service: she desired that France and England should by concert cut off all commerce with the Scots, till they should do justice to their injured sovereign.[76] She now dispatched Leighton into Scotland to offer both her good offices, and the assistance of her forces, to Mary; but as she apprehended the entrance of French troops into the kingdom, she desired that the controversy between the queen of Scots and her subjects might by that princess be referred entirely to her arbitration, and that no foreign succours should be introduced into Scotland.[77]

But Elizabeth had not leisure to exert fully her efforts in favour of Mary. The regent made haste to assemble forces; and notwithstanding that his army was inferior in number to that of the queen of Scots, he took the field against her. A battle was fought at Langside near Glasgow, which was entirely decisive in favour of the regent; and though Murray, after his victory, stopped the bloodshed, yet was the action followed by a total dispersion of the queen's party. That unhappy princess fled southwards from the field of battle with great precipitation, and came, with a few attendants, to the borders of England. She here deliberated concerning her next measures, which would probably prove so important to her future happiness or misery. She found it impossible to remain in her own kingdom: she had an aversion, in her present wretched condition, to return into France, where she had formerly appeared with so much splendour; and she was not, besides, provided with a vessel, which could safely convey her thither: the late generous behaviour of Elizabeth made her hope for protection, and even assistance, from that quarter;[78] and as the present fears from her domestic enemies were the most urgent, she overlooked all other considerations, and embraced the resolution of taking shelter in England. She embarked on board a fishing-boat in

[76] Keith, p. 462.

[77] *Ibid.*, p. 473, in the notes. Anderson, IV, 26.

[78] Samuel Jebb, *De vita et rebus gestis Mariae Scotorum Reginae . . .* , I, 420.

Galloway, and landed the same day at Workington in Cumberland, about thirty miles from Carlisle; whence she immediately
dispatched a messenger to London; notifying her arrival, desiring leave to visit Elizabeth, and craving her protection, in consequence of former professions of friendship made her by that
princess.

Elizabeth now found herself in a situation, when it was become necessary to take some decisive resolution with regard to
her treatment of the queen of Scots; and as she had hitherto,
contrary to the opinion of Cecil,[79] attended more to the motives
of generosity than of policy;[80] she was engaged by that prudent
minister to weigh anew all the considerations, which occurred
in this critical conjuncture. He represented, that the party
which had dethroned Mary, and had at present assumed the
government of Scotland, was always attached to the English
alliance, and was engaged, by all the motives of religion and
of interest, to persevere in their connection with Elizabeth:
that though Murray and his friends might complain of some
unkind usage during their banishment in England, they would
easily forget these grounds of quarrel, when they reflected, that
Elizabeth was the only ally on whom they could safely rely, and
that their own queen, by her attachment to the catholic faith,
and by her other connections, excluded them entirely from the
friendship of France, and even from that of Spain: that Mary,
on the other hand, even before her violent breach with her
protestant subjects, was in secret entirely governed by the
counsels of the house of Guise; much more would she implicitly
comply with their views, when, by her own ill conduct, the
power of that family and of the zealous catholics was become
her sole resource and security: that her pretensions to the
English crown would render her a dangerous instrument in
their hands; and, were she once able to suppress the protestants
in her own kingdom, she would unite the Scottish and English
catholics, with those of all foreign states, in a confederacy

[79] [William Cecil, Lord Burghley (1520–1598), "the ablest and most labori-
ous secretary" of Elizabeth, according to Dictionary of National Biography.]
[80] Cabala, p. 140.

against the religion and government of England: that it behoved Elizabeth, therefore, to proceed with caution in the design of restoring her rival to the throne; and to take care, both that this enterprise, if undertaken, should be effected by English forces alone, and that full securities should beforehand be provided for the reformers and the reformation in Scotland: that above all, it was necessary to guard carefully the person of that princess; lest, finding this unexpected reserve in the English friendship, she should suddenly take the resolution of flying into France, and should attempt, by foreign force, to recover possession of her authority: that her desperate fortunes and broken reputation fitted her for any attempt; and her resentment, when she should find herself thus deserted by the queen, would concur with her ambition and her bigotry, and render her an unrelenting, as well as powerful, enemy to the English government: that if she were once abroad, in the hands of enterprising catholics, the attack on England would appear to her as easy as that on Scotland; and the only method, she must imagine, of recovering her native kingdom, would be to acquire that crown, to which she would deem herself equally entitled: that a neutrality in such interesting situations, though it might be pretended, could never, without the most extreme danger, be upheld by the queen; and the detention of Mary was equally requisite, whether the power of England were to be employed in her favour, or against her: that nothing, indeed, was more becoming a great prince than generosity; yet the suggestions of this noble principle could never, without imprudence, be consulted in such delicate circumstances as those in which the queen was at present placed; where her own safety, and the interests of her people, were ultimately concerned in every resolution which she embraced: that though the example of successful rebellion, especially in a neighbouring country, could nowise be agreeable to any sovereign, yet Mary's imprudence had been so great, perhaps her crimes so enormous, that the insurrection of subjects, after such provocation, could no longer be regarded as a precedent against other princes: that it was first necessary for Elizabeth to ascertain, in a regular and satisfactory manner, the extent of Mary's guilt, and thence to determine the degree of protection which she ought to afford her against her discontented subjects: that as no glory could surpass that of defending oppressed innocence, it was equally infamous to patronize vice and murder on the throne; and the contagion of such dishonour would extend itself to all who countenanced or supported it: And that, if the crimes of the Scottish princess should, on inquiry, appear as great and certain as was affirmed and believed, every measure against her, which policy should dictate, would thence be justified; or if she should be found innocent, every enterprise, which friendship should inspire, would be acknowledged laudable and glorious.

Agreeably to these views, Elizabeth resolved to proceed in a seemingly generous, but really cautious, manner with the queen of Scots; and she immediately sent orders to lady Scrope, sister to the duke of Norfolk,[81] a lady who lived in the neighbourhood, to attend on that princess. Soon after, she dispatched to her lord Scrope[82] himself, warden of the marches, and Sir Francis Knolles,[83] vice-chairman. They found Mary already lodged in the castle of Carlisle; and, after expressing the queen's sympathy with her in her late misfortunes, they told her, that her request of being allowed to visit their sovereign, and of being admitted to her presence, could not at present be complied with: till she had cleared herself of her husband's murder, of which she was so strongly accused. Elizabeth could not without dishonour, show her any countenance, or appear indifferent to the assassination of so near a kinsman.[84] So unexpected a check threw Mary into tears; and the necessity of her situation extorted from her a declaration, that she would willingly justify herself to her sister from all imputations, and would submit

[81] [Thomas Howard III, fourth Duke of Norfolk of the Howard house (1536–1572).]

[82] [Henry le Scrope, ninth Baron Scrope of Bolton (1534–1592), Warden of the West Marches. Lady Scrope was Margaret, daughter of Henry Howard, Earl of Surrey, the poet.]

[83] [Sir Francis Knollys (1514?–1596), a trusted friend and aid of both Elizabeth and Cecil.]

[84] Anderson, IV, 54, 66, 82, 83, 86.

her cause to the arbitration of so good a friend.[85] Two days after she sent lord Herreis[86] to London with a letter to the same purpose.

This concession, which Mary could scarcely avoid, without an acknowledgment of guilt, was the point expected and desired by Elizabeth: she immediately dispatched Midlemore to the regent of Scotland; requiring him both to desist from the farther prosecution of his queen's party, and send some persons to London to justify his conduct with regard to her. Murray might justly be startled at receiving a message so violent and imperious; but as his domestic enemies were numerous and powerful, and England was the sole ally which he could expect among foreign nations, he was resolved rather to digest the affront, than provoke Elizabeth by a refusal. He also considered, that though that queen had hitherto appeared partial to Mary, many political motives evidently engaged her to support the king's cause in Scotland; and it was not to be doubted but so penetrating a princess would in the end discover this interest, and would at least afford him a patient and equitable hearing. He therefore replied, that he would himself take a journey to England, attended by other commissioners; and would willingly submit the determination of his cause to Elizabeth.[87]

Lord Herreis now perceived that his mistress had advanced too far in her concessions: he endeavoured to maintain, that Mary could not, without diminution of her royal dignity, submit to a contest with her rebellious subjects before a foreign prince; and he required either present aid from England, or liberty for his queen to pass over into France. Being pressed, however, with the former agreement before the English council, he again renewed his consent; but in a few days he began anew to recoil; and it was with some difficulty that he was brought to acquiesce in the first determination.[88] These fluctuations,

85 *Ibid.*, pp. 10, 55, 87.

86 [John of Terregles, Master of Maxwell and fourth Baron Herreis (1512?–1583).]

87 Anderson, IV, 13–16.

88 *Ibid.*, pp. 16–20.

which were incessantly renewed, shewed his visible reluctance
to the measures pursued by the court of England.

The queen of Scots discovered no less aversion to the trial
proposed; and it required all the artifice and prudence of Elizabeth to make her persevere in the agreement to which she at
first consented. This latter princess still said to her, that she
desired not, without Mary's consent or approbation, to enter
into the question, and pretended only, as a friend, to hear her
justification: that she was confident there would be found no
difficulty in refuting all the calumnies of her enemies; and even
if her apology should fall short of full conviction, Elizabeth
was determined to support her cause, and procure her some
reasonable terms of accommodation: and that it was never
meant, that she should be cited to a trial on the accusation of
her rebellious subjects; but, on the contrary, that they should
be summoned to appear, and to justify themselves for their
conduct towards her.[89] Allured by these plausible professions,
the queen of Scots agreed to vindicate herself by her own commissioners, before commissioners appointed by Elizabeth.

During these transactions, lord Scrope and Sir Francis
Knolles, who resided with Mary at Carlisle, had leisure to study
her character, and make report of it to Elizabeth. Unbroken
by her misfortunes, resolute in her purpose, active in her enterprises, she aspired to nothing but victory; and was determined
to endure any extremity, to undergo any difficulty, and to try
every fortune, rather than abandon her cause, or yield the
superiority to her enemies. Eloquent, insinuating, affable; she
had already convinced all those who approached her, of the
innocence of her past conduct; and as she declared her fixed
purpose to require aid of her friends all over Europe, and even
to have recourse to infidels and barbarians, rather than fail of
vengeance against her persecutors, it was easy to foresee the
danger to which her charms, her spirit, her address, if allowed
to operate with their full force, would expose them.[90] The court
of England, therefore, who, under pretence of guarding her,

89 *Ibid.,* pp. 11, 12, 13, 109, 110.
90 *Ibid.,* IV, 54, 71, 72, 74, 78, 92.

had already, in effect, detained her prisoner, were determined to watch her with still greater vigilance. As Carlisle, by its situation on the borders, afforded her great opportunities of contriving her escape, they removed her to Bolton, a seat of lord Scrope's in Yorkshire; and the issue of the controversy between her and the Scottish nation was regarded as a subject more momentous to Elizabeth's security and interests, than it had hitherto been apprehended.

The commissioners, appointed by the English court for the examination of this great cause, were the duke of Norfolk, the earl of Sussex,[91] and Sir Ralph Sadler;[92] and York was named as the place of conference. Lesley bishop of Ross,[93] the lords Herreis, Levingstone,[94] and Boyde,[95] with three persons more, appeared as commissioners from the queen of Scots. The earl of Murray, regent, the earl of Morton, the bishop of Orkney, lord Lindesey, and the abbot of Dunfermling,[96] were appointed commissioners from the king and kingdom of Scotland. Secretary Lidington,[97] George Buchanan,[98] the famous poet and historian, with some others, were named as their assistants.

It was a great circumstance in Elizabeth's glory, that she was thus chosen umpire between the factions of a neighboring kingdom, which had, during many centuries, entertained the most violent jealousy and animosity against England; and her felicity was equally rare, in having the fortunes and fame of so dangerous a rival, who had long given her the greatest inquietude, now entirely at her disposal. Some circumstances of her late conduct

[91] [Thomas Radcliffe, third Earl of Sussex, also Baron Fitzwalter (1526?–1583), lord lieutenant and lord president of the north.]

[92] [Sir Ralph Sadler, Sadleir, or Sadleyer (1507–1587), paymaster-general and adviser to Sussex.]

[93] [Presumably John Lesley or Leslie (1527–1596).]

[94] [William Livingstone, sixth Baron Livingstone (d. 1592), a partisan of Mary despite being a protestant.]

[95] [Robert Boyd, fourth Lord Boyd (d. 1590), a member of the Scottish privy council.]

[96] [Not identified by the editors.]

[97] [William Maitland of Lethington (1528–1573), Mary's secretary.]

[98] [George Buchanan (1506–1582), secretary for the Scottish commission.]

had discovered a bias towards the side of Mary: her prevailing
interests led her to favour the enemies of that princess: the professions of impartiality, which she had made, were open and
frequent; and she had so far succeeded, that each side accused
her commissioners of partiality towards their adversaries.[99] She
herself appears, by the instructions given them, to have fixed
no plan for the decision; but she knew that the advantages
which she should reap, must be great, whatever issue the cause
might take. If Mary's crimes could be ascertained by undoubted
proof, she could for ever blast the reputation of that princess,
and might justifiably detain her for ever a prisoner in England:
if the evidence fell short of conviction, it was intended to restore
her to the throne, but with such strict limitations as would
leave Elizabeth perpetual arbiter of all differences between the
parties in Scotland, and render her in effect absolute mistress
of the kingdom.[100]

Mary's commissioners, before they gave in their complaints
against her enemies in Scotland, entered a protest, that their
appearance in the cause should nowise affect the independence
of her crown, or be construed as a mark of subordination to
England: the English commissioners received this protest, but
with a reserve to the claim of England. The complaint of that
princess was next read, and contained a detail of the injuries
which she had suffered since her marriage with Bothwel: that
her subjects had taken arms against her, on pretence of freeing
her from captivity; that when she put herself into their hands,
they had committed her to close custody in Lochlevin; had
placed her son, an infant, on her throne; had again taken arms
against her after her deliverance from prison; had rejected all
her proposals for accommodation; had given battle to her
troops; and had obliged her, for the safety of her person, to
take shelter in England.[101] The earl of Murray, in answer
to this complaint, gave a summary and imperfect account of
the late transactions: that the earl of Bothwel, the known

99 Anderson, Vol. IV, pt. ii, p. 40.
100 *Ibid.*, pp. 14, 15ff. Goodall, II, 110.
101 Anderson, Vol. IV, pt. ii, p. 52. Goodall, II, 128. Haynes, p. 478.

murderer of the late king, had, a little after committing that crime, seized the person of the queen, and led her to Dunbar; that he acquired such influence over her, as to gain her consent to marry him, and he had accordingly procured a divorce from his former wife, and had pretended to celebrate his nuptials with the queen; that the scandal of this transaction, the dishonour which it brought on the nation, the danger to which the infant prince was exposed from the attempts of that audacious man, had obliged the nobility to take arms, and oppose his criminal enterprises: that after Mary, in order to save him, had thrown herself into their hands, she still discovered such a violent attachment to him, that they found it necessary, for their own and the public safety, to confine her person, during a season, till Bothwel and the other murderers of her husband could be tried and punished for their crimes: and that, during this confinement, she had voluntarily, without compulsion or violence, merely from disgust at the inquietude and vexations attending power, resigned her crown to her only son, and had appointed the earl of Murray regent during the minority[102] The queen's answer to this apology was obvious: that she did not know, and never could suspect, that Bothwel, who had been acquitted by a jury, and recommended to her by all the nobility for her husband, was the murderer of the king; that she ever was, and still continues desirous, that if he be guilty he may be brought to condign punishment; that her resignation of the crown was extorted from her by the well-grounded fears of her life, and even by direct menaces of violence; and that Throgmorton, the English ambassador, as well as others of her friends, had advised her to sign that paper, as the only means of saving herself from the last extremity, and had assured her that a consent, given under these circumstances, could never have any validity.[103]

So far the queen of Scots seemed plainly to have the advantage in the contest: and the English commissioners might have been surprised that Murray had made so weak a defence, and had suppressed all the material imputations against that

102 Anderson, Vol. IV, pt. ii, 64ff. Goodall, II, 144.
103 Anderson, Vol. IV, pt. ii, pp. 60ff. Goodall, II, 162.

princess, on which his party had ever so strenuously insisted; had not some private conferences previously informed them of the secret. Mary's commissioners had boasted that Elizabeth, from regard to her kinswoman, and from her desire of maintaining the rights of sovereigns, was determined, how criminal soever the conduct of that princess might appear, to restore her to the throne;[104] and Murray, reflecting on some past measures of the English court, began to apprehend that there were but too just grounds for these expectations. He believed that Mary, if he would agree to conceal the most violent part of the accusation against her, would submit to any reasonable terms of accommodation; but if he once proceeded so far as to charge her with the whole of her guilt, no composition could afterwards take place; and should she ever be restored, either by the power of Elizabeth, or the assistance of her other friends, he and his party must be exposed to her severe and implacable vengeance.[105] He resolved, therefore, not to venture rashly on a measure which it would be impossible for him to recal; and he privately paid a visit to Norfolk and the other English commissioners, confessed his scruples, laid before them the evidence of the queen's guilt, and desired to have some security for Elizabeth's protection, in case that evidence should, upon examination, appear entirely satisfactory. Norfolk was not secretly displeased with these scruples of the regent.[106] He had ever been a partisan of the queen of Scots: secretary Lidington, who began also to incline to that party, and was a man of singular address and capacity, had engaged him to embrace farther views in her favour, and even to think of espousing her: and though that duke confessed,[107] that the proofs against Mary seemed to be unquestionable, he encouraged Murray in his present resolution, not to produce them publicly in the conferences before the English commissioners.[108]

Norfolk, however, was obliged to transmit to court the queries

---

[104] Anderson, Vol. IV, pt. ii, p. 45. Goodall, II, 127.
[105] Anderson, Vol. IV, pt. ii, pp. 47, 48. Goodall, II, 159.
[106] Crawford, p. 92. Melville, pp. 94, 95. Haynes, p. 574.
[107] Anderson, Vol. IV, pt. ii, p. 77.
[108] *Ibid.*, pp. 57, 77. *State Trials*, I, 76.

proposed by the regent. These queries consisted of four particulars: Whether the English commissioners had authority from their sovereign to pronounce sentence against Mary, in case her guilt should be fully proved before them? Whether they would promise to exercise that authority, and proceed to an actual sentence? Whether the queen of Scots, if she were found guilty, should be delivered into the hands of the regent, or, at least, be so secured in England, that she never should be able to disturb the tranquillity of Scotland? and, Whether Elizabeth would also, in that case, promise to acknowledge the young king, and protect the regent in his authority?[109]

Elizabeth, when these queries, with the other transactions, were laid before her, began to think that they pointed towards a conclusion more decisive and more advantageous than she had hitherto expected. She determined, therefore, to bring the matter into full light; and under pretext that the distance from her person retarded the proceedings of her commissioners, she ordered them to come to London, and there continue the conferences. On their appearance, she immediately joined in commission with them some of the most considerable of her council; Sir Nicholas Bacon, lord keeper, the earls of Arundel and Leicester, lord Clinton,[110] admiral, and Sir William Cecil, secretary.[111] The queen of Scots, who knew nothing of these secret motives, and who expected that fear or decency would still restrain Murray from proceeding to any violent accusation against her, expressed an entire satisfaction in this adjournment; and declared that the affair, being under the immediate inspection of Elizabeth, was now in the hands where she most desired to rest it.[112] The conferences were accordingly continued at Hampton-court; and Mary's commissioners, as before, made no scruple to be present at them.

109 Anderson, Vol. IV, pt. ii, p. 55. Goodall, II, 130.

110 [Sir Nicholas Bacon (1509–1579), member of the privy council and lord keeper of the great seal; Henry Fitzalen, twelfth Earl of Arundel (1511?–1580); Robert Dudley, Earl of Leicester (1532–1588), a member of the privy council and a romantic favorite of Elizabeth; Edward Fiennes de Clinton, ninth Lord Clinton and Saye, Earl of Lincoln, lord high admiral.]

111 Anderson, Vol. IV, pt. ii, p. 99.

112 Anderson, p. 95. Goodall, II, 177, 179.

The queen, meanwhile, gave a satisfactory answer to all Murray's demands, and declared, that though she wished and hoped, from the present inquiry, to be entirely convinced of Mary's innocence, yet if the event should prove contrary, and that princess should appear guilty of her husband's murder, she should, for her own part, deem her ever after unworthy of a throne.[113] The regent, encouraged by this declaration, opened more fully his charge against the queen of Scots; and, after expressing his reluctance to proceed to that extremity, and protesting that nothing but the necessity of self-defence, which must not be abandoned for any delicacy, could have engaged him in such a measure, he proceeded to accuse her in plain terms of participation and consent in the assassination of the king.[114] The earl of Lenox too appeared before the English commissioners; and imploring vengeance for the murder of his son, accused Mary as an accomplice with Bothwel in that enormity.[115]

When this charge was so unexpectedly given in, and copies of it were transmitted to the bishop of Ross, lord Herries, and the other commissioners of Mary, they absolutely refused to return an answer; and they grounded their silence on very extraordinary reasons: they had orders, they said, from their mistress, if any thing were advanced that might touch her honour, not to make any defence, as she was a sovereign princess, and could not be subject to any tribunal; and they required that she should previously be admitted to Elizabeth's presence, to whom, and to whom alone, she was determined to justify her innocence.[116] They forgot that the conferences were at first begun, and were still continued, with no other view than to clear her from the accusations of her enemies; that Elizabeth had ever pretended to enter into them only as her friend, by her own consent and approbation, not as assuming any jurisdiction over her; that this princess had, from the beginning, refused to admit her to her presence, till she should vindicate herself from the crimes

113 Goodall, II, 199.
114 Anderson, Vol. IV, pt. ii, pp. 115ff. Goodall, II, 206.
115 Anderson, Vol. IV, pt. ii, p. 123. Goodall, II, 208.
116 Anderson, Vol. IV, pt. ii, pp. 125ff. Goodall, II, 184, 211, 217.

imputed to her; that she had therefore discovered no new signs
of partiality by her perseverance in that resolution; and that
though she had granted an audience to the earl of Murray and
his collegues, she had previously conferred the same honour
on Mary's commissioners;[117] and her conduct was so far entirely
equal to both parties.[118]

As the commissioners of the queen of Scots refused to give
in any answer to Murray's charge, the necessary consequence
seemed to be, that there could be no farther proceedings in the
conference. But though this silence might be interpreted as a
presumption against her, it did not fully answer the purpose
of those English ministers who were enemies to that princess.
They still desired to have in their hands the proofs of her guilt;
and, in order to draw them with decency from the regent, a
judicious artifice was employed by Elizabeth. Murray was called
before the English commissioners; and reproved by them, in
the queen's name, for the atrocious imputations which he had
the temerity to throw upon his sovereign: but though the earl
of Murray, they added, and the other commissioners, had so
far forgotten the duty of allegiance to their prince, the queen
never would overlook what she owed to her friend, her neigh-
bour, and her kinswoman; and she therefore desired to know
what they could say in their own justification.[119] Murray, thus
urged, made no difficulty in producing the proofs of his charge
against the queen of Scots; and among the rest, some love-letters

117 Lesley's *Negociations,* in Anderson, III, 25. Haynes, p. 487.

118* Mary's complaints of the queen's partiality in admitting Murray to a
conference, was a mere pretext, in order to break off the conference. She
indeed employs that reason in her order for that purpose, (see Goodall, II,
184), but in her private letter, her commissioners are directed to make use of
that order to prevent her honour from being attacked. Goodall, II, 183. It
was therefore the accusation only she was afraid of. Murray was the least
obnoxious of all her enemies. He was abroad when her subjects rebelled,
and reduced her to captivity: he had only accepted of the regency, when
voluntarily proffered him by the nation. His being admitted to queen
Elizabeth's presence was therefore a very bad foundation for a quarrel, or
for breaking off the conference; and was plainly a mere pretence.

119 Anderson, Vol. IV, pt. ii, p. 147. Goodall, II, 233.

and sonnets of her's to Bothwel, written all in her own hand, and two other papers, one written in her own hand, another subscribed by her, and written by the earl of Huntley;[120] each of which contained a promise of marriage with Bothwel, made before the pretended trial and acquittal of that nobleman.

All these important papers had been kept by Bothwel in a silver box or casket, which had been given him by Mary, and which had belonged to her first husband, Francis; and though the princess had enjoined him to burn the letters as soon as he had read them, he had thought proper carefully to preserve them as pledges of her fidelity, and had committed them to the custody of sir James Balfour, deputy-governor of the castle of Edinburgh. When that fortress was besieged by the associated lords, Bothwel sent a servant to receive the casket from the hands of the deputy-governor. Balfour delivered it to the messenger; but as he had at that time received some disgust from Bothwel, and was secretly negociating an agreement with the ruling party, he took care, by conveying private intelligence to the earl of Morton, to make the papers be intercepted by him. They contained incontestible proofs of Mary's criminal correspondence with Bothwel, of her consent to the king's murder, and of her concurrence in the violence which Bothwel pretended to commit upon her.[121] Murray fortified this evidence by some testimonies of correspondent facts;[122] and he added, some time after, the dying confession of one Hubert, or French Paris, as he was called, a servant of Bothwel's, who had been executed for the king's murder, and who directly charged the queen with her being accessary to that criminal enterprise.[123]

Mary's commissioners had used every expedient to ward this blow which they saw coming upon them, and against which, it appears, they were not provided with any proper defence. As soon as Murray opened his charge, they endeavoured to turn

[120] [George Gordon, fifth Earl of Huntly (d. 1576), lord high chancellor of Scotland under Mary.]
[121] Anderson, II, 115. Goodall, II, 1.
[122] Anderson, Vol. II, pt. ii, pp. 165ff, Goodall, II, 243.
[123] Anderson, II, 192. Goodall, II, 76.

the conferences from an inquiry into a negociation; and though informed by the English commissioners that nothing could be more dishonourable for their mistress, than to enter into a treaty with such undutiful subjects, before she had justified herself from those enormous imputations which had been thrown upon her, they still insisted that Elizabeth should settle terms of accommodation between Mary and her enemies in Scotland.[124] They maintained that, till their mistress had given in her answer to Murray's charge, his proofs could neither be called for nor produced:[125] and finding that the English commissioners were still determined to proceed in the method which had been projected, they finally broke off the conferences, and never would make any reply. These papers, at least translations of them, have since been published. The objections made to their authenticity are, in general, of small force: but were they ever so specious, they cannot now be hearkened to; since Mary, at the time when the truth could have been fully cleared, did, in effect, ratify the evidence against her, by recoiling from the inquiry at the very critical moment, and refusing to give an answer to the accusation of her enemies.[126]

But Elizabeth, though she had seen enough for her own satisfaction, was determined that the most eminent persons of

124 Anderson, Vol. IV, pt. ii, pp. 135, 139. Goodall, II, 224.

125 Anderson, Vol. IV, pt. ii, pp. 139, 145. Goodall, II, 228.

126* We shall not enter into a long discussion concerning the authenticity of these letters: we shall only remark in general, that the chief objections against them are, that they are supposed to have passed through the earl of Morton's hands, the least scrupulous of all Mary's enemies; and that they are, to the last degree, indecent, and even somewhat inelegant, such as it is not likely she would write. But to these presumptions we may oppose the following considerations. (1.) Though it be not difficult to counterfeit a subscription, it is very difficult, and almost impossible, to counterfeit several pages, so as to resemble exactly the hand-writing of any person. These letters were examined and compared with Mary's hand-writing, by the English privy-council, and by a great many of the nobility, among whom were several partisans of that princess. They might have been examined by the bishop of Ross, Herreis, and others of Mary's commissioners. The regent must have expected that they would be very critically examined by them: and had they not been able to stand that test, he was only preparing a scene of confusion to himself. Bishop Lesly expressly declines the comparing of the

her court should also be acquainted with these transactions, and should be convinced of the equity of her proceedings. She

---

hands, which he calls no legal proof. Goodall, II, 389. (2.) The letters are very long, much longer than they needed to have been, in order to serve the purposes of Mary's enemies; a circumstance which increased the difficulty, and exposed any forgery the more to the risk of a detection. (3.) They are not so gross and palpable as forgeries commonly are, for they still left a pretext for Mary's friends to assert, that their meaning was strained to make them appear criminal. See Goodall, II, 361. (4.) There is a long contract of marriage, said to be written by the earl of Huntley, and signed by the queen, before Bothwel's acquittal. Would Morton, without any necessity, have thus doubled the difficulties of the forgery and the danger of detection? (5.) The letters are indiscreet; but such was, apparently, Mary's conduct at that time: they are inelegant; but they have a careless, natural air, like letters hastily written between familiar friends. (6.) They contain such a variety of particular circumstances as nobody could have thought of inventing, especially as they must necessarily have afforded her many means of detection. (7.) We have not the originals of the letters, which were in French: we have only a Scotch and Latin translation from the original, and a French translation professedly done from the Latin. Now it is remarkable that the Scotch translation is full of Gallicisms, and is clearly a translation from a French original: such as "make fault," *faire des fautes;* "make it seem that I believe," *faire semblant de le croire;* "make brek," *faire breche;* "this is my first journey," *c'est ma premiere journée;* "have you not desire to laugh," *n'avez vous pas envie de rire;* "the place will hold unto the death," *la place tiendra jusqu' à la mort;* "he may not come forth of the house this long time," *il ne peut pas sortir du logis de long tems;* "to make me advertisement," *faire m'avertir;* "put order to it," *mettre ordre celà;* "discharge your heart," *decharger votre cœur;* "make gud watch," *faites bonne garde,* &c. (8.) There is a conversation which she mentions between herself and the king one evening: but Murray produced before the English commissioners the testimony of one Crawford, a gentleman of the earl of Lenox, who swore that the king, on her departure from him, gave him an account of the same conversation. (9.) There seems very little reason why Murray and his associates should run the risk of such a dangerous forgery, which must have rendered them infamous, if detected; since their cause, from Mary's known conduct, even without these letters, was sufficiently good and justifiable. (10.) Murray exposed these letters to the examination of persons qualified to judge of them; the Scotch council, the Scotch parliament, queen Elizabeth and her council, who were possessed of a great number of Mary's genuine letters. (11.) He gave Mary herself an opportunity of refuting and exposing him, if she had chosen to lay hold of it. (12.) The letters tally so well with all the other parts of her conduct during that transaction, that these proofs throw the strongest light on each other. (13.) The duke of Norfolk, who had examined

ordered her privy-council to be assembled; and, that she might render the matter more solemn and authentic, she summoned,

---

these papers, and who favoured so much the queen of Scots that he intended to marry her, and in the end lost his life in her cause, yet believed them authentic, and was fully convinced of her guilt. This appears not only from his letters above mentioned to queen Elizabeth and her ministers, but by his secret acknowledgment to Bannister, his most trusty confident. See *State Trials*, I, 81. In the conferences between the duke, secretary Lidington, and the bishop of Ross, all of them zealous partisans of that princess, the same thing is always taken for granted. *Ibid.*, pp. 74, 75. See farther MS. in the Advocates' library, A. 3. 28. p. 314, from the Cottonian library Calig. c. 9. Indeed the duke's full persuasion of Mary's guilt, without the least doubt or hesitation, could not have had place, if he had found Lidington or the bishop of Ross of a different opinion, or if they had ever told him that these letters were forged. It is to be remarked, that Lidington, being one of the accomplices, knew the whole bottom of the conspiracy against king Henry, and was besides, a man of such penetration, that nothing could escape him in such interesting events. (14.) I need not repeat the presumption drawn from Mary's refusal to answer. The only excuse for her silence is, that she suspected Elizabeth to be a partial judge: it was not indeed the interest of that princess to acquit and justify her rival and competitor; and we accordingly find that Lidington, from the secret information of the duke of Norfolk, informed Mary, by the bishop of Ross, that the queen of England never meant to come to a decision; but only to get into her hands the proofs of Mary's guilt, in order to blast her character. See *State Trials*, I, 77. But this was a better reason for declining the conference altogether, than for breaking it off on frivolous pretences, the very moment the chief accusation was unexpectedly opened against her. Though she could not expect Elizabeth's final decision in her favour, it was of importance to give a satisfactory answer, if she had any, to the accusation of the Scotch commissioners. That answer could have been dispersed for the satisfaction of the public, of foreign nations, and of posterity. And surely, after the accusation and proofs were in queen Elizabeth's hands, it could do no harm to give in the answers. Mary's information, that the queen never intended to come to a decision, could be no obstacle to her justification. (15.) The very disappearance of these letters is a presumption of their authenticity. That event can be accounted for no way but from the care of king James's friends, who were desirous to destroy every proof of his mother's crimes. The disappearance of Morton's narrative, and of Crawford's evidence, from the Cottonian library, Calig. c. i. must have proceeded from a like cause. See MS. in the Advocates' library, A. 3. 29, p. 88.

I find an objection made to the authenticity of the letters, drawn from the vote of the Scotch privy-council, which affirms the letters to be written and subscribed by queen Mary's own hand; whereas the copies given in to the

along with them, the earls of Northumberland, Westmoreland, Shrewsbury, Worcester, Huntingdon, and Warwic. All the proceedings of the English commissioners were read to them: the evidences produced by Murray were perused: a great number of letters, written by Mary to Elizabeth, were laid before them,

---

parliament a few days after, were only written, not subscribed. See Goodall, II, 64, 67. But it is not considered that this circumstance is of no manner of force: there were certainly letters, true or false, laid before the council; and whether the letters were true or false, this mistake proceeds equally from the inaccuracy or blunder of the clerk. The mistake may be accounted for: the letters were only written by her: the second contract with Bothwel was only subscribed. A proper accurate distinction was not made; and they are all said to be written and subscribed. A late writer, Mr. Goodall, has endeavoured to prove that these letters clash with chronology, and that the queen was not in the places mentioned in the letters, on the days there assigned: to confirm this, he produces charters and other deeds signed by the queen, where the date and place do not agree with the letters. But it is well known that the date of charters, and such like grants, is no proof of the real day on which they were signed by the sovereign. Papers of that kind commonly pass through different offices: the date is affixed by the first office, and may precede very long the day of the signature.

The account given by Morton of the manner in which the papers came into his hands, is very natural. When he gave it to the English commissioners, he had reason to think it would be canvassed with all the severity of able adversaries, interested in the highest degree to refute it. It is probable, that he could have confirmed it by many circumstances and testimonies; since they declined the contest.

The sonnets are inelegant; insomuch that both Brantome and Ronsard, who knew queen Mary's style, were assured, when they saw them, that they could not be of her composition. Jebb, II, 478. But no person is equal in his productions, especially one whose style is so little formed as Mary's must be supposed to be. Not to mention that such dangerous and criminal enterprises leave little tranquillity of mind for elegant, poetical compositions.

In a word, queen Mary might easily have conducted the whole conspiracy against her husband, without opening her mind to any one person except Bothwel, and without writing a scrap of paper about it; but it was very difficult to have conducted it so that her conduct should not betray her to men of discernment. In the present case her conduct was so gross, as to betray her to every body; and fortune threw into her enemies hands papers, by which they could convict her. The same infatuation and imprudence, which happily is the usual attendant of great crimes, will account for both. It is proper to observe, that there is not one circumstance of the foregoing narrative, contained in the history, that is taken from Knox, Buchanan, or even Thuanus, or indeed from any suspected authority.

and the hand-writing compared with that of the letters delivered in by the regent: the refusal of the queen of Scots' commissioners to make any reply, was related: and on the whole, Elizabeth told them, that, as she had from the first, thought it improper that Mary, after such horrid crimes were imputed to her, should be admitted to her presence before she had, in some measure, justified herself from the charge; so now, when her guilt was confirmed by so many evidences, and all answer refused, she must, for her part, persevere more steadily in that resolution.[127] Elizabeth next called in the queen of Scots' commissioners, and, after observing that she deemed it much more decent for their mistress to continue the conferences, than to require the liberty of justifying herself in person, she told them, that Mary might either send her reply by a person whom she trusted, or deliver it herself to some English nobleman, whom Elizabeth should appoint to wait upon her: but as to her resolution of making no reply at all, she must regard it as the strongest confession of guilt; nor could they ever be deemed her friends who advised her to that method of proceeding.[128] These topics she enforced still more strongly in a letter which she wrote to Mary herself.[129]

The queen of Scots had no other subterfuge from these pressing remonstrances, than still to demand a personal interview with Elizabeth: a concession which, she was sensible, would never be granted;[130] because Elizabeth knew that this expedient could decide nothing; because it brought matters to extremity, which that princess desired to avoid; and because it had been refused from the beginning, even before the commencement of the conferences. In order to keep herself better in countenance, Mary thought of another device. Though the conferences were broken off, she ordered her commissioners to accuse the earl of Murray and his associates as the murderers of the king:[131] but this accusation, coming so late, being extorted merely by a complaint of Murray's, and being unsupported by any proof,

127 Anderson, Vol. IV, pt. ii, pp. 170ff. Goodall, II, 254.

128 Anderson, Vol. IV, pt. ii, pp. 179ff. Goodall, II, 268.

129 Anderson, Vol. IV, pt. ii, p. 183. Goodall, II, 269.

130 *Cabala*, p. 157.

131 Goodall, II, 280.

could only be regarded as an angry recrimination upon her enemy.[132] She also desired to have copies of the papers given in by the regent; but as she still persisted in her resolution to make

[132]* Unless we take this angry accusation, advanced by queen Mary, to be an argument of Murray's guilt, there remains not the least presumption which should lead us to suspect him to have been anywise an accomplice in the king's murder. That queen never pretended to give any proof of the charge; and her commissioners affirmed at the time, that they themselves knew of none, though they were ready to maintain its truth by their mistress's orders, and would produce such proof as she should send them. It is remarkable that, at that time, it was impossible for either her or them to produce any proof; because the conferences before the English commissioners were previously broken off.

It is true, the bishop of Ross, in an angry pamphlet, written by him under a borrowed name (where it is easy to say any thing), affirms, that lord Herreis, a few days after the king's death, charged Murray with the guilt, openly to his face, at his own table. This latter nobleman, as Lesly relates the matter, affirmed, that Murray riding in Fife with one of his servants, the evening before commission of that crime, said to him among other talk, "This night ere morning the lord Darnley shall lose his life." See Anderson, I, 75. But this is only a heresay of Lesly's, concerning a heresay of Herreis's; and contains a very improbable fact. Would Murray, without any use or necessity, communicate to a servant such a dangerous and important secret, merely by way of conversation? We may also observe, that lord Herreis himself was one of queen Mary's commissioners who accused Murray. Had he ever heard this story, or given credit to it, was not that the time to have produced it? and not have affirmed, as he did, that he, for his part, knew nothing of Murray's guilt. See Goodall, II, 307.

The earls of Huntley and Argyle accuse Murray of this crime; but the reason which they assign is ridiculous. He had given his consent to Mary's divorce from the king; therefore he was the king's murderer. See Anderson, Vol. IV, pt. ii, p. 192. It is a sure argument, that these earls knew no better proof against Murray, otherwise they would have produced it, and not have insisted on so absurd a presumption. Was not this also the time for Huntley to deny his writing Mary's contract with Bothwel, if that paper had been a forgery?

Murray could have no motive to commit that crime. The king, indeed, bore him some ill-will; but the king himself was to become so despicable, both from his own ill conduct and the queen's aversion to him, that he could neither do good nor harm to any body. To judge by the event, in any case, is always absurd, especially in the present. The king's murder, indeed, procured Murray the regency: but much more Mary's ill conduct and imprudence, which he could not possibly foresee, and which never would have happened, had she been entirely innocent.

no reply before the English commissioners, this demand was finally refused her.[133]

As Mary had thus put an end to the conferences, the regent expressed great impatience to return into Scotland; and he complained, that his enemies had taken advantage of his absence, and had thrown the whole government into confusion. Eliza-

---

[133]* Goodall, II, 253, 283, 289, 310, 311. Haynes, I, 492. I believe there is no reader of common sense who does not see from the narrative in the text, that the author means to say, that queen Mary refuses constantly to answer before the English commissioners, but offers only to answer in person before queen Elizabeth in person, contrary to her practice during the whole course of the conference, till the moment the evidence of her being an accomplice in her husband's murder is unexpectedly produced. It is true, the author having repeated four or five times an account of this demand of being admitted to Elizabeth's presence, and having expressed his opinion, that, as it had been refused from the beginning, even before the commencement of the conferences, she did not expect it would now be complied with; thought it impossible his meaning could be misunderstood (as indeed it was impossible), and not being willing to tire his reader with continual repetitions, he mentions in a passage or two, simply, that she had refused to make any answer. I believe also, there is no reader of common sense who peruses Anderson or Goodall's collections, and does not see that, agreeably to this narrative, queen Mary insists unalterably and strenuously on not continuing to answer before the English commissioners, but insists to be heard in person, by queen Elizabeth in person; though once or twice, by way of bravado she says simply, that she will answer and refute her enemies, without inserting this condition, which still is understood. But there is a person [William Tytler] that has writ an *Enquiry historical and critical into the Evidence against Mary Queen of Scots;* and has attempted to refute the foregoing narrative. He quotes a single passage of the narrative, in which Mary is said simply to refuse answering; and then a single passage from Goodall, in which she boasts simply that she will answer; and he very civilly, and almost directly, calls the author a liar, on account of this pretended contradiction. That whole Enquiry, from beginning to end, is composed of such scandalous artifices; and from this instance, the reader may judge of the candour, fair dealing, veracity, and good manners of the Enquirer. There are, indeed, three events in our history, which may be regarded as touchstones of partymen. An English Whig, who asserts the reality of the popish plot, an Irish Catholic, who denies the massacre in 1641, and a Scotch Jacobite, who maintains the innocence of queen Mary, must be considered as men beyond the reach of argument or reason, and must be left to their prejudices.

beth therefore dismissed him; and granted him a loan of five thousand pounds to bear the charges of his journey.[134] During the conferences at York, the duke of Chatelrault arrived at London, in passing from France; and as the queen knew that he was engaged in Mary's party, and had very plausible pretensions to the regency of the king of Scots, she thought proper to detain him till after Murray's departure. But notwithstanding these marks of favour, and some other assistance which she secretly gave this latter nobleman,[135] she still declined acknowledging the young king, or treating with Murray as regent of Scotland.

Orders were given for removing the queen of Scots from Bolton, a place surrounded with catholics, to Tutbury in the county of Stafford; where she was put under the custody of the earl of Shrewsbury.[136] Elizabeth entertained hopes that this princess, discouraged by her misfortunes, and confounded by the late transactions, would be glad to secure a safe retreat from all the tempests with which she had been agitated; and she promised to bury every thing in oblivion, provided Mary would agree, either voluntarily to resign her crown, or to associate her son with her in the government; and the administration to remain, during his minority, in the hands of the earl of Murray.[137] But that high-spirited princess refused all treaty upon such terms, and declared that her last words should be those of a queen of Scotland. Besides many other reasons, she said, which fixed her in that resolution, she knew, that if, in the present emergence, she made such concessions, her submission would be universally deemed an acknowledgment of guilt, and would ratify all the calumnies of her enemies.[138]

Mary still insisted upon this alternative; either that Elizabeth

[134] Rymer, Bk. XV, p. 677.

[135] MS. in the Advocates' library. A. 3. 29, pp. 128, 129, 130 from Cottonian library, Calig. c. 1.

[136] [George Talbot, sixth Earl of Shrewsbury (1528?–1590), lord lieutenant of Yorkshire, Nottinghamshire, Derbyshire, and Staffordshire.]

[137] Goodall, II, 295.

[138] *Ibid.*, p. 301.

should assist her in recovering her authority, or should give her liberty to retire into France, and make trial of the friendship of other princes: and as she asserted that she had come voluntarily into England, invited by many former professions of amity, she thought that one or other of these requests could not, without the most extreme injustice, be refused her. But Elizabeth, sensible of the danger which attended both these proposals, was secretly resolved to detain her still a captive; and as her retreat into England had been little voluntary, her claim upon the queen's generosity appeared much less urgent than she was willing to pretend. Necessity, it was thought, would, to the prudent, justify her detention: her past misconduct would apologize for it to the equitable: and though it was foreseen, that compassion for Mary's situation, joined to her intrigues and insinuating behaviour, would, while she remained in England, excite the zeal of her friends, especially of the catholics, these inconveniencies were deemed much inferior to those which attended any other expedient. Elizabeth trusted also to her own address for eluding all those difficulties: she purposed to avoid breaking absolutely with the queen of Scots, to keep her always in hopes of an accommodation, to negotiate perpetually with her, and still to throw the blame of not coming to any conclusion, either on unforeseen accidents, or on the obstinacy and perverseness of others.[139]

---

[139] [As Hume suggests, it was many years before Elizabeth took any determinate action with regard to Mary. But when the latter was linked with a plot to murder Elizabeth herself, she was brought to trial (October 1586), and convicted. Even then Elizabeth appeared reluctant to execute Mary, as the Parliament demanded, but she did at last sign the death warrant, and Mary was executed February 8, 1587.]

## *From* Chapter XLV—James I

THE CROWN of England was never transmitted from father to son with greater tranquillity, than it passed from the family of Tudor to that of Stuart. During the whole reign of Elizabeth, the eyes of men had been employed in search of her successor; and when old age made the prospect of her death more immediate, there appeared none but the king of Scots, who could advance any just claim or pretension to the throne. He was great-grandson of Margaret, elder daughter of Henry VII. and, on the failure of the male-line, his hereditary right remained unquestionable. If the religion of Mary queen of Scots, and the other prejudices contracted against her, had formed any considerable obstacle to her succession; these objections, being entirely personal, had no place with regard to her son. Men also considered, that though the title, derived from blood, had been frequently violated since the Norman conquest, such licences had proceeded more from force or intrigue, than from any deliberate maxims of government. The lineal heir had still in the end prevailed; and both his exclusion and restoration had been commonly attended with such convulsions, as were sufficient to warn all prudent men not lightly to give way to such irregularities. If the will of Henry VIII. authorised by act of parliament, had tacitly excluded the Scottish line; the tyranny and caprices of that monarch had been so signal, that a settlement of this nature, unsupported by any just reason, had no authority with the people. Queen Elizabeth too, with her dying breath, had recognized the undoubted title of her kinsman James; and the whole nation seemed to dispose themselves with joy and pleasure for his reception. Though born and educated amidst a foreign and hostile people, men hoped, from his character of moderation and wisdom, that he would embrace the maxims of an English monarch; and the prudent foresaw greater advantages resulting from a union with Scotland, than disadvantages from submitting to a prince of that nation. The alacrity, with which the English looked towards the successor, had appeared so evident to Elizabeth, that, concurring with other causes, it affected her with the deepest melancholy; and that wise princess, whose penetration and experience had given her the greatest insight into human affairs, had not yet sufficiently weighed the ingratitude of courtiers, and levity of the people.

As victory abroad, and tranquillity at home, had attended this princess, she left the nation in such flourishing circumstances, that her successor possessed every advantage, except that of comparison with her illustrious name, when he mounted the throne of England. The king's journey from Edinburgh to London immediately afforded to the inquisitive some circumstances of comparison, which even the natural partiality in favour of their new sovereign could not interpret to his advantage. As he passed along, all ranks of men flocked about him from every quarter, allured by interest or curiosity. Great were the rejoicings, and loud and hearty the acclamations which resounded from all sides; and every one could remember how the affability and popular manners of their queen displayed themselves, amidst such concourse and exultation of her subjects. But James, though sociable and familiar with his friends and courtiers, hated the bustle of a mixt multitude; and though far from disliking flattery, yet was he still fonder of tranquillity and ease. He issued therefore a proclamation, forbidding this resort of people, on pretence of the scarcity of provisions, and other inconveniences, which, he said, would necessarily attend it.[1]

He was not, however, insensible to the great flow of affection which appeared in his new subjects; and being himself of an affectionate temper, he seems to have been in haste to make them some return of kindness and good offices. To this motive, probably, we are to ascribe that profusion of titles, which was observed in the beginning of his reign; when, in six weeks time

---

[1] White Kennet, *Compleat History of England,* p. 662.

after his entrance into the kingdom, he is computed to have bestowed knighthood on no less than two hundred and thirty-seven persons. If Elizabeth's frugality of honours, as well as of money, had formerly been repined at, it began now to be valued and esteemed: and every one was sensible that the king, by his lavish and premature conferring of favours, had failed of obliging the persons on whom he bestowed them. Titles of all kinds became so common, that they were scarcely marks of distinction; and being distributed, without choice or deliberation, to persons unknown to the prince, were regarded more as the proofs of facility and good-nature, than of any determined friendship or esteem.

. . . . . . . . . . . . .

Though the severities of Elizabeth towards the catholics had    1604
much weakened that party, whose genius was opposite to the prevailing spirit of the nation; like severities had had so little influence on the puritans, who were encouraged by that spirit, that no less than seven hundred and fifty clergymen of that party signed a petition to the king on his accession; and many more seemed willing to adhere to it.[2] They all hoped, that James, having received his education in Scotland, and having sometimes professed an attachment to the church established there, would at least abate the rigour of the laws enacted in support of the ceremonies, and against puritans; if he did not show more particular grace and encouragement to that sect. But the king's disposition had taken strongly a contrary bias. The more he knew the puritanical clergy, the less favour he bore to them. He had remarked in their Scottish brethren a violent turn towards republicanism, and a zealous attachment to civil liberty; principles nearly allied to that religious enthusiam with which they were actuated. He had found, that being mostly persons of low birth, and mean education, the same lofty pretensions which attended them in their familiar addresses to their Maker, of whom they believed themselves the peculiar favourites, in-

2 Thomas Fuller, *The Church History of Britain*, Bk. 10. Jeremy Collier, *An Ecclesiastical History of Great Britain . . . to the End of the Reign of Charles II*, II, 672.

duced them to use the utmost freedoms with their earthly sovereign. In both capacities, of monarch and of theologian, he had experienced the little complaisance which they were disposed to show him; whilst they controulled his commands, disputed his tenets, and, to his face, before the whole people, censured his conduct and behaviour. If he had submitted to the indignity of courting their favour, he treasured up, on that account, the stronger resentment against them, and was determined to make them feel, in their turn, the weight of his authority. Though he had often met with resistance and faction and obstinacy in the Scottish nobility, he retained no ill-will to that order; or rather showed them favour and kindness in England, beyond what reason and sound policy could well justify: But the ascendant, which the presbyterian clergy had assumed over him, was what his monarchical pride could never thoroughly digest.[3]

He dreaded likewise the popularity which attended this order of men in both kingdoms. As useless austerities and self-denial are imagined, in many religions, to render us acceptable to a benevolent Being, who created us solely for happiness, James remarked, that the rustic severity of these clergymen, and of their whole sect, had given them, in the eyes of the multitude, the appearance of sanctity and virtue. Strongly inclined himself to mirth and wine and sports of all kinds, he apprehended their censure for his manner of life, free and disengaged. And, being thus averse, from temper, as well as policy, to the sect of puritans, he was resolved, if possible, to prevent its farther growth in England.

But it was the character of James's councils, throughout

---

[3] James ventured to say, in his *Basilicon Doron,* published while he was in Scotland: "I protest before the great God, and since I am here as upon my Testament, it is no place for me to lie in, that ye shall never find with any Highland or Borderer Thieves greater ingratitude and more lies and vile perjuries, than with these fanatic spirits: And suffer not the principal of them to brook your land." King James's *Works* [i.e., James I, *Collected Works*], p. 161.

his whole reign, that they were more wise and equitable in their end, than prudent and political in the means. Though justly sensible that no part of civil administration required greater care or a nicer judgment than the conduct of religious parties; he had not perceived, that, in the same proportion as this practical knowledge of theology is requisite, the speculative refinements in it are mean and even dangerous in a monarch. By entering zealously into frivolous disputes, James gave them an air of importance and dignity, which they could not otherwise have acquired; and being himself enlisted in the quarrel, he could no longer have recourse to contempt and ridicule, the only proper method of appeasing it. The church of England had not yet abandoned the rigid doctrines of grace and predestination: The puritans had not yet separated themselves from the church, nor openly renounced episcopacy. Though the spirit of the parties was considerably different, the only appearing subjects of dispute were concerning the cross in baptism, the ring in marriage, the use of the surplice, and the bowing at the name of Jesus. These were the mighty questions which were solemnly agitated in the conference at Hampton-court between some bishops and dignified clergymen on the one hand, and some leaders of the puritanical party on the other; the king and his ministers being present.[4]

The puritans were here so unreasonable as to complain of a partial and unfair management of the dispute; as if the search after truth were in any degree the object of such conferences, and a candid indifference, so rare even among private inquirers in *philosophical* questions, could ever be expected among princes, and prelates, in a *theological* controversy. The king, it must be confessed, from the beginning of the conference, showed the strongest propensity to the established church, and frequently inculcated a maxim, which, though it has some foundation, is to be received with great limitations, "No bishop, no king." The bishops, in their turn, were very liberal of their

4 Fuller.

praises towards the royal disputant; and the archbishop of Canterbury said, that "undoubtedly his majesty spake by the special assistance of God's spirit."[5] A few alterations in the liturgy were agreed to, and both parties separated with mutual dissatisfaction.

.   .   .   .   .   .   .   .   .   .   .   .

The speech which the king made on opening the parliament, fully displays his character, and proves him to have possessed more knowledge and better parts than prudence or any just sense of decorum and propriety.[6] Though few productions of the age surpass this performance either in style or matter; it wants that majestic brevity and reserve, which becomes a king in his addresses to the great council of the nation. It contains, however, a remarkable stroke of candour, where he confesses his too great facility in yielding to the solicitations of suitors:[7] A fault which he promises to correct, but which adhered to him, and distressed him, during the whole course of his reign.

The first business, in which the commons were engaged, was of the utmost importance to the preservation of their privileges; and neither temper nor resolution were wanting in their conduct of it.

In former periods of the English government, the house of commons was of so small weight in the balance of the constitution, that little attention had been given, either by the crown, the people, or the house itself, to the choice and continuance of the members. It had been usual, after parliaments were prolonged beyond one session, for the chancellor to exert a discretionary authority of issuing new writs to supply the place of any members, whom he judged incapable of attending, either on account of their employment, their sickness, or other impediment. This practice gave that minister, and consequently the prince, an unlimited power of modelling at pleasure the rep-

5 Kennet, p. 665.

6 King James's *Works*, pp. 484, 485ff. *Journ.*, 22d March, 1603. Kennet, p. 668.

7 King James's *Works*, pp. 495, 496.

resentatives of the nation; yet so little jealousy had it created, that the commons, of themselves, without any court influence or intrigue, and contrary to some former votes of their own, confirmed it in the twenty-third of Elizabeth.[8] At that time, though some members, whose places had been supplied on account of sickness, having now recovered their health, appeared in the house, and claimed their seat; such was the authority of the chancellor, that, merely out of respect to him, his sentence was adhered to, and the new members were continued in their places. Here a most dangerous prerogative was conferred on the crown: But to show the genius of that age, or rather the channels in which power then ran, the crown put very little value on this authority; insomuch that two days afterwards the chancellor, of himself, resigned it back to the commons, and gave them power to judge of a particular vacancy in their house. And when the question, concerning the chancellor's new writs was again brought on the carpet towards the end of the session, the commons were so little alarmed at the precedent, that, though they re-admitted some old members, whose seats had been vacated, on account of slight indispositions, yet they confirmed the chancellor's sentence, in instances where the distemper appeared to have been dangerous and incurable.[9] Nor did they proceed any farther, in vindication of their privileges, than to vote, "that during the sitting of parliament, there do not, at any time, any writ go out for choosing or returning any member without the warrant of the house." In Elizabeth's reign we may remark, and the reigns preceding, sessions of parliament were not usually the twelfth part so long as the vacations; and during the latter, the chancellor's power, if he pleased to exert it, was confirmed, at least left, by this vote, as unlimited and unrestrained as ever.

In a subsequent parliament, the absolute authority of the queen was exerted in a manner still more open; and began for the first time to give alarm to the commons. New writs having

8 *Journ.*, 19th January, 1580.

9 *Journ.*, 18th March, 1580. See farther, Sir Simonds d'Ewes, *Journals of all the Parliaments during the Reign of Queen Elizabeth*, p. 430.

been issued by the chancellor when there was no vacancy, and a controversy arising upon that incident; the queen sent a message to the house, informing them, that it were impertinent for them to deal in such matters. These questions, she said, belonged only to the chancellor; and she had appointed him to confer with the judges, in order to settle all disputes with regard to elections. The commons had the courage, a few days after, to vote, "That it was a most perilous precedent, where two knights of a county were duly elected, if any new writ should issue out for a second election, without order of the house itself; that the discussing and adjudging of this and such like differences belonged only to the house; and that there should be no message sent to the lord chancellor, not so much as to inquire what he had done in the matter, because it was conceived to be a matter derogatory to the power and privilege of the house."[10] This is the most considerable, and almost only, instance of parliamentary liberty, which occurs during the reign of that princess.

.     .     .     .     .     .     .     .     .     .     .

When James summoned this parliament, he issued a proclamation;[11] in which among many general advices, which, like a kind tutor, he bestowed on his people, he strictly enjoins them not to choose any outlaw for their representative. And he adds; "If any person take upon him the place of knight, citizen, or burgess, not being duly elected, according to the laws and statutes in that behalf provided, and according to the purport, effect, and true meaning of this our proclamation, then every person so offending to be fined or imprisoned for the same." A proclamation here was plainly put on the same footing with a law, and that in so delicate a point as the right of elections: Most alarming circumstances, had there not been reason to believe, that this measure, being entered into so early in the king's reign, proceeding more from precipitation and mistake,

10 D'Ewes, p. 397.
11 11th January, 1604. Rymer, Bk. XVI, 561.

than from any serious design of invading the privileges of parliament.[12]

Sir Francis Goodwin[13] was chosen member for the county of Bucks; and his return, as usual, was made into chancery. The chancellor, pronouncing him an outlaw, vacated his seat, and issued writs for a new election.[14] Sir John Fortescue[15] was chosen in his place by the county: But the first act of the house was to reverse the chancellor's sentence, and restore sir Francis to his seat. At the king's suggestion, the lords desired a conference on the subject; but were absolutely refused by the commons, as the question entirely regarded their own privileges.[16] The commons, however, agreed to make a remonstrance to the king by the mouth of their speaker; in which they maintained, that though the returns were by form made into chancery, yet the sole right of judging with regard to elections belonged to the house itself, not to the chancellor.[17] James was not satisfied, and ordered a conference between the house and the judges, whose opinion in this case was opposite to that of the commons. This conference, he said, he commanded as an "absolute" king;[18]

[12] The duke of Sully tells us, that it was a maxim of James, that no prince in the first year of his reign, should begin any considerable undertaking: A maxim reasonable in itself, and very suitable to his cautious, not to say timid character. The facility with which he departed from this pretension, is another proof that his meaning was innocent. But had the privileges of parliament been at that time exactly ascertained, or royal power fully limited, could such an imagination ever have been entertained by him, as to think that his proclamations could regulate parliamentary elections?

[13] [Not identified by the editors.]

[14] Sir Ralph Winwood, *Memorials of Affairs of State in the Reign of Queen Elizabeth and King James I*, II, 18, 19.

[15] [Sir John Fortescue (1531?–1607), chancellor of the exchequer under Elizabeth.]

[16] *Journ.*, 26th March, 1604.

[17] *Journ.*, 3d April, 1604.

[18]* Sir Charles Cornwallis, the king's ambassador at Madrid, when pressed by the Duke of Lerma to enter into a league with Spain, said to that minister; "though his majesty was an *absolute* king, and therefore not bound to give an account to any, of his actions; yet that so gracious and

an epithet, we are apt to imagine, not very grateful to English ears, but one to which they had already been somewhat ac-

---

regardful a prince he was of the love and contentment of his own subjects, as I assured myself he would not think it fit to do any thing of so great consequence without acquainting them with his intentions." Winwood, II, 222. Sir Walter Raleigh has this passage in the Preface to his *History of the World*. "Philip II. by strong hand and main force, attempted to make himself not only an *absolute monarch* over the Netherlands, like unto the kings and monarchs of England and France, but Turk-like, to tread under his feet all their natural and fundamental laws, privileges, and ancient rights." We meet with this passage in sir John Davis's *Question concerning Impositions*, p. 161. "Thus we see by this comparison, that the king of England doth lay but his little finger upon his subjects, when other princes and states do lay their heavy loins upon their people: what is the reason of this difference? From whence cometh it? Assuredly not from a different power of prerogative: for the king of England is as absolute a monarch as any emperor or king in the world, and hath as many prerogatives, incident to his crown." Coke, in Cawdry's case, says, "That, by the ancient laws of this realm, England is an *absolute* empire and monarchy; and that the king is furnished with plenary and entire power, prerogative, and jurisdiction, and is supreme governor over all persons within this realm." Spencer, speaking of some grants of the English kings to the Irish corporations, says, "All which, though at the time of their first grant they were tolerable, and perhaps reasonable, yet now are most unreasonable and inconvenient. But all these will easily be cut off, with the superior power of her majesty's prerogative, against which her own grants are not to be pleaded or enforced." *State of Ireland*, p. 1537, edit. 1706. The same author in p. 1660, proposes a plan for the civilization of Ireland; that the queen should create a provost marshal in every county, who might ride about with eight or ten followers in search of stragglers and vagabonds; the first time he catches any, he may punish them more lightly, by the stocks; the second time, by whipping; but the third time he may hang them, without trial or process, on the first bough: and he thinks, that this authority may more safely be entrusted to the provost marshal than to the sheriff: because the latter magistrate, having a profit by the escheats of felons, may be tempted to hang innocent persons. Here a real, absolute, or rather despotic power is pointed out; and we may infer from all these passages, either that the word *absolute* bore a different sense from what it does at present, or that men's ideas of the English, as well as Irish government, were then different. This latter inference seems juster. The word, being derived from the French, bore always the same sense as in that language. An absolute monarchy, in Charles the first's answer to the nineteen propositions, is opposed to a limited; and the king of England is acknowledged not to be absolute: so much had matters changed even

customed from the mouth of Elizabeth.[19] He added, "That all their privileges were derived from his grant, and hoped they would not turn them against him";[20] a sentiment which, from her conduct, it is certain that princess had also entertained, and which was the reigning principle of her courtiers and ministers, and the spring of all her administration.

The commons were in some perplexity. Their eyes were now opened, and they saw the consequences of that power which had been assumed by the chancellor, and to which their predecessors had, in some instances, blindly submitted. "By this course," said a member, "the free election of the counties is taken away, and none shall be chosen but such as shall please the king and council. Let us, therefore, with fortitude, understanding, and sincerity, seek to maintain our privilege. This cannot be construed any contempt in us, but merely a maintenance of our common rights, which our ancestors have left us, and which it is just and fit for us to transmit to our posterity."[21] Another said,[22] "This may be called a *quo warranto* to seize all our liberties." "A chancellor," added a third, "by this course, may call a parliament consisting of what persons he pleases. Any suggestion, by any person, may be the cause of sending a new writ. It is come to this plain question, Whether the chancery or parliament ought to have authority?"[23]

Notwithstanding this watchful spirit of liberty, which now

---

before the civil war. In sir John Fortescue's treatise of absolute and limited monarchy, a book written in the reign of Edward the fourth, the word *absolute* is taken in the same sense as at present; and the government of England is also said not to be absolute. They were the princes of the house of Tudor chiefly, who introduced that administration, which had the appearance of absolute government. The princes before them were restrained by the barons; as those after them by the house of commons. The people had, properly speaking, little liberty in either of these ancient governments, but least, in the more ancient.

[19] Camden, in Kennet, p. 375.
[20] *Journ.*, 29th March, 5th April, 1604.
[21] *Journ.*, 30th March, 1604.
[22] *Ibid.*
[23] *Ibid.*

appeared in the commons, their deference for majesty was so great, that they appointed a committee to confer with the judges before the king and council. There the question of law began to appear, in James's eyes, a little more doubtful than he had hitherto imagined it; and in order to extricate himself with some honour, he proposed that both Goodwin and Fortescue should be set aside, and a writ be issued, by warrant of the house, for a new election. Goodwin gave his consent, and the commons embraced the expedient; but in such a manner, that, while they showed their regard for the king, they secured for the future the free possession of their seats, and the right which they claimed of judging solely in their own elections and returns.[24]

A power like this, so essential to the exercise of all their other powers, themselves so essential to public liberty, cannot fairly be deemed an encroachment in the commons; but must be regarded as an inherent privilege, happily rescued from that ambiguity which the negligence of some former parliaments had thrown upon it.

.    .    .    .    .    .    .    .    .    .    .    .

About this period the minds of men throughout Europe, especially in England, seem to have undergone a general, but insensible revolution. Though letters had been revived in the preceding age, they were chiefly cultivated by those of sedentary professions; nor had they, till now, begun to spread themselves, in any degree, among men of the world. Arts, both mechanical and liberal, were every day receiving great improvements. Navigation had extended itself over the whole globe. Travelling was

24* Even this parliament, which showed so much spirit and good-sense in the affair of Goodwin, made a strange concession to the crown, in their fourth session. Toby Mathews, a member, had been banished by order of the council upon direction from his majesty. The parliament not only acquiesced in this arbitrary proceeding, but issued writs for a new election. Such novices were they, as yet, in the principles of liberty! See *Journ.*, 14th February, 1609. Mathews was banished by the king, on account of his change of religion to popery. The king had an indulgence to those who had been educated catholics; but could not bear the new converts. It was probably the animosity of the commons against the papists, which made them acquiesce in this precedent, without reflecting on the consequences! The jealousy of Liberty, though roused, was not yet thoroughly enlightened.

secure and agreeable. And the general system of politics in Europe was become more enlarged and comprehensive.

In consequence of this universal fermentation, the ideas of men enlarged themselves on all sides; and the several constituent parts of the Gothic governments, which seem to have lain long unactive, began, every where, to operate and encroach on each other. On the continent, where the necessity of discipline had begotten standing armies, the princes commonly established an unlimited authority, and overpowered, by force or intrigue, the liberties of the people. In England, the love of freedom, which, unless checked, flourishes extremely in all liberal natures, acquired new force, and was regulated by more enlarged views, suitably to that cultivated understanding, which became, every day, more common among men of birth and education. A familiar acquaintance with the precious remains of antiquity excited, in every generous breast, a passion for a limited constitution, and begat an emulation of those manly virtues, which the Greek and Roman authors, by such animating examples, as well as pathetic expressions, recommend to us. The severe, though popular government of Elizabeth had confined this rising spirit within very narrow bounds: But when a new and a foreign family succeeded to the throne, and a prince less dreaded and less beloved, symptoms immediately appeared of a more free and independent genius in the nation.

Happily this prince possessed neither sufficient capacity to perceive the alteration, nor sufficient art and vigour to check it in its early advances. Jealous of regal, because conscious of little personal authority, he had established within his own mind a speculative system of absolute government, which few of his subjects, he believed, and none but traitors and rebels, would make any scruple to admit. On whichever side he cast his eye, every thing concurred to encourage his prejudices. When he compared himself with the other hereditary sovereigns of Europe, he imagined, that as he bore the same rank, he was entitled to equal prerogatives; not considering the innovations lately introduced by them, and the military force by which their authority was supported. In England, that power, almost unlimited, which had been exercised for above a century, especially during the late reign, he ascribed solely to royal birth and title; not to the prudence and spirit of the monarchs, nor to the conjunctures of the times. Even the opposition which he had struggled with in Scotland encouraged him still farther in his favourite notions; while he there saw, that the same resistance which opposed regal authority, violated all law and order, and made way either for the ravages of a barbarous nobility, or for the more intolerable insolence of seditious preachers. In his own person, therefore, he thought all legal power to be centered, by an hereditary and a divine right: And this opinion might have proved dangerous, if not fatal, to liberty, had not the firmness of the persuasion, and its seeming evidence, induced him to trust solely to his right, without making the smallest provision, either of force or politics, in order to support it.

Such were the opposite dispositions of parliament and prince, at the commencement of the Scottish line; dispositions just beginning to exist and to appear in the parliament,[25] but thoroughly established and openly avowed on the part of the prince.

.    .    .    .    .    .    .    .    .    .    .    .

The same spirit of independence, and perhaps not better judgment, appeared in the house of commons, when the ques-

[25]* At that time, men of genius and enlarged minds had adopted the principles of liberty, which were as yet pretty much unknown to the generality of the people. Sir Matthew Hales has published a remonstrance against the king's conduct towards the parliament during this session. The remonstrance is drawn with great force of reasoning and spirit of liberty; and was the production of sir Francis Bacon and sir Edwin Sandys, two men of the greatest parts and knowledge in England. It is drawn in the name of the commons; but as there is no hint of it in the journals, we must conclude, either that the authors, sensible that the strain of the piece was much beyond the principles of the age, had not ventured to present it to the house, or that it had been, for that reason, rejected. The dignity and authority of the commons are strongly insisted upon in this remonstrance; and it is there said, that their submission to the ill treatment which they received during the latter part of Elizabeth's reign, had proceeded from their tenderness towards her age and her sex. But the authors are mistaken in these facts: for the house received and submitted to as bad treatment in the beginning and middle of that reign. The government was equally arbitrary in Mary's reign, in Edward's, in Harry the eighth and seventh's. And the farther we go back into history, though there might be more of a certain irregular kind of liberty among the barons, the commons were still of less authority.

tion of supply was brought before them, by some members attached to the court. In vain it was urged, that, though the king received a supply which had been voted to Elizabeth, and which had not been collected before her death; yet he found it burthened with a debt contracted by the queen, equal to the full amount of it: That peace was not yet thoroughly concluded with Spain, and that Ireland was still expensive to him: That on his journey from Scotland amidst such a concourse of people, and on that of the queen and royal family, he had expended considerable sums: And that, as the courtiers had looked for greater liberalities from the prince on his accession, and had imposed on his generous nature; so the prince, in his turn, would expect, at the beginning, some mark of duty and attachment from his people, and some consideration of his necessities. No impression was made on the house of commons by these topics; and the majority appeared fully determined to refuse all supply. The burthen of government, at that time, lay surprisingly light upon the people: And that very reason, which to us, at this distance, may seem a motive of generosity, was the real cause why the parliament was, on all occasions, so remarkably frugal and reserved. They were not, as yet, accustomed to open their purses in so liberal a manner as their successors, in order to supply the wants of their sovereign; and the smallest demand, however requisite, appeared in their eyes unreasonable and exorbitant. The commons seem also to have been desirous of reducing the crown to still farther necessities, by their refusing a bill, sent down to them by the lords, for entailing the crown lands for ever on the king's heirs and successors.[26] The dissipation, made by Elizabeth, had probably taught James the necessity of this law, and shown them the advantage of refusing it.

In order to cover a disappointment with regard to supply, which might bear a bad construction, both at home and abroad, James sent a message to the house;[27] in which he told them, that he desired no supply; and he was very forward in refusing what was never offered him. Soon after, he prorogued the parliament, not without discovering, in his speech, visible marks of dissatis-

26 *The Parliamentary or Constitutional History of England,* V. 108.
27 *Journ.,* 26th June, 1604.

faction. Even so early in his reign, he saw reason to make public complaints of the restless and encroaching spirit of the puritanical party, and of the malevolence with which they endeavoured to inspire the commons. Nor were his complaints without foundation, or the puritans without interest; since the commons, now finding themselves free from the arbitrary government of Elizabeth, made application for a conference with the lords, and presented a petition to the king; the purport of both which was, to procure, in favour of the puritans, a relaxation of the ecclesiastical laws.[28]

28 [Antoine la Fèvre de] la Boderie, the French ambassador, says, that the house of commons was composed mostly of puritans (*Ambassades . . . 1606 jusqu'en 1611 . . .*, I, 81).

# *From* Chapter XLVI—James I

WE ARE now to relate an event, one of the most memorable that history has conveyed to posterity, and containing at once a singular proof both of the strength and weakness of the human mind; its widest departure from morals, and most steady attachment to religious prejudices. 'Tis the "Gunpowder treason" of which I speak; a fact as certain as it appears incredible.

The Roman catholics had expected great favour and indulgence on the accession of James, both as he was descended from Mary, whose life they believed to have been sacrificed to their cause, and as he himself, in his early youth, was imagined to have shown some partiality towards them, which nothing, they thought but interest and necessity had since restrained. It is pretended, that he had even entered into positive engagements to tolerate their religion, as soon as he should mount the throne of England; whether their credulity had interpreted in this sense some obliging expressions of the king's, or that he had employed such an artifice, in order to render them favourable to his title.[1] Very soon they discovered their mistake; and were at once surprised and enraged to find James, on all occasions, express his intention of strictly executing the laws enacted against them, and of persevering in all the rigorous measures of Elizabeth. Catesby,[2] a gentleman of good parts and of an ancient family, first thought of a most extraordinary method of revenge; and he opened his intention to Piercy,[3] a descendant of the illustrious house of Northumberland. In one of their conversations with regard to the distressed condition of the catholics, Piercy having broken into a sally of passion, and mentioned assassinating the king; Catesby took the opportunity of reveal-

1 *State Trials*, II, 201, 202, 203. Winwood, II, 49.
2 [Robert Catesby (1573–1605).]
3 [Thomas Percy (1560–1605), cousin of Henry Percy, ninth Earl of Northumberland.]

ing to him a nobler and more extensive plan of treason, which not only included a sure execution of vengeance, but afforded some hopes of restoring the catholic religion in England. In vain, said he, would you put an end to the king's life: He has children, who would succeed both to his crown and to his maxims of government. In vain would you extinguish the whole royal family: The nobility, the gentry, the parliament, are all infected with the same heresy, and could raise to the throne another prince and another family, who, besides their hatred to our religion, would be animated with revenge for the tragical death of their predecessors. To serve any good purpose, we must destroy, at one blow, the king, the royal family, the lords, the commons; and bury all our enemies in one common ruin. Happily, they are all assembled on the first meeting of the parliament; and afford us the opportunity of glorious and useful vengeance. Great preparations will not be requisite. A few of us, combining, may run a mine below the hall in which they meet; and choosing the very moment when the king harangues both houses, consign over to destruction these determined foes to all piety and religion. Meanwhile, we ourselves standing aloof, safe and unsuspected, shall triumph in being the instruments of divine wrath, and shall behold with pleasure those sacrilegious walls, in which were passed the edicts for proscribing our church and butchering her children, tost into a thousand fragments; while their impious inhabitants, meditating, perhaps, still new persecutions against us, pass from flames above to flames below, there for ever to endure the torments due to their offences.[4]

Piercy was charmed with this project of Catesby; and they agreed to communicate the matter to a few more, and among the rest to Thomas Winter,[5] whom they sent over to Flanders, in quest of Fawkes,[6] an officer in the Spanish service, with whose zeal and courage they were all thoroughly acquainted. When they enlisted any new conspirator, in order to bind him to

4 *History of the Gunpowder Treason.*

5 [Thomas Winter or Wintour (1572–1606); his confession is one of the most important sources of information regarding the gunpowder plot.]

6 [Guy Fawkes (1570–1606), son of Edward Fawkes of York; he became a soldier of fortune for Spain in 1593.]

secrecy, they always, together with an oath, employed the Communion, the most sacred rite of their religion.[7] And it is remarkable, that no one of these pious devotees ever entertained the least compunction with regard to the cruel massacre, which they projected, of whatever was great and eminent in the nation. Some of them only were startled by the reflection, that of necessity many catholics must be present; as spectators or attendants on the king, or as having seats in the house of peers: But Tesmond, a Jesuit, and Garnet, superior of that order in England, removed these scruples, and showed them how the interests of religion required, that the innocent should here be sacrificed with the guilty.

All this passed in the spring and summer of the year 1604; when the conspirators also hired a house in Piercy's name, adjoining to that in which the parliament was to assemble. Towards the end of that year they began their operations. That they might be less interrupted, and give less suspicion to the neighbourhood, they carried in store of provisions with them, and never desisted from their labour. Obstinate in their purpose, and confirmed by passion, by principle, and by mutual exhortation, they little feared death in comparison of a disappointment; and having provided arms, together with the instruments of their labour, they resolved there to perish in case of a discovery. Their perseverance advanced the work; and they soon pierced the wall, though three yards in thickness; but on approaching the other side, they were somewhat startled at hearing a noise, which they knew not how to account for. Upon inquiry, they found, that it came from the vault below the house of lords; that a magazine of coals had been kept there; and that, as the coals were selling off, the vault would be let to the highest bidder. The opportunity was immediately seized; the place hired by Piercy; thirty-six barrels of powder lodged in it; the whole covered up with faggots and billets; the doors of the cellar boldly flung open; and every body admitted, as if it contained nothing dangerous.

1605

Confident of success, they now began to look forward, and to

7 *State Trials*, I, 190, 198, 210.

plan the remaining part of their project. The king, the queen, prince Henry, were all expected to be present at the opening of parliament. The duke, by reason of his tender age, would be absent; and it was resolved, that Piercy should seize him, or assassinate him. The princess Elizabeth, a child likewise, was kept at lord Harrington's house at Warwickshire; and sir Everard Digby, Rookwood, Grant,[8] being let into the conspiracy, engaged to assemble their friends on pretence of a hunting match, and seizing that princess, immediately to proclaim her queen. So transported were they with rage against their adversaries, and so charmed with the prospect of revenge, that they forgot all care of their own safety; and trusting to the general confusion, which must result from so unexpected a blow, they foresaw not, that the fury of the people, now unrestrained by any authority, must have turned against them, and would probably have satiated itself, by an universal massacre of the catholics.

The day, so long wished for, now approached, on which the parliament was appointed to assemble. The dreadful secret, though communicated to above twenty persons, had been religiously kept, during the space of near a year and a half. No remorse, no pity, no fear of punishment, no hope of reward, had, as yet, induced any one conspirator either to abandon the enterprise or make a discovery of it. The holy fury had extinguished in their breast every other motive; and it was an indiscretion at last, proceeding chiefly from these very bigoted prejudices and partialities, which saved the nation.

Ten days before the meeting of parliament, lord Monteagle, a catholic, son to lord Morley,[9] received the following letter, which had been delivered to his servant by an unknown hand. "My Lord, Out of the love I bear to some of your friends, I have

---

8 [John Harington, first Baron Harington of Exton (d. 1613), who had charge of the princess by order of the privy seal; Sir Everard Digby (1578–1606); Ambrose Rookwood or Rokewode (1578?–1606); Grant has not been identified by the editors.]

9 [William Parker, eleventh Baron Morley (1575–1622), eldest son of Edward Parker, tenth Baron Morley (1555–1618), and Lady Elizabeth Monteagle.]

a care of your preservation. Therefore would advise you, as you tender your life, to devise some excuse to shift off your attendance at this parliament. For God and man have concurred to punish the wickedness of this time. And think not slightly of this advertisement; but retire yourself into your country, where you may expect the event in safety. For, though there be no appearance of any stir, yet, I say, they will receive a terrible blow this parliament, and yet they shall not see who hurts them. This counsel is not to be contemned, because it may do you good, and can do you no harm: For the danger is past as soon as you have burned the letter. And I hope God will give you the grace to make good use of it, unto whose holy protection I commend you."[10]

Monteagle knew not what to make of this letter; and though inclined to think it a foolish attempt to frighten and ridicule him, he judged it safest to carry it to lord Salisbury,[11] secretary of state. Though Salisbury too was inclined to pay little attention to it, he thought proper to lay it before the king, who came to town a few days after. To the king it appeared not so light a matter; and from the serious earnest style of the letter, he conjectured, that it implied something dangerous and important. A "terrible blow," and yet "the authors concealed"; a danger so "sudden," and yet so "great"; these circumstances seemed all to denote some contrivance by gunpowder; and it was thought advisable to inspect all the vaults below the houses of parliament. This care belonged to the earl of Suffolk,[12] lord chamberlain; who purposely delayed the search, till the day before the meeting of parliament. He remarked those great piles of wood and faggots, which lay in the vault under the upper house; and he cast his eye upon Fawkes, who stood in a dark corner, and passed himself for Piercy's servant. That daring and deter-

---

10 King James's *Works*, p. 227.

11 [Robert Cecil, first Earl of Salisbury and first Viscount Cranborne (1563?–1612), son of William Cecil (see p. 173).]

12 [Thomas Howard, first Earl of Suffolk and first Baron Howard de Walden (1561–1626), privy councillor and lord chamberlain of the household.]

mined courage, which so much distinguished this conspirator, even among those heroes in villiany, was fully painted in his countenance, and was not passed unnoticed by the chamberlain.[13] Such a quantity also of fuel, for the use of one who lived so little in town as Piercy, appeared a little extraordinary;[14] and upon comparing all circumstances, it was resolved that a more thorough inspection should be made. About midnight, sir Thomas Knevet,[15] a justice of peace, was sent with proper attendants; and before the door of the vault finding Fawkes, who had just finished all his preparations, he immediately seized him, and turning over the faggots, discovered the powder. The matches and every thing proper for setting fire to the train were taken in Fawkes's pocket; who finding his guilt now apparent, and seeing no refuge but in boldness and despair, expressed the utmost regret, that he had lost the opportunity of firing the powder at once, and of sweetening his own death by that of his enemies.[16] Before the council, he displayed the same intrepid firmness, mixed even with scorn and disdain; refusing to discover his accomplices, and showing no concern but for the failure of the enterprise.[17] This obstinacy lasted two or three days: But being confined to the Tower, left to reflect on his guilt and danger, and the rack being just shown to him; his courage, fatigued with so long an effort, and unsupported by hope or society, at last failed him; and he made a full discovery of all the conspirators.[18]

Catesby, Piercy, and the other criminals, who were in London, though they had heard of the alarm taken at a letter sent to Monteagle; though they had heard of the chamberlain's search; yet were resolved to persist to the utmost, and never abandon

13 King James's *Works*, p. 229.
14 *Ibid.*
15 [Thomas Knyvet, Lord Knyvet of Escrick (d. 1622), later a member of the privy council.]
16 King James's *Works*, p. 230.
17 Winwood, II, 173.
18 King James's *Works*, p. 231.

their hopes of success.[19] But at last, hearing that Fawkes was arrested, they hurried down to Warwickshire; where sir Everard Digby, thinking himself assured that success had attended his confederates, was already in arms, in order to seize the princess Elizabeth. She had escaped into Coventry; and they were obliged to put themselves on their defence against the country, who were raised from all quarters, and armed, by the sheriff. The conspirators, with all their attendants, never exceeded the number of eighty persons; and being surrounded on every side, could no longer entertain hopes, either of prevailing or escaping. Having therefore confessed themselves, and received absolution, they boldly prepared for death, and resolved to sell their lives as dear as possible to the assailants. But even this miserable consolation was denied them. Some of their powder took fire, and disabled them for defence.[20] The people rushed in upon them. Piercy and Catesby were killed by one shot. Digby, Rookwood, Winter, and others, being taken prisoners, were tried, confessed their guilt, and died, as well as Garnet, by the hands of the executioner. Notwithstanding this horrid crime, the bigoted catholics were so devoted to Garnet, that they fancied miracles to be wrought by his blood;[21] and in Spain he was regarded as a martyr.[22]

Neither had the desperate fortune of the conspirators urged them to this enterprise, nor had the former profligacy of their

[19]* Some historians have imagined, that the king had secret intelligence of the conspiracy, and that the letter to Monteagle was written by his direction, in order to obtain the praise of penetration in discovering the plot. But the known facts refute this supposition. That letter, being commonly talked of, might naturally have given an alarm to the conspirators, and made them contrive their escape. The visit of the lord chamberlain ought to have had the same effect. In short, it appears that nobody was arrested or inquired after, for some days, till Fawkes discovered the names of the conspirators. We may infer, however, from a letter in Winwood's *Memorials*, II, 171, that Salisbury's sagacity led the king in his conjectures, and that the minister, like an artful courtier, gave his master the praise of the whole discovery.

[20] *State Trials*, I, 199. *Discourse of the Manner*, etc., pp. 69, 70.

[21] Winwood, II, 300.

[22] *Ibid.*

lives prepared them for so great a crime. Before that audacious attempt, their conduct seems, in general, to be liable to no reproach. Catesby's character had entitled him to such regard, that Rookwood and Digby were seduced by their implicit trust in his judgment; and they declared, that, from the motive alone of friendship to him, they were ready, on any occasion, to have sacrificed their lives.[23] Digby himself was as highly esteemed and beloved as any man in England; and he had been particularly honoured with the good opinion of queen Elizabeth.[24] It was bigoted zeal alone, the most absurd of prejudices masqued with reason, the most criminal of passions covered with the appearance of duty, which seduced them into measures, that were fatal to themselves, and had so nearly proved fatal to their country.[25]

The lords Mordaunt and Stourton, two catholics, were fined, the former ten thousand pounds, the latter four thousand, by the star-chamber; because their absence from parliament had begotten a suspicion of their being acquainted with the conspiracy. The earl of Northumberland was fined thirty thousand pounds, and detained several years prisoner in the Tower; because, not to mention other grounds of suspicion, he had admitted Piercy into the number of gentlemen pensioners, without his taking the requisite oaths.[26]

The king, in his speech to the parliament observed, that, though religion had engaged the conspirators in so criminal an attempt, yet ought we not to involve all the Roman catholics in the same guilt, or suppose them equally disposed to commit such enormous barbarities. Many holy men, he said, and our ancestors among the rest, had been seduced to concur with that

---

[23] *State Trials,* I, 201.

[24] Anthony à Wood, *Athenae Oxoniensis,* II, fol. 254.

[25] Digby, after his condemnation, said in a letter to his wife: "Now for my intention, let me tell you, that if I had thought there had been the least sin in the plot, I would not have been of it for all the world; and no other cause drew me, to hazard my fortune and life, but zeal to God's religion." He expresses his surprise to hear that any catholics had condemned it. Digby's *Papers,* published by secretary Coventry.

[26] Camden in Kennet, p. 692.

church in her scholastic doctrines; who yet had never admitted her seditious principles, concerning the pope's power of dethroning kings, or sanctifying assassination. The wrath of Heaven is denounced against crimes, but innocent error may obtain its favour; and nothing can be more hateful than the uncharitableness of the puritans, who condemn alike to eternal torments, even the most inoffensive partisans of popery. For his part, he added, that conspiracy, however atrocious, should never alter, in the least, his plan of government: While with one hand he punished guilt; with the other, he would still support and protect innocence.[27] After this speech, he prorogued the parliament till the 22d of January.[28]

The moderation, and, I may say, magnanimity, of the king, immediately after so narrow an escape from a most detestable conspiracy, was nowise agreeable to his subjects. Their animosity against popery, even before this provocation, had risen to a great pitch; and it had perhaps been more prudent in James, by a little dissimulation to have conformed himself to it. His theological learning, confirmed by disputation, had happily fixed his judgment in the protestant faith; yet was his heart a little biassed by the allurements of Rome, and he had been well pleased, if the making of some advances could have affected an union with that ancient mother-church. He strove to abate the acrimony of his own subjects against the religion of their fathers: He became himself the object of their diffidence and aversion. Whatever measures he embraced; in Scotland to introduce prelacy, in England to enforce the authority of the established church, and support its rites and ceremonies, were interpreted as so many steps towards popery; and were represented by the puritans as symptoms of idolatry and superstition. Ignorant of

---

[27] King James's *Works*, pp. 503, 504.

[28] The parliament, this session, passed an act obliging every one to take the oath of allegiance: a very moderate test, since it decided no controverted points between the two religions, and only engaged the persons who took it to abjure the pope's power of dethroning kings. See King James's *Works*, p. 250.

the consequences, or unwilling to sacrifice to politics his inclination, which he called his conscience, he persevered in the same
measures, and gave trust and preferment, almost indifferently,
to his catholic and protestant subjects. And finding his person,
as well as his title, less obnoxious to the church of Rome, than
those of Elizabeth, he gradually abated the rigour of those laws,
which had been enacted against that church, and which were so
acceptable to his bigoted subjects. But the effects of these dispositions on both sides became not very sensible till towards the
conclusion of his reign.

1606    At this time, James seems to have possessed the affections even
of his English subjects, and, in a tolerable degree, their esteem
and regard. Hitherto their complaints were chiefly levelled
against his too great constancy in his early friendships; a quality, which, had it been attended with more oeconomy, the wise
would have excused, and the candid would even, perhaps, have
applauded. His parts, which were not despicable, and his learning, which was great, being highly extolled by his courtiers and
gownmen, and not yet tried in the management of any delicate
affairs, for which he was unfit, raised a high idea of him in the
world; nor was it always through flattery or insincerity that he
received the title of the second Solomon. A report, which was
suddenly spread about this time, of his being assassinated,
visibly struck a great consternation into all orders of men.[29]
The commons also abated, this session, somewhat of their excessive frugality, and granted him an aid, payable in four years,
of three subsidies and six fifteenths, which sir Francis Bacon
said in the house,[30] might amount to about four hundred thousand pounds: and for once the king and parliament parted in
friendship and good humour. The hatred which the catholics
so visibly bore him, gave him, at this time, an additional value
in the eyes of his people. The only considerable point, in which
the commons incurred his displeasure, was by discovering their

29 Kennet, p. 696.
30 *Journ.*, 20th May, 1606.

constant good-will to the puritans, in whose favour they desired a conference with the lords:[31] which was rejected.

. . . . . . . . . .

A petition was moved in the lower house for a more rigorous   1607
execution of the laws against popish recusants, and an abatement towards protestant clergymen, who scrupled to observe the ceremonies. Both these points were equally unacceptable to the king; and he sent orders to the house to proceed no farther in that matter. The commons were inclined, at first, to consider these orders as a breach of privilege: But they soon acquiesced, when told that this measure of the king's was supported by many precedents during the reign of Elizabeth.[32] Had they been always disposed to make the precedents of that reign the rule of their conduct, they needed never have had any quarrel with any of their monarchs.

. . . . . . . . . .

The little concern which James took in foreign affairs, renders   1610
the domestic occurrences, particularly those of parliament, the most interesting of his reign. A new session was held this spring; the king full of hopes of receiving supply; the commons, of circumscribing his prerogative. The earl of Salisbury, now created treasurer on the death of the earl of Dorset, laid open the king's necessities, first to the peers, then to a committee of the lower house.[33] He insisted on the unavoidable expence incurred in supporting the navy, and in suppressing a late insurrection in Ireland: He mentioned three numerous courts which the king was obliged to maintain, for himself, for the queen, and for the prince of Wales: He observed, that queen Elizabeth, though a single woman, had received very large supplies in the years preceding her death, which alone were expensive to her: And he remarked, that, during her reign, she had alienated many of the crown lands; an expedient which, though it supplied her present necessities, without laying burthens on her people, extreme-

---

[31] *Journ.*, 5th April, 1606.
[32] *Journ.*, 16th, 17th June, 1607.
[33] *Journ.*, 17th February, 1609. Kennet, p. 681.

ly multiplied the necessities of her successor. From all these causes he thought it nowise strange, that the king's income should fall short so great a sum as eighty-one thousand pounds of his stated and regular expence; without mentioning contingencies, which ought always to be esteemed a fourth of the yearly charges. And as the crown was now necessarily burthened with a great and urgent debt of 300,000 pounds, he thence inferred the absolute necessity of an immediate and large supply from the people. To all these reasons, which James likewise urged in a speech addressed to both houses, the commons remained inexorable. But, not to shock the king with an absolute refusal, they granted him one subsidy and one fifteenth; which would scarcely amount to a hundred thousand pounds. And James received the mortification of discovering, in vain, all his wants, and of begging aid of subjects who had no reasonable indulgence or consideration for him.

Among the many causes of disgust and quarrel, which now daily and unavoidably multiplied between prince and parliament, this article of money is to be regarded as none of the least considerable. After the discovery and conquest of the West-Indies, gold and silver became every day more plentiful in England, as well as in the rest of Europe; and the price of all commodities and provisions rose to a height beyond what had been known since the declension of the Roman empire. As the revenue of the crown rose not in proportion,[34] the prince was insensibly reduced to poverty amidst the general riches of his subjects, and required additional funds, in order to support the same magnificence and force which had been maintained by former monarchs. But, while money thus flowed into England, we may observe, that, at the same time, and probably from that very cause, arts and industry of all kinds received a mighty increase; and elegance in every enjoyment of life became better known, and more cultivated among all ranks of people. The king's servants, both civil and military, his courtiers, his min-

[34] Besides the great alienation of the crown lands, the fee-farm rents never increased, and the other lands were let on long leases, and at a great undervalue, little or nothing above the old rent.

isters, demanded more ample supplies from the impoverished prince, and were not contented with the same simplicity of living, which had satisfied their ancestors. The prince himself began to regard an increase of pomp and splendour as requisite to support the dignity of his character, and to preserve the same superiority above his subjects, which his predecessors had enjoyed. Some equality too, and proportion to the other sovereigns of Europe, it was natural for him to desire; and as they had universally enlarged their revenue, and multiplied their taxes, the king of England deemed it reasonable that his subjects, who were generally as rich as theirs, should bear with patience some additional burthens and impositions.

Unhappily for the king, those very riches, with the increasing knowledge of the age, bred opposite sentiments in his subjects; and, begetting a spirit of freedom and independence, disposed them to pay little regard either to the entreaties or menaces of their sovereign. While the barons possessed their former immense property and extensive jurisdictions, they were apt, at every disgust, to endanger the monarch, and throw the whole government into confusion: But this confusion often, in its turn, proved favourable to the monarch, and made the nation again submit to him, in order to re-establish justice and tranquillity. After the power of alienations, as well as the increase of commerce, had thrown the balance of property into the hands of the commons, the situation of affairs, and the dispositions of men became susceptible of a more regular plan of liberty; and the laws were not supported singly by the authority of the sovereign. And though in that interval, after the decline of the peers, and before the people had yet experienced their force, the princes assumed an exorbitant power, and had almost annihilated the constitution under the weight of their prerogative; as soon as the commons recovered from their lethargy, they seem to have been astonished at the danger, and were resolved to secure liberty by firmer barriers, than their ancestors had hitherto provided for it.

Had James possessed a very rigid frugality, he might have warded off this crisis somewhat longer; and waiting patiently for a favourable opportunity to increase and fix his revenue, might have secured the extensive authority transmitted to him. On the other hand, had the commons been inclined to act with more generosity and kindness towards their prince, they might probably have turned his necessities to good account, and have bribed him to depart peaceably from the more dangerous articles of his prerogative. But he was a foreigner, and ignorant of the arts of popularity; they were soured by religious prejudices, and tenacious of their money: And, in this situation, it is no wonder, that, during this whole reign, we scarcely find an interval of mutual confidence and friendship between prince and parliament.

The king, by his prerogative alone, had some years before altered the rates of the customs, and had established higher impositions on several kinds of merchandise. This exercise of power will naturally, to us, appear arbitrary and illegal; yet, according to the principles and practices of that time, it might admit of some apology. The duties of tonnage and poundage were at first granted to the crown, by a vote of parliament, and for a limited time; and as the grant frequently expired and was renewed, there could not then arise any doubt concerning the origin of the king's right to levy these duties; and this imposition, like all others, was plainly derived from the voluntary consent of the people. But as Henry V. and all the succeeding sovereigns, had the revenue conferred on them for life, the prince, so long in possession of these duties, began gradually to consider them as his own proper right and inheritance, and regarded the vote of parliament as a mere formality, which rather expressed the acquiescence of the people in his prerogative, than bestowed any new gift of revenue upon him.

The parliament, when it first granted poundage to the crown, had fixed no particular rates: The imposition was given as a shilling a pound, or five *per cent.* on all commodities: It was left to the king himself, and the privy council, aided by the advice of such merchants as they should think proper to consult, to fix the value of goods, and thereby the rates of the customs: And as that value had been settled before the discovery of the West-

Indies, it was become much inferior to the prices which almost all commodities bore in every market in Europe; and consequently, the customs on many goods, though supposed to be five *per cent.* was in reality much inferior. The king, therefore, was naturally led to think that rates which were now plainly false, ought to be corrected;[35] that a valuation of commodities, fixed by one act of the privy council, might be amended by another; that if his right to poundage were inherent in the crown, he should also possess, of himself, the right of correcting its inequalities; if this duty were granted by the people, he should at least support the spirit of the law, by fixing a new and a juster valuation of all commodities. But besides this reasoning, which seems plausible, if not solid, the king was supported in that act of power by direct precedents, some in the reign of Mary, some in the beginning of Elizabeth.[36] Both these princesses had, without consent of parliament, altered the rates of commodities; and as their impositions had, all along, been submitted to without a murmur, and still continued to be levied, the king had no reason to apprehend, that a farther exertion of the same authority would give any occasion of complaint. That less umbrage might be taken, he was moderate in the new rates, which he established: The customs, during his whole reign, rose only from 127,000 pounds a year to 190,000; though, besides the increase of the rates, there was a sensible increase of commerce and industry during that period: Every commodity, besides, which might serve to the subsistence of the people, or might be considered as a material of manufactures, was exempted from the new impositions of James:[37] But all this caution could not prevent the complaints of the commons. A spirit of liberty had now taken possession of the house: The leading members, men of an independent genius and large views, began to regulate their opinions, more by the future consequences which they

[35] Winwood, II, 438.

[36] *Journ.*, 18th April, 5th and 10th May, 1614, etc., 26th February, 1625. See also sir John Davis's [*i.e.,* Davies'] *Question Concerning Impositions,* pp. 127, 128.

[37] Davies, *Question Concerning Impositions.*

foresaw, than by the former precedents which were set before them; and they less aspired at maintaining the ancient constitution, than at establishing a new one, and a freer, and a better. In their remonstrances to the king on this occasion, they observed it to be a general opinion, "That the reasons of that practice might be extended much farther, even to the utter ruin of the ancient liberty of the kingdom, and the subjects' right of property in their lands and goods."[38] Though expressly forbidden by the king to touch his prerogative, they passed a bill abolishing these impositions; which was rejected by the house of lords.

.    .    .    .    .    .    .    .    .    .    .

Amidst all these attacks, some more, some less violent, on royal prerogative, the king displayed, as openly as ever, all his exalted notions of monarchy and the authority of princes. Even in a speech to the parliament, where he begged for supply, and where he should naturally have used every art to ingratiate himself with that assembly, he expressed himself in these terms: "I conclude, then, the point, touching the power of kings, with this axiom of divinity, that, as to dispute *what God may do,* is blasphemy, but *what God wills,* that divines may lawfully and do ordinarily dispute and discuss; so is it sedition in subjects to dispute what a king may do in the heighth of his power. But just kings will ever be willing to declare what they will do, if they will not incur the curse of God. I will not be content, that my power be disputed upon; but I shall ever be willing to make the reason appear of my doings, and rule my actions according to *my* laws."[39] Notwithstanding the great extent of prerogative in that age, these expressions would probably give some offence. But we may observe, that, as the king's despotism was more speculative than practical, so the independency of the commons was, at this time, the reverse; and though strongly supported by their present situation, as well as disposition, was too new and

[38] *Journ.,* 23d May, 1610.
[39] King James's *Works,* p. 531.

recent to be as yet founded on systematical principles and opinions.[40]

[40]* It may not be unworthy of observation, that James, in a book called *The true laws of free Monarchies,* which he published a little before his accession to the crown of England, affirmed, "That a good king, although he be above the law, will subject and frame his actions thereto, for example's sake to his subjects, and of his own free-will, but not as subject or bound thereto." In another passage, "According to the fundamental law already alleged, we daily see, that in the parliament (which is nothing else but the head-court of the king and his vassals) the laws are but craved by his subjects, and only made by him at their rogation, and with their advice. For albeit the king *make daily* statutes and ordinances, enjoining such pains thereto as he thinks meet, without any advice of parliament or estates; yet it lies in the power of no parliament to make any kind of law or statute, without his sceptre be to it, for giving it the force of a law." King James's *Works,* p. 202. It is not to be supposed, that, at such a critical juncture, James had so little sense as, directly, in so material a point, to have openly shocked what were the universal established principles of that age: on the contrary, we are told by historians, that nothing tended more to facilitate his accession, than the good opinion entertained of him by the English, on account of his learned and judicious writings. The question, however, with regard to the royal power was, at this time, become a very dangerous point; and without employing ambiguous, insignificant terms, which determined nothing, it was impossible to please both king and parliament. Dr. Cowell, who had magnified the prerogative in words too intelligible, fell this session under the indignation of the commons. *Parliamentary History,* V, 221. The king himself, after all his magnificent boasts, was obliged to make his escape through a distinction, which he framed between a king *in abstracto* and a king *in concreto:* an abstract king, he said, had all power; but a concrete king was bound to observe the laws of the country, which he governed. King James's *Works,* p. 533. But how bound? By conscience only? Or might his subjects resist him and defend their privileges? This he thought not fit to explain. And so difficult is it to explain that point, that, to this day, whatever liberties may be used by private inquirers, the laws have, very prudently, thought proper to maintain a total silence with regard to it.

# *From* Chapter XLVII—James I

1614   WHEN THE commons were assembled, they discovered an extraordinary alarm, on account of the rumour which was spread
abroad concerning "undertakers."[1] It was reported, that several
persons, attached to the king, had entered into a confederacy;
and having laid a regular plan for the new elections had distributed their interest all over England, and had undertaken to
secure a majority for the court. So ignorant were the commons,
that they knew not this incident to be the first infallible symp-
tom of any regular or established liberty. Had they been contented to follow the maxims of their predecessors, who, as the
earl of Salisbury said to the last parliament, never, but thrice in
six hundred years, refused a supply;[2] they needed not dread that
the crown should ever interest itself in their elections. Formerly,
the kings even insisted, that none of their household should be
elected members; and though the charter was afterwards declared void, Henry VI. from his great favour to the city of York,
conferred a peculiar privilege on its citizens, that they should
be exempted from this trouble.[3] It is well known, that, in ancient
times, a seat in the house being considered as a burthen, attended neither with honour nor profit, it was requisite for the
counties and boroughs to pay fees to their representatives. About
this time a seat began to be regarded as an honour, and the
country-gentlemen contended for it; though the practice of levy-

[1] *Parliamentary History,* V, 286. Kennet, p. 696. *Journ.,* 12th April, 2d
May, 1614, etc. Franklyn [i.e., Thomas Frankland], *The Annals of King
James I and King Charles I,* p. 48.

[2] *Journ.,* 17th February, 1609. It appears, however, that Salisbury was
somewhat mistaken in this fact: And if the kings were not oftener refused
supply by the parliament, it was only because they would not often expose
themselves to the hazard of being refused: But it is certain that English
parliaments did anciently carry their frugality to an extreme, and seldom
could be prevailed upon to give the necessary support to government.

[3] Sir Edward Coke, *Institutes,* "Charters of Exemption," pt. 4, chap. 1.

ing wages for parliament-men was not altogether discontinued. It was not till long after, when liberty was thoroughly established, and popular assemblies entered into every branch of public business, that the members began to join profit to honour, and the crown found it necessary to distribute among them all the considerable offices of the kingdom.

So little skill or so small means had the courtiers, in James's reign, for managing elections, that this house of commons showed rather a stronger spirit of liberty than the foregoing; and instead of entering upon the business of supply, as urged by the king, who made them several liberal offers of grace,[4] they immediately resumed the subject which had been opened last parliament, and disputed his majesty's power of levying new customs and impositions, by the mere authority of his prerogative. It is remarkable, that, in their debates on this subject, the courtiers frequently pleaded, as a precedent, the example of all the other hereditary monarchs in Europe, and particularly mentioned the kings of France and Spain; nor was this reasoning received by the house, either with surprise or indignation.[5] The members of the opposite party, either contented themselves with denying the justness of the inference, or they disputed the truth of the observation.[6] And a patriot member in particular, sir Roger Owen,[7] even in arguing against the impositions, frankly allowed, that the king of England was endowed with as ample a power and prerogative as any prince in Christendom.[8] The nations on the continent, we may observe, enjoyed still, in that age, some small remains of liberty; and the English were possessed of little more.

The commons applied to the lords for a conference with regard to the new impositions. A speech of Neile,[9] bishop of Lincoln, reflecting on the lower house, begat some altercation with

4 *Journ.*, 11th April, 1614.
5 *Journ.*, 21st May, 1614.
6 *Journ.*, 12th, 21st May, 1614.
7 [Sir Roger Owen (1573–1617), member from Shropshire.]
8 *Journ.*, 18th April, 1614.
9 [Richard Neil (1562–1640), archbishop of York.]

the peers;[10] and the king seized the opportunity of dissolving immediately, with great indignation, a parliament which had shown so firm a resolution of retrenching his prerogative, without communicating, in return, the smallest supply to his necessities. He carried his resentment so far as even to throw into prison some of the members, who had been the most forward in their opposition to his measures.[11] In vain did he plead, in excuse for this violence, the example of Elizabeth and other princes of the line of Tudor, as well as Plantagenet. The people and the parliament, without abandoning for ever all their liberties and privileges, could acquiesce in none of these precedents, how ancient and frequent soever. And were the authority of such precedents admitted, the utmost that could be inferred is, that the constitution of England was, at that time, an inconsistent fabric, whose jarring and discordant parts must soon destroy each other, and from the dissolution of the old, beget some new form of civil government more uniform and consistent.

---

[10]* *Parliamentary History*, V, 290. So little fixed at this time were the rules of parliament, that the commons complained to the peers of a speech made in the upper house by the bishop of Lincoln; which it belonged only to that house to censure, and which the other could not regularly be supposed to be acquainted with. These at least are the rules established since the parliament became a real seat of power, and scene of business. Neither the king must take notice of what passes in either house, nor either house of what passes in the other, till regularly informed of it. The commons, in their famous protestation [of] 1621, fixed this rule with regard to the king, though at present they would not bind themselves by it. But as liberty was yet new, those maxims, which guard and regulate it, were unknown and unpractised.

[11] Kennet, p. 696.

## *From* Chapter XLVIII—James I

[JAMES]FIRST tried the expedient of a benevolence or free-gift 1621
from individuals; pretending the urgency of the case, which
would not admit of leisure for any other measure: But the
jealousy of liberty was now rouzed, and the nation regarded
these pretended benevolences as real extortions, contrary to law,
and dangerous to freedom, however authorised by ancient precedent. A parliament was found to be the only resource which
could furnish any large supplies; and writs were accordingly
issued for summoning that great council of the nation.[1]

1* This parliament is remarkable for being the epoch, in which were first
regularly formed, though without acquiring these denominations, the parties
of court and country; parties, which have ever since continued, and which,
while they oft threaten the total dissolution of the government, are the real
causes of its permanent life and vigour. In the ancient feudal constitution,
of which the English partook with other European nations, there was a
mixture, not of authority and liberty, which we have since enjoyed in this
island, and which now subsist uniformly together; but of authority and
anarchy, which perpetually shocked with each other, and which took place
alternately, according as circumstances were more or less favourable to
either of them. A parliament composed of barbarians, summoned from their
fields and forests, uninstructed by study, conversation, or travel; ignorant of
their own laws and history, and unacquainted with the situation of all
foreign nations; a parliament called precariously by the king, and dissolved
at his pleasure; sitting a few days, debating a few points prepared for them,
and whose members were impatient to return to their own castles, where
alone they were great, and to the chase, which was their favourite amusement: such a parliament was very little fitted to enter into a discussion of all
the questions of government, and to share, in a regular manner, the legal
administration. The name, the authority of the king alone appeared, in the
common course of government; in extraordinary emergencies, he assumed,
with still better reason, the sole direction; the imperfect and unformed laws
left, in every thing, a latitude of interpretation; and when the ends, pursued
by the monarch were, in general, agreeable to his subjects, little scruple or
jealousy was entertained with regard to the regularity of the means. During
the reign of an able, fortunate, or popular prince, no member of either
house, much less of the lower, durst think of entering into a formed party,

In this parliament, there appeared, at first, nothing but duty, and submission on the part of the commons; and they seemed

---

in opposition to the court; since the dissolution of the parliament must, in a few days, leave him unprotected, to the vengeance of his sovereign, and to those stretches of prerogative, which were then so easily made, in order to punish an obnoxious subject. During an unpopular and weak reign, the current commonly ran so strong against the monarch, that none durst enlist themselves in the court party; or if the prince was able to engage any considerable barons on his side, the question was decided with arms in the field, not by debates or arguments in a senate or assembly. And upon the whole, the chief circumstance, which, during ancient times, retained the prince in any legal form of administration, was, that the sword, by the nature of the feudal tenures, remained still in the hands of his subjects; and this irregular and dangerous check had much more influence than the regular and methodical limits of the laws and constitution. As the nation could not be compelled, it was necessary that every public measure of consequence, particularly that of levying new taxes, should seem to be adopted by common consent and approbation.

The princes of the house of Tudor, partly by the vigour of their administration, partly by the concurrence of favourable circumstances, had been able to establish a more regular system of government; but they drew the constitution so near to despotism, as diminished extremely the authority of the parliament. The senate became, in a great degree, the organ of royal will and pleasure: opposition would have been regarded as a species of rebellion: and even religion, the most dangerous article in which innovations could be introduced, had admitted, in the course of a few years, four several alterations, from the authority alone of the sovereign. The parliament was not then the road to honour and preferment: the talents of popular intrigue and eloquence were uncultivated and unknown: and though that assembly still preserved authority, and retained the privilege of making laws and bestowing public money, the members acquired not, upon that account, either with prince or people, much more weight and consideration. What powers were necessary for conducting the machine of government, the king was accustomed, of himself, to assume. His own revenues supplied him with money sufficient for his ordinary expences. And when extraordinary emergencies occurred, the prince needed not to solicit votes in parliament, either for making laws or imposing taxes, both of which were now become requisite for public interest and preservation.

The security of individuals, so necessary to the liberty of popular councils, was totally unknown in that age. And as no despotic princes, scarcely even the eastern tyrants, rule entirely without the concurrence of some assemblies, which supply both advice and authority; little, but a mercenary force, seems then to have been wanting towards the establishment of a simple monarchy in England. The militia, though more favourable to regal authority, than

determined to sacrifice every thing, in order to maintain a good correspondence with their prince. They would allow no men-

---

the feudal institutions, was much inferior, in this respect, to disciplined armies; and if it did not preserve liberty to the people, it preserved at least the power, if ever the inclination should arise of recovering it.

But so low, at that time, ran the inclination towards liberty, that Elizabeth, the last of that arbitrary line, herself no less arbitrary, was yet the most renowned and most popular of all the sovereigns that had filled the throne of England. It was natural for James to take the government as he found it, and to pursue her measures, which he heard so much applauded; nor did his penetration extend so far as to discover, that neither his circumstances nor his character could support so extensive an authority. His narrow revenues and little frugality began now to render him dependent on his people, even in the ordinary course of administration: their increasing knowledge discovered to them that advantage, which they had obtained; and made them sensible of the inestimable value of civil liberty. And as he possessed too little dignity to command respect, and too much good-nature to impress fear, a new spirit discovered itself every day in the parliament; and a party, watchful of a free constitution, was regularly formed in the house of commons.

But notwithstanding these advantages acquired to liberty, so extensive was royal authority, and so firmly established in all its parts, that it is probable the patriots of that age would have despaired of ever resisting it, had they not been stimulated by religious motives, which inspire a courage unsurmountable by any human obstacle.

The same alliance which has ever prevailed between kingly power and ecclesiastical authority, was now fully established in England; and while the prince assisted the clergy in suppressing schismatics and innovators, the clergy, in return, inculcated the doctrine of an unreserved submission and obedience to the civil magistrate. The genius of the church of England, so kindly to monarchy, forwarded the confederacy; its submission to episcopal jurisdiction; its attachment to ceremonies, to order, and to a decent pomp and splendor of worship; and in a word, its affinity to the tame superstition of the catholics, rather than to the wild fanaticism of the puritans.

On the other hand, opposition to the church, and the persecutions under which they laboured, were sufficient to throw the puritans into the country party, and to beget political principles little favourable to the high pretensions of the sovereign. The spirit too of enthusiasm; bold, daring and, uncontrolled; strongly disposed their minds to adopt republican tenets; and inclined them to arrogate, in their actions and conduct, the same liberty, which they assumed in their rapturous flights and ecstasies. Ever since the first origin of that sect, through the whole reign of Elizabeth as well as of James, *puritanical* principles had been understood in a double sense, and expressed the opinions favourable both to political and to ecclesiastical

tion to be made of the new customs or impositions, which had been so eagerly disputed in the former parliament:[2] The imprisonment of the members of that parliament was here, by some, complained of; but, by the authority of the graver and more prudent part of the house, that grievance was buried in oblivion:[3] And, being informed that the king had remitted several considerable sums to the palatine, the commons, without a negative, voted him two subsidies,[4] and that too, at the very beginning of the session, contrary to the maxims frequently adopted by their predecessors.

Afterwards, they proceeded, but in a very temperate manner, to the examination of grievances. They found, that patents had been granted to sir Giles Mompesson and sir Francis Michel, for licensing inns and ale-houses; that great sums of money had been exacted, under pretext of these licenses; and that such innkeepers as presumed to continue their business, without satisfying the rapacity of the patentees, had been severely punished by fine, imprisonment, and vexatious prosecutions.

The same persons had also procured a patent, which they shared with sir Edward Villiers, brother to Buckingham,[5] for the sole making of gold and silver thread and lace, and had

---

liberty. And as the court, in order to discredit all parliamentary opposition, affixed the denomination of puritans to its antagonists; the religious puritans willingly adopted this idea, which was so advantageous to them, and which confounded their cause with that of the patriots or country party. Thus were the civil and ecclesiastical factions regularly formed; and the humour of the nation during that age, running strongly towards fanatical extravagancies, the spirit of civil liberty gradually revived from its lethargy, and by means of its religious associate, from which it reaped more advantage than honour, it secretly enlarged its dominion over the greater part of the kingdom. (This Note was in the first editions a part of the text; but the author omitted it, in order to avoid, as much as possible, the style of dissertation in the body of his history. The passage, however, contains views so important, that, he thought it might be admitted as a note.)

2 *Journ.*, 5th December, 1621.

3 *Journ.*, 12th, 16th February, 1620.

4 *Journ.*, 16th February, 1620.

5 [Sir Edward Villiers (1585?–1626), half-brother of George Villiers, first Duke of Buckingham (1592–1628), who was a favorite of both James and Charles.]

obtained very extraordinary powers for preventing any rivalship in these manufactures: They were armed with authority to search for all goods, which might interfere with their patent; and even to punish, at their own will and discretion, the makers, importers, and venders of such commodities. Many had grievously suffered by this exorbitant jurisdiction; and the lace, which had been manufactured by the patentees was universally found to be adulterated, and to be composed more of copper than of the precious metals.

These grievances the commons represented to the king; and they met with a very gracious and very cordial reception. He semed even thankful for the information given him; and declared himself ashamed, that such abuses, unknowingly to him, had creeped into his administration. "I assure you," said he, "had I before heard these things complained of, I would have done the office of a just king, and out of parliament have punished them, as severely, and peradventure more, than you now intend to do."[6] A sentence was passed for the punishment of Michel and Mompesson.[7] It was executed on the former. The latter broke prison and escaped. Villiers was, at that time, sent purposely on a foreign employment; and his guilt being less enormous, or less apparent, than that of the others, he was the more easily protected by the credit of his brother, Buckingham.[8]

Encouraged by this success, the commons carried their scrutiny, and still with a respectful hand, into other abuses of importance. The great seal was, at that time, in the hands of the celebrated Bacon,[9] created viscount St. Albans; a man univer-

6 Franklyn, p. 51. John Rushworth, *Historical Collections*, I, 25.

7 Franklyn, p. 52. Rushworth, I, 27.

8 Yelverton, the attorney-general, was accused by the commons for drawing the patents for these monopolies, and for supporting them. He apologised for himself, that he was forced by Buckingham, and that he supposed it to be the king's pleasure. The lords were so offended at these articles of defence, though necessary to the attorney-general, that they fined him 10,000 pounds to the king, 5,000 to the duke. The fines, however, were afterwards remitted. Franklyn, p. 55. Rushworth, I, 31, 32, etc.

9 [Bacon (1561–1626) was made solicitor general in 1607, attorney general in 1613, privy councillor in 1616, lord keeper in 1617, and lord chancellor in 1618.]

sally admired for the greatness of his genius, and beloved for the courteousness and humanity of his behaviour. He was the great ornament of his age and nation; and nought was wanting to render him the ornament of human nature itself, but that strength of mind which might check his intemperate desire of preferment, that could add nothing to his dignity, and might restrain his profuse inclination to expence, that could be requisite neither for his honour nor entertainment. His want of oeconomy, and his indulgence to servants, had involved him in necessities; and, in order to supply his prodigality, he had been tempted to take bribes, by the title of presents, and that in a very open manner, from suitors in chancery. It appears, that it had been usual for former chancellors to take presents; and it is pretended, that Bacon, who followed the same dangerous practice, had still, in the seat of justice, preserved the integrity of a judge, and had given just decrees against those very persons, from whom he had received the wages of iniquity. Complaints rose the louder on that account, and at last reached the house of commons, who sent up an impeachment against him to the peers. The chancellor, conscious of guilt, deprecated the vengeance of his judges, and endeavoured, by a general avowal, to escape the confusion of a stricter inquiry. The lords insisted on a particular confession of all his corruptions. He acknowledged twenty-eight articles; and was sentenced to pay a fine of 40,000 pounds, to be imprisoned in the Tower during the king's pleasure, to be for ever incapable of any office, place, or employment, and never again to sit in parliament, or come within the verge of the court.

This dreadful sentence, dreadful to a man of nice sensibility to honour, he survived five years; and, being released in a little time from the Tower, his genius, yet unbroken, supported itself amidst involved circumstances and a depressed spirit, and shone out in literary productions, which have made his guilt or weaknesses be forgotten or overlooked by posterity. In consideration of his great merit, the king remitted his fine, as well as all the other parts of his sentence, conferred on him a large pension of 1,800 pounds a year, and employed every expedient to alleviate

the weight of his age and misfortunes. And that great philosopher, at last, acknowledged with regret, that he had too long
neglected the true ambition of a fine genius; and, by plunging
into business and affairs, which require much less capacity, but
greater firmness of mind, than the pursuits of learning, had
exposed himself to such grievous calamities.[10]

The commons had entertained the idea, that they were the
great patrons of the people, and that the redress of all grievances
must proceed from them; and to this principle they were chiefly
beholden for the regard and consideration of the public. In
the execution of this office, they now kept their ears open to
complaints of every kind; and they carried their researches into
many grievances, which, though of no great importance, could
not be touched on, without sensibly affecting the king and his
ministers. The prerogative seemed every moment to be invaded;
the king's authority, in every article, was disputed; and James,
who was willing to correct the abuses of his power, would not
submit to have his power itself questioned and denied. After
the house, therefore, had sitten near six months, and had, as
yet, brought no considerable business to a full conclusion, the
king, resolved, under pretence of the advanced season, to inter-
rupt their proceedings; and he sent them word, that he was determined, in a little time, to adjourn them till next winter.
The commons made application to the lords, and desired them
to join in a petition for delaying the adjournment; which was
refused by the upper house. The king regarded this project of
a joint petition as an attempt to force him from his measures:
He thanked the peers for their refusal to concur in it, and told
them, that, if it were their desire, he would delay the adjournment, but would not so far comply with the request of the
lower house.[11] And thus, in these great national affairs, the same
peevishness, which, in private altercations, often raises a quar-

10 It is thought, that appeals from chancery to the house of peers first
came into practice, while Bacon held the great seal. Appeals, under the
form of *writs of error*, had long before lain against the courts of law. Sir
William Blackstone, *Commentaries on the Laws of England*, III, 454.

11 Rushworth, I, 35.

rel from the smallest beginnings, produced a mutual coldness and disgust between the king and the commons.

During the recess of parliament, the king used every measure to render himself popular with the nation, and to appease the rising ill-humour of their representatives. He had voluntarily offered the parliament to circumscribe his own prerogative, and to abrogate for the future his power of granting monopolies. He now recalled all the patents of that kind, and redressed every article of grievance, to the number of thirty-seven, which had ever been complained of in the house of commons.[12] But he gained not the end which he proposed. The disgust, which had appeared at parting, could not so suddenly be dispelled. He had likewise been so imprudent as to commit to prison sir Edwin Sandys,[13] without any known cause, besides his activity and vigour in discharging his duty as a member of parliament. And, above all, the transactions in Germany were sufficient, when joined to the king's cautions, negociations, and delays, to inflame that jealousy of honour and religion which prevailed throughout the nation.[14] This summer, the ban of the empire had been published against the elector palatine; and the execution of it was committed to the duke of Bavaria.[15] The Upper Palatinate[16] was, in a little time, conquered by that prince; and measures were taking in the empire for bestowing on him the elec-

[12] Rushworth, I, 36. Kennet, p. 733.

[13] *Journ.*, 1st December, 1621.

[14] To show to what degree the nation was inflamed with regard to the Palatinate, there occurs a remarkable story this session. One Floyd, a prisoner in the Fleet, a catholic, had dropped some expressions, in private conversation, as if he were pleased with the misfortunes of the palatine and his wife. The commons were in a flame, and, pretending to be a court of judicature and of record, proceeded to condemn him to a severe punishment. The house of lords checked this encroachment; and, what was extraordinary, considering the present humour of the lower house, the latter acquiesced in the sentiments of the peers. This is almost the only pretension of the English commons, in which they have not prevailed. Happily for the nation, they have been successful in almost all the other claims. See *Parliamentary History*, V, 428, 429ff. *Journ.*, 4th, 8th, 12th May, 1621.

[15] Franklyn, p. 73.

[16] [A principality in the Rhine valley.]

toral dignity, of which the palatine was despoiled. Frederic[17] now lived with his numerous family, in poverty and distress, either in Holland or at Sedan, with his uncle the duke of Boüillon; and throughout all the new conquests, in both the Palatinates, as well as in Bohemia, Austria, and Lusatia,[18] the progress of the Austrian arms was attended with rigours and severities, exercised against the professors of the reformed religion.

The zeal of the commons immediately moved them, upon their assembling, to take all these transactions into consideration. They framed a remonstrance, which they intended to carry to the king. They represented, that the enormous growth of the Austrian power threatened the liberties of Europe; that the progress of the catholic religion in England bred the most melancholy apprehensions lest it should again acquire an ascendant in the kingdom; that the indulgence of his majesty towards the professors of that religion had encouraged their insolence and temerity; that the uncontroulled conquests, made by the Austrian family in Germany, raised mighty expectations in the English papists; but above all, that the prospect of the Spanish match[19] elevated them so far as to hope for an entire toleration, if not the final re-establishment of their religion. The commons, therefore, entreated his majesty, that he would immediately undertake the defence of the palatine, and maintain it by force of arms; that he would turn his sword against Spain, whose armies and treasures were the chief support of the catholic interest in Europe; that he would enter into no negociation for the marriage of his son but with a protestant princess; that the children of popish recusants should be taken from their parents,

17 [Frederick V (1596–1632), elector palatine of the Rhine and king of Bohemia; he married Elizabeth, daughter of James, in 1613. He was crowned king of Bohemia on Nov. 4, 1619, but a year later (Nov. 8, 1620) his troops were routed by Tilly, general for the Catholic league. Frederick and his family fled to Holland, where he remained a pensioner of the Dutch states-general for the remainder of his life.]

18 [Region between Elbe and Oder rivers, in eastern Germany.]

19 [Negotiations to marry the Prince of Wales (Charles I) to the Spanish infanta, Maria, were being carried on.]

and be committed to the care of protestant teachers and school-masters; and that the fines and confiscations, to which the catholics were by law liable, should be levied with the utmost severity.[20]

By this *bold* step, unprecedented in England for many years, and scarcely ever heard of in peaceable times, the commons attacked at once all the king's favourite maxims of government; his cautious and pacific measures, his lenity towards the Romish religion, and his attachment to the Spanish alliance, from which he promised himself such mighty advantages. But what most disgusted him was, their seeming invasion of his prerogative, and their pretending, under colour of advice, to direct his conduct in such points, as had even been acknowledged to belong solely to the management and direction of the sovereign. He was, at that time, absent at Newmarket; but as soon as he heard of the intended remonstrance of the commons, he wrote a letter to the speaker, in which he sharply rebuked the house for openly debating matters far above their reach and capacity, and he strictly forbade them to meddle with any thing that regarded his government, or deep matters of state, and especially not to touch on his son's marriage with the daughter of Spain, nor to attack the honour of that king, or any other of his friends and confederates. In order the more to intimidate them, he mentioned the imprisonment of sir Edwin Sandys; and though he denied that the confinement of that member had been owing to any offence committed in the house, he plainly told them, that he thought himself fully entitled to punish every misdemeanor in parliament, as well during its sitting as after its dissolution; and that he intended thenceforward to chastise any man, whose insolent behaviour there should minister occasion of offence.[21]

This *violent* letter, in which the king, though he here imitated former precedents, may be thought not to have acted altogether on the defensive, had the effect which might naturally have been expected from it: The commons were inflamed, not

20 Franklyn, pp. 58, 59. Rushworth, I, 40, 41. Kennet, p. 737.
21 Franklyn, p. 60. Rushworth, I, 43. Kennet, p. 741.

terrified. Secure of their own popularity, and of the bent of the nation towards a war with the catholics abroad, and the persecution of popery at home, they little dreaded the menaces of a prince, who was unsupported by military force, and whose gentle temper would, of itself, so soon disarm his severity. In a new remonstrance, therefore, they still insisted on their former remonstrance and advice; and they maintained, though in respectful terms, that they were entitled to interpose with their counsel in all matters of government; that, to possess entire freedom of speech, in their debates on public business, was their ancient and undoubtful right, and an inheritance transmitted to them from their ancestors; and that, if any member abused this liberty, it belonged to the house alone, who were witnesses of his offence, to inflict a proper censure upon him.[22]

*So vigorous* an answer was nowise calculated to appease the king. It is said, when the approach of the committee who were to present it was notified to him, he ordered twelve chairs to be brought: For that there were so many kings a coming.[23] His answer was prompt and sharp. He told the house, that their remonstrance was more like a denunciation of war than an address of dutiful subjects; that their pretension to inquire into all state-affairs, without exception, was such a *plenipotence* as none of their ancestors, even during the reign of the weakest princes, had ever pretended to; that public transactions depended on a complication of views and intelligence, with which they were entirely unacquainted; that they could not better show their wisdom, as well as duty, than by keeping within their proper sphere;[24] and that, in any business which depended on his prerogative, they had no title to interpose with their advice, except when he was pleased to desire it. And he concluded with these memorable words: "And though we cannot allow of your style, in mentioning your ancient and undoubted right and

22 Franklyn, p. 60. Rushworth, I, 44. Kennet, p. 741.

23 Kennet, p. 43.

24 *Ne sutor ultra crepidam* ["Let the cobbler stick to his last"]. This expression is imagined to be insolent and disobliging: But it was a Latin proverb familiarly used on all occasions.

inheritance, but would rather have wished that ye had said, that your privileges were derived from the grace and permission of our ancestors and us (for the most of them grew from precedents, which shows rather a toleration than inheritance); yet we are pleased to give you our royal assurance, that as long as you contain yourself within the limits of your duty, we will be as careful to maintain and preserve your lawful liberties and privileges as ever any of our predecessors were, nay, as to preserve our own royal prerogative."[25]

This open pretension of the king's naturally gave great alarm to the house of commons. They saw their title to every privilege, if not plainly denied, yet considered at least as precarious. It might be forfeited by abuse, and they had already abused it. They thought proper, therefore, immediately to oppose pretension to pretension. They framed a protestation, in which they repeated all their former claims for freedom of speech, and an unbounded authority to interpose with their advice and council. And they asserted, "That the liberties, franchises, privileges, and jurisdictions of parliament, are the ancient and undoubted birth-right and inheritance of the subjects of England."[26]

---

[25] Franklyn, pp. 62, 63, 64. Rushworth, I, 46, 47ff. Kennet, p. 743.

[26]* This protestation is so remarkable, that it may not be improper to give it in its own words. "The commons now assembled in parliament, being justly occasioned thereunto, concerning sundry liberties, franchises, and privileges, of parliament, amongst others, here mentioned, do make this protestation following: that the liberties, franchises, and jurisdictions of parliament are the ancient and undoubted birth-right and inheritance of the subjects of England; and that the urgent and arduous affairs concerning the king, state, and defence of the realm and of the church of England; and the maintenance and making of laws, and redress of mischiefs and grievances, which daily happen within this realm, are proper subjects and matter of council and debate in parliament; and that in the handling and proceeding of those businesses, every member of the house of parliament hath, and, of right ought to have, freedom of speech to propound, treat, reason, and bring to conclusion the same; and that the commons in parliament have like liberty and freedom to treat of these matters, in such order as in their judgment shall seem fittest; and that every member of the said house hath like freedom from all impeachment, imprisonment, and molestation (other than by censure of the house itself) for or concerning any speaking, reasoning, or declaring of any matter or matters touching the parliament or parliament-business. And that if any of the said members be

The king, informed of these increasing heats and jealousies in the house, hurried to town. He sent immediately for the journals of the commons; and, with his own hand, before the council, he tore out this protestation;[27] and ordered his reasons to be inserted in the council-book. He was doubly displeased, he said, with the protestation of the lower house, on account of the manner of framing it, as well as of the matter which it contained. It was tumultuously voted, at a late hour, and in a thin house; and it was expressed in such general and ambiguous terms, as might serve for a foundation to the most enormous claims, and to the most unwarrantable usurpations upon his prerogative.[28]

The meeting of the house might have proved dangerous after so violent a breach. It was no longer possible, while men were in such a temper, to finish any business. The king, therefore, prorogued the parliament, and soon after dissolved it by proclamation; in which he also made an apology to the public for his whole conduct.

The leading members of the house, sir Edward Coke and sir Robert Philips,[29] were committed to the tower; Selden, Pym, and Mallory, to other prisons.[30] As a lighter punishment, sir Dudley Digges, sir Thomas Crew, sir Nathaniel Rich, sir James Perrot,[31] joined in commission with others, were sent to Ire-

---

complained of and questioned for any thing done or said in parliament, the same is to be shown to the king by the advice and assent of all the commons assembled in parliament, before the king give credence to any private information." Franklyn, p. 65. Rushworth, I, 53. Kennet, p. 747. Coke, p. 77.

27 *Journ.*, 18th December, 1621.

28 Franklyn, p. 65.

29 [Sir Edward Coke (1552–1634), best known, perhaps, for his *Institutes* a series of law commentaries; Sir Robert Philips (1586?–1638), member, at this time, for Bath.]

30 Franklyn, p. 66. Rushworth, I, 55. [John Selden (1584–1654), a noted jurist before beginning his political career in 1621; John Pym (1584–1643), member for Calne; Mallory has not been identified by the editors.]

31 [Sir Dudley Digges (1583–1639), member for Tewkesbury; Sir Thomas Crew, member for the borough of Northampton, later (1623), speaker of the House of Commons; Sir Nathaniel Rich (1585–1636), member for East Retford; Sir James Perrot (1571–1637), member for Haverfordwest.]

land, in order to execute some business.[32] The king, at that time, enjoyed, at least exercised, the prerogative of employing any man, even without his consent, in any branch of public service.

Sir John Savile,[33] a powerful man in the house of commons, and a zealous opponent of the court, was made comptroller of the household, a privy counsellor, and soon after a baron.[34] This event is memorable; as being the first instance, perhaps, in the whole history of England, of any king's advancing a man on account of parliamentary interest, and of opposition to his measures. However irregular this practice, it will be regarded by political reasoners, as one of the most early and most infallible symptoms of a regular established liberty.

The king having thus, with so rash and indiscreet a hand, torn off that sacred veil which had hitherto covered the English constitution, and which threw an obscurity upon it, so advantageous to royal prerogative, every man began to indulge himself in political reasonings and inquiries; and the same factions which commenced in parliament were propagated throughout the nation. In vain did James, by reiterated proclamations, forbid the discoursing of state affairs.[35] Such proclamations, if they had any effect, served rather to inflame the curiosity of the public. And, in every company or society, the late transactions became the subject of argument and debate.

All history, said the partisans of the court, as well as the history of England, justify the king's position with regard to the origin of popular privileges; and every reasonable man must allow, that, as monarchy is the most simple form of government, it must first have occurred to rude and uninstructed mankind. The other complicated and artificial additions were the succes-

32 Franklyn, p. 66. Rushworth, I, 55.

33 [John Savile, first Baron Savile of Pontefract (1556–1630).]

34 Kennet, p. 749.

35 Franklyn, p. 56. Rushworth, I, 21, 36, 55. The king also, in imitation of his predecessors, gave rules to preachers. Franklyn, p. 70. The pulpit was at that time much more dangerous than the press. Few people could read, and still fewer were in the practice of reading.

sive invention of sovereigns and legislators; or, if they were
obtruded on the prince by seditious subjects, their origin must
appear, on that very account, still more precarious and unfavourable. In England, the authority of the king, in all the
exterior forms of government, and in the common style of law,
appears totally absolute and sovereign; nor does the real spirit
of the constitution, as it has ever discovered itself in practice,
fall much short of these appearances. The parliament is created
by his will; by his will it is dissolved. It is his will alone, though
at the desire of both houses, which gives authority to laws. To
all foreign nations, the majesty of the monarch seems to merit
sole attention and regard. And no subject, who has exposed
himself to royal indignation, can hope to live with safety in the
kingdom; nor can he even leave it, according to law, without
the consent of his master. If a magistrate, environed with such
power and splendour, should consider his authority as sacred,
and regard himself as the anointed of heaven, his pretensions
may bear a very favourable construction. Or, allowing them to
be merely pious frauds, we need not be surprised, that the same
stratagem which was practised by Minos, Numa, and the most
celebrated legislators of antiquity, should now, in these restless
and inquisitive times, be employed by the king of England. Subjects are not raised above that quality, though assembled in
parliament. The same humble respect and deference is still due
to their prince. Though he indulges them in the privilege of
laying before him their domestic grievances, with which they
are supposed to be best acquainted, this warrants not their bold
intrusion into every province of government. And, to all judicial examiners, it must appear, "That the lines of duty are as
much transgressed by a more independent and less respectful
exercise of acknowledged powers, as by the usurpation of such
as are new and unusual."

The lovers of liberty, throughout the nation, reasoned after
a different manner. It is in vain, said they, that the king traces
up the English government to its first origin, in order to represent the privileges of parliament as dependent and precarious:
Prescription, and the practice of so many ages, must, long ere

this time have given a sanction to these assemblies, even though they had been derived from an origin no more dignified than that which he assigns them. If the written records of the English nation, as asserted, represent parliaments to have arisen from the consent of monarchs, the principles of human nature, when we trace grovernment a step higher, must show us, that monarchs themselves owe all their authority to the voluntary submission of the people. But, in fact, no age can be shown, when the English government was altogether an unmixed monarchy: And, if the privileges of the nation have, at any period, been overpowered by violent irruptions of foreign force or domestic usurpation; the generous spirit of the people has ever seized the first opportunity of re-establishing the ancient government and constitution. Though in the style of the laws, and in the usual forms of administration, royal authority may be represented as sacred and supreme; whatever is essential to the exercise of sovereign and legislative power must still be regarded as equally divine and inviolable. Or, if any distinction be made in this respect, the preference is surely due to those national councils, by whose interposition the exorbitancies of tyrannical power are restrained, and that sacred liberty is preserved, which heroic spirits, in all ages, have deemed more precious than life itself. Nor is it sufficient to say, that the mild and equitable administration of James affords little occasion, or no occasion of complaint. How moderate soever the exercise of his prerogative, how exact soever his observance of the laws and constitution; "If he founds his authority on arbitrary and dangerous principles, it is requisite to watch him with the same care, and to oppose him with the same vigour, as if he had indulged himself in all the excesses of cruelty and tyranny."

Amidst these disputes, the wise and moderate in the nation endeavoured to preserve, as much as possible, an equitable neutrality between the opposite parties; and the more they reflected on the course of public affairs, the greater difficulty they found in fixing just sentiments with regard to them. On the one hand, they regarded the very rise of parties as a happy prognostic of the establishment of liberty; nor could they ever expect to enjoy, in a mixed government, so invaluable a bless-ing, without suffering that inconvenience, which, in such gov-ernments, has ever attended it. But, when they considered, on the other hand, the necessary aims and pursuits of both parties, they were struck with apprehension of the consequences, and could discover no feasible plan of accommodation between them. From long practice, the crown was now possessed of so exorbitant a prerogative, that it was not sufficient for liberty to remain on the defensive, or endeavour to secure the little ground which was left her: It was become necessary to carry on an offensive war, and to circumscribe, within more narrow, as well as more exact bounds, the authority of the sovereign. Upon such provocation, it could not but happen that the prince, however just and moderate, would endeavour to repress his opponents; and, as he stood upon the very brink of arbitrary power, it was to be feared that he would, hastily and unknow-ingly, pass those limits, which were not precisely marked by the constitution. The turbulent government of England, ever fluc-tuating between privilege and prerogative, would afford a variety of precedents, which might be pleaded on both sides. In such delicate questions, the people must be divided: The arms of the state were still in their hands: A civil war must ensue; a civil war, where no party or both parties would justly bear the blame, and where the good and virtuous would scarcely know what vows to form; were it not that liberty, so necessary to the perfection of human society, would be sufficient to bias their affections towards the side of its defenders.

## *From* Chapter XLIX—James I

1624    THE KING, having broken with Spain, was obliged to concert new measures; and, without the assistance of parliament, no effectual step of any kind could be taken. The benevolence, which, during the interval, had been rigorously exacted for recovering the Palatinate, though levied for so popular an end, had procured to the king less money than ill-will from his subjects.[1] Whatever discouragements, therefore, he might receive from his ill agreement with former parliaments, there was a necessity of summoning once more this assembly: And, it might be hoped, that the Spanish alliance, which gave such umbrage, being abandoned, the commons would now be better satisfied with the king's administration. In his speech to the houses, James dropped some hints of his causes of complaint against Spain; and he graciously condescended to ask the advice of parliament, which he had ever before rejected, with regard to the conduct of so important an affair as his son's marriage.[2] Buckingham delivered, to a committee of lords and commons, a long narrative, which he pretended to be true and complete, of every step taken in the negociations with Philip:[3] But partly by the suppression of some facts, partly by the false colouring laid on others, this narrative was calculated entirely to mislead the parliament, and to throw on the court of Spain the reproach of artifice and insincerity. He said that, after many years nego-

[1] To show by what violent measures benevolences were usually raised, Robert Johnston tells us, in his *Historia rerum Britannicarum,* that Barnes, a citizen of London, was the first who refused to contribute any thing; upon which the treasurer sent him word, that he must immediately prepare himself to carry by post a dispatch into Ireland. The citizen was glad to make his peace, by paying a hundred pounds; and no one durst afterwards refuse the benevolence required. See farther, Coke, p. 80.

[2] Franklyn, p. 79. Rushworth, I, 115. Kennet, p. 778.

[3] [Philip IV, who succeeded his father, Philip III, in 1621.]

ciation, the king found not himself any nearer his purpose; and that Bristol[4] had never brought the treaty beyond general professions and declarations: That the prince, doubting the good intentions of Spain, resolved at last to take a journey to Madrid, and put the matter to the utmost trial: That he there found such artificial dealing as made him conclude all the steps taken towards the marriage to be false and deceitful: That the restitution of the Palatinate, which had ever been regarded by the king as an essential preliminary, was not seriously intended by Spain: And that, after enduring much bad usage, the prince was obliged to return to England, without any hopes, either of obtaining the infanta, or of restoring the elector palatine.[5]

This narrative, which, considering the importance of the occasion, and the solemnity of that assembly to which it was delivered, deserves great blame, was yet vouched for truth by the prince of Wales, who was present; and the king himself lent it, indirectly, his authority, by telling the parliament that it was by his orders Buckingham laid the whole affair before them. The conduct of these princes it is difficult fully to excuse. It is in vain to plead the youth and inexperience of Charles; unless his inexperience and youth, as is probable,[6] if not certain, really led him into error, and made him swallow all the falsities of Buckingham. And though the king was here hurried from his own measures by the impetuosity of others; nothing should

4 [John Digby, first Earl of Bristol (1580–1653), ambassador to Spain.]

5 Franklyn, pp. 89, 90, 91ff. Rushworth, I, 119, 120ff. *Parliamentary History*, VI, 20, 21ff.

6* The moment the prince embarked at St. Andero's, he said, to those about him, that it was folly in the Spaniards to use him so ill, and allow him to depart: a proof that the duke had made him believe they were insincere in the affair of the marriage and the Palatinate: for, as to his reception, in other respects, it had been altogether unexceptionable. Besides, had not the prince believed the Spaniards to be insincere, he had no reason to quarrel with them, though Buckingham had. It appears, therefore, that Charles himself must have been deceived. The multiplied delays of the dispensation, though they arose from accident, afforded Buckingham a plausible pretext for charging the Spaniards with insincerity.

have induced him to prostitute his character, and seem to vouch the impostures, at least false colourings, of his favourite, of which he had so good reason to entertain a suspicion.[7]

Buckingham's narrative, however artfully disguised, contained so many contradictory circumstances, as were sufficient to open the eyes of all reasonable men; but it concurred so well with the passions and prejudices of the parliament, that no scruple was made of immediately adopting it.[8] Charmed with having obtained at length the opportunity, so long wished for, of going to war with papists, they little thought of future consequences; but immediately advised the king to break off both treaties with Spain, as well that which regarded the marriage, as that for the restitution of the Palatinate.[9] The people, ever greedy of war, till they suffer by it, displayed their triumph at these violent measures by public bonfires and rejoicings, and by insults on the Spanish ministers. Buckingham was now the favourite of the public, and of the parliament. Sir Edward Coke, in the house of commons, called him the Saviour of the nation.[10] Every place resounded with his praises. And he himself, intoxicated by a popularity which he enjoyed so little time, and which he so ill deserved, violated all duty to his indulgent master, and entered into cabals with the puritanical members, who had ever opposed the royal authority. He even encouraged schemes for abolishing the order of bishops, and selling the dean and chapter lands, in order to defray the expences of a Spanish war. And the king, though he still entertained projects for temporising, and for forming an accommodation with Spain, was so borne down by the torrent of popular prejudices, conducted and increased by Buckingham, that he was at last obliged, in a speech to parliament, to declare in favour of hostile measures,

[7] It must, however, be confessed, that the king afterwards warned the house not to take Buckingham's narrative for his, though it was laid before them by his order. *Parliamentary History*, VI, 104. James was probably ashamed to have been carried so far by his favourite.

[8] *Parliamentary History*, VI, 75.

[9] Franklyn, p. 98. Rushworth, I, 128. *Parliamentary History*, VI, 103.

[10] Clarendon [i.e., Edward Hyde, Earl of Clarendon], *History of the Rebellion*, I, 6.

if they would engage to support him.[11] Doubts of their sincerity in this respect, doubts which the event showed not to be ill-grounded, had probably been one cause of his former pacific and dilatory measures.

In his speech on this occasion, the king began with lamenting his own unhappiness, that, having so long valued himself on the epithet of the pacific monarch, he should now, in his old age, be obliged to exchange the blessings of peace for the inevitable calamities of war. He represented to them the immense and continued expense requisite for military armaments; and besides supplies, from time to time, as they should become necessary, he demanded a vote of six subsidies and twelve fifteenths, as a proper stock before the commencement of hostilities. He told them of his intolerable debts, chiefly contracted by the sums remitted to the Palatine;[12] but he added, that he did not insist on any supply for his own relief, and that it was sufficient for him, if the honour and security of the public were provided for. To remove all suspicion, he, who had ever strenuously maintained his prerogative, and who had even extended it into some points esteemed doubtful, now made an imprudent concession, of which the consequences might have proved fatal to royal authority: He voluntarily offered, that the money voted should be paid to a committe of parliament, and should be issued by them, without being entrusted to his management.[13]

[11] Franklyn, pp. 94, 95. Rushworth, I, 129, 130.

[12]* Among other particulars, he mentions a sum of eighty thousand pounds borrowed from the king of Denmark. In a former speech to the parliament, he told them, that he had expended five hundred thousand pounds in the cause of the Palatine, besides the voluntary contribution given him by the people. See Franklyn, p. 50. But what is more extraordinary, the treasurer, in order to show his own good services, boasts to the parliament, that, by his contrivance, sixty thousand pounds had been saved in the article of exchange in the sums remitted to the Palatine. This seems a great sum, nor is it easy to conceive whence the king could procure such vast sums as would require a sum so considerable to be paid in exchange. From the whole, however, it appears, that the king had been far from neglecting the interests of his daughter and son-in-law, and had even gone far beyond what his narrow revenue could afford.

[13] Rushworth, I, 137.

The commons willingly accepted of this concession, so unusual in an English monarch; they voted him only three subsidies and three fifteenths:[14] And they took no notice of the complaints which he made of his own wants and necessities.

Advantage was also taken of the present good agreement between the king and parliament, in order to pass the bill against monopolies, which had formerly been encouraged by the king, but which had failed by the rupture between him and the last house of commons. This bill was conceived in such terms as to render it merely declaratory; and all monopolies were condemned as contrary to law and to the known liberties of the people. It was there supposed, that every subject of England had entire power to dispose of his own actions, provided he did no injury to any of his fellow-subjects; and that no prerogative of the king, no power of any magistrate, nothing but the authority alone of laws, could restrain that unlimited freedom. The full prosecution of this noble principle into all its natural consequences, has at last, through many contests, produced that singular and happy government which we enjoy at present.[15]

.    .    .    .    .    .    .    .    .    .    .

This session an address was also made, very disagreeable to the king, craving the severe execution of the laws against cath-

[14] Less than three hundred thousand pounds.

[15*] How little this principle had prevailed, during any former period of the English government, particularly during the last reign, which was certainly not so perfect a model of liberty as most writers would represent it, will easily appear from many passages in the history of that reign. But the ideas of men were much changed, during about twenty years of a gentle and peaceful administration. The commons, though James, of himself, had recalled all patents of monopolies, were not contented without a law against them, and a declaratory law too; which was gaining a great point, and establishing principles very favourable to liberty: but they were extremely grateful, when Elizabeth, upon petition (after having once refused their requests) recalled a few of the most oppressive patents; and employed some soothing expressions towards them.

The parliament had surely reason, when they confessed, in the seventh of James, that he allowed them more freedom of debate, than ever was indulged by any of his predecessors. His indulgence in this particular, joined to his easy temper, was probably one cause of the great power assumed by the commons. Monsieur de la Boderie, in his dispatches, I, 449, mentions the liberty of speech in the house of commons as a new practice.

olics. His answer was gracious and condescending;[16] though he declared against persecution, as being an improper measure for the suppression of any religion, according to the received maxim, "That the blood of the martyrs was the seed of the church." He also condemned an entire indulgence of the catholics; and seemed to represent a middle course, as the most humane and most politic. He went so far as even to affirm, with an oath, that he never had entertained any thoughts of granting a toleration to these religionists.[17] The liberty of exercising their worship in private houses, which he had secretly agreed to in the Spanish treaty, did not appear to him deserving that name; and it was probably by means of this explication, he thought that he had saved his honour. And as Buckingham, in his narrative,[18] confessed, that the king had agreed to a temporary suspension of the penal laws against the catholics, which he distinguished from a toleration, a term at that time extremely odious, James naturally deemed his meaning to be sufficiently explained, and feared not any reproach of falsehood or duplicity, on account of this asseveration. After all these transactions, the parliament was prorogued by the king, who let fall some hints, though in gentle terms, of the sense which he entertained of their unkindness, in not supplying his necessities.[19]

*     *     *     *     *     *     *     *     *     *     *     1625

[James'] reign was now drawing towards a conclusion. With peace, so successfully cultivated, and so passionately loved by this monarch, his life also terminated. This spring he was seized with a tertian ague; and, when encouraged by his courtiers with the common proverb, that such a distemper, during that season, was health for a king, he replied, that the proverb was meant of a young king. After some fits, he found himself extremely weakened, and sent for the prince, whom he exhorted to bear a tender affection for his wife, but to preserve a constancy in religion; to protect the church of England; and to

16 Franklyn, pp. 101, 102.
17 See farther, Franklyn, p. 87.
18 *Parliamentary History*, VI, p. 37.
19 Franklyn, p. 103.

extend his care towards the unhappy family of the palatine.[20] With decency and courage he prepared himself for his end; and he expired on the 27th of March, after a reign over England of twenty-two years and some days; and in the fifty-ninth year of his age. His reign over Scotland was almost of equal duration with his life. In all history, it would be difficult to find a reign less illustrious, yet more unspotted and unblemished, than that of James in both kingdoms.

No prince, so little enterprising and so inoffensive, was ever so much exposed to the opposite extremes of calumny and flattery, of satire and panegyric. And the factions, which began in his time, being still continued, have made his character be as much disputed to this day, as is commonly that of princes who are our contemporaries. Many virtues, however, it must be owned, he was possessed of; but scarce any of them pure, or free from the contagion of the neighbouring vices. His generosity bordered on profusion, his learning on pedantry, his pacific disposition on pusillanimity, his wisdom on cunning, his friendship on light fancy and boyish fondness. While he imagined that he was only maintaining his own authority, he may perhaps be suspected in a few of his actions, and still more of his pretensions, to have somewhat encroached on the liberties of his people: While he endeavoured, by an exact neutrality, to acquire the good-will of all his neighbours, he was able to preserve fully the esteem and regard of none. His capacity was considerable; but fitter to discourse on general maxims than to conduct any intricate business: His intentions were just; but more adapted to the conduct of private life, than to the government of kingdoms. Awkward in his person, and ungainly in his manners, he was ill qualified to command respect; partial and undiscerning in his affections, he was little fitted to acquire general love. Of a feeble temper more than of a frail judgment: Exposed to our ridicule from his vanity; but exempt from our hatred by his freedom from pride and arrogance. And upon the whole, it may be pronounced of his character, that all his qual-

20 Rushworth, I, 155.

ities were sullied with weakness and embellished by humanity. Of political courage he certainly was destitute; and thence chiefly is derived the strong prejudice which prevails against his personal bravery: An inference, however, which must be owned, from general experience, to be extremely fallacious.

# *From* the Appendix to the Reign of James I

WHAT CHIEFLY renders the reign of James memorable, is the commencement of the English colonies in America; colonies established on the noblest footing that has been known in any age or nation. The Spaniards, being the first discoverers of the new world, immediately took possession of the precious mines which they found there; and, by the allurement of great riches, they were tempted to depopulate their own country, as well as that which they conquered; and added the vice of sloth to those of avidity and barbarity, which had attended their adventurers in those renowned enterprises. That fine coast was entirely neglected, which reaches from St. Augustin to Cape Breton, and which lies in all the temperate climates, is watered by noble rivers, and offers a fertile soil, but nothing more, to the industrious planter. Peopled gradually from England by the necessitous and indigent, who, at home, increased neither wealth nor populousness, the colonies, which were planted along that tract, have promoted the navigation, encouraged the industry, and even perhaps multiplied the inhabitants of their mother-country. The spirit of independency, which was reviving in England, here shone forth in its full lustre, and received new accession from the aspiring character of those, who, being discontented with the established church and monarchy, had sought for freedom amidst those savage desarts.

Queen Elizabeth had done little more than give a name to the continent of Virginia; and, after her planting one feeble colony, which quickly decayed, that country was entirely abandoned. But when peace put an end to the military enterprises against Spain, and left ambitious spirits no hopes of making any longer such rapid advances towards honour and fortune, the nation began to second the pacific intentions of its monarch, and to seek a surer, though slower expedient, for acquiring riches and glory. In 1606, Newport[1] carried over a colony, and began a settlement; which the company erected by patent for that purpose in London and Bristol, took care to supply with yearly recruits of provisions, utensils, and new inhabitants. About 1609, Argal[2] discovered a more direct and shorter passage to Virginia; and left the track of the ancient navigators, who had first directed their course southwards to the tropic, sailed westward by means of the trade-winds, and then turned northward, till they reached the English settlements. The same year, five hundred persons under Sir Thomas Gates and Sir George Somers[3] were embarked for Virginia. Somers's ship, meeting with a tempest, was driven into the Bermudas, and laid the foundation of a settlement in those islands. Lord Delawar[4] afterwards undertook the government of the English colonies: but notwithstanding all his care, seconded by supplies from James, and by money raised from the first lottery ever known in the kingdom, such difficulties attended the settlement of these countries, that, in 1614, there were not alive more than four hundred men, of all that had been sent thither. After supplying themselves with provisions more immediately necessary for the support of life, the new planters began the cultivating of tobacco; and James, notwithstanding his antipathy to that drug, which he affirmed to be pernicious to men's morals as well as their health,[5] gave them permission to enter it in England; and he inhibited by proclamation all importation of it from Spain.[6] By degrees, new colonies were established in that

1 [Christopher Newport (1565?–1617); between 1606 and 1611, Newport made five voyages to Virginia, the fourth by way of Bermuda. See footnote 3, below.]

2 [Sir Samuel Argall (d. 1626), deputy governor of Virginia.]

3 [Thomas Gates (d. 1621), governor of Virginia; Sir George Somers or Summers (1554–1610), leader of the expedition and hence credited with the rediscovery (after Juan Bermudes, 1515) of the Bermudas. Newport was a member of this expedition.]

4 [Thomas West, third or twelfth Baron de la Warr (1577–1618), first governor of Virginia.]

5 Rymer, Bk. XVII, p. 621.

6 Rymer, Bk. XVIII, pp. 621, 633.

continent, and gave new names to the places where they settled, leaving that of Virginia to the province first planted. The island of Barbadoes was also planted in this reign.

Speculative reasoners, during that age, raised many objections to the planting of those remote colonies; and foretold, that, after draining their mother-country of inhabitants, they would soon shake off her yoke, and erect an independent government in America: but time has shown, that the views, entertained by those who encouraged such generous undertakings, were more just and solid. A mild government and great naval force have preserved, and may still preserve during some time, the dominion of England over her colonies. And such advantages have commerce and navigation reaped from these establishments, that more than four of the English shipping is at present computed to be employed in carrying on the traffic with the American settlements.

Agriculture was anciently very imperfect in England. The sudden transitions so often mentioned by historians, from the lowest to the highest price of grain, and the prodigious inequality of its value in different years, are sufficient proofs, that the produce depended entirely on the seasons, and that art had as yet done nothing to fence against the injuries of the heavens. During this reign, considerable improvements were made, as in most arts, so in this, the most beneficial of any. A numerous catalogue might be formed of books and pamphlets treating of husbandry, which were written about this time. The nation, however, was still dependent on foreigners for daily bread; and though its exportation of grain now forms a considerable branch of its commerce, notwithstanding its probable increase of people, there was, in that period, a regular importation from the Baltic as well as from France; and if it ever stopped, the bad consequences were sensibly felt by the nation. Sir Walter Raleigh in his observations computes, that two millions went out at one time for corn. It was not till the fifth of Elizabeth, that the exportation of corn had been allowed in England; and

Camden observes, that agriculture, from that moment, received new life and vigour.

The endeavours of James, or, more properly speaking, those of the nation, for promoting trade, were attended with greater success than those for the encouragement of learning. Though the age was by no means destitute of eminent writers, a very bad taste in general prevailed during that period; and the monarch himself was not a little infected with it.

On the origin of letters among the Greeks, the genius of poets and orators, as might naturally be expected, was distinguished by an amiable simplicity, which, whatever rudeness may sometimes attend it, is so fitted to express the genuine movements of nature and passion, that the compositions possessed of it must ever appear valuable to the discerning part of mankind. The glaring figures of discourse, the pointed antithesis, the unnatural conceit, the jingle of words; such false ornaments were not employed by early writers; not because they were rejected, but because they scarcely ever occurred to them. An easy unforced strain of sentiment runs through their compositions; though at the same time we may observe, that amidst the most elegant simplicity of thought and expression, one is sometimes surprised to meet with a poor conceit, which had presented itself unsought for, and which the author had not acquired critical observation enough to condemn.[7] A bad taste seizes with avidity these frivolous beauties, and even perhaps a good taste, ere surfeited by them: they multiply every day more and more in the fashionable compositions: nature and good sense are neglected: laboured ornaments studied and admired:

---

[7] The name of Polynices, one of Oedipus's sons, means in the original "much quarrelling." In the altercations between the two brothers, in Aeschylus, Sophocles, and Euripides, this conceit is employed; and it is remarkable, that so poor a conundrum could not be rejected by any of these three poets, so justly celebrated for their taste and simplicity. What could Shakespeare have done worse? Terence has his *inceptio est amentium, non amantium.* Many similar instances will occur to the learned. It is well known, that Aristotle treats very seriously of puns, divides them into several classes, and recommends the use of them to orators.

and a total degeneracy of style and language prepares the way for barbarism and ignorance. Hence the Asiatic manner was found to depart so much from the simple purity of Athens: hence that tinsel eloquence which is observable in many of the Roman writers, from which Cicero himself is not wholly exempted, and which so much prevails in Ovid, Seneca, Lucan, Martial, and the Plinys.

On the revival of letters, when the judgment of the public is yet raw and unformed, this false glitter catches the eye, and leaves no room, either in eloquence or poetry, for the durable beauties of solid sense and lively passion. The reigning genius is then diametrically opposite to that which prevails on the first origin of arts. The Italian writers, it is evident, even the most celebrated, have not reached the proper simplicity of thought and composition; and in Petrarch, Tasso, Guarini, frivolous witticisms and forced conceits are but too predominant. The period during which letters were cultivated in Italy, was so short as scarcely to allow leisure for correcting this adulterated relish.

The more early French writers are liable to the same reproach. Voiture, Balzac, even Corneille, have too much affected those ambitious ornaments, of which the Italians in general, and the least pure of the ancients supplied them with so many models. And it was not till late, that observation and reflection give rise to a more natural turn of thought and composition among that elegant people.

A like character may be extended to the first English writers; such as flourished during the reigns of Elizabeth and James, and even till long afterwards. Learning, on its revival in this island, was attired in the same unnatural garb which it wore at the time of its decay among the Greeks and Romans. And, what may be regarded as a misfortune, the English writers were possessed of great genius before they were endowed with any degree of taste, and by that means gave a kind of sanction to those forced turns and sentiments which they so much affected. Their distorted conceptions and expressions are attended with such

vigour of mind, that we admire the imagination which produced them, as much as we blame the want of judgment which
gave them admittance. To enter into an exact criticism of the
writers of that age, would exceed our present purpose. A short
character of the most eminent, delivered with the same freedom
which history exercises over kings and ministers, may not be
improper. The national prepossessions, which prevail, will perhaps render the former liberty not the least perilous for an
author.

If Shakespeare be considered as a *man,* born in a rude age,
and educated in the lowest manner, without any instruction,
either from the world or from books, he may be regarded as a
prodigy: if represented as a *poet,* capable of furnishing a proper
entertainment to a refined or intelligent audience, we must
abate much of this eulogy. In his compositions, we regret, that
many irregularities, and even absurdities, should so frequently
disfigure the animated and passionate scenes intermixed with
them; and at the same time, we perhaps admire the more those
beauties, on account of their being surrounded with such de-
formities. A striking peculiarity of sentiment, adapted to a
single character, he frequently hits, as it were by inspiration;
but a reasonable propriety of thought he cannot for any time
uphold. Nervous and picturesque expressions, as well as descriptions, abound in him; but it is in vain we look either for purity
or simplicity of diction. His total ignorance of all theatrical art
and conduct, however material a defect; yet, as it affects the
spectator, rather than the reader, we can more easily excuse,
than that want of taste which often prevails in his productions,
and which gives way, only by intervals, to irradiations of genius.
A great and fertile genius he certainly possessed, and one enriched equally with a tragic and comic vein; but he ought to
be cited as a proof, how dangerous it is to rely on these advantages alone for attaining an excellence in the finer arts.[8] And

8 *Invenire etiam barbari solent, disponere et ornare non nisi eruditus*
["Even barbarians are wont to discover, but not to arrange and embellish
unless learned"]–Pliny.

there may even remain a suspicion, that we over-rate, if possible, the greatness of his genius; in the same manner as bodies often appear more gigantic, on account of their being disproportioned and misshapen. He died in 1616, aged fifty-three years.

Jonson[9] possessed all the learning which was wanting to Shakespeare, and wanted all the genius of which the other was possessed. Both of them were equally deficient in taste and elegance, in harmony and correctness. A servile copyist of the ancients, Jonson translated into bad English the beautiful passages of the Greek and Roman authors, without accommodating them to the manners of his age and country. His merit has been totally eclipsed by that of Shakespeare, whose rude genius prevailed over the rude art of his contemporary. The English theatre has ever since taken a strong tincture of Shakespeare's spirit and character; and thence it has proceeded, that the nation has undergone from all its neighbours, the reproach of barbarism, from which its valuable productions in some other parts of learning would otherwise have exempted it. Jonson had a pension of a hundred marks from the king, which Charles afterwards augmented to a hundred pounds. He died in 1637, aged sixty-three.

Fairfax[10] has translated Tasso with an elegance and ease, and, at the same time with an exactness, which for that age are surprising. Each line in the original is faithfully rendered by a correspondent line in the translation. Harrington's[11] translation of Ariosto is not likewise without its merit. It is to be regretted that these poets should have imitated the Italians in their stanza, which has a prolixity and uniformity in it that displeases in long performances. They had otherwise, as well as Spenser,[12] who went before them, contributed much to the polishing and refining of English versification.

In Donne's[13] satires, when carefully inspected, there appear

9 [Ben Jonson (1573?–1637), playwright and poet.]
10 [Edward Fairfax (d. 1635) translated Tasso's *Gerusalemme Liberata*.]
11 [Sir John Harington (1561–1612) translated Ariosto's *Orlando Furioso*.]
12 [Edmund Spenser (1552–1599), poet.]
13 [John Donne (1573–1631), poet and dean of St. Paul's.]

some flashes of wit and ingenuity; but these totally suffocated and buried by the hardest and most uncouth expression that is any-where to be met with.

If the poetry of the English was so rude and imperfect during that age, we may reasonably expect that their prose would be liable still to greater objections. Though the latter appears the more easy, as it is the more natural method of composition; it has ever in practice been found the more rare and difficult; and there scarcely is an instance in any language, that it has reached a degree of perfection before the refinement of poetical numbers and expression. English prose, during the reign of James, was written with little regard to the rules of grammar, and with a total disregard to the elegance and harmony of the period. Stuffed with Latin sentences and quotations, it likewise imitated those inversions which, however forcible and graceful in the ancient languages, are entirely contrary to the idiom of the English. I shall indeed venture to affirm, that, whatever uncouth phrases and expressions occur in old books, they were chiefly owing to the unformed taste of the author; and that the language, spoken in the courts of Elizabeth and James, was very little different from that which we meet with at present in good company. Of this opinion the little scraps of speeches which are found in the parliamentary journals, and which carry an air so opposite to the laboured orations, seem to be a sufficient proof; and there want not productions of that age, which, being written by men who were not authors by profession, retain a very natural manner, and may give us some idea of the language which prevailed among men of the world. I shall particularly mention Sir John Davis's *Discovery,* Throgmorton's, Essex's, and Nevil's letters. In a more early period, Cavendish's life of cardinal Wolsey, the pieces that remain of bishop Gardiner, and Anne Boleyn's letter to the king, differ little or nothing from the language of our time.

The great glory of literature in this island, during the reign of James, was lord Bacon. Most of his performances were composed in Latin; though he possessed neither the elegance of that, nor of his native tongue. If we consider the variety of talents displayed by this man; as a public speaker, a man of business, a wit, a courtier, a companion, an author, a philosopher; he is justly the object of great admiration. If we consider him merely as an author and philosopher, the light in which we view him at present, though very estimable, he was yet inferior to his co-temporary Galilaeo, perhaps even to Kepler. Bacon pointed out at a distance the road to true philosophy: Galilaeo both pointed it out to others, and made himself considerable advances in it. The Englishman was ignorant of geometry: the Florentine revived that science, excelled in it, and was the first that applied it, together with experiment, to natural philosophy. The former rejected, with the most positive disdain, the system of Copernicus: the latter fortified it with new proofs, derived both from reason and the senses. Bacon's style is stiff and rigid: his wit, though often brilliant, is also often unnatural and far-fetched; and he seems to be the original of those pointed similies and long-spun allegories, which so much distinguish the English authors: Galilaeo is a lively and agreeable, though somewhat a prolix writer. But Italy, not united in any single government, and perhaps satiated with that literary glory which it has possessed both in ancient and modern times, has too much neglected the renown which it has acquired by giving birth to so great a man. That national spirit which prevails among the English, and which forms their great happiness, is the cause why they bestow on all their eminent writers, and on Bacon among the rest, such praises and acclamations, as may often appear partial and excessive. He died in 1626, in the sixty-sixth year of his age.

If the reader of Raleigh's history[14] can have the patience to wade through the Jewish and Rabbinical learning which compose the half of the volume, he will find, when he comes to the Greek and Roman story, that his pains are not unrewarded. Raleigh is the best model of that ancient style, which some writers would affect to revive at present. He was beheaded in 1618, aged sixty-six years.

14 [Sir Walter Raleigh (1552?–1618) wrote a *History of the World*.]

Camden's history[15] of queen Elizabeth may be esteemed good composition, both for style and matter. It is written with simplicity of expression, very rare in that age, and with a regard to truth. It would not perhaps be too much to affirm, that it is among the best historical productions which have yet been composed by any Englishman. It is well known that the English have not much excelled in that kind of literature. He died in 1623, aged seventy-three years.

We shall mention the king himself at the end of these English writers; because that is *his* place, when considered as an author. It may safely be affirmed, that the mediocrity of James's talents in literature, joined to the great change in national taste, is one cause of that contempt under which his memory labours, and which is often carried by party-writers to a great extreme. It is remarkable how different from ours were the sentiments of the ancients with regard to learning. Of the first twenty Roman emperors, counting from Caesar to Severus, above the half were authors; and though few of them seem to have been eminent in that profession, it is always remarked to their praise, that by their example they encouraged literature. Not to mention Germanicus, and his daughter Agrippina, persons so nearly allied to the throne, the greater part of the classic writers, whose works remain, were men of the highest quality. As every human advantage is attended with inconveniences, the change of men's ideas in this particular may probably be ascribed to the invention of printing; which has rendered books so common, that even men of slender fortunes can have access to them.

That James was but a middling writer may, be allowed: that he was a contemptible one, can by no means be admitted. Whoever will read his Basilicon Doron, particularly the two last books, the true law of free monarchies, his answer to cardinal Perron, and almost all his speeches and messages to parliament, will confess him to have possessed no mean genius. If he wrote

15 [William Camden (1551–1623), antiquarian and historian, author of *Annales rerum Anglicarum et Hibernicaruma regnante Elizabetha, ad annum Salutis MDXXXIX.*]

concerning witches and apparitions; who, in that age, did not admit the reality of these fictitious beings? If he has composed a commentary on the Revelations, and proved the pope to be antichrist; may not a similar reproach be extended to the famous Napier; and even to Newton,[16] at a time when learning was much more advanced than during the reign of James? From the grossness of its superstitions, we may infer the ignorance of an age; but never should pronounce concerning the folly of an individual, from his admitting popular errors, consecrated by the appearance of religion.

Such a superiority do the pursuits of literature possess above every other occupation, that even he who attains but a mediocrity in them, merits the pre-eminence above those that excel the most in the common and vulgar professions. The speaker of the house of commons is usually an eminent lawyer; yet the harangue of his majesty will always be found much superior to that of the speaker, in every parliament during this reign.

Every science, as well as polite literature, must be considered as being yet in its infancy. Scholastic learning and polemical divinity retarded the growth of all true knowledge. Sir Henry Saville,[17] in the preamble of that deed by which he annexed a salary to the mathematical and astronomical professors in Oxford, says, that geometry was almost totally abandoned and unknown in England.[18] The best learning of that age was the study of the ancients. Casaubon,[19] eminent for this species of knowledge, was invited over from France by James, and encouraged by a pension of three hundred pounds a year, as well as by church preferments.[20] The famous Antonio di Dominis,

---

[16] [John Napier or Neper, eighth laird of Murchiston (1550–1617), inventor of logarithms, and a passionate Protestant, author of *A Plaine Discovery of the Whole Revelation of Saint John*. Newton's speculative theological writings include *Observations upon the Prophecies of Holy Writ, particularly the Prophecies of Daniel and the Apocalypse of St. John*.]

[17] [Sir Henry Savile (1549–1622), a mathematician himself, established the two Savilian chairs of geometry and astronomy at Oxford in 1619.]

[18] Rymer, Bk. XVII, p. 217.

[19] [Isaac Casaubon (1559–1614).]

[20] Rymer, Bk. XVII, p. 709.

archbishop of Spalatro,[21] no despicable philosopher, came likewise into England, and afforded great triumph to the nation, by their gaining so considerable a proselyte from the papists. But the mortification followed soon after: the archbishop, though advanced to some ecclesiastical preferments,[22] received not encouragement sufficient to satisfy his ambition: he made his escape into Italy, where he died in confinement.

21 [Marco Antonio Dominis (1566–1624); while in England, Dominis published (1619) Paul Sarpi's *History of the Council of Trent,* a manuscript copy of which he had surreptitiously obtained in Venice.]

22 Rymer, Bk. XVII, p. 95.

# *From* Chapter L—Charles I

1625    No SOONER had Charles taken into his hands the reins of government, than he showed an impatience to assemble the great council of the nation; and he would gladly, for the sake of dispatch,
have called together the same parliament, which had sitten
under his father, and which lay at that time under prorogation.
But being told that this measure would appear unusual, he issued writs for summoning a new parliament on the 7th of
May; and it was not without regret that the arrival of the princess Henriettta,[1] whom he had espoused by proxy, obliged him
to delay, by repeated prorogations, their meeting till the eighteenth of June, when they assembled at Westminster for the
dispatch of business. The young prince, unexperienced and impolitic, regarded as sincere all the praises and caresses with
which he had been loaded, while active in procuring the rupture with the house of Austria. And besides that he laboured
under great necessities, he hastened with alacrity to a period
when he might receive the most undoubted testimony of the
dutiful attachment of his subjects. His discourse to the parliament was full of simplicity and cordiality. He lightly mentioned
the occasion which he had for supply.[2] He employed no intrigue
to influence the suffrages of the members. He would not even
allow the officers of the crown, who had seats in the house, to
mention any particular sum which might be expected by him.
Secure of the affections of the commons, he was resolved that
their bounty should be entirely their own deed; unasked, un-
solicited; the genuine fruit of sincere confidence and regard.

     The house of commons accordingly took into consideration
the business of supply. They knew that all the money granted
by the last parliament had been expended on naval and military

---

   1 [Henrietta Maria (1609–1669), youngest daughter of Henry IV of France
by his second wife, Marie de Medicis.]

   2 Rushworth, I, 171. *Parliamentary History*, VI, 346. Franklyn, p. 108.

armaments; and that great anticipations were likewise made on the revenues of the crown. They were not ignorant that Charles was loaded with a large debt, contracted by his father, who had borrowed money both from his own subjects, and from foreign princes. They had learned by experience, that the public revenue could with difficulty maintain the dignity of the crown, even under the ordinary charges of government. They were sensible, that the present war was, very lately, the result of their own importunate applications and entreaties, and that they had solemnly engaged to support their sovereign in the management of it. They were acquainted with the difficulty of military enterprises, directed against the whole house of Austria; against the king of Spain, possessed of the greatest riches and most extensive dominions of any prince in Europe; against the emperor Ferdinand,[3] hitherto the most fortunate monarch of his age, who had subdued and astonished Germany by the rapidity of his victories. Deep impressions they saw, must be made by the English sword, and a vigorous offensive war be waged against these mighty potentates, ere they would resign a principality, which they had now fully subdued, and which they held in secure possession, by its being surrounded with all their other territories.

To answer, therefore, all these great and important ends; to satisfy their young king in the first request which he made them; to prove their sense of the many royal virtues, particularly oeconomy, with which Charles was endowed; the house of commons, conducted by the wisest and ablest senators that had ever flourished in England, thought proper to confer on the king a supply of two subsidies, amounting to 112,000 pounds.[4]

This measure, which discovers rather a cruel mockery of Charles than any serious design of supporting him, appears so extraordinary, when considered in all its circumstances, that it naturally summons up our attention, and raises an inquiry

---

[3] [Ferdinand II (1578–1637), Emperor of the Holy Roman Empire, 1619–1637.]

[4] A subsidy was now fallen to about 56,000 pounds. *Cabala*, p. 224, first edition.

concerning the causes of a conduct, unprecedented in an English parliament. So numerous an assembly, composed of persons of various dispositions, was not, it is probable, wholly influenced by the same motives; and few declared openly their true reason. We shall, therefore, approach nearer to the truth, if we mention all the views which, the present conjuncture could suggest to them.

It is not to be doubted but spleen and ill-will against the duke of Buckingham had an influence with many. So vast and rapid a fortune, so little merited, could not fail to excite public envy; and, however men's hatred might have been suspended for a moment, while the duke's conduct seemed to gratify their passions and their prejudices, it was impossible for him long to preserve the affections of the people. . . .

However the ill-humour of the commons might have been increased by these considerations, we are not to suppose them the sole motives. The last parliament of James, amidst all their joy and festivity, had given him a supply very disproportioned to his demand and to the occasion. And, as every house of commons, which was elected during forty years, succeeded to all the passions and principles of their predecessors; we ought rather to account for this obstinacy from the general situation of the kingdom during that whole period, than from any circumstances which attended this particular conjuncture. . . .

The nation was very little accustomed at that time to the burden of taxes, and had never opened their purses in any degree for supporting their sovereign. Even Elizabeth, notwithstanding her vigour and frugality, and the necessary wars in which she was engaged, had reason to complain of the commons in this particular; nor could the authority of that princess, which was otherwise almost absolute, ever extort from them the requisite supplies. Habits, more than reason, we find, in every thing, to be the governing principle of mankind. . . .

The puritanical party, though disguised, had a great authority over the kingdom; and many of the leaders among the commons had secretly embraced the rigid tenets of that sect. All these were disgusted with the court, both by the prevalence of the principles of civil liberty essential to their party, and on account of the restraint under which they were held by the established hierarchy.

.        .        .        .        .        .        .        .        .

To all these causes we must yet add another of considerable moment. The house of commons, we may observe, was almost entirely governed by a set of men of the most uncommon capacity and the largest views: men, who were now formed into a regular party, and united, as well by fixed aims and projects, as by the hardships which some of them had undergone in prosecution of them. Among these we may mention the names of Sir Edward Coke, Sir Edwin Sandys, Sir Robert Philips, Sir Francis Seymour, Sir Dudley Digges, Sir John Elliot, Sir Thomas Wentworth, Mr. Selden, and Mr. Pym. Animated with a warm regard to liberty, these generous patriots saw with regret an unbounded power exercised by the crown, and were resolved to seize the opportunity, which the king's necessities offered them, of reducing the prerogative within more reasonable compass. Though their ancestors had blindly given way to practices and precedents favourable to kingly power, and had been able, notwithstanding, to preserve some small remains of liberty; it would be impossible, they thought, when all these pretensions were methodized and prosecuted by the increasing knowledge of the age, to maintain any shadow of popular government, in opposition to such unlimited authority in the sovereign. It was necessary to fix a choice: either to abandon entirely the privileges of the people, or to secure them by firmer and more precise barriers than the constitution had hitherto provided for them. In this dilemma, men of such aspiring geniuses, and such independent fortunes, could not long deliberate: they boldly embraced the side of freedom, and resolved to grant no supplies to their necessitous prince, without extorting concessions in favour of civil liberty. The end, they esteemed beneficent and noble; the means, regular and constitutional. To grant or refuse supplies was the undoubted privilege of the commons. And as all human governments, particularly those of a mixed frame, are in continual fluctuation, it was as natural in their opinion, and allowable, for popular assemblies to take advantage of favourable incidents, in order to secure the subject; as for the monarchs, in order to extend their own authority.

.    .    .    .    .    .    .    .    .    .    .

Charles now found himself obliged to depart from that delicacy, which he had formerly maintained. By himself or his ministers, he entered into a particular detail, both of the alliances which he had formed, and of the military operations which he had projected.[5] He told the parliament, that, by a promise of subsidies, he had engaged the king of Denmark to take part in the war; that this monarch intended to enter Germany by the north, and to rouze to arms those princes, who impatiently longed for an opportunity of asserting the liberty of the empire; that Mansfeldt[6] had undertaken to penetrate with an English army into the Palatinate, and by that quarter to excite the members of the evangelical union; that the states must be supported in the unequal warfare which they maintained with Spain; that no less a sum than 700,000 pounds a year had been found, by computation, requisite for all these purposes; that the maintenance of the fleet and the defence of Ireland, demanded an annual expense of 400,000 pounds; that he himself had already exhausted and anticipated, in the public service, his whole revenue, and had scarcely left sufficient for the daily subsistence of himself and his family,[7] that on his accession to the crown, he found a debt of above 300,000 pounds, contracted by his father in support of the palatine; and that, while prince of Wales, he had himself contracted debts, notwithstanding his great frugality, to the amount of 70,000 pounds, which he had expended entirely on naval and military armaments. After mentioning all these facts, the king even condescended to use entreaties. He said, that this request was the first that he had ever made them; that he was young and in the commencement

---

[5] Sir William Dugdale, *A Short View of the Late Troubles in England* . . . , pp. 25, 26.

[6] [Ernst Graf von Mansfield (*ca.* 1580–1626), furnished by James I with men and money for the recovery of the Palatinate.]

[7] *Parliamentary History,* VI, 396.

of his reign; and, if he now met with kind and dutiful usage, it would endear to him the use of parliaments, and would for ever preserve an entire harmony between him and his people.[8]

To these reasons the commons remained inexorable. Notwithstanding that the king's measures, on the supposition of a foreign war, which they had constantly demanded, were altogether unexceptionable, they obstinately refused any farther aid. Some members favourable to the court having insisted on an addition of two fifteenths to the former supply, even this pittance was refused;[9] though it was known that a fleet and army were lying at Portsmouth in great want of pay and provisions; and that Buckingham, the admiral, and the treasurer of the navy, had advanced on their own credit near a hundred thousand pounds for the sea-service.[10]

. . . . . . . . . . . .

Charles, having failed of so rich a prize,[11] was obliged again to have a recourse to a parliament. Though the ill success of his enterprises diminished his authority, and showed every day more plainly the imprudence of the Spanish war; though the increase of his necessities rendered him more dependent, and more exposed to the encroachments of the commons; he was resolved to try once more that regular and constitutional expedient for supply. Perhaps too, a little political art, which at that time he practised, was much trusted to. He had named four popular leaders, sheriffs of counties; Sir Edward Coke, Sir Robert Philips, Sir Thomas Wentworth, and Sir Francis Seymour;[12]

1626

---

8 Rushworth, I, 177, 178 ff. *Parliamentary History*, VI, 399. Franklyn, pp. 108, 109. *Journ.*, 10th August, 1625.

9 Rushworth, I, 190.

10 *Parliamentary History*, VI, 390.

11 [Some Spanish galleons that escaped the English fleet.]

12 [Thomas Wentworth, first Earl of Strafford (1593–1641), who later became lord lieutenant of Ireland as well as trusted adviser to Charles. He was impeached by the House of Commons and, with the reluctant consent of Charles, executed (May 12, 1641); see below, Chap. LIV (p. 344). Francis Seymour, first Baron Seymour of Trowbridge (1590?–1664), member for Wiltshire.]

and, though the question had been formerly much contested,[13] he thought that he had by that means incapacitated them from being elected members. But his intention being so evident, rather put the commons more upon their guard. Enow of patriots still remained to keep up the ill-humour of the house; and men needed but little instruction or rhetoric to recommend to them practices, which increased their own importance and consideration. The weakness of the court also could not more evidently appear, than by its being reduced to use so ineffectual an expedient, in order to obtain an influence over the commons.

The views, therefore, of the last parliament were immediately adopted; as if the same men had been every where elected, and no time had intervened since their meeting. When the king laid before the house his necessities, and asked for supply, they immediately voted him three subsidies and three fifteenths; and though they afterwards added one subsidy more, the sum was little proportioned to the greatness of the occasion, and ill fitted to promote those views of success and glory, for which the young prince, in his first enterprise, so ardently longed. But this circumstance was not the most disagreeable one. The supply was only voted by the commons. The passing of that vote into a law was reserved till the end of the session.[14] A condition was thereby made, in a very undisguised manner, with their sovereign. Under colour of redressing grievances, which during this short reign could not be very numerous, they were to proceed in regulating and controlling every part of government which displeased them: and if the king either cut them short in this undertaking, or refused compliance with their demands, he must not expect any supply from the commons. Great dissatisfaction was expressed by Charles at a treatment, which he deemed so harsh and undutiful.[15] But his urgent necessities

---

[13] It is always an express clause in the writ of summons, that no sheriff shall be chosen; but the contrary practice had often prevailed. D'Ewes, p. 38. Yet still great doubts were entertained on this head. See *Journ.*, 9th April, 1614.

[14] *Journ.*, 27th March, 1626.

[15] *Parliamentary History*, VI, 449. Rushworth, I, 224.

obliged him to submit; and he waited with patience, observing to what side they would turn themselves.

.    .    .    .    .    .    .    .    .    .    .    .

Besides a more stately style which Charles in general affected to this parliament than to the last, he went so far, in a message, as to threaten the commons, that, if they did not furnish him with supplies, he should be obliged to try "new counsels." This language was sufficiently clear: yet, lest any ambiguity should remain, Sir Dudley Carleton,[16] vice-chamberlain, took care to explain it. "I pray you consider," said he, "what these new counsels are or may be. I fear to declare those that I conceive. In all Christian kingdoms, you know that parliaments were in use anciently, by which those kingdoms were governed in a most flourishing manner; until the monarchs began to know their own strength, and, seeing the turbulent spirit of their parliaments, at length they, by little and little, began to stand on their prerogatives, and at last overthrew the parliaments, throughout Christendom, except here only with us.—Let us be careful then to preserve the king's good opinion of parliaments, which bringeth such happiness to the nation, and makes us envied of all others, while there is this sweetness between his majesty and the commons; lest we lose the repute of a free people by our turbulency in parliament."[17] These imprudent suggestions rather gave warning than struck terror. A precarious liberty, the commons thought, which was to be preserved by unlimited complaisance, was no liberty at all. And it was necessary, while yet in their power, to secure the constitution by such invincible barriers, that no king or minister should ever, for the future, dare to speak such a language to any parliament, or even entertain such a project against them.

.    .    .    .    .    .    .    .    .    .    .    .

The next attack made by the commons, had it prevailed, would have proved decisive. They were preparing a remon-

16 [Dudley Carleton, Viscount Dorchester (1573–1632), also a privy councillor.]

17 Rushworth, I, 359. Bulstrode Whitlocke, *Memorials of the English Affairs. . .*, p. 6.

strance against the levying of tonnage and poundage without consent of parliament. This article, together with the new impositions laid on merchandise by James, constituted near half of the crown-revenues; and by depriving the king of these resources, they would have reduced him to total subjection and dependance. While they retained such a pledge, besides the supply already promised, they were sure that nothing could be refused them. Though after canvassing the matter near three months, they found themselves utterly incapable of fixing any legal crime upon the duke,[18] they regarded him as an unable and perhaps a dangerous minister; and they intended to present a petition, which would then have been equivalent to a command, for removing him from his majesty's person and councils.[19]

The king was alarmed at the yoke which he saw prepared for him. Buckingham's sole guilt, he thought, was the being his friend and favourite.[20] All the other complaints against him were mere pretences. A little before, he was the idol of the people. No new crime had since been discovered. After the most diligent inquiry, prompted by the greatest malice, the smallest appearance of guilt could not be fixed upon him. What idea, he asked, must all mankind entertain of his honour, should he sacrifice his innocent friend to pecuniary considerations? What farther authority should he retain in the nation, were he capable, in the beginning of his reign, to give, in so signal an instance, such matter of triumph to his enemies, and discouragement to his adherents? To-day, the commons pretend to wrest his minister from him. Tomorrow, they will attack some branch of his prerogative. By their remonstrances, and promises, and protestations, they had engaged the crown in a war. As soon as they saw a retreat impossible, without waiting for new incidents, without covering themselves with new pretences, they immediately deserted him, and refused him all reasonable supply. It

18 [Buckingham.]
19 Rushworth, I, 400. Franklyn, p. 199.
20 Franklyn, p. 178.

was evident, that they desired nothing so much as to see him plunged in inextricable difficulties, of which they intended to take advantage. To such deep perfidy, to such unbounded usurpations, it was necessary to oppose a proper firmness and resolution. All encroachments on supreme power could only be resisted sucessfully on the first attempt. The sovereign authority was, with some difficulty, reduced from its ancient and legal height; but when once pushed downwards, it soon became contemptible, and would easily, by the continuance of the same effort, now encouraged by success, be carried to the lowest extremity.

Prompted by these plausible motives, Charles was determined immediately to dissolve the parliament. When this resolution was known, the house of peers, whose compliant behaviour entitled them to some authority with him, endeavoured to interpose;[21] and they petitioned him, that he would allow the parliament to sit some time longer. "Not a moment longer," cried the king hastily;[22] and he soon after ended the session by a dissolution.

As this measure was foreseen, the commons took care to finish and disperse their remonstrance, which they intended as a justification of their conduct to the people. The king, likewise, on his part, published a declaration, in which he gave the reasons of his disagreement with the parliament, and of their sudden dissolution, before they had time to conclude any one act.[23] These papers furnished the partisans on both sides with ample matter of apology or of recrimination. But all impartial men judged "*That* the commons, though they had not as yet violated any law, yet, by their unpliableness and independence, were insensibly changing, perhaps improving, the spirit and genius, while they preserved the forms of the constitution: and *that* the king was acting altogether without any plan; running

[21] Rushworth, I, 398.

[22] Sir William Sanderson, *A Complete History of the Life and Reign of Charles I . . .* , p. 58.

[23] Franklyn, p. 203 ff. *Parliamentary History*, VII, 300.

on in a road surrounded on all sides with the most dangerous precipices, and concerting no proper measures, either for submitting to the obstinacy of the commons, or for subduing it."

. . . . . . . . . . . .

The "new counsels," which Charles had mentioned to the parliament, were now to be tried, in order to supply his necessities. Had he possessed any military force, on which he could rely, it is not improbable, that he had at once taken off the mask, and governed without any regard to parliamentary privileges: so high an idea had he received of kingly prerogative, and so contemptible a notion of the rights of those popular assemblies, from which, he very naturally thought, he had met with such ill usage. But his army was new levied, ill paid, and worse disciplined; no-wise superior to the militia, who were much more numerous, and who were in a great measure under the influence of the country-gentlemen. It behoved him, therefore, to proceed cautiously, and to cover his enterprises under the pretence of ancient precedents, which, considering the great authority commonly enjoyed by his predecessors, could not be wanting to himself.

A commission was openly granted, to compound with the catholics, and agree for dispensing with the penal laws enacted against them.[24] By this expedient, the king both filled his coffers, and gratified his inclination of giving indulgence to these religionists: but he could not have employed any branch of prerogative which would have been more disagreeable, or would have appeared more exceptionable to his protestant subjects.

From the nobility he desired assistance: from the city he required a loan of a hundred thousand pounds. The former contributed slowly: but the latter, covering themselves under many pretences and excuses, gave him at last a flat refusal.[25]

In order to equip a fleet, a distribution, by order of council, was made to all the maritime towns; and each of them was required, with the assistance of the adjacent counties, to arm so

24 Rushworth, I, 413. Whitlocke, p. 7.
25 Rushworth, I, 415. Franklyn, p. 206.

many vessels as were appointed them.[26] The city of London was rated at twenty ships. This is the first appearance, in Charles's reign, of ship-money; a taxation which had once been imposed by Elizabeth, but which afterwards, when carried some steps farther by Charles, created such violent discontents.

Of some, loans were required:[27] to others the way of benevolence was proposed: methods supported by precedent, but always invidious, even in times more submissive and compliant. In the most absolute governments, such expedients would be regarded as irregular and unequal.

These counsels for supply were conducted with some moderation; till news arrived, that a great battle was fought between the king of Denmark and count Tilly,[28] the Imperial general; in which the former was totally defeated. Money now, more than ever, became necessary, in order to repair so great a breach in the alliance, and to support a prince, who was so nearly allied to Charles, and who had been engaged in the war chiefly by the intrigues, solicitations, and promises of the English monarch. After some deliberation, an act of council was passed; importing, that as the urgency of affairs admitted not the way of parliament, the most speedy, equal, and convenient method of supply was by a *general loan* from the subject, according as every man was assessed in the rolls of the last subsidy. That precise sum was required, which each would have paid, had the vote of four subsidies passed into a law: but care was taken to inform the people, that the sums exacted were not to be called subsidies, but loans.[29] Had any doubt remained, whether forced loans, however authorised by precedent, and even by statute, were a violation of liberty, and must, by necessary consequence, render all parliaments superfluous; this was the proper expedient for opening the eyes of the whole nation. The example of Henry

26 Rushworth, *ut supra.*

27 *Ibid.*, I, 416.

28 [Johann Tzerclaes Tilly (1559–1632), general of the Catholic League in the Thirty Years' War.]

29 Rushworth, I, 418. Whitlocke, p. 8.

VIII. who had once, in his arbitrary reign, practised a like method of levying a regular supply, was generally deemed a very insufficient authority.

The commissioners appointed to levy these loans, among other articles of secret instruction, were enjoined, "If any shall refuse to lend, and shall make delays or excuses, and persist in his obstinacy, that they examine him upon oath, whether he has been dealt with to deny or refuse to lend, or make an excuse for not lending? Who has dealt with him, and what speeches or persuasions were used to that purpose? And that they also shall charge every such person, in his majesty's name, upon his allegiance, not to disclose to any one what his answer was."[30] So violent an inquisitorial power, so impracticable an attempt at secrecy, were the objects of indignation, and even, in some degree, of ridicule.

That religious prejudices might support civil authority, sermons were preached by Sibthorpe and Manwaring,[31] in favour of the general loan; and the court industriously spread them over the kingdom. Passive obedience was there recommended in its full extent, the whole authority of the state was represented as belonging to the king alone, and all limitations of law and a constitution were rejected as seditious and impious.[32]

.    .    .    .    .    .    .    .    .    .    .

While the king, instigated by anger and necessity, thus employed the whole extent of his prerogative, the spirit of the people was far from being subdued. Throughout England, many refused these loans; some were even active in encouraging their neighbors to insist upon their common rights and priv-

30 Rushworth, I, 419. Franklyn, p. 207.

31 [Robert Sibthorp or Sybthorppe, D.D. (d. 1662); Roger Manwaring or Maynwaring (1590–1653), bishop of St. David's. Sibthorp said in a sermon on Feb. 22, 1626-7, that "if princes command anything which subjects may not performe, because it is against the laws of God, or of nature, or impossible, yet subjects are bound to undergoe the punishment without either resistance or railing and reviling; and so yield a passive obedience, where they cannot exhibit an active one."]

32 Rushworth, I, 422. Franklyn, p. 208.

ileges. By warrant of the council *these* were thrown into prison.[33] Most of them with patience submitted to confinement, or applied by petition to the king, who commonly released them. Five gentlemen alone, Sir Thomas Darnel, Sir John Corbet, Sir Walter Earl, Sir John Heveningham, and Sir Edmond Hambden, had spirit enough, at their own hazard and expence, to defend the public liberties, and to demand releasement, not as a favour from the court, but as their due, by the laws of their country.[34] No particular cause was assigned of their commitment. The special command alone of the king and council was pleaded; and it was asserted, that, by law, this was not sufficient reason for refusing bail or releasement to the prisoners.

This question was brought to a solemn trial, before the king's bench; and the whole kingdom was attentive to the issue of a cause, which was of much greater consequence than the event of many battles.

By the debates on this subject, it appeared, beyond controversy, to the nation, that their ancestors had been so jealous of personal liberty, as to secure it against arbitrary power in the crown, by six[35] several statutes, and by an article[36] of the great charter itself, the most sacred foundation of the laws and constitution. But the kings of England, who had not been able to prevent the enacting of these laws, had sufficient authority, when the tide of liberty was spent, to obstruct their regular execution; and they deemed it superfluous, to attempt the formal repeal of statutes which they found so many expedients and pretences to elude. Turbulent and seditious times frequently occurred, when the safety of the people absolutely required the confinement of factious leaders; and by the genius of the old constitution, the prince, of himself, was accustomed to assume every branch of prerogative, which was found necessary for

[33] Rushworth, I, 429. Franklyn, p. 210.

[34] Rushworth, I, 458. Franklyn, p. 224. Whitlocke, p. 8.

[35] 25 Edw. III. cap. 4; 28 Edw. III. cap. 3; 37 Edw. III. cap. 18; 38 Edw. III. cap. 9; 42 Edw. III. cap. 3; 1 Richard II. cap. 12.

[36] Chap. 29.

the preservation of public peace and of his own authority. Expediency, at other times, would cover itself under the appearance of necessity; and, in proportion as precedents multiplied, the will alone of the sovereign was sufficient to supply the place of expediency, of which he constituted himself the sole judge. In an age and nation where the power of a turbulent nobility prevailed, and where the king had no settled military force, the only means that could maintain public peace, was the exertion of such prompt and discretionary powers in the crown; and the public itself had become so sensible of the necessity, that those ancient laws in favour of personal liberty, while often violated, had never been challenged or revived, during the course of near three centuries. Though rebellious subjects had frequently, in the open field, resisted the king's authority; no person had been found so bold, while confined and at mercy, as to set himself in opposition to regal power, and to claim the protection of the constitution, against the will of the sovereign. It was not till this age, when the spirit of liberty was universally diffused, when the principles of government were nearly reduced to a system, when the tempers of men, more civilized, seemed less to require those violent exertions of prerogative, that these five gentlemen above mentioned, by a noble effort, ventured, in this national cause, to bring the question to a final determination. And the king was astonished to observe, that a power, exercised by his predecessors, almost without interruption, was found, upon trial, to be directly opposite to the clearest laws, and supported by few undoubted precedents in courts of judicature. These had scarcely, in any instance, refused bail upon commitments by special command of the king; because the persons committed had seldom or never dared to demand it; at least to insist on their demand.

1627    Sir Randolf Crew,[37] chief justice, had been displaced, as unfit for the purposes of the court: Sir Nicholas Hyde,[38] esteemed more obsequious, had obtained that high office: yet the judges, by his direction, went no farther than to remand the gentlemen to

37 [Ranulphe or Randolph Crew or Crewe (1558–1646).]
38 [Nicholas Hyde or Hide (d. 1631).]

prison, and refuse the bail which was offered.[39] Heathe,[40] the attorney-general, insisted, that the court, in imitation of the judges in the 34th of Elizabeth,[41] should enter a general judgment that no bail could be granted, upon a commitment by the king or council.[42] But the judges wisely declined complying. The nation, they saw, was already to the last degree, exasperated. In the present disposition of men's minds, universal complaints prevailed, as if the kingdom were reduced to slavery. And the most invidious prerogative of the crown, it was said, that of imprisoning the subject, is here openly and solemnly, and in numerous instances, exercised for the most invidious purpose; in order to extort loans, or rather subsidies, without consent of parliament.

[39] Rushworth, I, 462.
[40] [Sir Robert Heath (1575–1649).]
[41] State Trials, VII, 147.
[42] Ibid., p. 161.

# *From* Chapter LI—Charles I

1628   THERE was reason to apprehend some disorder or insurrection from the discontents which prevailed among the people in England. Their liberties, they believed, were ravished from them; illegal taxes extorted; their commerce, which had met with a severe check from the Spanish, was totally annihilated by the French war; those military honours transmitted to them from their ancestors, had received a grievous stain, by two unsuccessful and ill-conducted expeditions; scarce an illustrious family but mourned, from the last of them, the loss of a son or brother; greater calamities were dreaded from the war with these powerful monarchies, concurring with the internal disorders under which the nation laboured. And these ills were ascribed, not to the refractory disposition of the two former parliaments, to which they were partly owing; but solely to Charles's obstinacy, in adhering to the counsels of Buckingham; a man nowise entitled, by his birth, age, services, or merit, to that unlimited confidence reposed in him. To be sacrificed to the interest, policy, and ambition of the great, is so much the common lot of the people, that they may appear unreasonable who would pretend to complain of it: but to be the victim of the frivolous gallantry of a favourite, and of his boyish caprices, seemed the object of peculiar indignation.

In this situation, it may be imagined, the king and the duke dreaded, above all things, the assembling of a parliament: but so little foresight had they possessed in their enterprising schemes, that they found themselves under an absolute necessity of embracing that expedient. . . .

The views of the popular leaders were much more judicious and profound. When the commons assembled, they appeared to be men of the same independent spirit with their predecessors, and possessed of such riches, that their property was computed

to surpass three times that of the house of peers;[1] they were
deputed by boroughs and counties, enflamed, all of them, by the
late violations of liberty; many of the members themselves had
been cast into prison, and had suffered by the measures of the
court; yet, notwithstanding these circumstances, which might
prompt them to embrace violent resolutions, they entered upon
business with perfect temper and decorum. They considered,
that the king, disgusted at these popular assemblies, and little
prepossessed in favour of their privileges, wanted but a fair
pretence for breaking with them, and would seize the first opportunity offered by any incident, or any undutiful behaviour
of the members. He fairly told them, in his first speech, that,
"if they should not do their duties, in contributing to the necessities of the state, he must, in discharge of his conscience, use
those other means which God had put into his hands, in order
to save that which the follies of some particular men may otherwise put in danger. Take not this for a threatening," added the
king, "for I scorn to threaten any but my equals; but as an
admonition from him who, by nature and duty, has most care
of your preservation and prosperity."[2] The lord keeper, by the
king's direction, subjoined, "This way of parliamentary supplies,
as his majesty told you, he hath chosen, not as the only way,
but as the fittest; not because he is destitute of others, but because it is most agreeable to the goodness of his own most
gracious disposition, and to the desire and weal of his people.
If this be deferred, necessity and the sword of the enemy make
way for the others. Remember his majesty's admonition, I say,
remember it."[3] From these avowed maxims, the commons foresaw, that, if the least handle were afforded, the king would
immediately dissolve them, and would thenceforward deem himself justified for violating, in a manner still more open, all the
ancient forms of the constitution. No remedy could then be
looked for, but from insurrections and civil war, of which the

[1] Sanderson, p. 106. Clement Walker, *The History of Independency* . . . ,
p. 339.

[2] Rushworth, I, 477. Franklyn, p. 233.

[3] Rushworth, I, 479. Franklyn, p. 234.

issue would be extremely uncertain, and which must, in all events, prove calamitous to the nation. To correct the late disorders in the administration required some new laws, which would, no doubt, appear harsh to a prince, so enamoured of his prerogative; and it was requisite to temper, by the decency and moderation of their debates, the rigour, which must necessarily attend their determinations. Nothing can give us a higher idea of the capacity of those men who now guided the commons, and of the great authority, which they had acquired, than the forming and executing of so judicious and so difficult a plan of operations.

.   .   .   .   .   .   .   .   .   .   .   .   .

The supply, though voted, was not, as yet, passed into a law; and the commons resolved to employ the interval, in providing some barriers to their rights and liberties so lately violated. They knew, that their own vote, declaring the illegality of the former measures, had not, of itself, sufficient authority to secure the constitution against future invasion. Some act to that purpose must receive the sanction of the whole legislature; and they appointed a committee to prepare the model of so important a law. By collecting into one effort all the dangerous and oppressive claims of his prerogative, Charles had exposed them to the hazard of one assault; and had farther, by presenting a nearer view of the consequences attending them, rouzed the independent genius of the commons. Forced loans, benevolences, taxes without consent of parliament, arbitrary imprisonments, the billeting of soldiers, martial law; these were the grievances complained of, and against these an eternal remedy was to be provided. The commons pretended not, as they affirmed, to any unusual powers or privileges: they aimed only at securing those which had been transmitted them from their ancestors: and their law they resolved to call a *petition of right;* as implying that it contained a corroboration or explanation of the ancient constitution, not any infringement of royal prerogative, or acquisition of new liberties.

.   .   .   .   .   .   .   .   .   .   .   .   .

The king could easily see the consequence of these proceedings. Though he had offered, at the beginning of the session, to give his consent to any law for the security of the rights and liberties of the people; he had not expected that such inroads would be made on his prerogative. In order, therefore, to divert the commons from their intention, he sent a message, wherein he acknowledged past errors, and promised that, hereafter, there should be no just cause of complaint. And he added, "That the affairs of the kingdom press him so, that he could not continue the session above a week or two longer: and if the house be not ready, by that time, to do what is fit for themselves, it shall be their own fault."[4] On a subsequent occasion, he asked them, "Why demand explanations, if you doubt not the performance of the statutes, according to their true meaning? Explanations will hazard an encroachment upon the prerogative. And it may well be said, What need a new law to confirm an old, if you repose confidence in the declarations which his majesty made to both houses?"[5] The truth is, the great charter and the old statutes were sufficiently clear in favour of personal liberty: but as all kings of England had ever, in cases of necessity or expediency, been accustomed, at intervals, to elude them; and as Charles, in a complication of instances, had lately violated them; the commons judged it requisite to enact a new law, which might not be eluded or violated, by any interpretation, construction, or contrary precedent. Nor was it sufficient, they thought, that the king promised to return into the way of his predecessors. His predecessors, in all times, had enjoyed too much discretionary power; and by his recent abuse of it, the whole world had reason to see the necessity of entirely retrenching it.

The king still persevered in his endeavours to elude the petition. He sent a letter to the house of lords, in which he went so far as to make a particular declaration, "That neither he nor his privy-council shall or will, at any time hereafter, commit or command to prison, or otherwise restrain, any man for not lending money, or for any other cause, which, in his conscience, he thought not to concern the public good, and the safety of king and people." And he farther declared, "That he never

[4] *State Trials*, VII, 193.
[5] *Ibid.*, p. 196. Rushworth, I, 556.

would be guilty of so base an action as to pretend any cause, of whose truth he was not fully satisfied."[6] But this promise, though enforced to the commons by the recommendation of the upper house, made no more impression than all the former messages.

Among the other evasions of the king, we may reckon the proposal of the house of peers, to subjoin, to the intended petition of right, the following clause: "We humbly present this petition to your majesty, not only with a care of preserving our own liberties, but with due regard to leave entire that *sovereign power*, with which your majesty is entrusted for the protection, safety, and happiness of your people."[7] Less penetration than was possessed by the leaders of the house of commons, could easily discover how captious this clause was, and how much it was calculated to elude the whole force of the petition.

These obstacles, therefore, being surmounted, the petition of right passed the commons, and was sent to the upper house.[8] The

[6] *State Trials*, VII, 198. Rushworth, I, 560. *Parliamentary History*, VIII, 111.

[7] *State Trials*, VII, 199. Rushworth, I, 561. *Parliamentary History*, VIII, 116. Whitlocke, p. 10.

[8]* *This petition is of so great importance, that we shall here give it at length:* Humbly shew unto our sovereign lord the king, the lords spiritual and temporal, and commons, in parliament assembled, That, whereas it is declared and enacted by a statute made in the time of the reign of king Edward I. commonly called *Statutum de tallagio non concedendo*, that no tallage or aid shall be levied by the king or his heirs in this realm, without the good will and assent of the archbishops, bishops, earls, barons, knights, burgesses, and other the freemen of the commonalty of this realm: and, by authority of parliament holden in the five and twentieth year of the reign of king Edward III. it is declared and enacted, That, from thenceforth, no person shall be compelled to make any loans to the king against his will, because such loans were against reason, and the franchise of the land: and, by other laws of this realm, it is provided, that none should be charged by any charge or imposition called a benevolence, or by such like charge: by which the statutes before-mentioned, and other the good laws and statutes of this realm, your subjects have inherited this freedom, that they should not be compelled to continue to any tax, tallage, aid, or other like charge, not set by common consent in parliament.

II. Yet nevertheless, of late divers commissions directed to sundry com-

peers, who were probably well pleased in secret that all their
solicitations had been eluded by the commons, quickly passed

---

missioners in several counties, with instructions, have issued; by means
whereof your people have been in divers places assembled, and required to
lend certain sums of money unto your majesty, and many of them, upon
their refusal so to do, have had an oath administered unto them not war-
rantable by the laws or statutes of this realm, and have been constrained
to become bound to make appearance and give attendance before your
privy-council, and in other places, and others of them have been therefore
imprisoned, confined, and sundry other ways molested and disquieted: and
divers other charges have been laid and levied upon your people, in several
counties, by lord-lieutenants, deputy-lieutenants, commissioners for musters,
justices of peace, and others, by command or direction from your majesty,
or your privy council, against the laws and free customs of this realm.

III. And whereas also, by the statute called "The great charter of the liberties of England," it is declared and enacted, That no freeman may be
taken or imprisoned, or be disseized of his freehold or liberties, or his free
customs, or be outlawed or exiled, or in any manner destroyed, but by the
lawful judgment of his peers, or by the law of the land.

IV. And, in the eight and twentieth year of the reign of king Edward III.
it was declared and enacted, by authority of parliament, That no man, of
what estate or condition that he be, should be put out of his land or tene-
ments, nor taken, nor imprisoned, nor disherited, nor put to death, without being brought to answer by due process of law.

V. Nevertheless, against the tenor of the said statutes, and other the good
laws and statutes of your realm to that end provided, divers of your subjects have of late been imprisoned without any cause showed: and, when,
for their deliverance, they were brought before justice, by your majesty's
writs of *Habeas Corpus,* there to undergo, and receive as the court should
order, and their keepers commanded to certify the causes of their detainer,
no cause was certified, but that they were detained by your majesty's special
command, signified by the lords of your privy council, and yet were returned
back to several prisons, without being charged with any thing to which they
might make answer according to the law.

VI. And whereas of late great companies of soldiers and mariners have
been dispersed into divers counties of the realm, and the inhabitants, against
their wills, have been compelled to receive them into their houses, and
there to suffer them to sojourn, against the laws and customs of this realm,
and to the great grievance and vexation of the people.

VII. And whereas also, by authority of parliament, in the five and twentieth year of the reign of king Edward III. it is declared and enacted, That
no man shall be fore-judged of life or limb against the form of the Great
Charter and law of the land: and, by the said Great Charter, and other the

the petition without any material alteration; and nothing but the royal assent was wanting to give it the force of a law. The king accordingly came to the house of peers; sent for the com-

laws and statutes of this your realm, no man ought to be judged to death but by the laws established in this your realm, either by the customs of the same realm, or by acts of parliament: and whereas no offender, of what kind soever, is exempted from the proceedings to be used, and punishments to be inflicted by the laws and statutes of this your realm: nevertheless, of late divers commissions, under your majesty's great seal, have issued forth, by which certain persons have been assigned and appointed commissioners, with power and authority to proceed within the land, according to the justice of martial law, against such soldiers and mariners, or other dissolute persons joining with them, as should commit any murther, robber, felony, mutiny, or other outrage or misdemeanor whatsoever, and by such summary course and order as is agreeable to martial law, and as is used in armies in time of war, to proceed to the trial and condemnation of such offenders, and them to cause to be executed and put to death according to the law martial.

VIII. By pretext whereof some of your majestys' subjects have been by some of the said commissioners put to death, when and where, if, by the laws and statutes of the land, they had deserved death, by the same laws and statutes also they might, and by no other ought, to have been judged and executed.

IX. And also sundry grievous offenders, by colour thereof claiming an exemption, have escaped the punishments due to them by the laws and statutes of this your realm, by reason that divers of your officers and ministers of justice have unjustly refused or forborne to proceed against such offenders according to the same laws and statutes, upon pretence that the said offenders were punishable only by martial law, and by authority of such commissions as aforesaid; which commissions, and all other of like nature, are wholly and directly contrary to the said laws and statutes of this your realm.

X. They do therefore humbly pray your most excellent majesty, That no man hereafter be compelled to make or yield any gift, loan, benevolence, tax, or such like charge, without common consent, by act of parliament: and that none be called to make answer, or take such oath, or to give attendance, or be confined, or otherwise molested or disquieted, concerning the same, or for refusal thereof: and that no freeman, in any such manner as is before mentioned, be imprisoned or detained: and that your majesty would be pleased to remove the said soldiers and mariners, and that people may not be so burthened in time to come; and that the aforesaid commissions, for proceeding by martial law, may be revoked and annulled: and that hereafter no commissions of like nature may issue forth, to any person or persons whatsoever, to be executed as foresaid, lest, by colour of them, any

mons; and, being seated in his chair of state, the petition was read to him. Great was now the astonishment of all men, when, instead of the usual concise, and clear form, by which a bill is either confirmed or rejected, Charles said, in answer to the petition, "The king willeth, that right be done according to the laws and customs of the realm, and that the statutes be put into execution; that his subjects may have no cause to complain of any wrong or oppression, contrary to their just rights and liberties, to the preservation whereof he holds himself in con- science as much obliged as of his own prerogative."[9]

It is surprising, that Charles, who had seen so many instances of the jealousy of the commons, who had himself so much roused that jealousy by his frequent evasive messages during this session, could imagine that they would rest satisfied with an answer so vague and undeterminate. It was evident, that the unusual form alone of the answer must excite their attention; that the disappointment must inflame their anger; and that therefore it was necessary, as the petition seemed to bear hard on royal prerogative, to come early to some fixed resolution, either gracefully to comply with it, or courageously to reject it.

It happened as might have been foreseen. The commons returned in very ill humour. Usually, when in that disposition, their zeal for religion, and their enmity against the unfortunate catholics, ran extremely high. But they had already, in the beginning of the session, presented their petition of religion, and had received a satisfactory answer; though they expected,

---

of your majesty's subjects be destroyed, or put to death, contrary to the laws and franchise of the land.

XI. All which they most humbly pray of your most excellent majesty, as their rights and liberties, according to the laws and statutes of this realm: and that your majesty would also vouchsafe to declare, That the awards, doings, and proceedings to the prejudice of your people, in any of the premises, shall not be drawn hereafter into consequence or example: and that your majesty would be also graciously pleased, for the further com- fort and safety of your people, to declare your royal will and pleasure, that in the things aforesaid, all your officers and ministers shall serve you according to the laws and statutes of this realm, as they tender the honour of your majesty, and the prosperity of this kingdom. *Stat.* 17 Car. chap. 14.

[9] *State Trials*, VII, 212. Rushworth, I, 590.

that the execution of the laws against papists would, for the future, be no more exact and rigid, than they had hitherto found it. To give vent to their present indignation, they fell with their utmost force, on Dr. Manwaring.

There is nothing, which tends more to excuse, if not justify, the extreme rigour of the commons towards Charles, than his open encouragement and avowal of such general principles as were altogether incompatible with a limited government. Manwaring had preached a sermon, which the commons found, upon inquiry, to be printed by special command of the king;[10] and, when this sermon was looked into, it contained doctrines subversive of all civil liberty. It taught, that, though property was commonly lodged in the subject, yet, whenever any exigency required supply, all property was transferred to the sovereign; that the consent of parliament was not necessary for the imposition of taxes; and that the divine laws required compliance with every demand, how irregular soever, which the prince should make upon his subjects.[11] For these doctrines the commons impeached Manwaring. The sentence, pronounced upon him by the peers, was, that he should be imprisoned during the pleasure of the house, be fined a thousand pounds to the king, make submission and acknowledgment for his offence, be suspended during three years, be incapable of holding any ecclesiastical dignity or secular office, and that his book be called in and burnt.[12]

It may be worthy of notice, that no sooner was the session ended, than this man, so justly obnoxious to both houses, received a pardon, and was promoted to a living of considerable value.[13] Some years after, he was raised to the see of St. Asaph. If the republican spirit of the commons increased, beyond all reasonable bounds, the monarchical spirit of the court, this latter, carried to so high a pitch, tended still farther to augment

10 *Parliamentary History,* VIII, 206.

11 Rushworth, I, 585, 594. *Parliamentary History,* VIII, 168, 169, 170 ff. James Welwood, *Memoirs of the most Material Transactions in England* ... , p. 44.

12 Rushworth, I, 65. *Parliamentary History,* VIII, 212.

13 Rushworth, I, 635. Whitlocke, p. 11.

the former. And thus extremes were every where affected, and the just medium was gradually deserted by all men.

From Manwaring, the house of commons proceeded to censure the conduct of Buckingham, whose name hitherto they had cautiously forborn to mention.[14] In vain did the king send them a message, in which he told them, that the session was drawing near to a conclusion; and desired, that they would not enter upon new business, nor cast any aspersions on his government and ministry.[15] Though the court endeavoured to explain and soften this message by a subsequent message;[16] as Charles was apt hastily to correct any hasty step, which he had taken; it served rather to inflame than appease the commons: as if the method of their proceedings had here been prescribed to them. It was foreseen, that a great tempest was ready to burst on the duke; and in order to divert it, the king thought proper, upon a joint application of the lords and commons,[17] to endeavour giving them satisfaction with regard to the petition of right. He came, therefore, to the house of peers, and pronouncing the usual form of words, "Let it be law as is desired," gave full sanction and authority to the petition. The acclamations, with which the house resounded, and the universal joy diffused over the nation, showed how much this petition had been the object of all men's vows and expectations.[18]

It may be affirmed, without any exaggeration, that the king's assent to the petition of right produced such a change in the government, as was almost equivalent to a revolution; and by circumscribing, in so many articles, the royal prerogative, gave additional security to the liberty of the subject.

.     .     .     .     .     .     .     .     .     .     .

The following interval, between the second and third parliament, was distinguished by so many exertions of prerogative, that men had little leisure to attend to the affair of tonnage and                1629

---

[14] Rushworth, I, 607.

[15] *Ibid.*, p. 605.

[16] *Ibid.*, p. 610. *Parliamentary History*, VIII, 197.

[17] Rushworth, I, 613. *Journ.*, 7th June, 1628. *Parliamentary History*, VIII, 201.

[18] Rushworth, I, 613.

poundage, where the abuse of power in the crown might seem to be of a more disputable nature. But after the commons, during the precedent session, had remedied all these grievances by means of their petition of right, which they deemed so necessary; they afterwards proceeded to take the matter into consideration, and they showed the same intention, as formerly, of exacting, in return for the grant of this revenue, very large compliances on the part of the crown. Their sudden prorogation prevented them from bringing their pretensions to a full conclusion.

When Charles opened this session, he had foreseen, that the same controversy would arise; and he therefore took care, very early, among many mild and reconciling expressions, to inform the commons, "That he had not taken these duties as appertaining to his hereditary prerogative; but that it ever was, and still is, his meaning to enjoy them as a gift of his people: and that, if he had hitherto levied tonnage and poundage, he pretended to justify himself only by the necessity of so doing, not by any right which he assumed."[19] This concession, which probably arose from the king's moderate temper, now freed from the impulse of Buckingham's violent counsels,[20] might have satisfied the commons, had they entertained no other view than that of ascertaining their own powers and privileges. But they carried their pretensions much higher. They insisted, as a necessary preliminary, that the king should once entirely desist from levying these duties; after which, they were to take it into consideration, how far they would restore him to the possession of a revenue, of which he had clearly divested himself. But, besides that this extreme rigour had never been exercised towards any of his predecessors, and many obvious inconveniencies must follow from the intermission of the customs; there were other reasons which deterred Charles from complying with so hard a condition. It was probable, that the commons might renew their former project of making this revenue only temporary, and thereby reducing their prince to perpetual dependence; they certainly would cut off the new impositions which Mary and

19 Rushworth, I, 644. *Parliamentary History*, VIII, 256, 346.
20 [The Duke of Buckingham was assassinated on August 23, 1628.]

Elizabeth, but especially James, had levied, and which formed no despicable part of the public revenue; and they openly declared, that they had, at present, many important pretensions, chiefly with regard to religion; and if compliance were refused, no supply must be expected from the commons.

It is easy to see in what an inextricable labyrinth Charles was now involved. By his own concessions, by the general principles of the English government, and by the form of every bill which had granted this duty, tonnage and poundage was derived entirely from the free gift of the people; and, consequently, might be withdrawn at their pleasure. If unreasonable in their refusal, they still refused nothing but what was their own. If public necessity required this supply, it might be thought also to require the king's compliance with those conditions, which were the price of obtaining it. Though the motive for granting it had been the enabling of the king to guard the seas; it did not follow, that because he guarded the seas, he was therefore entitled to this revenue, without farther formality: since the people had still reserved to themselves the right of judging how far that service merited such a supply. But Charles, notwithstanding his public declaration, was far from assenting to this conclusion in its full extent. The plain consequence, he saw, of all these rigours, and refinements, and inferences, was, that he, without any public necessity, and without any fault of his own, must, of a sudden, even from his accession, become a magistrate of a very different nature from any of his predecessors, and must fall into a total dependence on subjects over whom former kings, especially those immediately preceding, had exercised an authority almost unlimited. Entangled in a chain of consequences, which he could not easily break, he was inclined to go higher, and rather deny the first principle, than admit of conclusions which to him appeared so absurd and unreasonable. Agreeably to the ideas hitherto entertained both by natives and foreigners, the monarch he esteemed the essence and soul of the English government; and whatever other power pretended to annihilate, or even abridge the royal authority, must necessarily, he thought, either in its nature or exercise, be deemed no better than an usurpation. Willing to preserve the ancient harmony of the constitution, he had ever intended to comply, as far as he *easily* could, with the ancient forms of administration: but when these forms appeared to him, by the inveterate obstinacy of the commons, to have no other tendency than to disturb that harmony, and to introduce a new constitution; he concluded, that, in this violent situation, what was subordinate must necessarily yield to what was principal, and the privileges of the people, for a time, give place to royal prerogative. From the rank of a monarch, to be degraded into a slave of his insolent, ungrateful subjects, seemed, of all indignities, the greatest; and nothing, in his judgment, could exceed the humiliation attending such a state, but the meanness of tamely submitting to it, without making some efforts to preserve the authority transmitted to him by his predecessors.

Though these were the king's reflections and resolutions before the parliament assembled, he did not immediately break with them, upon their delay in voting him this supply. He thought that he could better justify any strong measure which he might afterwards be obliged to take, if he allowed them to carry to the utmost extremities their attacks upon his government and prerogative.[21] He contented himself, for the present, with soliciting the house by messages and speeches. But the commons, instead of hearkening to his solicitations, proceeded to carry their scrutiny into his management of religion,[22] which was the only grievance to which, in their opinion, they had not as yet, by their petition of right, applied a sufficient remedy.

It was not possible that this century, so fertile in religious sects and disputes, could escape the controversy concerning fatalism and free-will, which, being strongly interwoven both with philosophy and theology, had, in all ages, thrown every school and every church into such inextricable doubt and perplexity. The first reformers in England, as in other European countries, had embraced the most rigid tenets of predestination

21 Rushworth, I, 642.
22 Rushworth, I, 651. Whitlocke, p. 12.

and absolute decrees, and had composed, upon that system, all the articles of their religious creed. But these principles having met with opposition from Arminius and his sectaries, the controversy was soon brought into this island, and began here to diffuse itself. The Arminians,[23] finding more encouragement from the superstitious spirit of the church than from the fanaticism of the puritans, gradually incorporated themselves with the former; and some of that sect, by the indulgence of James and Charles, had attained the highest preferments in the hierarchy. But their success with the public had not been altogether answerable to that which they met with in the church and the court. Throughout the nation, they still lay under the reproach of innovation and heresy. The commons now levelled against them their formidable censures, and made them the objects of daily invective and declamation. Their protectors were stigmatised; their tenets canvassed; their views represented as dangerous and pernicious. To impartial spectators surely, if any such had been at that time in England, it must have given great entertainment, to see a popular assembly, inflamed with faction and enthusiasm, pretend to discuss questions to which the greatest philosophers, in the tranquillity of retreat, had never hitherto been able to find any satisfactory solution.

Amidst that complication of disputes in which men were then involved, we may observe, that the appellation "puritan" stood for three parties, which, though commonly united, were yet actuated by very different views and motives. There were the political puritans, who maintained the highest principles of civil liberty; the puritans in discipline, who were averse to the ceremonies and episcopal government of the church; and the doctrinal puritans, who rigidly defended the speculative system of the first reformers. In opposition to all these, stood

23 [Jacobus Arminius (Jacob Harmensen or Hermansz), Dutch theologian and founder of Arminianism. Arminius opposed the Dutch Calvinists' doctrine of predestination, maintaining rather a conditional election in which the offer of salvation could be accepted or rejected by one's free will. The English Puritans generally maintained the doctrine of predestination.]

the court party, the hierarchy, and the Arminians; only with this distinction, that the latter sect, being introduced a few years before, did not, as yet, comprehend all those who were favourable to the church and to monarchy. But, as the controversies on every subject grew daily warmer, men united themselves more intimately with their friends, and separated themselves wider from their antagonists; and the distinction gradually became quite uniform and regular.

This house of commons, which, like all the preceding during the reigns of James and Charles, and even of Elizabeth, was much governed by the puritanical party, thought that they could not better serve their cause, than by branding and punishing the Arminian sect, which, introducing an innovation in the church, were the least favoured and least powerful of all their antagonists. From this measure it was easily foreseen, that, besides gratifying the animosity of the doctrinal puritans, both the puritans in discipline, and those in politics, would reap considerable advantages. Laud, Neile, Montague,[24] and other bishops, who were the chief supporters of episcopal government, and the most zealous partisans of the discipline and ceremonies of the church, were all supposed to be tainted with Arminianism. The same men and their disciples were the strenuous preachers of passive obedience, and of entire submission to princes; and if these could once be censured, and be expelled the church and court, it was concluded, that the hierarchy would receive a mortal blow, the ceremonies be less rigidly insisted on, and the king, deprived of his most faithful friends, be obliged to abate those high claims of prerogative, on which at present he insisted.

But Charles, besides a view of the political consequences which must result from a compliance with such pretensions, was strongly determined, from principles of piety and conscience, to oppose them. Neither the dissipation incident to

---

24 [William Laud (1573–1645), archbishop of Canterbury; Richard Neile (1562–1640), archbishop of York; Richard Montagu or Montague (1577–1641), bishop of Chichester.]

youth, nor the pleasures attending a high fortune, had been able to prevent this virtuous prince from embracing the most sincere sentiments of religion; and that character which, in that religious age, should have been of infinite advantage to him, proved in the end the chief cause of his ruin: merely because the religion adopted by him was not of that precise mode and sect which *began* to prevail among his subjects. His piety, though remote from popery, had a tincture of superstition in it; and, being averse to the gloomy spirit of the puritans, was represented by them as tending towards the abominations of antichrist. Laud also had unfortunately acquired a great ascendant over him: and as all those prelates, obnoxious to the commons, were regarded as his chief friends and most favourite courtiers; he was resolved not to disarm and dishonour himself, by abandoning them to the resentment of his enemies. Being totally unprovided with military force, and finding a refractory independent spirit to prevail among the people; the most solid basis of his authority, he thought, consisted in the support which he received from the hierarchy.

.    .    .    .    .    .    .    .    .    .    .    .

Oliver Cromwell,[25] at that time a young man of no account in the nation, is mentioned in these debates as complaining of one who, he was told, preached flat popery.[26] It is amusing to observe the first words of this fanatical hypocrite correspond so exactly to his character.

The inquiries and debates concerning tonnage and poundage went hand in hand with these theological or metaphysical controversies. The officers of the custom-house were summoned before the commons, to give an account by what authority they had seized the goods of merchants, who had refused to pay these duties: the barons of the exchequer were questioned concerning their decrees on that head.[27] One of the sheriffs of London was committed to the Tower for his activity in supporting the offi-

25 [Oliver Cromwell (1599–1658), later Protector of the Commonwealth.]
26 Rushworth, I, 655. *Parliamentary History*, VIII, 289.
27 Rushworth, I, 654. *Parliamentary History*, VIII, 301.

cers of the custom-house: the goods of Rolles, a merchant, and member of the house, being seized for his refusal to pay the duties, complaints were made of this violence, as if it were a breach of privilege:[28] Charles supported his officers in all these measures; and the quarrel grew every day higher between him and the commons.[29] Mention was made in the house of impeaching Sir Richard Weston, the treasurer;[30] and the king began to entertain thoughts of finishing the session by a dissolution.

Sir John Elliot[31] framed a remonstrance against levying tonnage and poundage without consent of parliament, and offered it to the clerk to read. It was refused. He read it himself. The question being then called for, the speaker, Sir John Finch,[32] said, "That he had a command from the king to adjourn, and to put no question."[33] Upon which he rose and left the chair. The whole house was in an uproar. The speaker was pushed back into the chair, and forcibly held in it by Hollis and Valentine,[34] till a short remonstrance was framed, and was passed by acclamation rather than by vote. Papists and Arminians were there declared capital enemies to the commonwealth. Those who levied tonnage and poundage were branded with the same epithet. And even the merchants who should voluntarily pay these duties, were denominated betrayers of English liberty, and public enemies. The doors being locked, the gentleman usher

[28] Rushworth, I, 653.

[29] *Ibid.,* p. 658.

[30] *Parliamentary History,* VIII, 326. [Richard Weston, first Earl of Portland (1577–1635).]

[31] [Sir John Eliot (1592–1632), member for the county of Cornwall.]

[32] [John Finch, Baron Finch of Fordwich (1584–1660), also lord keeper.]

[33] The king's power of adjourning, as well as proroguing the parliament, was and is never questioned. In the 19th of the late king, the judges determined, that the adjournment by the king kept the parliament in *statu quo* until the next sitting; but that then no committees were to meet: but if the adjournment be by the house, then the committees and other matters do continue. *Parliamentary History,* V, 466.

[34] [Denzil Hollis (1599–1680), member for the borough of St. Michael in Cornwall; Benjamin Valentine (d. 1652?), member for the borough of St. Germans.]

of the house of lords, who was sent by the king, could not get admittance till this remonstrance was finished. By the king's order, he took the mace from the table, which ended their proceedings.[35] And a few days after the parliament was dissolved.

[35] Rushworth, I, 660. Whitlocke, p. 12.

# *From* Chapter LII—Charles I

THERE now opens to us a new scene. Charles, naturally disgusted with parliaments, who, he found, were determined to proceed against him with unmitigated rigour, both in invading his prerogative, and refusing him all supply, resolved not to call any more, till he should see greater indications of a compliant disposition in the nation. Having lost his great favourite, Buckingham, he became his own minister; and never afterwards reposed in any one such unlimited confidence. As he chiefly follows his own genius and disposition, his measures are henceforth less rash and hasty; though the general tenor of his administration still wants somewhat of being entirely legal, and perhaps more of being entirely prudent.

.     .     .     .     .     .     .     .     .     .     .

1632  The council of York had been first erected, after a rebellion, by a patent from Henry VIII. without any authority of parliament; and this exercise of power, like many others, was indulged to that arbitrary monarch. This council had long acted chiefly as a criminal court; but, besides some innovations, introduced by James, Charles thought proper, some time after Wentworth was made president, to extend its powers, and to give it a large civil jurisdiction, and that in some respects, discretionary.[1] It is not improbable that the king's intention was only to prevent inconveniencies, which arose from the bringing of every cause, from the most distant parts of the kingdom, into Westminster-hall: but the consequence, in the mean time, of this measure, was the putting of all the northern counties out of the protection of ordinary law, and subjecting them to an authority somewhat arbitrary. Some irregular acts of that council were, this year, complained of.[2]

1633  The court of star-chamber extended its authority; and it was

[1] Rushworth, II, 158, 159ff. Franklyn, p. 412.
[2] Rushworth, II, 202, 203.

matter of complaint, that it encroached upon the jurisdiction of the other courts; imposing heavy fines and inflicting severe punishment, beyond the usual course of justice. Sir David Foulis[3] was fined five thousand pounds, chiefly because he had dissuaded a friend from compounding with the commissioners of knighthood.[4]

. . . . . . . . . . . . . . . .

Ship-money was now introduced. The first writs of this kind had been directed to sea-port towns only: but ship-money was at this time levied on the whole kingdom; and each county was rated at a particular sum, which was afterwards assessed upon individuals.[5] The amount of the whole tax was very moderate, little exceeding two hundred thousand pounds: it was levied upon the people with equality: the money was entirely expended on the navy, to the great honour and advantage of the kingdom: as England had no military force, while all the other powers of Europe were strongly armed, a fleet seemed absolutely necessary for her security: and it was obvious that a navy must be built and equipped at leisure, during peace; nor could it possibly be fitted out on a sudden emergence, when the danger became urgent: yet all these considerations could not reconcile the people to the imposition. It was entirely arbitrary: by the same right any other tax might be imposed: and men thought a powerful fleet, though very desirable both for the credit and safety of the kingdom, but an unequal recompence for their liberties, which, they apprehended, were thus sacrificed to the obtaining of it.

England, it must be owned, was, in this respect, unhappy in its present situation, that the king had entertained a very different idea of the constitution, from that which *began,* in general, to prevail among his subjects. He did not regard national privileges as so sacred and inviolable, that nothing but the most extreme necessity could justify an infringement of them. He considered himself as the supreme magistrate, to whose care heaven,

1634

3 [David Foulis (d. 1642), a member of the council of the north.]
4 Rushworth, II, 215, 216ff.
5 *Ibid.,* pp. 257, 258 ff.

by his birth-right, had committed his people, whose duty it was to provide for their security and happiness, and who was vested with ample discretionary powers for that salutary purpose. If the observance of ancient laws and customs was consistent with the present convenience of government, he thought himself obliged to comply with that rule; as the easiest, the safest, and what procured the most prompt and willing obedience. But when a change of circumstances, especially if derived from the obstinacy of the people, required a new plan of administration, national privileges, he thought, must yield to supreme power; nor could any order of the state oppose any right to the will of the sovereign, directed to the good of the public.[6] That these principles of government were derived from the uniform tenor of the English laws, it would be rash to affirm. The fluctuating nature of the constitution, the impatient humour of the people, and the variety of events had, no doubt, in different ages, produced exceptions and contradictions. These observations alone may be established on both sides, *that* the appearances were sufficiently strong in favour of the king to apologise for his following such maxims; and *that* public liberty must be so precarious under this exorbitant prerogative, as to render an opposition not only excusable, but laudable, in the people.[7]

. . . . . . . . . . .

1635    Charles had imitated the example of Elizabeth and James, and had issued proclamations forbidding the landed gentlemen

[6] *Ibid.*, IV, 535, 542.

[7]* Here is a passage of Sir John Davis's *Question concerning Impositions*, p. 131. "This power of laying on arbitrarily new impositions being a prerogative in point of government, as well as in point of profit, it cannot be restrained or bound by act of parliament; it cannot be limited by any certain or fixt rule of law, no more than the course of a pilot upon the sea, who must turn the helm, or bear higher or lower sail, according to the wind or weather; and therefore it may be properly said, that the king's prerogative in this point, is as strong as *Samson*; it cannot be bound: for though an act of parliament be made to restrain it, and the king doth give his consent unto it, as *Samson* was bound with his own consent, yet if the *Philistines* come; that is, if any just or important occasion do arise, it cannot hold or

and the nobility to live idly in London, and ordering them to retire to their country-seats.[8] For disobedience to this edict, many were indicted by the attorney-general, and were fined in the star-chamber.[9] This occasioned discontents; and the sentences were complained of, as illegal. But if proclamations had authority, of which nobody pretended to doubt, must they not be put in execution? In no instance, I must confess, does it more evidently appear, what confused and uncertain ideas were, during that age, entertained concerning the English constitution.

.    .    .    .    .    .    .    .    .    .    .    .    .

This year, John Hambden[10] acquired, by his spirit and courage, universal popularity throughout the nation, and has merited great renown with posterity, for the bold stand which he made, in defence of the laws and liberties of his country. After the imposing of ship-money, Charles, in order to discourage all opposition, had proposed this question to the judges; "Whether, in a case of necessity, for the defence of the kingdom, he might not impose this taxation; and whether he were not sole judge of the necessity?" These guardians of law and liberty replied, with great complaisance, "That in a case of necessity he might impose that taxation, and that he was sole judge of the necessity":[11] Hambden had been rated at twenty shillings, for an

**1637**

---

restrain the prerogative; it will be as thread, and broken as easy as the bonds of *Samson*—The king's prerogatives are the sun-beams of the crown, and as inseparable from it as the sun-beams from the sun: the king's crown must be taken from him; *Samson's* hair must be cut out, before his courage can be any jot abated. Hence it is that neither the king's act, nor any act of parliament, can give away his prerogative."

8 Rushworth, II, 144.

9 *Ibid.*, p. 288.

10 [John Hampden (1594–1643), according to the *Dictionary of National Biography*, was assessed at 31s. 6d. for estates in Buckinghamshire, and 20s. for those in the parish of Stoke Mandeville, "and without doubt similar sums for his lands in other parishes. As he possessed property in some dozen parishes, the total amount of the sum demanded from Hampden must have been nearer £20 than 20s." The 20s. amount was widely mentioned, however, as, for example, by Edmund Burke in his speech on American taxation.]

11 Rushworth, II, 355. Whitlocke, p. 24.

estate which he possessed in the county of Buckingham: yet notwithstanding this declared opinion of the judges, notwithstanding the great power, and sometimes rigorous maxims of the crown, notwithstanding the small prospect of relief from parliament; he resolved, rather than tamely submit to so illegal an imposition, to stand a legal prosecution, and expose himself to all the indignation of the court. The case was argued during twelve days, in the exchequer-chamber, before all the judges of England; and the nation regarded, with the utmost anxiety, every circumstance of this celebrated trial. The event was easily foreseen: but the principles, and reasonings, and behaviour of the parties, engaged in the trial, were much canvassed and inquired into; and nothing could equal the favour paid to the one side, except the hatred which attended the other.

It was urged by Hambden's counsel, and by his partisans in the nation, that the plea of necessity was in vain introduced into a trial of law; since it was the nature of necessity to abolish all law, and, by irresistible violence, to dissolve all the weaker and more artificial ties of human society. Not only the prince, in cases of extreme distress, is exempted from the ordinary rules of administration: all orders of men are then levelled; and any individual may consult the public safety by any expedient, which his situation enables him to employ. But to produce so violent an effect, and so hazardous to every community, an ordinary danger or difficulty is not sufficient; much less, a necessity, which is merely fictitious and pretended. Where the peril is urgent and extreme, it will be palpable to every member of the society; and though all ancient rules of government are in that case abrogated, men will readily, of themselves, submit to that irregular authority, which is exerted for their preservation. But what is there in common between such suppositions, and the present condition of the nation? England enjoys a profound peace with all her neighbours: and what is more, all her neighbours are engaged in furious and bloody wars among themselves, and by their mutual enmities farther ensure her tranquillity. The very writs themselves, which are issued for the levying of ship-money, contradict the supposition of necessity, and pretend only that the seas are infested with pirates; a slight and temporary inconvenience, which may well await a legal supply from parliament. The writs likewise allow several months for equipping the ships; which proves a very calm and deliberate species of necessity, and one that admits of delay much beyond the forty days requisite for summoning that assembly. It is strange too, that an extreme necessity which is always apparent, and usually comes to a sudden crisis, should now have continued, without interruption, for near four years, and should have remained, during so long a time, invisible to the whole kingdom. And as to the pretension, that the king is sole judge of the necessity; what is that but to subject all the privileges of the nation to his arbitrary will and pleasure? To expect that the public will be convinced by such reasoning, must aggravate the general indignation; by adding, to violence against men's persons and their property, so cruel a mockery of their understanding.

In vain are precedents of ancient writs produced: these writs, when examined, are only found to require the sea-ports, sometimes at their own charge, sometimes at the charge of the counties, to send their ships for the defence of the nation. Even the prerogative, which empowered the crown to issue such writs, is abolished, and its exercise almost entirely discontinued, from the time of Edward III.;[12] and all the authority, which remained, or was afterwards exercised, was to press ships into the public service, to be paid for by the public. How wide are these precedents from a power of obliging the people, at their own charge, to build new ships, to victual and pay them, for the public; nay, to furnish money to the crown for that purpose! What security either against the farther extension of this claim, or against diverting to other purposes the public money, so levied? The plea of necessity would warrant any other taxation as well as that of ship-money: wherever any difficulty shall occur, the administration, instead of endeavouring to elude or overcome it by gentle and prudent measures, will instantly represent it as a

12 *State Trials*, V, 245, 255. Thomas May, *History of the Long Parliament*, p. 18. Sir Philip Warwick, *Memoirs of the Reigne of King Charles I . . .* , p. 62.

reason for infringing all ancient laws and institutions: and if such maxims and such practices prevail, what has become of national liberty? What authority is left to the great charter, to the statutes, and to that very petition of right, which, in the present reign, had been so solemnly enacted by the concurrence of the whole legislature?

The defenceless condition of the kingdom while unprovided with a navy; the inability of the king, from his established revenues, with the utmost care and frugality, to equip and maintain one; the impossibility of obtaining, on reasonable terms, any voluntary supply from parliament: all these are reasons of state, not topics of law. If these reasons appear to the king so urgent as to dispense with the legal rules of government; let him enforce his edicts, by his court of star-chamber, the proper instrument of irregular and absolute power; not prostitute the character of his judges by a decree, which is not, and cannot possibly be legal. By this means the boundaries, at least, will be kept more distinct between ordinary law and extraordinary exertions of prerogative; and men will know, that the national constitution is only suspended during a present and difficult emergence, but has not undergone a total and fundamental alteration.

Notwithstanding these reasons, the prejudiced judges, four excepted,[13] gave sentence in favour of the crown. Hambden, however, obtained by the trial the end for which he had so generously sacrificed his safety and his quiet: the people were rouzed from their lethargy, and became sensible of the danger, to which their liberties were exposed. These national questions were canvassed in every company; and the more they were examined, the more evidently did it appear to many, that liberty was totally subverted, and an unusual and arbitrary authority exercised over the kingdom. Slavish principles, they said, concur with illegal practices; ecclesiastical tyranny gives aid to civil usurpation; iniquitous taxes are supported by arbitrary punishments; and all the privileges of the nation, transmitted through so

[13] See *State Trials:* article Ship-money, which contains the speeches of four judges in favour of Hambden.

many ages, secured by so many laws, and purchased by the blood of so many heroes and patriots, now lie prostrate at the feet of the monarch. What though public peace and national industry increased the commerce and opulence of the kingdom? This advantage was temporary, and due alone, not to any encouragement given by the crown, but to the spirit of the English, the remains of their ancient freedom. What though the personal character of the king, amidst all his misguided counsels, might merit indulgence, or even praise? He was but one man; and the privileges of the people, the inheritance of millions, were too valuable to be sacrificed to his prejudices and mistakes. Such, or more severe, were the sentiments promoted by a great party in the nation: no excuse on the king's part, or alleviation, how reasonable soever, could be hearkened to or admitted: and to redress these grievances, a parliament was impatiently longed for; or any other incident, however calamitous, that might secure the people against those oppressions, which they felt, or the greater ills, which they apprehended, from the combined encroachments of church and state.

# *From* Chapter LIII—Charles I

THE GRIEVANCES, under which the English laboured, when considered in themselves, without regard to the constitution, scarcely deserve the name; nor were they either burthensome on the people's properties, or any way shocking to the natural humanity of mankind. Even the imposition of ship-money, independent of the consequences, was a great and evident advantage to the public; by the judicious use, which the king made of the money levied by that expedient. And though it was justly apprehended, that such precedents, if patiently submitted to, would end in a total disuse of parliaments, and in the establishment of arbitrary authority; Charles dreaded no opposition from the people, who are not commonly much affected with consequences, and require some striking motive, to engage them in a resistance of established government. All ecclesiastical affairs were settled by law and uninterrupted precedent; and the church was become a considerable barrier to the power, both legal and illegal, of the crown. Peace too, industry, commerce, opulence; nay, even justice and lenity of administration, notwithstanding some very few exceptions: all these were enjoyed by the people; and every other blessing of government, except liberty, or rather the present exercise of liberty and its proper security.[1] It seemed probable, therefore, that affairs might long have continued on the same footing in England, had it not been for the neighbourhood of Scotland; a country more turbulent, and less disposed to submission and obedience. It was thence the commotions first arose; and it is therefore time for us to return thither, and to give an account of the state of affairs in that kingdom.

Though the pacific, and not unskilful government of James, and the great authority which he had acquired, had much

[1] Clarendon, pp. 74, 75.

allayed the feuds among the great families, and had established law and order throughout the kingdom; the Scottish nobility were still possessed of the chief power and influence over the people. Their property was extensive; their hereditary jurisdictions and the feudal tenures increased their authority; and the attachment of the gentry to the heads of families established a kind of voluntary servitude under the chieftains. Besides that long absence had much loosened the king's connections with the nobility, who resided chiefly at their country-seats; they were, in general, at this time, though from slight causes, much disgusted with the court. Charles, from the natural piety or superstition of his temper, was extremely attached to the ecclesiastics: and as it is natural for men to persuade themselves, that their interest coincides with their inclination; he had established it as a fixed maxim of policy, to increase the power and the authority of that order. The prelates, he thought, established regularity and discipline among the clergy; the clergy inculcated obedience and loyalty among the people: and as that rank of men had no separate authority, and no dependence but on the crown; the royal power, it would seem, might with the greater safety, be entrusted in their hands. Many of the prelates, therefore, were raised to the chief dignities of the state:[2] Spotswood, archbishop of the St. Andrews,[3] was created chancellor: nine of the bishops were privy councellors: the bishop of Ross aspired to the office of treasurer: some of the prelates possessed places in the exchequer: and it was even endeavoured to revive the first institution of the college of justice, and to share equally between the clergy and laity the whole judicial authority.[4] These advantages, possessed by the church, and which the

2 Rushworth, II, 386. Thomas May, [probably his *History of the Parliament of England Which Began on 3 Nov. 1640, with a Short and Necessary View of Some Precedent Years* (known as the *History of the Long Parliament*)], p. 29.

3 [John Spottiswood or Spotswood (1565–1639), author of the *History of the Church and State of Scotland from the year of our Lord 203 to the end of the reign of King James VI, 1625*.]

4 Henry Guthry, *Memoirs of Scottish Affairs, Civil and Ecclesiastical . . .* , p. 14. Gilbert Burnet, *Memoires of . . . James and William, Dukes of Hamilton*, pp. 29, 30.

bishops did not always enjoy with suitable modesty, disgusted the haughty nobility, who, deeming themselves much superior in rank and quality to this new order of men, were displeased to find themselves inferior in power and influence. Interest joined itself to ambition, and begat a jealousy, lest the episcopal sees, which, at the reformation, had been pillaged by the nobles, should again be enriched at the expence of that order. By a most useful and beneficial law, the impropriations had already been ravished from the great men: competent salaries had been assigned to the impoverished clergy from the tithes of each parish: and what remained, the proprietor of the land was empowered to purchase at a low valuation.[5] The king likewise, warranted by ancient law and practice, had declared for a general resumption of all crown-lands, alienated by his predecessors; and though he took no step towards the execution of this project, the very pretension to such power had excited jealousy and discontent.[6]

Notwithstanding the tender regard which Charles bore to the whole church, he had been able, in Scotland, to acquire only the affection of the superior rank among the clergy. The ministers in general equalled, if not exceeded, the nobility, in their prejudices against the court, against the prelates, and against episcopal authority.[7] Though the establishment of the hierarchy might seem advantageous to the inferior clergy, both as it erected dignities to which all of them might aspire, and as it bestowed a lustre on the whole body, and allured men of family into it; these views had no influence on the Scottish ecclesiastics. In the present disposition of men's minds, there was another circumstance, which drew consideration, and counterbalanced power and riches, the usual foundations of distinction among men; and that was, the fervour of piety, and the rhetoric, however barbarous, of religious lectures and discourses. Checked by the prelates in the licence of preaching, the clergy regarded episcopal jurisdiction both as tyranny and an usurpa-

5 King's Declaration, p. 7. Franklyn, p. 611.
6 King's Declaration, p. 6.
7 Burnet, *Memoires*, pp. 29, 30.

tion, and maintained a parity among ecclesiastics to be a divine privilege, which no human law could alter or infringe. While such ideas prevailed, the most moderate exercise of authority would have given disgust; much more, that extensive power, which the king's indulgence encouraged the prelates to assume. The jurisdiction of presbyteries, synods, and other democratical courts, was, in a manner, abolished by the bishops; and the general assembly itself had not been summoned for several years.[8] A new oath was arbitrarily imposed on intrants, by which they swore to observe the articles of Perth, and submit to the liturgy and canons. And in a word, the whole system of church government, during a course of thirty years, had been changed by means of the innovations, introduced by James and Charles.

.    .    .    .    .    .    .    .    .    .    .

All men, however, began to unite and to encourage each other, in opposition to the religious innovations introduced into the kingdom. Petitions to the council were signed and presented by persons of the highest quality: the women took part, and, as was usual, with violence: the clergy, every where, loudly declaimed against popery and the liturgy, which they represented as the same. The pulpits resounded with vehement invectives against antichrist: and the populace, who first opposed the service, was often compared to Balaam's ass, an animal, in itself, stupid and senseless, but whose mouth had been opened by the Lord, to the admiration of the whole world.[9] In short, fanaticism mingling with faction, private interest with the spirit of liberty, symptoms appeared, on all hands, of the most dangerous insurrection and disorder.

The primate, a man of wisdom and prudence, who was all along averse to the introduction of the liturgy, represented to the king the state of the nation: the earl of Traquaire,[10] the treasurer, set out for London, in order to lay the matter more

8 May, p. 29.

9 King's Declaration, p. 31.

10 [John Stewart, first Earl of Traquair (d. 1659), lord high treasurer of Scotland.]

fully before him: every circumstance, whether the condition of England or of Scotland were considered, should have engaged him to desist from so hazardous an attempt: yet was Charles inflexible. In his whole conduct of this affair, there appear no marks of the good sense, with which he was endowed: a lively instance of that species of character, so frequently to be met with; where there are found parts and judgment in every discourse and opinion; in many actions, indiscretion and imprudence. Men's views of things are the result of their understanding alone: their conduct is regulated by their understanding, their temper, and their passions.

To so violent a combination of a whole kingdom, Charles had nothing to oppose but a proclamation; in which he pardoned all past offences, and exhorted the people to be more obedient for the future, and to submit peaceably to the use of the liturgy. This proclamation was instantly encountered with a public protestation, presented by the earl of Hume and lord Lindsey:[11] and this was the first time that men of quality had appeared in any violent act of opposition.[12] But this proved a crisis. The insurrection, which had been advancing by a gradual and slow progress, now blazed up at once. No disorder, however, attended it. On the contrary, a new order immediately took place. Four *tables,* as they were called, were formed in Edinburgh. One consisted of nobility, another of gentry, a third of ministers, a fourth of burgesses. The table of gentry was divided into many subordinate tables, according to their different counties. In the hands of the four tables, the whole authority of the kingdom was placed. Orders were issued by them, and every where obeyed, with the utmost regularity.[13] And among the first acts of their government was the production of the *covenant.*

This famous covenant consisted first of a renunciation of

1638

11 [James Home of Coldingknows, third Earl of Home (d. 1666); John Lindsay, tenth Baron Lindsay of the Byres, first Earl of Lindsay, afterwards known as John Crawford-Lindsay, seventeenth Earl of Crawford (1596–1678).]
12 King's Declaration, pp. 47, 48ff. Guthry, p. 28. May, p. 37.
13 Clarendon, I, 111. Rushworth, II, 734.

popery, formerly signed by James in his youth, and composed of many invectives, fitted to inflame the minds of men against their fellow-creatures, whom heaven has enjoined them to cherish and to love. There followed a bond of union, by which the subscribers obliged themselves to resist religious innovations, and to defend each other against all opposition whatsoever: and all this, for the greater glory of God, and the greater honour and advantage of their king and country.[14] The people, without distinction of rank or condition, of age or sex, flocked to the subscription of this covenant: few, in their judgment, disapproved of it; and still fewer durst openly condemn it. The king's ministers and counsellors themselves were, most of them, seized by the general contagion. And none but rebels to God, and traitors to their country, it was thought, would withdraw themselves from so salutary and so pious a combination.

The treacherous, the cruel, the unrelenting Philip [II], accompanied with all the terrors of a Spanish inquisition, was scarcely, during the preceding century, opposed in the Low Countries with more determined fury, than was now, by the Scots, the mild, the humane Charles, attended with his inoffensive liturgy.

The king began to apprehend the consequences. He sent the marquis of Hamilton,[15] as commissioner, with authority to treat with the covenanters. He required the covenant to be renounced and recalled: and he thought, that on his part he had made very satisfactory concessions, when he offered to suspend the canons and the liturgy, till, in a fair and legal way, they could be received; and so to model the high commission, that it should no longer give offence to his subjects.[16] Such general declarations could not well give content to any, much less to those who carried so much higher their pretensions. The covenanters found themselves seconded by the zeal of the whole nation. Above sixty thousand people were assembled in a tumul-

14 King's Declaration, pp. 57, 58. Rushworth, II, 734. May, p. 38.

15 [James Hamilton, third Marquis and first Duke of Hamilton in the Scottish peerage (1606–1649).]

16 Rushworth, II, 754ff.

tuous manner in Edinburgh and the neighbourhood. Charles possessed no regular forces in either of his kingdoms. And the discontents in England, though secret, were believed so violent, that the king, it was thought, would find it very difficult to employ in such a cause the power of that kingdom. The more, therefore, the popular leaders in Scotland considered their situation, the less apprehension did they entertain of royal power, and the more rigorously did they insist on entire satisfaction. In answer to Hamilton's demand of renouncing the covenant, they plainly told him, that they would sooner renounce their baptism.[17] And the clergy invited the commissioner himself to subscribe it, by informing him, "With what peace and comfort it had filled the hearts of all God's people; what resolutions and beginnings of reformation of manners were sensibly perceived in all parts of the nation, above any measure they had ever before found or could have expected; how great glory the Lord had received thereby; and what confidence they had, that God would make Scotland a blessed kingdom."[18]

Hamilton returned to London: made another fruitless journey, with new concessions, to Edinburgh: returned again to London; and was immediately sent back with still more satisfactory concessions. The king was now willing entirely to abolish the canons, the liturgy, and the high commission court. He was even resolved to limit extremely the power of the bishops, and was content if on any terms he could retain that order in the church of Scotland.[19] And to ensure all these gracious offers, he gave Hamilton authority to summon first an assembly, then a parliament, where every national grievance might be redressed and remedied. These successive concessions of the king, which yet came still short of the rising demands of the malcontents, discovered his own weakness, encouraged their insolence, and gave no satisfaction. The offer, however, of an assembly and a parliament, in which they expected to be entirely masters, was willingly embraced by the covenanters.

Charles, perceiving what advantage his enemies had reaped

17 King's Declaration, p. 87.
18 *Ibid.*, p. 88. Rushworth, II, 751.
19 King's Declaration, p. 137. Rushworth, II, 762.

from their covenant, resolved to have a covenant on his side;
and he ordered one to be drawn up for that purpose. It consisted of the same violent renunciation of popery above mentioned; which, though the king did not approve of it, he thought
it safest to adopt, in order to remove all the suspicions entertained against him. As the covenanters, in their bond of mutual
defence against all opposition, had been careful not to except
the king; Charles had formed a bond, which was annexed to
this renunciation, and which expressed the duty and loyalty
of the subscribers to his majesty.[20] But the covenanters, perceiving that this new covenant was only meant to weaken and
divide them, received it with the utmost scorn and detestation.
And without delay they proceeded to model the future assembly, from which such great achievements were expected.[21]

.     .     .     .     .     .     .     .     .     .     .

The assembly met at Glasgow: and, besides a great concourse
of the people, all the nobility and gentry of any family or interest were present, either as members, assessors, or spectators; and
it was apparent, that the resolutions, taken by the covenanters,
could here meet with no manner of opposition. A firm determination had been entered into of utterly abolishing episcopacy; and as a preparative to it, there was laid before the pres-
bytery of Edinburgh, and solemnly read in all the churches of
the kingdom, an accusation against the bishops, as guilty, all
of them, of heresy, simony, bribery, perjury, cheating, incest,
adultery, fornication, common swearing, drunkenness, gaming,
breach of the sabbath, and every other crime that had occurred
to the accusers.[22] The bishops sent a protest, declining the
authority of the assembly; the commissioner too protested
against that court, as illegally constituted and elected; and, in
his majesty's name, dissolved it. This meaure was foreseen, and
little regarded. The court still continued to sit, and to finish
their business.[23] All the acts of assembly, since the accession of
James to the crown of England, were, upon pretty reasonable

20 King's Declaration, p. 140ff.
21 Rushworth, II, 772.
22 King's Declaration, p. 218. Rushworth, II, 787.
23 May, p. 44.

grounds, declared null and invalid. The acts of parliament, which affected ecclesiastical affairs, were supposed, on that very account, to have no manner of authority. And thus episcopacy, the high commission, the articles of Perth, the canons, and the liturgy, were abolished and declared unlawful: and the whole fabric, which James and Charles, in a long course of years, had been rearing with so much care and policy, fell at once to the ground.

1639    Charles had agreed to reduce episcopal authority so much, that it would no longer have been of any service to support the crown; and this sacrifice of his own interests he was willing to make, in order to attain public peace and tranquillity. But he could not consent entirely to abolish an order, which he thought as essential to the being of a Christian church, as his Scottish subjects deemed it incompatible with that sacred institution. This narrowness of mind, if we would be impartial, we must either blame or excuse equally on both sides; and thereby anticipate, by a little reflection, that judgment which time, by introducing new subjects of controversy, will undoubtedly render quite familiar to posterity.

So great was Charles's aversion to violent and sanguinary measures, and so strong his affection to his native kingdom, that, it is probable, the contest in his breast would be nearly equal between these laudable passions, and his attachment to the hierarchy. The latter affection, however, prevailed for the time, and made him hasten those military preparations which he had projected for subduing the refractory spirit of the Scottish nation. By regular oeconomy, he had not only paid all the debts contracted during the Spanish and French wars, but had amassed a sum of two hundred thousand pounds, which he reserved for any sudden exigency. The queen had great interest with the catholics, both from the sympathy of religion, and from the favours and indulgences which she had been able to procure to them. She now employed her credit, and persuaded them, that it was reasonable to give large contributions, as a mark of their duty to the king, during this urgent necessity.[24]

24 Rushworth, III, 1329. Franklyn, p. 767.

A considerable supply was obtained by this means; to the great scandal of the puritans, who were offended at seeing the king on such good terms with the papists, and repined that others should give what they themselves were disposed to refuse him.

Charles's fleet was formidable and well supplied. Having put five thousand land-forces on board, he entrusted it to the marquis of Hamilton, who had orders to sail to the Frith [i.e., Firth] of Forth, and to cause a diversion in the forces of the malcontents. An army was levied of near twenty thousand foot, and above three thousand horse, and was put under the command of the earl of Arundel,[25] a nobleman of great family, but celebrated neither for military nor political abilities. The earl of Essex,[26] a man of strict honour, and extremely popular, especially among the soldiery, was appointed lieutenant-general: the earl of Holland[27] was general of the horse. The king himself joined the army, and he summoned all the peers of England to attend him. The whole had the appearance of a splendid court, rather than of a military armament; and in this situation, carrying more show than real force with it, the camp arrived at Berwic.[28]

The Scottish army was as numerous as that of the king, but inferior in cavalry. The officers had more reputation and experience; and the soldiers, though undisciplined and ill-armed, were animated as well by the national aversion to England, and the dread of becoming a province to their old enemy, as by an unsurmountable fervour of religion. The pulpits had extremely assisted the officers in levying recruits, and had thundered out anathemas against all those "who went not out to assist the Lord against the mighty."[29] Yet so prudent were the leaders of the malcontents, that they immediately sent submissive messages to the king, and craved to be admitted to a treaty.

Charles knew that the force of the covenanters was considerable, their spirits high, their zeal furious; and that, as they

25 [Thomas Howard, second Earl of Arundel (1584–1646).]

26 [Robert Devereux, third Earl of Essex (1591–1649).]

27 [Henry Rich, first Earl of Holland (1590–1649).]

28 Clarendon, I, 115, 116, 117.

29 Burnet, *Memoires*.

were not yet daunted by any ill success, no reasonable terms could be expected from them. With regard therefore to a treaty, great difficulties occurred on both sides. Should he submit to the pretensions of the malcontents, besides that the prelacy must be sacrificed to their religious prejudices, such a check would be given to royal authority, which had, very lately, and with much difficulty, been thoroughly established in Scotland, that he must expect, ever after, to retain, in that kingdom, no more than the appearance of majesty. The great men, having proved, by so sensible a trial, the impotence of law and prerogative, would return to their former licentiousness: the preachers would retain their innate arrogance: and the people, unprotected by justice, would recognize no other authority than that which they found to domineer over them. England also, it was much to be feared, would imitate so bad an example; and having already a strong propensity towards republican and puritanical factions, would expect, by the same seditious practices, to attain the same indulgence. To advance so far, without bringing the rebels to a total submission, at least to reasonable concessions, was to promise them, in all future time, an impunity for rebellion.

On the other hand, Charles considered that Scotland was never before, under any of his ancestors, so united, and so animated in its own defence; yet had often been able to foil or elude the force of England, combined heartily in one cause, and enured by long practice to the use of arms. How much greater difficulty should he find, at present, to subdue, by violence, a people inflamed with religious prejudices; while he could only oppose to them a nation enervated by long peace, and lukewarm in his service; or, what was more to be dreaded, many of them engaged in the same party with the rebels.[30] Should the war be only protracted beyond a campaign, (and who could expect to finish it in that period?) his treasures would fail him; and for supply, he must have recourse to an English parliament, which, by fatal experience, he had ever found more ready to encroach on the prerogatives, than to supply the neces-

[30] Rushworth, III, 936.

sities, of the crown. And what if he receive a defeat from the rebel army? This misfortune was far from being impossible. They were engaged in a national cause, and strongly actuated by mistaken principles. His army was retained entirely by pay, and looked on the quarrel with the same indifference which naturally belongs to mercenary troops, without possessing the discipline by which such troops are commonly distinguished. And the consequences of a defeat, while Scotland was enraged and England discontented, were so dreadful, that no motive should persuade him to hazard it.

It is evident that Charles had fallen into such a situation, that, which ever side he embraced, his errors must be dangerous: no wonder, therefore, he was in great perplexity. But he did worse than embrace the worst side: for, properly speaking, he embraced no side at all. He concluded a sudden pacification, in which it was stipulated, that he should withdraw his fleet and army; that within eight and forty hours the Scots should dismiss their forces; that the king's forts should be restored to him; his authority be acknowledged; and a general assembly and a parliament be immediately summoned, in order to compose all differences.[31] What were the *reasons* which engaged the king to admit such strange articles of peace, it is in vain to inquire: for there scarcely could be any. The *causes* of that event may admit of a more easy explication.

The malcontents had been very industrious in representing to the English the grievances under which Scotland laboured, and the ill counsels which had been suggested to their sovereign. Their liberties, they said, were invaded: the prerogatives of the crown extended beyond all former precedent: illegal courts erected: the hierarchy exalted at the expence of national privileges: and so many new superstitions introduced by the haughty tyrannical prelates, as begat a just suspicion that a project was seriously formed for the restoration of popery. The king's conduct, surely, in Scotland, had been, in every thing, except in establishing the ecclesiastical canons, more legal than in England; yet was there such a general resemblance in the com-

31 *Ibid.*, p. 945.

plaints of both kingdoms, that the English readily assented to all the representations of the Scottish malcontents, and believed that nation to have been driven, by oppression, into the violent counsels which they had embraced. So far, therefore, from being willing to second the king in subduing the free spirit of the Scots; they rather pitied that unhappy people, who had been pushed to those extremities: and they thought that the example of such neighbours, as well as their assistance, might some time be advantageous to England, and encourage her to recover, by a vigorous effort, her violated laws and liberties. The gentry and nobility, who, without attachment to the court, without command in the army, attended in great numbers the English camp, greedily seized, and propagated, and gave authority to these sentiments: a retreat, very little honourable, which the earl of Holland, with a considerable detachment of the English forces, had made before a detachment of the Scottish, caused all these humours to blaze up at once: and the king, whose character was not sufficiently vigorous or decisive, and who was apt, from facility, to embrace hasty counsels, suddenly assented to a measure which was recommended by all about him, and which favoured his natural propension towards the misguided subjects of his native kingdom.[32]

Charles, having so far advanced in pacific measures, ought, with a steady resolution, to have prosecuted them, and have submitted to every tolerable condition demanded by the assembly and parliament; nor should he have recommenced hostilities, but on account of such enormous and unexpected pretensions, as would have justified his cause, if possible, to the whole English nation. So far, indeed, he adopted this plan, that he agreed, not only to confirm his former concessions, of abrogating the canons, the liturgy, the high commission, and the articles of Perth; but also to abolish the order itself of bishops, for which he had so zealously contended.[33] But this concession was gained by the utmost violence which he could impose on his disposition and prejudices: he even secretly retained an intention of

32 Clarendon, I, 122, 123, May p. 46.
33 Rushworth, III, 946.

seizing favourable opportunities, in order to recover the ground
which he had lost.[34] And one step farther he could not prevail
with himself to advance. The assembly, when it met, paid no
deference to the king's prepossessions, but gave full indulgence
to their own. They voted episcopacy to be unlawful in the
church of Scotland: he was willing to allow it contrary to the
constitutions of that church. They stigmatised the liturgy and
canons as popish: he agreed simply to abolish them. They denominated the high commission, tyranny: he was content to set
it aside.[35] The parliament, which sat after the assembly, advanced pretensions which tended to diminish the civil power
of the monarch; and, what probably affected Charles still more,
they were proceeding to ratify the acts of assembly, when, by
the king's instructions,[36] Traquaire, the commissioner, prorogued them. And on account of these claims, which might have
been foreseen, was the war renewed with great advantages on
the side of the covenanters, and disadvantages on that of the
king.

No sooner had Charles concluded the pacification without
conditions, than the necessity of his affairs, and his want of
money, obliged him to disband his army; and as the soldiers had
been held together solely by mercenary views, it was not possible, without great trouble, and expence, and loss of time,
again to assemble them. The more prudent covenanters had
concluded, that their pretensions being so contrary to the interests, and still more to the inclinations of the king, it was
likely that they should again be obliged to support their cause
by arms; and they were therefore careful in dismissing their
troops, to preserve nothing but the appearance of a pacific disposition. The officers had orders to be ready on the first summons: the soldiers were warned not to think the nation secure
from an English invasion: and the religious zeal which animated all ranks of men, made them immediately fly to their
standards as soon as the trumpet was sounded by their spiritual

[34] Burnet, *Memoires,* p. 154. Rushworth, III, 951.
[35] *Ibid.,* p. 958ff.
[36] *Ibid.,* p. 955.

and temporal leaders. The credit which, in their last expedition, they had acquired, by obliging their sovereign to depart from all his pretensions, gave courage to every one in undertaking this new enterprise.[37]

1640    The king, with great difficulty, found means to draw together an army; but soon discovered, that all savings being gone, and great debts contracted, his revenue would be insufficient to support them. An English parliament, therefore, formerly so unkind and intractable, must now, after above eleven years' intermission, after the king had tried many irregular methods of taxation, after multiplied disgusts given to the puritanical party, be summoned to assemble, amidst the most pressing necessities of the crown.

As the king resolved to try, whether this house of commons would be more compliant than their predecessors, and grant him supply on any reasonable terms; the time appointed for the meeting of parliament was late, and very near the time allotted for opening the campaign against the Scots. After the past experience of their ill-humour, and of their encroaching disposition, he thought that he could not in prudence trust them with a long session, till he had seen some better proofs of their good intentions: the urgency of the occasion, and the little time allowed for debate, were reasons which he reserved against the malcontents in the house: and an incident had happened, which, he believed, had now furnished him with still more cogent arguments.

The earl of Traquaire had intercepted a letter, written to the king of France by the Scottish malcontents; and had conveyed this letter to the king. Charles, partly repenting of the large concessions made to the Scots, partly disgusted at their fresh insolence and pretensions, seized this opportunity of breaking with them. He had thrown into the Tower lord Loudon,[38] commissioner from the covenanters; one of the persons who had signed the treasonable letter.[39] And he now laid the matter before the parliament, whom he hoped to inflame

37 Clarendon, I, 125. Rushworth, III, 1023.
38 [John Campbell, first Earl of Loudoun (1598–1663).]
39 Clarendon, I, 129. Rushworth, III, 956. May, p. 56.

by the resentment, and alarm by the danger, of this application
to a foreign power. By the mouth of the lord keeper, Finch, he
discovered his wants, and informed them, that he had been able
to assemble his army, and to subsist them, not by any revenue
which he possessed, but by means of a large debt of above three
hundred thousand pounds which he had contracted, and for
which he had given security upon the crown-lands. He represented, that it was necessary to grant supplies for the immediate
and urgent demands of his military armaments: that the season
was far advanced, the time precious, and none of it must be lost
in deliberation: that though his coffers were empty, they had
not been exhausted by unnecessary pomp, or sumptuous build-
ings, or any other kind of magnificence: that whatever supplies
had been levied on his subjects, had been employed for their
advantage and preservation, and like vapours rising out of the
earth, and gathered into a cloud, had fallen in sweet and re-
freshing showers on the same fields, from which they had, at first,
been exhaled: that though he desired such immediate assistance
as might prevent, for the time, a total disorder in the government, he was far from any intention of precluding them from
their right to inquire into the state of the kingdom, and to offer
him petitions for the redress of their grievances: that as much as
was possible of this season should afterwards be allowed them
for that purpose: that as he expected only such supply at present
as the current service necessarily required, it would be requisite
to assemble them again next winter, when they should have full
leisure to conclude whatever business had, this session, been left
imperfect and unfinished: that the parliament of Ireland had
twice put such trust in his good intentions, as to grant him,
in the beginning of the session, a large supply, and had ever
experienced good effects from the confidence reposed in him,
and that, in every circumstance, his people should find his conduct suitable to a just, pious, and gracious king, and such as
was calculated to promote an entire harmony between prince
and parliament.[40]

However plausible these topics, they made small impression
on the house of commons. By some illegal, and several suspi-

40 Rushworth, III, 1114.

cious measures of the crown, and by the courageous opposition which particular persons, amidst dangers and hardships, had made to them; the minds of men, throughout the nation, had taken such a turn as to ascribe every honour to the refractory opposers of the king and the ministers. These were the only patriots, the only lovers of their country, the only heroes, and, perhaps too, the only true Christians. A reasonable compliance with the court was slavish dependence; a regard to the king, servile flattery; a confidence in his promises, shameful prostitution. This general cast of thought, which has, more or less, prevailed in England, during near a century and a half, and which has been the cause of much good and much ill in public affairs, never predominated more than during the reign of Charles. The present house of commons, being entirely composed of country-gentlemen, who came into parliament with all their native prejudices about them, and whom the crown had no means of influencing, could not fail to contain a majority of these stubborn patriots.

Affairs likewise, by means of the Scottish insurrection, and the general discontents in England, were drawing so near to a crisis, that the leaders of the house, sagacious and penetrating, began to foresee the consequences, and to hope, that the time, so long wished for, was now come, when royal authority must fall into a total subordination under popular assemblies, and when public liberty must acquire a full ascendant. By reducing the crown to necessities, they had hitherto found, that the king had been pushed into violent counsels, which had served extremely the purposes of his adversaries: and by multiplying these necessities, it was foreseen, that his prerogative, undermined on all sides, must, at last, be overthrown, and be no longer dangerous to the privileges of the people. Whatever, therefore, tended to compose the differences between king and parliament, and to preserve the government uniformly in its present channel, was zealously opposed by these popular leaders; and their past conduct and sufferings gave them credit sufficient to effect all their purposes.

The house of commons, moved by these and many other obvious reasons, instead of taking notice of the king's complaints against his Scottish subjects, or his applications for supply, entered immediately upon grievances; and a speech, which Pym made them on that subject, was much more hearkened to, than that which the lord keeper had delivered to them in the name of their sovereign. The subject of Pym's harangue has been sufficiently explained above; where we gave an account of all the grievances, imaginary in the church, more real in the state, of which the nation, at that time, so loudly complained.[41] The house began with examining the behaviour of the speaker the last day of the former parliament; when he refused, on account of the king's command, to put the question: and they declared it a breach of privilege. They proceeded next to inquire into the imprisonment and prosecution of Sir John Elliot, Hollis, and Valentine.[42] the affair of ship-money was canvassed: and plentiful subject of inquiry was suggested on all hands. Grievances were regularly classed under three heads; those with regard to privileges of parliament, to the property of the subject, and to religion.[43] The king, seeing a large and inexhaustible field opened, pressed them again for supply; and finding his message ineffectual, he came to the house of peers, and desired their good offices with the commons. The peers were sensible of the king's urgent necessities; and thought that supply, on this occasion, ought, both in reason and in decency, to go before grievances. They ventured to represent their sense of the matter to the commons; but their intercession did harm. The commons had always claimed, as their peculiar province, the granting of supplies; and, though the peers had here gone no farther than offering advice, the lower house immediately thought proper to vote so unprecedented an interposition to be a breach of privilege.[44] Charles, in order to bring the matter of supply to some issue, solicited the house by new messages: and finding that ship-money gave great alarm and disgust; besides informing them, that he never intended to make a constant revenue of it, that all the money levied had been regularly, with

41 Clarendon, I, 133. Rushworth, III, 1131. May, p. 60.
42 Rushworth, III, 1136.
43 *Ibid.*, p. 1147.
44 Clarendon, I, 134.

other great sums, expended on equipping the navy; he now went so far as to offer them a total abolition of that obnoxious claim, by any law, which the commons should think proper to present to him. In return, he only asked, for his necessities, a supply of twelve subsidies, about six hundred thousand pounds, and that payable in three years; but, at the same time, he let them know, that, considering the situation of his affairs, a delay would be equivalent to a denial.[45] The king, though the majority was against him, never had more friends in any house of commons; and the debate was carried on for two days, with great zeal and warmth on both sides.

.    .    .    .    .    .    .    .    .    .    .

The king was in great doubt and perplexity. He saw, that his friends in the house were outnumbered by his enemies, and that the same counsels were still prevalent, which had ever bred such opposition and disturbance. Instead of hoping that any supply would be granted him, to carry on war against the Scots, whom the majority of the house regarded as their best friends and firmest allies; he expected every day, that they would present him an address for making peace with those rebels. And if the house met again, a vote, he was informed, would certainly pass, to blast his revenue of ship-money; and thereby renew all the opposition, which, with so much difficulty, he had surmounted, in levying that taxation. Where great evils lie on all sides, it is difficult to follow the best counsel; nor is it any wonder, that the king, whose capacity was not equal to situations of such extreme delicacy, should hastily have formed and executed the resolution of dissolving this parliament: a measure, however, of which he soon after repented, and which the subsequent events, more than any convincing reason, inclined every one to condemn. The last parliament, which ended with such rigour and violence, had yet, at first, covered their intentions with greater appearance of moderation than this parliament had hitherto assumed.

.    .    .    .    .    .    .    .    .    .    .

The king issued a declaration, in order to convince his people of the necessity, which he lay under, of dissolving the last parlia-

45 Clarendon, I, 135. Rushworth, III, 1154.

ment.[46] The chief topic, on which he insisted, was, that the commons imitated the bad example of all their predecessors of late years, in making continual encroachments on his authority, in censuring his whole administration and conduct, in discussing every circumstance of public government, and in their indirect bargaining and contracting with their king for supply; as if nothing ought to be given him but what he should purchase, either by quitting somewhat of his royal prerogative, or by diminishing and lessening his standing revenue. These practices, he said, were contrary to the maxims of their ancestors; and these practices were totally incompatible with monarchy.[47]

---

[46] Rushworth, III, 1166.

[47]* We shall here make use of the liberty, allowed in a note, to expatiate a little on the present subject. It must be confessed that the king, in this declaration, touched upon that circumstance in the English constitution, which it is most difficult, or rather altogether impossible, to regulate by laws, and which must be governed by certain delicate ideas of propriety and decency, rather than by any exact rule or prescription. To deny the parliament all right of remonstrating against what they esteem grievances, were to reduce that assembly to a total insignificancy, and to deprive the people of every advantage, which they could reap from popular councils. To complain of the parliament's employing the power of taxation, as the means of extorting concessions from their sovereign, were to expect, that they would entirely disarm themselves, and renounce the sole expedient, provided by the constitution, for ensuring to the kingdom a just and legal administration. In different periods of English story, there occur instances of their remonstrating with their princes in the freest manner, and sometimes of their refusing supply, when disgusted with any circumstance of public conduct. 'Tis, however, certain, that this power, though essential to parliaments, may easily be abused, as well by the frequency and minuteness of their remonstrances, as by their intrusion into every part of the king's counsels and determinations. Under colour of advice, they may give disguised orders; and in complaining of grievances, they may draw to themselves every power of government. Whatever measure is embraced, without consulting them, may be pronounced an oppression of the people; and, till corrected, they may refuse the most necessary supplies to their indigent sovereign. From the very nature of this parliamentary liberty, it is evident, that it must be left unbounded by law: for who can foretel, how frequently grievances may occur, or what part of administration may be affected by them? From the nature too of the human frame, it may be expected, that this liberty would be exerted in its full extent, and no branch of authority be allowed to remain unmolested in the hands of the prince: for will the weak limitations of re-

The king, disappointed of parliamentary subsidies, was obliged to have recourse to other expedients, in order to supply his urgent necessities. The ecclesiastical subsidies served him in

---

spect and decorum be sufficient to restrain human ambition, which so frequently breaks through all the prescriptions of law and justice?

But here it is observable, that the wisdom of the English constitution, or rather the concurrence of accidents, has provided, in different periods, certain irregular checks to this privilege of parliament, and thereby maintained, in some tolerable measure, the dignity and authority of the crown.

In the ancient constitution, before the beginning of the seventeenth century, the meetings of parliament were precarious, and were not frequent. The sessions were short; and the members had no leisure, either to get acquainted with each other, or with public business. The ignorance of the age made men more submissive to that authority which governed them. And above all, the large demesnes of the crown, with the small expence of government during that period, rendered the prince almost independent, and taught the parliament to preserve great submission and duty towards him.

In our present constitution, many accidents, which have rendered governments, every where, as well as in Great Britain, much more burthensome than formerly, have thrown into the hands of the crown the disposal of a large revenue, and have enabled the king, by the private interest and ambition of the members, to restrain the public interest and ambition of the body. While the opposition (for we must still have an opposition, open or disguised) endeavours to draw every branch of administration under the cognizance of parliament, the courtiers reserve a part to the disposal of the crown; and the royal prerogative, though deprived of its ancient powers, still maintains a due weight in the balance of the constitution.

It was the fate of the house of Stuart to govern England at a period, when the former source of authority was already much diminished, and before the latter began to flow in any tolerable abundance. Without a regular and fixed foundation, the throne perpetually tottered; and the prince sat upon it anxiously and precariously. Every expedient, used by James and Charles, in order to support their dignity, we have seen attended with sensible inconveniences. The majesty of the crown, derived from ancient powers and prerogatives, procured respect, and checked the approaches of insolent intruders: but it begat in the king so high an idea of his own rank and station, as made him incapable of stooping to popular courses, or submitting, in any degree, to the controul of parliament. The alliance with the hierarchy strengthened law by the sanction of religion: but it enraged the puritanical party, and exposed the prince to the attacks of enemies, numerous, violent, and implacable. The memory too of these two kings, from like causes, has been attended, in some degree, with the same infelicity, which pursued them during the whole course of their lives. Though it must be confessed, that

some stead; and it seemed but just, that the clergy should contribute to a war, which was in a great measure, of their own raising.[48] He borrowed money from his ministers and courtiers; and so much was he beloved among them, that above three hundred thousand pounds were subscribed in a few days: though nothing surely could be more disagreeable to a prince, full of dignity, than to be a burthen on his friends, instead of being a support to them. Some attempts were made towards forcing a loan from the citizens; but still repelled by the spirit of liberty, which was now become unconquerable.[49] A loan of forty thousand pounds was extorted from the Spanish merchants, who had bullion in the Tower, exposed to the attempts of the king. Coat and conduct-money for the soldiery was levied on the counties; an ancient practice,[50] but supposed to be abolished by the petition of right. All the pepper was bought from the East-India Company upon trust, and sold, at a great discount, for ready money.[51] A scheme was proposed for coining two or three hundred thousand pounds of base money.[52] Such were

---

their skill in government was not proportioned to the extreme delicacy of their situation; a sufficient indulgence has not been given them, and all the blame, by several historians, has been unjustly thrown on *their* side. Their violations of law, particularly those of Charles, are, in some few instances, transgressions of a plain limit, which was marked out to royal authority. But the encroachments of the commons, though in the beginning less positive and determinate, are no less discernible by good judges, and were equally capable of destroying the just balance of the constitution. While they exercised the powers transmitted to them, in a manner more independent, and less compliant, than had ever before been practised; the kings were, perhaps imprudently, but, as they imagined, from necessity, tempted to assume powers, which had scarcely ever been exercised, or had been exercised in a different manner, by the crown. And from the shock of these opposite pretensions, together with religious controversy, arose all the factions, convulsions, and disorders, which attended that period. (This Note was, in the first editions, a part of the text.)

[48] May, p. 48.
[49] Rushworth, III, 1181.
[50] *Ibid.*, I, 168.
[51] May, p. 63.
[52] Rushworth, III, 1216. May, p. 63.

332     DAVID HUME: PHILOSOPHICAL HISTORIAN

the extremities to which Charles was reduced. The fresh difficulties, which, admist the present distresses, were, every day,
raised, with regard to the payment of ship-money, obliged
him to exert continual acts of authority, augmented the discontents of the people, and increased his indigence and
necessities.[53]

The present expedients, however, enabled the king, though
with great difficulty, to march his army, consisting of nineteen
thousand foot and two thousand horse.[54] The earl of Northumberland was appointed general: the earl of Strafford, who
was called over from Ireland, lieutenant-general: lord Conway,
general of the horse.[55] A small fleet was thought sufficient to
serve the purposes of this expedition.

So great are the effects of zeal and unanimity, that the Scottish army, though somewhat superior, were sooner ready than
the king's; and they marched to the borders of England. To
engage them to proceed, besides their general knowledge of the
secret discontents of that kingdom, lord Saville had forged a
letter, in the name of six noblemen the most considerable of
England, by which the Scots were invited to assist their neighbours, in procuring a redress of grievances.[56] Notwithstanding
these warlike preparations and hostile attempts, the covenanters
still preserved the most pathetic and most submissive language;
and entered England, they said, with no other view, than to
obtain access to the king's presence, and lay their humble petition at his royal feet. At Newburn upon Tyne, they were opposed
by a detachment of four thousand five hundred men under
Conway, who seemed resolute to dispute with them the passage
of the river. The Scots first entreated them, with great civility,
not to stop them in their march to their gracious sovereign; and

[53] Rushworth, III, 1173, 1182, 1184, 1199, 1200, 1203, 1204.

[54] *Ibid.*, p. 1279.

[55] [Algernon Percy, tenth Earl of Northumberland (1602–1668), general of
all forces south of the Trent and a member of the council of regency; on
Strafford; see note 12, p. 273; Edward Conway, Viscount Conway, son of
Sir John Conway (d. 1631?).]

[56] John Nalson, *Impartial Collection of the Great Affairs of State . . . ,*
II, 427.

then attacked them with great bravery, killed several, and chased the rest from their ground. Such a panic seized the whole English army, that the forces at Newcastle fled immediately to Durham; and not yet thinking themselves safe, they deserted that town, and retreated into Yorkshire.[57]

The Scots took possession of Newcastle; and though sufficiently elated with their victory, they preserved exact discipline, and persevered in their resolution of paying for every thing, in order still to maintain the appearance of an amicable correspondence with England. They also dispatched messengers to the king, who was arrived at York; and they took care, after the advantage, which they had obtained, to redouble their expressions of loyalty, duty, and submission to his person, and they even made apologies, full of sorrow and contrition, for their late victory.[58]

Charles was in a very distressed condition. The nation was universally and highly discontented. The army was discouraged, and began likewise to be discontented, both from the contagion of general disgust, and as an excuse for their misbehaviour, which they were desirous of representing rather as want of will than of courage to fight. The treasury too was quite exhausted, and every expedient or supply had been tried to the uttermost. No event had happened, but what might have been foreseen as necessary, at least as very probable; yet such was the king's situation, that no provision could be made, nor was even any resolution taken, against such an exigency.

In order to prevent the advance of the Scots upon him, the king agreed to a treaty, and named sixteen English noblemen, who met with eleven Scottish commissioners at Rippon. The earls of Hertford, Bedford, Salisbury, Warwic, Essex, Holland, Bristol, and Berkshire, the lords of Kimbolton, Wharton, Dunsmore, Paget, Broke, Saville, Paulet, and Howard of Escric, were chosen by the king; all of them popular men, and consequently supposed nowise averse to the Scottish invasion, or unacceptable to that nation.[59]

57 Clarendon, I, 143.
58 Rushworth, III, 1255.
59 Clarendon, I, 155.

# *From* Chapter LIV—Charles I

THE CAUSES of disgust which, for above thirty years, had daily been multiplying in England, were now come to full maturity, and threatened the kingdom with some great revolution or convulsion. The uncertain and undefined limits of prerogative and privilege had been eagerly disputed during that whole period; and in every controversy between prince and people, the question, however doubtful, had always been decided by each party in favour of its own pretensions. Too lightly, perhaps, moved by the appearance of necessity, the king had even assumed powers incompatible with the principles of limited government, and had rendered it impossible for his most zealous partisans entirely to justify his conduct, except by topics so unpopular, that they were more fitted, in the present disposition of men's minds, to inflame, than appease, the general discontent. Those great supports of public authority, law and religion, had likewise, by the unbounded compliance of judges and prelates, lost much of their influence over the people; or rather had in a great measure gone over to the side of faction, and authorised the spirit of opposition and rebellion. The nobility, also, whom the king had no means of retaining by offices and preferments suitable to their rank, had been seized with the general discontent, and unwarily threw themselves into the scale, which already began too much to preponderate. Sensible of some encroachments which had been made by royal authority, men entertained no jealousy of the commons, whose enterprises, for the acquisition of power, had ever been covered with the appearance of public good, and had hitherto gone no farther than some disappointed efforts and endeavours. The progress of the Scottish malcontents reduced the crown to an entire dependence for supply: their union with the popular party in England brought great accession of authority to the latter: the near prospect of success rouzed all latent murmurs and pretensions which had hitherto been held in such violent constraint: and the torrent of general inclination and opinion ran so strongly against the court, that the king was in no situation to refuse any reasonable demands of the popular leaders, either for defining or limiting the powers of his prerogative. Even many exorbitant claims, in his present situation, would probably be made, and must necessarily be complied with.

The triumph of the malcontents over the church was not yet so immediate or certain. Though the political and religious puritans mutually lent assistance to each other, there were many who joined the former, yet declined all connexion with the latter. The hierarchy had been established in England ever since the reformation: the Romish church, in all ages, had carefully maintained that form of ecclesiastical government: the ancient fathers too bore testimony to episcopal jurisdiction: and though parity may seem at first to have had place among Christian pastors, the period, during which it prevailed, was so short, that few undisputed traces of it remained in history. The bishops and their more zealous partisans inferred thence the divine indefeizable right of prelacy: others regarded that institution as venerable and useful: and if the love of novelty led some to adopt the new rites and discipline of the puritans, the reverence to antiquity retained many in their attachment to the liturgy and government of the church. It behoved, therefore, the zealous innovators in parliament to proceed with some caution and reserve. By promoting all measures which reduced the powers of the crown, they hoped to disarm the king, whom they justly regarded, from principle, inclination, and policy, to be the determined patron of the hierarchy. By declaiming against the supposed encroachments and tyranny of the prelates, they endeavoured to carry the nation, from a hatred of their persons, to an opposition against their office and character. And when men were enlisted in party, it would not be difficult, they thought, to lead them by degrees into many measures, for which they formerly entertained the greatest aversion. Though the new sectaries composed not, at first, the majority of the nation, they were inflamed, as is usual among innovators, with extreme zeal for their opinions. Their unsurmountable passion, disguised to themselves, as well as to others, under the appearance of holy fervours, was well qualified to make proselytes, and to seize the minds of the ignorant multitude. And one furious enthusiast was able, by his active industry, to surmount the indolent efforts of many sober and reasonable antagonists.

When the nation, therefore, was so generally discontented, and little suspicion was entertained of any design to subvert the church and monarchy; no wonder that almost all elections ran in favour of those, who, by their high pretensions to piety and patriotism, had encouraged the national prejudices. It is a usual compliment to regard the king's inclination in the choice of a speaker; and Charles had intended to advance Gardiner, recorder of London,[1] to that important trust: but so little interest did the crown, at that time, possess in the nation, that Gardiner was disappointed of his election, not only in London, but in every other place where it was attempted: and the king was obliged to make the choice of speaker fall on Lenthal,[2] a lawyer of some character, but not sufficiently qualified for so high and difficult an office.[3]

The eager expectations of men with regard to a parliament,[4] summoned at so critical a juncture, and during such general discontents; a parliament which, from the situation of public affairs, could not be abruptly dissolved, and which was to execute every thing left unfinished by former parliaments; these motives, so important and interesting, engaged the attendance of all the members; and the house of commons was never observed to be, from the beginning, so full and numerous.

.    .    .    .    .    .    .    .    .    .    .

The universal discontent which prevailed in England against the court, was all pointed towards the earl of Strafford; though

---

[1] [Sir Thomas Gardiner (1591–1652).]

[2] [William Lenthal (1591–1662), member for Woodstock; he was unanimously elected speaker.]

[3] Clarendon, I, 169.

[4] [This is the Long Parliament; it began on November 3, 1640, and ended on March 16, 1660.]

without any particular reason, but because he was the minister of state whom the king most favoured and most trusted. His extraction was honourable, his paternal fortune considerable: yet envy attended his sudden and great elevation. And his former associates in popular counsels, finding that he owed his advancement to the desertion of their cause, represented him as the great apostate of the commonwealth, whom it behoved them to sacrifice as a victim to public justice.

Strafford, sensible of the load of popular prejudices under which he laboured, would gladly have declined attendance in parliament; and he begged the king's permission to withdraw himself to his government of Ireland, at least to remain at the head of the army in Yorkshire; where many opportunities, he hoped, would offer, by reason of his distance, to elude the attacks of his enemies. But Charles, who had entire confidence in the earl's capacity, thought, that his counsels would be extremely useful during the critical session which approached. And when Strafford still insisted on the danger of his appearing amidst so many enraged enemies, the king, little apprehensive that his own authority was so suddenly to expire, promised him protection, and assured him, that not a hair of his head should be touched by the parliament.[5]

No sooner was Strafford's arrival known, than a concerted attack was made upon him in the house of commons. Pym, in a long, studied discourse, divided into many heads after his manner, enumerated all the grievances under which the nation laboured; and, from a complication of such oppressions, inferred, that a deliberate plan had been formed of changing entirely the frame of government, and subverting the ancient laws and liberties of the kingdom.[6] Could any thing, he said, increase our indignation against so enormous and criminal a project, it would be to find, that, during the reign of the best of princes, the constitution had been endangered by the worst of ministers, and that the virtues of the king had been seduced by wicked and pernicious counsel. We must inquire, added he,

[5] Whitlocke, p. 36.
[6] *Ibid.*

from what fountain these waters of bitterness flow; and though doubtless many evil counsellors will be found to have contributed their endeavours, yet there is one who challenges the infamous pre-eminence, and who, by his courage, enterprise, and capacity, is entitled to the first place among these betrayers of their country. He is the earl of Strafford, lieutenant of Ireland, and president of the council of York, who in both places, and in all other provinces where he has been entrusted with authority, has raised ample monuments of tyranny, and will appear, from a survey of his actions, to be the chief promoter of every arbitrary council. Some instances of imperious expressions, as well as actions, were given by Pym; who afterwards entered into a more personal attack of that minister, and endeavoured to expose his whole character and manners. The austere genius of Strafford, occupied in the pursuits of ambition, had not rendered his breast altogether inaccessible to the tender passions, or secured him from the dominion of the fair; and in that sullen age, when the irregularities of pleasure were more reproachful than the most odious crimes, these weaknesses were thought worthy of being mentioned, together with his treasons, before so great an assembly. And, upon the whole, the orator concluded, that it belonged to the house to provide a remedy proportionable to the disease, and to prevent the farther mischiefs justly to be apprehended from the influence which this man had acquired over the measures and counsels of their sovereign.[7]

Sir John Clotworthy, an Irish gentleman, Sir John Hotham[8] of Yorkshire, and many others, entered into the same topics: and, after several hours spent in bitter invective, when the doors were locked, in order to prevent all discovery of their purpose; it was moved, in consequence of the resolution secretly taken, that Strafford should immediately be impeached of high treason. This motion was received with universal approbation; nor was there, in all the debate, one person that offered to stop

[7] Clarendon, I, 172.

[8] [John Clotworthy, first Lord Masserene (d. 1665); John Hotham (d. 1645), member for Beverly.]

the torrent by any testimony in favour of the earl's conduct. Lord Falkland[9] alone, though known to be his enemy, modestly desired the house to consider whether it would not better suit the gravity of their proceedings, first to digest, by a committee, many of those particulars, which had been mentioned, before they sent up an accusation against him. It was ingeniously answered by Pym, that such a delay might probably blast all their hopes, and put it out of their power to proceed any farther in the prosecution: that when Strafford should learn, that so many of his enormities were discovered, his conscience would dictate his condemnation; and so great was his power and credit, he would immediately procure the dissolution of the parliament, or attempt some other desperate measure for his own preservation: that the commons were only accusers, not judges; and it was the province of the peers to determine, whether such a complication of enormous crimes, in one person, did not amount to the highest crime known by the law.[10] Without farther debate, the impeachment was voted: Pym was chosen to carry it up to the lords: most of the house accompanied him on so agreeable an errand: and Strafford, who had just entered the house of peers, and who little expected so speedy a prosecution, was immediately, upon this general charge, ordered into custody, with several symptoms of violent prejudice in his judges, as well as in his prosecutors.

In the inquiry concerning grievances, and in the censure of past measures, Laud could not long escape the severe scrutiny of the commons; who were led too, in their accusation of that prelate, as well by their prejudices against his whole order, as by the extreme antipathy, which his intemperate zeal had drawn upon him. After a deliberation, which scarcely lasted half an hour, an impeachment of high treason was voted against this subject, the first, both in rank and in favour, throughout the kingdom. Though this incident, considering the example of Strafford's impeachment and the present disposition of the nation and parliament, needed be no surprise to him; yet was

9 [Lucius Cary, second Viscount Falkland (1610?–1643).]
10 Clarendon, I, 174.

he betrayed into some passion, when the accusation was presented. "The commons themselves," he said, "though his accusers, did not believe him guilty of the crimes with which they charged him": an indiscretion, which, next day, upon more mature deliberation, he desired leave to retract; but so little favourable were the peers, that they refused him this advantage or indulgence. Laud also was immediately, upon this general charge, sequestered from parliament, and committed to custody.[11]

.    .    .    .    .    .    .    .    .    .    .

Thus, in a few weeks, this house of commons, not opposed, or rather seconded by the peers, had produced such a revolution in the government, that the two most powerful and most favoured ministers of the king were thrown into the Tower, and daily expected to be tried for their life: two other ministers had, by flight alone, saved themselves from a like fate: all the king's servants saw that no protection could be given them by their master: a new jurisdiction was erected in the nation; and before that tribunal all those trembled, who had before exulted most in their credit and authority.

What rendered the power of the commons more formidable, was, the extreme prudence with which it was conducted. Not content with the authority, which they had acquired by attacking these great ministers, they were resolved to render the most considerable bodies of the nation obnoxious to them. Though the idol of the people, they determined to fortify themselves likewise with terrors, and to overawe those who might still be inclined to support the falling ruins of monarchy.

.    .    .    .    .    .    .    .    .    .    .

It may be worth observing, that all historians, who lived near that age, or what perhaps is more decisive, all authors, who have casually made mention of those public transactions, still represent the civil disorders and convulsions, as proceeding from religious controversy, and consider the political disputes about power and liberty as entirely subordinate to the other. It is

11 *Ibid.*, p. 177. Whitlocke, p. 38. Rushworth, III, 1365.

true, had the king been able to support government, and at the same time, to abstain from all invasion of national privileges, it seems not probable that the puritans ever could have acquired such authority as to overturn the whole constitution: yet so entire was the subjection into which Charles was now fallen, that, had not the wound been poisoned by the infusion of theological hatred, it must have admitted of an easy remedy. Disuse of parliaments, imprisonments and prosecution of members, ship-money, an arbitrary administration; these were loudly complained of: but the grievances which tended chiefly to inflame the parliament and nation, especially the latter, were the surplice, the rails placed about the altar, the bows exacted on approaching it, the liturgy, the breach of the sabbath, embroidered copes, lawn sleeves, the use of the ring in marriage, and of the cross in baptism. On account of these, were the popular leaders content to throw the government into such violent convulsions; and, to the disgrace of that age, and of this island, it must be acknowledged, that the disorders in Scotland entirely, and those in England mostly, proceeded from so mean and contemptible an origin.[12]

Some persons, partial to the patriots of this age, have ventured to put them in balance with the most illustrious characters of antiquity; and mentioned the names of Pym, Hambden, Vane, as a just parallel to those of Cato, Brutus, Cassius. Profound capacity, indeed, undaunted courage, extensive enterprise; in these particulars, perhaps the Roman do not much surpass the English worthies: but what a difference, when the discourse, conduct, conversation, and private as well as public behaviour, of both are inspected! Compare only one circumstance, and consider its consequences. The leisure of those noble ancients was

12 Lord Clarendon, I, 233, says, that the parliamentary party were not agreed about the entire abolition of episcopacy: they were only the "root and branch men," as they were called, who insisted on that measure. But those who were willing to retain bishops, insisted on reducing their authority to a low ebb; as well as on abolishing the ceremonies of worship and vestments of the clergy. The controversy, therefore, between the parties was almost wholly theological, and that of the most frivolous and ridiculous kind.

totally employed in the study of Grecian eloquence and philosophy; in the cultivation of polite letters and civilized society: the whole discourse and language of the moderns were polluted with mysterious jargon, and full of the lowest and most vulgar hypocrisy.

Charles, in the former part of his reign, had endeavoured to overcome the intractable and encroaching spirit of the commons, by a perseverance in his own measures, by a stately dignity of behaviour, and by maintaining, at their utmost height, and even perhaps stretching beyond former precedent, the rights of his prerogative. Finding, by experience, how unsuccessful those measures had proved, and observing the low condition to which he was now reduced, he resolved to alter his whole conduct, and to regain the confidence of his people, by pliableness, by concessions, and by a total conformity to their inclinations and prejudices. It may safely be averred, that this new extreme into which the king, for want of proper counsel or support, was fallen, became no less dangerous to the constitution, and pernicious to public peace, than the other, in which he had so long and so unfortunately persevered.

The pretensions with regard to tonnage and poundage were revived, and with certain assurance of success by the commons.[13] The levying of these duties, as formerly without consent of parliament, and even increasing them at pleasure, was such an incongruity in a free constitution, where the people, by their fundamental privileges, cannot be taxed but by their own consent, as could no longer be endured by these jealous patrons of liberty. In the preamble, therefore, to the bill, by which the commons granted these duties to the king, they took care, in the strongest and most positive terms, to assert their own right

---

[13] It appears not that the commons, though now entirely masters, abolished the new impositions of James, against which they had formerly so loudly complained: a certain proof that the rates of customs, settled by that prince, were in most instances just, and proportioned to the new price of commodities. They seem rather to have been low. See *Journ.*, 10th August, 1625.

of bestowing this gift, and to divest the crown of all independent title of assuming it. And that they might increase, or rather finally fix, the entire dependence and subjection of the king, they voted these duties only for two months; and afterwards, from time to time, renewed their grant for very short periods.[14] Charles, in order to show that he entertained no intention ever again to separate himself from his parliament, passed this important bill, without any scruple or hesitation.[15]

With regard to the bill for triennial parliaments, he made a little difficulty. By an old statute, passed during the reign of Edward III. it had been enacted, that parliaments should be held once every year, or more frequently if necessary: but as no provision had been made in case of failure, and no precise method pointed out for execution; this statute had been considered merely as a general declaration, and was dispensed with at pleasure. The defect was supplied by those vigilant patriots, who now assumed the reins of government. It was enacted, that if the chancellor, who was first bound under severe penalties, failed to issue writs by the third of September in every third year, any twelve or more of the peers should be empowered to exert this authority: in default of the peers, that the sheriffs, mayors, bailiffs, &c. should summon the voters: and in their default, that the voters themselves should meet and proceed to the election of members, in the same manner as if writs had been regularly issued from the crown. Nor could the parliament, after it was assembled, be adjourned, prorogued, or dissolved, without their own consent, during the space of fifty days. By this bill, some of the noblest and most valuable prerogatives of the crown were retrenched; but at the same time nothing could be more necessary than such a statute, for completing a regular plan of law and liberty. A great reluctance to assemble parlia-

[14] It was an instruction given by the house to the committee which framed one of these bills, to take care that the rates upon exportation may be as light as possible; and upon importation, as heavy as trade will bear: a proof that the nature of commerce began now to be understood. *Journ.*, 1st June, 1641.

[15] Clarendon, I, 208.

ments must be expected in the king; where these assemblies, as of late, establish it as a maxim to carry their scrutiny into every part of government. During long intermissions of parliament, grievances and abuses, as was found by recent experience, would naturally creep in; and it would even become necessary for the king and council to exert a great discretionary authority, and, by acts of state, to supply, in every emergence, the legislative power, whose meeting was so uncertain and precarious. Charles, finding that nothing less would satisfy his parliament and people, at last gave his assent to this bill, which produced so great an innovation in the constitution.[16] Solemn thanks were presented him by both houses. Great rejoicings were expressed both in the city and throughout the nation. And mighty professions were every where made of gratitude and mutual returns of supply and confidence. This concession of the king, it must be owned, was not entirely voluntary: it was of a nature too important to be voluntary. The sole inference which his partisans were entitled to draw from the submissions so frankly made to present necessity, was, that he had certainly adopted a new plan of government, and for the future was resolved, by every indulgence, to acquire the confidence and affections of his people.

.     .     .     .     .     .     .     .     .     .     .

1641     Thus perished, in the forty-ninth year of his age, the earl of Strafford,[17] one of the most eminent personages that has appeared in England. Though his death was loudly demanded as a satisfaction to justice, and an atonement for the many violations of the constitution; it may safely be affirmed, that the sentence, by which he fell, was an enormity greater than the worst of those which his implacable enemies prosecuted with so much cruel industry. The people, in their rage, had totally mistaken the proper object of their resentment. All the necessities, or, more properly speaking, the difficulties, by which the king had been induced to use violent expedients for raising supply, were the result of measures previous to Strafford's

16 *Ibid.*, p. 209. Whitlocke, p. 39. Rushworth, V, 189.
17 [Strafford was executed on May 12, 1641.]

favour; and if they arose from ill conduct, he at least was entirely innocent. Even those violent expedients themselves, which occasioned the complaint that the constitution was subverted, had been, all of them, conducted, so far as appeared, without his counsel or assistance. And whatever his private advice might be,[18] this salutary maxim he failed not, often and publicly, to inculcate in the king's presence, that, if any inevitable necessity ever obliged the sovereign to violate the laws, this license ought to be practised with extreme reserve, and, as soon as possible, a just atonement be made to the constitution, for any injury which it might sustain from such dangerous precedents.[19] The first parliament after the restoration reversed the bill of attainder; and even a few weeks after Strafford's execution, this very parliament remitted to his children the more severe consequences of his sentence: as if conscious of the violence, with which the prosecution had been conducted.

In vain did Charles expect, as a return for so many instances of unbounded compliance, that the parliament would at last show him some indulgence, and would cordially fall into that unanimity, to which, at the expense of his own power, and of his friend's life, he so earnestly courted them. All his concessions were poisoned by their suspicion of his want of cordiality; and the supposed attempt to engage the army against them, served with many as a confirmation of this jealousy. It was natural for the king to seek some resource, while all the world seemed to desert him, or combine against him; and this probably was the utmost of that embryo-scheme which was formed with regard to the army. But the popular leaders still insisted, that a desperate plot was laid to bring up the forces immediately, and offer violence to the parliament: a design of which Piercy's[20] evidence

18 That Strafford was secretly no enemy to arbitrary counsels, appears from some of his letters and dispatches, particularly Vol. II, p. 60, where he seems to wish that a standing army were established.

19 Rushworth, IV, 567, 568, 569, 570.

20 [Henry Percy, Lord Percy of Alnwick (d. 1659), whose letter to his brother, the Earl of Northumberland, served as evidence of the "first army plot"— a royalist plan to bring the army to London. Percy claimed he sought only to procure the army's declaration for the king.]

acquits the king, and which the near neighborhood of the Scottish army seems to render absolutely impracticable.[21] By means, however, of these suspicions, was the same implacable spirit still kept alive; and the commons, without giving the king any satisfaction in the settlement of his revenue, proceeded to carry their inroads, with great vigour, into his now defenceless prerogative.[22]

The two ruling passions of this parliament, were zeal for liberty, and an aversion to the church; and to both of these, nothing could appear more exceptionable, than the court of high commission, whose institution rendered it entirely arbitrary, and assigned to it the defence of the ecclesiastical establishment. The star-chamber also was a court, which exerted high discretionary powers; and had no precise rule or limit, either with regard to the causes which came under its jurisdiction, or the decisions which it formed. A bill unanimously passed the houses to abolish these two courts; and, in them, to annihilate the principal and most dangerous articles of the king's prerogative. By the same bill, the jurisdiction of the council was regulated, and its authority abridged.[23] Charles hesitated before he gave his assent. But finding that he had gone too far to retreat, and that he possessed no resource in case of a rupture, he at last affixed the royal sanction to this excellent bill. But to show the parliament, that he was sufficiently apprised of the importance of his grant, he observed to them, that this statute altered in a great measure the fundamental laws, ecclesiastical and civil, which many of his predecessors had established.[24]

[21] The project of bringing up the army to London, according to Piercy, was proposed to the king; but he rejected it as foolish: because the Scots, who were in arms, and lying in their neighbourhood, must be at London as soon as the English army. This reason is so solid and convincing, that it leaves no room to doubt of the veracity of Piercy's evidence; and consequently acquits the king of this terrible plot of bringing up the army, which made such a noise at the time, and was a pretence for so many violences.

[22] Clarendon, I, 266.

[23] *Ibid.*, pp. 283, 284. Whitlocke, p. 47. Rushworth, III, 1383, 1384.

[24] Rushworth, V. 307.

By removing the star-chamber, the king's power of binding
the people by his proclamations was indirectly abolished; and
that important branch of prerogative, the strong symbol of arbitrary power, and unintelligible in a limited constitution, being
at last removed, left the system of government more consistent
and uniform. The star-chamber alone was accustomed to punish
infractions of the king's edicts: but as no courts of judicature
now remained, except those in Westminster-hall, which take
cognizance only of common and statute law, the king may
thenceforth issue proclamations, but no man is bound to obey
them. It must, however, be confessed, that the experiment here
made by the parliament, was not a little rash and adventurous.
No government, at that time, appeared in the world, nor is perhaps to be found in the records of any history, which subsisted
without the mixture of some arbitrary authority, committed
to some magistrate; and it might reasonably, beforehand, appear
doubtful, whether human society could ever reach that state
of perfection, as to support itself with no other controul than
the general and rigid maxims of law and equity. But the parliament justly thought, that the king was too eminent a magistrate to be trusted with discretionary power, which he might so
easily turn to the destruction of liberty. And in the event it has
hitherto been found, that, though some sensible inconveniencies
arise from the maxim of adhering strictly to law, yet the advantages overbalance them, and should render the English grateful
to the memory of their ancestors, who, after repeated contests, at
last established that noble though dangerous principle.

. . . . . . . . . . .

In short, if we take a survey of the transactions of this memorable parliament, during the first period of its operations, we
shall find that, excepting Strafford's attainder, which was a complication of cruel iniquity, their merits, in other respects, so
much outweigh their mistakes, as to entitle them to praise from
all lovers of liberty. Not only were former abuses remedied, and
grievances redressed: great provision, for the future, was made
by law against the return of like complaints. And if the means by

which they obtained such advantages, savour often of artifice, sometimes of violence; it is to be considered, that revolutions of government cannot be effected by the mere force of argument and reasoning: and that factions being once excited, men can neither so firmly regulate the tempers of others, nor their own, as to insure themselves against all exorbitances.

# *From* Chapter LV—Charles I

THE ENGLISH parliament was now assembled; and discovered, in every vote, the same dispositions in which they had separated. The exalting of their own authority, the diminishing of the king's, were still the objects pursued by the majority. Every attempt which had been made to gain the popular leaders, and by offices to attach them to the crown, had failed of success, either for want of skill in conducting it, or by reason of the slender preferments, which it was then in the king's power to confer. The ambitious and enterprising patriots disdained to accept, in detail, of a precarious power; while they deemed it so easy, by one bold and vigorous assault, to possess themselves for ever of the entire sovereignty. Sensible that the measures which they had hitherto pursued, rendered them extremely obnoxious to the king; were many of them in themselves exceptionable; some of them, strictly speaking, illegal; they resolved to seek their own security, as well as greatness, by enlarging popular authority in England. The great necessities to which the king was reduced; the violent prejudices which generally, throughout the nation, prevailed against him; his facility in making the most important concessions; the example of the Scots, whose encroachments had totally subverted monarchy: all these circumstances farther instigated the commons in their invasion of royal prerogative. And the danger to which the constitution seemed to have been so lately exposed, persuaded many, that it never could be sufficiently secured, but by the entire abolition of that authority which had invaded it.

But this project, it had not been in the power, scarcely in the intention, of the popular leaders to execute, had it not been for the passion which seized the nation for presbyterian discipline, and for the wild enthusiasm which at that time accompanied it. The license which the parliament had bestowed on this spirit, by checking ecclesiastical authority; the countenance and encouragement with which they had honoured it; had already diffused its influence to a wonderful degree: and all orders of men had drunk deep of the intoxicating poison. In every discourse or conversation, this mode of religion entered; in all business it had a share; every elegant pleasure or amusement it utterly annihilated; many vices or corruptions of mind it promoted; even diseases and bodily distempers were not totally exempted from it; and it became requisite, we are told, for all physicians to be expert in the spiritual profession, and, by theological considerations, to allay those religious terrors with which their patients were so generally haunted. Learning itself, which tends so much to enlarge the mind, and humanise the temper, rather served on this occasion to exalt that epidemical frenzy which prevailed. Rude as yet, and imperfect, it supplied the dismal fanaticism with a variety of views, founded it on some coherency of system, enriched it with different figures of elocution; advantages with which a people, totally ignorant and barbarous, had been happily unacquainted.

From policy, at first, and inclination, now from necessity, the king attached himself extremely to the hierarchy: for like reasons, his enemies were determined, by one and the same effort, to overpower the church and monarchy.

While the commons were in this disposition, the Irish rebellion was the event which tended most to promote the views in which all their measures terminated. A horror against the papists, however innocent, they had constantly encouraged; a terror from the conspiracies of that sect, however improbable, they had at all times endeavoured to excite. Here was broken out a rebellion, dreadful and unexpected; accompanied with circumstances the most detestable of which there ever was any record: and what was the peculiar guilt of the Irish catholics, it was no difficult matter, in the present disposition of men's minds, to attribute to that whole sect, who were already so much the object of general abhorrence. Accustomed, in all invectives, to join the prelatical party with the papists, the people immediately supposed this insurrection to be the result of their united counsels. And when they heard that the Irish rebels pleaded the king's commission for all their acts of violence; bigotry, ever credulous and malignant, assented without scruple to that gross imposture, and loaded the unhappy prince with the whole enormity of a contrivance so barbarous and inhuman.[1]

By the difficulties and distresses of the crown, the commons,

[1] It is now so universally allowed, notwithstanding some muttering to the contrary, that the king had no hand in the Irish rebellion, that it will be superfluous to insist on a point which seems so clear. I shall only suggest a very few arguments, among an infinite number which occur. (1) Ought the affirmation of perfidious, infamous rebels ever to have passed for any authority? (2) Nobody can tell us what the words of the pretended commission were. That commission which we find in Rushworth, V, 400, and in Milton's *Works,* Toland's edition, is plainly an imposture; because it pretends to be dated in October 1641, yet mentions facts which happened not till some months after. It appears that the Irish rebels, observing some inconsistence in their first forgery, were obliged to forge this commission anew, yet could not render it coherent or probable. (3) Nothing could be more obviously pernicious to the king's cause than the Irish rebellion; because it increased his necessities, and rendered him still more dependent on the parliament, who had before sufficiently shown on what terms they would assist him. (4) The instant the king heard of the rebellion, which was a very few days after its commencement, he wrote to the parliament, and gave over to them the management of the war. Had he built any projects on that rebellion, would he not have waited some little time to see how they would succeed? Would he presently have adopted a measure which was evidently so hurtful to his authority? (5) What can be imagined to be the king's projects? To raise the Irish to arms, I suppose, and bring them over to England for his assistance. But is it not plain, that the king never intended to raise war in England? Had that been his intention, would he have rendered the parliament perpetual? Does it not appear, by the whole train of events, that the parliament forced him into the war? (6) The king conveyed to the justices intelligence which ought to have prevented the rebellion. (7) The Irish catholics, in all their future transactions with the king, where they endeavour to excuse their insurrection, never had the assurance to plead his commission. Even among themselves they dropped that pretext. It appears that Sir Phelim O'Neale, chiefly, and he only at first, promoted that imposture. See Thomas Carte, *Life of James, Duke of Ormonde,* III, 100, 111, 112, 114, 115, 121, 132, 137. (8) O'Neale himself confessed the imposture on his trial and at his execution. See Nalson, II, 528. Maguire, at his execution, made a like confession. (9) It is ridiculous to mention the justification which Charles II. gave to the marquis of Antrim, as if he had acted by his father's commission. Antrim had no hand in the first rebellion and the massacre. He joined not the rebels till two years after: it was with the king's consent; and he did important service, in sending over a body of men to Montrose.

who possessed alone the power of supply, had aggrandised themselves; and it seemed a peculiar happiness, that the Irish rebellion had succeeded, at so critical a juncture, to the pacification
of Scotland. That expression of the king's, by which he committed to them the care of Ireland, they immediately laid hold
of, and interpreted in the most unlimited sense. They had, on
other occasions, been gradually encroaching on the executive
power of the crown, which forms its principal and most natural
branch of authority; but, with regard to Ireland, they at once
assumed it, fully and entirely, as if delivered over to them by
a regular gift or assignment. And to this usurpation the king was
obliged passively to submit; both because of his inability to
resist, and lest he should still more expose himself to the reproach of favouring the progress of that odious rebellion.

 . . . . . . . . . .

To make the attack on royal authority by regular approaches,
it was thought proper to frame a general remonstrance of the
state of the nation; and accordingly, the committee, which, at
the first meeting of parliament, had been chosen for that purpose, and which had hitherto made no progress in their work,
received fresh injunctions to finish that undertaking.

The committee brought into the house that remonstrance,
which has become so memorable, and which was soon afterwards attended with such important consequences. It was not
addressed to the king; but was openly declared to be an appeal
to the people. The harshness of the matter was equalled by the
severity of the language. It consists of many gross falsehoods,
intermingled with some evident truths: malignant insinuations
are joined to open invectives: loud complaints of the past,
accompanied with jealous prognostications of the future. Whatever unfortunate, whatever invidious, whatever suspicious
measure had been embraced by the king from the commencement of his reign, is insisted on and aggravated with
merciless rhetoric: the unsuccessful expeditions to Cadiz and
the isle of Rhé, are mentioned: the sending of ships to
France for the suppression of the hugonots: the forced loans:
the illegal confinement of men for not obeying illegal com-

mands: the violent dissolution of four parliaments: the arbitrary government which always succeeded: the questioning, fining, and imprisoning of members for their conduct in the house: the levying of taxes without consent of the commons: the introducing of superstitious innovations into the church, without authority of law: in short, every thing which, either with or without reason, had given offence, during the course of fifteen years, from the accession of the king to the calling of the present parliament. And, though all these grievances had been already redressed, and even laws enacted for future security against their return, the praise of these advantages was ascribed, not to the king, but to the parliament who had extorted his consent to such salutary statutes. Their own merits too, they asserted, towards the king, were no less eminent, than towards the people. Though they had seized his whole revenue, rendered it totally precarious, and made even their temporary supplies be paid to their own commissioners, who were independent of him; they pretended, that they had liberally supported him in his necessities. By an insult still more egregious, the very giving of money to the Scots, for levying war against their sovereign, they represented as an instance of their duty towards him. And all their grievances, they said, which amounted to no less than a total subversion of the constitution, proceeded entirely from the formed combination of a popish faction, who had ever swayed the king's counsels, who had endeavoured, by an uninterrupted effort, to introduce their superstition into England and Scotland, and who had now, at last, excited an open and bloody rebellion in Ireland.[2]

This remonstrance, so full of acrimony and violence, was a plain signal for some farther attacks intended on royal prerogative, and a declaration, that the concessions already made, however important, were not to be regarded as satisfactory. What pretensions would be advanced, how unprecedented, how unlimited, were easily imagined; and nothing less was foreseen, whatever ancient names might be preserved, than

2 Rushworth, V, 438. Nalson, II, 694.

354 DAVID HUME: PHILOSOPHICAL HISTORIAN

an abolition, almost total, of the monarchical government of England. The opposition, therefore, which the remonstrance met with in the house of commons, was great. For above fourteen hours, the debate was warmly managed; and from the weariness of the king's party, which probably consisted chiefly of the elderly people, and men of cool spirits, the vote was at last carried by a small majority of eleven.[3] Some time after, the remonstrance was ordered to be printed and published, without being carried up to the house of peers, for their assent and concurrence.

As soon as the remonstrance of the commons was published, the king dispersed an answer to it. In this contest he lay under great disadvantages. Not only the ears of the people were extremely prejudiced against him; the best topics, upon which he could justify, at least apologise for his former conduct, were such as it was not safe or prudent for him at this time to employ. So high was the national idolatry towards parliaments, that to blame the past conduct of these assemblies, would have been very ill received by the generality of the people. So loud were the complaints against regal usurpations, that, had the king asserted the prerogative of supplying, by his own authority, the deficiencies in government, arising from the obstinacy of the commons, he would have increased the clamours with which the whole nation already resounded. Charles, therefore, contented himself with observing in general, that even during that period so much complained of, the people enjoyed a great measure of happiness, not only comparatively, in respect of their neighbours, but even in respect of those times, which were justly accounted the most fortunate. He made warm protestations of sincerity in the reformed religion; he promised indulgence to tender consciences with regard to the ceremonies of the church; he mentioned his great concessions to national liberty; he blamed the infamous libels every where dispersed against his person and the national religion; he complained of

[3] Whitlocke, p. 49. Dugdale, p. 71. Nalson, II, 668.

the general reproaches thrown out in the remonstrance with regard to ill counsels, though he had protected no minister from parliamentary justice, retained no unpopular servant, and conferred offices on no one who enjoyed not a high character and estimation in the public. "If, notwithstanding this," he adds, "any malignant party shall take heart, and be willing to sacrifice the peace and happiness of their country to their own sinister ends and ambition, under whatever pretence of religion and conscience; if they shall endeavour to lessen my reputation and interest, and to weaken my lawful power and authority; if they shall attempt, by discountenancing the present laws, to loosen the bands of government, that all disorder and confusion may break in upon us; I doubt not but God, in his good time, will discover them to me, and that the wisdom and courage of my high court of parliament will join with me in their suppression and punishment."[4] Nothing shows more evidently the hard situation in which Charles was placed, than to observe, that he was obliged to confine himself within the limits of civility towards subjects, who had transgressed all bounds of regard, and even of good manners, in the treatment of their sovereign.

. . . . . . . . . . .

A few days after the king was betrayed into another indiscretion, much more fatal: an indiscretion, to which all the ensuing disorders and civil wars ought immediately and directly to be ascribed. This was the impeachment of lord Kimbolton and the five members.

When the commons employed, in their remonstrance, language so severe and indecent, they had not been actuated entirely by insolence and passion: their views were more solid and prefound. They considered, that, in a violent attempt, such as an invasion of the ancient constitution, the more leisure was afforded the people to reflect, the less would they be inclined to second that rash and dangerous enterprise; that the peers would certainly refuse their concurrence, nor were there any hopes of prevailing on them, but by instigating the populace to

4 Nalson, II, 748.

tumult and disorder; that the employing of such odious means for so invidious an end, would, at long-run, lose them all their popularity, and turn the tide of favour to the contrary party; and that, if the king only remained in tranquillity, and cautiously eluded the first violence of the tempest, he would, in the end, certainly prevail, and be able at least to preserve the ancient laws and constitution. They were therefore resolved, if possible, to excite him to some violent passion; in hopes that he would commit indiscretions, of which they might make advantage.

It was not long before they succeeded beyond their fondest wishes. Charles was enraged to find that all his concessions but increased their demands; that the people, who were returning to a sense of duty towards him, were again roused to sedition and tumults; that the blackest calumnies were propagated against him, and even the Irish massacre ascribed to his counsels and machinations; and that a method of address was adopted, not only unsuitable towards so great a prince, but which no private gentleman could bear without resentment. When he considered all these increasing acts of insolence in the commons, he was apt to ascribe them, in a great measure, to his own indolence and facility. The queen and the ladies of the court farther stimulated his passion, and represented, that, if he exerted the vigour, and displayed the majesty of a monarch, the daring usurpations of his subjects would shrink before him. Lord Digby,[5] a man of fine parts, but full of levity, and hurried on by precipitate passions, suggested like counsels; and Charles, who, though commonly moderate in his temper, was ever disposed to hasty resolutions, gave way to the fatal importunity of his friends and servants.[6]

Herbert,[7] attorney general, appeared in the house of peers, and, in his majesty's name, entered an accusation of high treason against lord Kimbolton and five commoners, Hollis, Sir Arthur

5 [Presumably Lord John Digby. See note 4, p. 249 above.]
6 Clarendon, II, 360.
7 [Sir Edward Herbert (1591?–1657).]

Hazlerig, Hambden, Pym, and Strode.[8] The articles were, That they had traitorously endeavoured to subvert the fundamental laws and government of the kingdom, to deprive the king of his regal power, and to impose on his subjects an arbitrary and tyrannical authority; that they had endeavoured by many foul aspersions on his majesty and his government, to alienate the affections of his people, and make him odious to them; that they had attempted to draw his late army to disobedience of his royal commands, and to side with them in their traitorous designs; that they had invited and encouraged a foreign power to invade the kingdom; that they had aimed at subverting the rights and very being of parliament; that in order to complete their traitorous designs, they had endeavoured, as far as in them lay, by force and terror, to compel the parliament to join with them, and, to that end, had actually raised and countenanced tumults against the king and parliament; and that they had traitorously conspired to levy, and actually had levied, war against the king.[9]

The whole world stood amazed at this important accusation, so suddenly entered upon, without concert, deliberation, or reflection. Some of these articles of accusation, men said, to judge by appearance, seem to be common between the impeached members and the parliament; nor did these persons appear any farther active in the enterprises, of which they were accused, than so far as they concurred with the majority in their votes and speeches. Though proofs might, perhaps, be produced, of their privately inviting the Scots to invade England; how could such an attempt be considered as treason, after the act of oblivion which had passed, and after that both houses, with the king's concurrence, had voted that nation three hundred thousand pounds for their brotherly assistance! While the house

8 [Arthur Hesilrige or Haselrig (d. 1661); William Strode (1599?–1645), member for Beeralston. For Hollis, Hampden and Pym, see pp. 300, 305, and 243, respectively. Lord Kimbolton has not been identified by the editors.]

9 Whitlocke, p. 50. Rushworth, V, 473. Nalson, II, 811. Franklyn, p. 906.

of peers are scarcely able to maintain their independency, or to reject the bills sent them by the commons; will they ever be permitted by the populace, supposing them inclined, to pass a sentence, which must totally subdue the lower house, and put an end to their ambitious undertakings? These five members, at least Pym, Hambden, and Hollis, are the very heads of the popular party; and if these be taken off, what fate must be expected by their followers, who are many of them accomplices in the same treason? The punishment of leaders is ever the last triumph over a broken and routed party; but surely was never before attempted, in opposition to a faction, during the full tide of its power and success.

But men had not leisure to wonder at the indiscretion of this measure: their astonishment was excited by new attempts, still more precipitate and imprudent. A serjeant at arms, in the king's name, demanded of the house the five members; and was sent back without any positive answer. Messengers were employed to search for them and arrest them. Their trunks, chambers, and studies, were sealed and locked. The house voted all these acts of violence to be breaches of privilege, and commanded every one to defend the liberty of the members.[10] The king, irritated by all this opposition, resolved next day to come in person to the house, with an intention to demand, perhaps seize in their presence, the persons whom he had accused.

This resolution was discovered to the countess of Carlisle, sister to Northumberland,[11] a lady of spirit, wit, and intrigue.[12] She privately sent intelligence to the five members; and they had time to withdraw, a moment before the king entered. He was accompanied by his ordinary retinue to the number of about two hundred, armed as usual, some with halberts, some with walking swords. The king left them at the door, and he himself advanced alone through the hall; while all the mem-

10 Whitlocke, p. 50. Rushworth, V, 474, 475.

11 [Lucy Hay, Countess of Carlisle (1599–1660), a popular figure in the court of Charles, and the subject of poems by Carew, Herrick, Cartwright, Wallis, and others.]

12 Whitlocke, p. 51. Warwick, p. 204.

bers rose to receive him. The speaker withdrew from his chair, and the king took possession of it. The speech which he made was as follows: "Gentlemen, I am sorry for this occasion of coming to you. Yesterday, I sent a serjeant at arms, to demand some, who, by my order, were accused of high treason. Instead of obedience, I received a message. I must here declare to you, that, though no king, that ever was in England, could be more careful of your privileges than I shall be, yet in cases of treason no person has privilege. Therefore, am I come to tell you, that I must have these men wheresoever I can find them. Well, since I see all the birds are flown, I do expect that you will send them to me as soon as they return. But I assure you, on the word of a king, I never did intend any force, but shall proceed against them in a fair and legal way: for I never meant any other. And now since I see I cannot do what I came for, I think this is no unfit occasion to repeat what I have said formerly, that whatever I have done in favour and to the good of my subjects, I do intend to maintain it."[13]

When the king was looking around for the accused members, he asked the speaker, who stood below, whether any of these persons were in the house? The speaker, falling on his knee, prudently replied: "I have, sir, neither eyes to see, nor tongue to speak in this place, but as the house is pleased to direct me, whose servant I am. And I humbly ask pardon, that I cannot give any other answer to what your majesty is pleased to demand of me."[14]

The commons were in the utmost disorder; and, when the king was departing, some members cried aloud, so as he might hear them, "Privilege! privilege!" And the house immediately adjourned till next day.[15]

When the house of commons met, they affected the greatest dismay; and adjourning themselves for some days, ordered a committee to sit in merchant-taylors hall in the city. The com-

13 Whitlocke, p. 50.
14 *Ibid.*, May, Bk. II, p. 20.
15 Whitlocke, p. 51.

mittee made an exact inquiry into all circumstances attending the king's entry into the house: every passionate speech, every menacing gesture of any, even the meanest, of his attendants, was recorded and aggravated. An intention of offering violence to the parliament, of seizing the accused members in the very house, and of murdering all who should make resistance, was inferred. And that unparalleled breach of privilege, so it was called, was still ascribed to the counsel of papists and their adherents. This expression, which then recurred every moment in speeches and memorials, and which, at present, is so apt to excite laughter in the reader, begat at that time the deepest and most real consternation throughout the kingdom.

. . . . . . . . . . . .

The house again met; and, after confirming the votes of their committee, instantly adjourned, as if exposed to the most imminent perils from the violence of their enemies. This practice they continued for some time. When the people, by these affected panics, were wrought up to a sufficient degree of rage and terror, it was thought proper, that the accused members should, with a triumphant and military procession, take their seats in the house. The river was covered with boats, and other vessels, laden with small pieces of ordnance, and prepared for fight. Skippon, whom the parliament had appointed, by their own authority, major-general of the city-militia,[16] conducted the members, at the head of this tumultuary army, to Westminster-hall. And when the populace, by land and by water, passed Whitehall, they still asked with insulting shouts, "What has become of the king and his cavaliers? And whither are they fled?"[17]

The king, apprehensive of danger from the enraged multitude, had retired, to Hampton-court, deserted by all the world, and overwhelmed with grief, shame, and remorse, for the fatal measures into which he had been hurried. His distressed situation he could no longer ascribe to the rigours of destiny, or the malignity of enemies: his own precipitancy and indiscretion

16 Nalson, II, 833.
17 Whitlocke, p. 52. Dugdale, p. 82. Clarendon, II, 380.

must bear the blame of whatever disasters should henceforth befal him. The most faithful of his adherents, between sorrow and indignation, were confounded with reflections on what had happened, and what was likely to follow. Seeing every prospect blasted, faction triumphant, the discontented populace inflamed to a degree of fury, they utterly despaired of success, in a cause, to whose ruin friends and enemies seemed equally to conspire.

. . . . . . . . . . . . .

By the flight, or terror, or despondency of the king's party, an undisputed majority remained every where to their opponents; and the bills sent up by the commons, which had hitherto stopped with the peers, and would certainly have been rejected, now passed, and were presented for the royal assent. These were, the pressing bill with its preamble, and the bill against the votes of the bishops in parliament. The king's authority was at that time reduced to the lowest ebb. The queen too, being secretly threatened with an impeachment, and finding no resource in her husband's protection, was preparing to retire into Holland. The rage of the people was, on account of her religion, as well as her spirit and activity, universally levelled against her. Usage, the most contumelious, she had hitherto borne with silent indignation. The commons, in their fury against priests, had seized her very confessor; nor would they release him upon her repeated applications. Even a visit of the prince to his mother had been openly complained of, and remonstrances against it had been presented to her.[18] Apprehensive of attacks still more violent, she was desirous of facilitating her escape; and she prevailed with the king to pass these bills, in hopes of appeasing, for a time, the rage of the multitude.[19]

These new concessions, however important, the king immediately found to have no other effect, than had all the preceding ones: they were made the foundation of demands still more exorbitant. From the facility of his disposition, from the weakness of his situation, the commons believed that he could now

18 Nalson, II, 512.
19 Clarendon, II, 428.

refuse them nothing. And they regarded the least moment of relaxation, in their invasion of royal authority, as highly impolitic, during the uninterrupted torrent of their successes. The very moment they were informed of these last acquisitions, they affronted the queen, by opening some intercepted letters written to her by lord Digby: they carried up an impeachment against Herbert, attorney-general, for obeying his master's commands in accusing their members.[20] And they prosecuted, with fresh vigour, their plan of the militia, on which they rested all future hopes of an uncontrouled authority.

The commons were sensible that monarchical government, which, during so many ages, had been established in England, would soon regain some degree of its former dignity, after the present tempest was overblown; nor would all their new-invented limitations be able totally to suppress an authority, to which the nation had ever been accustomed. The sword alone, to which all human ordinances must submit, could guard their acquired power, and fully ensure to them personal safety against the rising indignation of their sovereign. This point, therefore, became the chief object of their aims. A large magazine of arms being placed in the town of Hull, they dispatched thither Sir John Hotham, a gentleman of considerable fortune in the neighbourhood, and of an ancient family; and they gave him the authority of governor. They sent orders to Goring, governor of Portsmouth,[21] to obey no commands but such as he should receive from the parliament. Not content with having obliged the king to displace Lunsford, whom he had appointed governor of the Tower,[22] they never ceased soliciting him, till he had also displaced Sir John Biron,[23] a man of unexceptionable character, and had bestowed that command on Sir John Coniers,[24] in whom alone, they said, they could repose confidence. After

20 Rushworth, V, 489. Clarendon, II, 385.

21 [George Goring, Baron Goring (1608–1657).]

22 Rushworth, V, 459. [Sir Thomas Lunsford (1610?–1653?), colonel in the royal army, lieutenant of the Tower.]

23 [John Byron, first Lord Byron (d. 1652).]

24 [John Conyers, not further identified by the editors.]

making a fruitless attempt, in which the peers refused their concurrence, to give public warning, that the people should put themselves in a posture of defence against the enterprises of "papists and other ill-affected persons,"[25] they now resolved, by a bold and decisive stroke, to seize at once the whole power of the sword, and to confer it entirely on their own creatures and adherents.

The severe votes, passed in the beginning of this parliament, against lieutenants and their deputies, for exercising powers assumed by all their predecessors, had totally disarmed the crown, and had not left in any magistrate military authority, sufficient for the defence and security of the nation. To remedy this inconvenience now appeared necessary. A bill was introduced and passed the two houses, which restored to lieutenants and deputies the same powers, of which the votes of the commons had bereaved them; but at the same time the names of all the lieutenants were inserted in the bill; and these consisted entirely of men, in whom the parliament could confide. And for their conduct, they were accountable, by the express terms of the bill, not to the king, but to the parliament.

The policy pursued by the commons, and which had hitherto succeeded to admiration, was, to astonish the king by the boldness of their enterprises, to intermingle no sweetness with their severity, to employ expressions no less violent than their pretensions, and to make him sensible in what little estimation they held both his person and his dignity. To a bill so destructive of royal authority, they prefixed, with an insolence seemingly wanton, a preamble equally dishonourable to the personal character of the king. These are the words: "Whereas there has been of late a most dangerous and desperate design upon the house of commons, which we have just cause to believe an effect of the bloody counsels of papists and other ill-affected persons, who have already raised a rebellion in the kingdom of Ireland. And whereas, by reason of many discoveries, we cannot but fear they will proceed, not only to stir up the like rebellions

25 Nalson, II, 850.

and insurrections in this kingdom of England; but also to back them with forces from abroad, &c."[26]

Here Charles first ventured to put a stop to his concessions; and that not by a refusal, but a delay. When this demand was made; a demand which, if granted, the commons justly regarded as the last they should ever have occasion to make; he was at Dover, attending the queen and the princess of Orange,[27] in their embarcation. He replied, that he had not now leisure to consider a matter of so great importance, and must therefore respite his answer till his return.[28] The parliament instantly dispatched another message to him, with solicitations still more importunate. They expressed their great grief on account of his majesty's answer to their just and necessary petition. They represented, that any delay, during dangers and distractions so great and pressing, was not less unsatisfactory and destructive than an absolute denial. They insisted, that it was their duty to see put in execution a measure so necessary for public safety. And they affirmed, that the people, in many counties, had applied to them for that purpose, and, in some places, were of themselves, and by their own authority, providing against those urgent dangers with which they were threatened.[29]

Even after this insolence, the king durst not venture upon a flat denial. Besides excepting to the preamble, which threw such dishonour upon him, and protesting the innocence of his intentions when he entered the house of commons; he only desired that the military authority, if it were defective, should first be conferred upon the crown; and he promised to bestow commissions, but such as should be revocable at pleasure, on the same persons whom the parliament had named in the bill.[30] By a former message he had expressed his wishes, that they would lay before him, in one view, all the concessions which

26 Rushworth, V, 519.

27 [Mary, Princess Royal of England and Princess of Orange (1631–1660), eldest daughter of Charles I and Queen Henrietta Maria.]

28 Rushworth, V, 521.

29 *Ibid.*

30 *Ibid.*

they deemed requisite for the settlement of the nation. They pretended that they were exposed to perils so dreadful and imminent, that they had not leisure for such a work.[31] The expedient proposed by the king seemed a sufficient remedy during this emergence; and yet maintained the prerogatives of the crown entire and unbroken.

But the intentions of the commons were wide of this purpose, and their panics could be cured by one remedy alone. They instantly replied, that the dangers and distempers of the nation were such as could endure no longer delay; and, unless the king speedily complied with their demands, they should be constrained, for the safety of prince and people, to dispose of the militia by the authority of both houses, and were resolved to do it accordingly. They asserted, that those parts of the kingdom which had, from their own authority, put themselves in a posture of defence during these prevailing fears and jealousies, had acted suitably to the declarations and directions of both houses, and conformably to the laws of the kingdom. And while they thus menaced the king with their power, they invited him to fix his residence at London, where they knew he would be entirely at mercy.[32]

"I am so much amazed at this message," said the king in his prompt reply, "that I know not what to answer. You speak of jealousies and fears! Lay your hands on your hearts, and ask yourselves, whether I may not likewise be disturbed with fears and jealousies: and if so, I assure you that this message has nothing lessened them.

"As to the militia, I thought so much of it before I gave that answer, and am so much assured that the answer is agreeable to what in justice or reason you can ask, or I in honour grant, that I shall not alter it in any point.

"For my residence near you, I wish it might be safe and honourable, and that I had no cause to absent myself from Whitehall: ask yourselves whether I have not.[33]

31 *Ibid.*, pp. 516, 517.
32 *Ibid.*, Pt. III, Vol. I, chap. 4, p. 523.
33 *Ibid.*, V, 524.

"What would you have? Have I violated your laws? Have I denied to pass any bill for the ease and security of my subjects? I do not ask what you have done for me.

"Have any of my people been transported with fears and apprehensions? I offer as free and general a pardon as yourselves can devise. All this considered, there is a judgment of Heaven upon this nation, if these distractions continue.

"God so deal with me and mine as all my thoughts and intentions are upright for the maintenance of the true protestant profession, and for the observance and preservation of the laws; and I hope God will bless and assist those laws for *my* preservation."[34]

No sooner did the commons despair of obtaining the king's consent to their bill, than they instantly voted, that those who advised his majesty's answer were enemies to the state, and mischievous projectors against the safety of the nation; that this denial is of such dangerous consequence, that, if his majesty persist in it, it will hazard the peace and tranquillity of all his kingdoms, unless some speedy remedy be applied by the wisdom and authority of both houses; and that such of the subjects as have put themselves in a posture of defence against the common danger, have done nothing but what is justifiable, and approved by the house.[35]

Lest the people might be averse to the seconding of all these usurpations, they were plied anew with rumours of danger, with the terrors of invasion, with the dread of English and Irish papists; and the most unaccountable panics were spread throughout the nation. Lord Digby having entered Kingston in a coach and six, attended by a few livery-servants, the intelligence was conveyed to London; and it was immediately voted, that he had appeared in a hostile manner, to the terror and affright of his majesty's subjects, and had levied war against the king and kingdom.[36] Petitions from all quarters loudly demanded of parliament to put the nation in a posture of defence;

34 *Ibid.*, p. 532.
35 *Ibid.*, Pt. III, Vol. I, chap. 4, p. 524.
36 Clarendon. Rushworth, Pt. III, Vol. I, chap. 2, p. 495.

and the county of Stafford, in particular, expressed such dread of an insurrection among the papists, that every man, they said, was constrained to stand upon his guard, not even daring to go to church unarmed.[37]

That the same violence by which he had so long been oppressed, might not still reach him, and extort his consent to the militia bill, Charles had resolved to remove farther from London: and accordingly, taking the prince of Wales[38] and the duke of York[39] along with him, he arrived, by slow journies, at York, which he determined for some time to make the place of his residence. The distant parts of the kingdom, being removed from that furious vortex of new principles and opinions which had transported the capital, still retained a sincere regard for the church and monarchy; and the king here found marks of attachment beyond what he had before expected.[40] From all quarters of England, the prime nobility and gentry, either personally, or by messages and letters, expressed their duty towards him; and exhorted him to save himself and them from that ignominious slavery with which they were threatened. The small interval of time which had passed since the fatal accusation of the members, had been sufficient to open the eyes of many, and to recover them from the astonishment with which at first they had been seized. One rash and passionate attempt of the king's seemed but a small counterbalance to so many acts of deliberate violence, which had been offered to him and every branch of the legislature: and, however sweet the sound of liberty, many resolved to adhere to that moderate freedom transmitted them from their ancestors, and now better secured by such important concessions; rather than, by engaging in a giddy search after more independence, run a manifest risk, either of incurring a cruel subjection, or abandoning all law and order.

Charles, finding himself supported by a considerable party

37 Dugdale, p. 89.
38 [Charles, later Charles II (1630–1685).]
39 [James, later James II (1633–1701), second son of Charles I and Queen Henrietta Maria.]
40 Warwick, p. 203.

in the kingdom, began to speak in a firmer tone, and to retort the accusations of the commons with a vigour which he had not before exerted. Notwithstanding their remonstrances, and menaces, and insults, he still persisted in refusing their bill; and they proceeded to frame an ordinance, in which, by the authority of the two houses, without the king's consent, they named lieutenants for all the counties, and conferred on them the command of the whole military force, of all the guards, garrisons, and forts of the kingdom. He issued proclamations against this manifest usurpation; and as he professed a resolution strictly to observe the law himself, so was he determined, he said, to oblige every other person to pay it a like obedience. The name of the king was so essential to all laws, and so familiar in all acts of executive authority, that the parliament was afraid, had they totally omitted it, that the innovation would be too sensible to the people. In all commands, therefore, which they conferred, they bound the persons to obey the orders of his majesty, signified by both houses of parliament. And, inventing a distinction, hitherto unheard of, between the office and the person of the king; those very forces which they employed against him, they levied in his name, and by his authority.[41]

It is remarkable how much the topics of argument were now reversed between the parties. The king, while he acknowledged his former error, of employing a plea of necessity, in order to infringe the laws and constitution, warned the parliament not to imitate an example on which they threw such violent blame; and the parliament, while they clothed their personal fears or ambition under the appearance of national and imminent danger, made unknowingly an apology for the most exceptionable part of the king's conduct. That the liberties of the people were no longer exposed to any peril from royal authority, so narrowly circumscribed, so exactly defined, so much unsupported by revenue and by military power, might be maintained upon very plausible topics: but that the danger, allowing it to have any existence, was not of that kind; great, urgent, inevitable; which

41 Rushworth, V, 526.

dissolves all laws, and levels all limitations, seems apparent from the simplest view of these transactions. So obvious indeed was the king's present inability to invade the constitution, that the fears and jealousies which operated on the people, and pushed them so furiously to arms, were undoubtedly not of a civil, but of a religious nature. The distempered imaginations of men were agitated with a continual dread of popery, with a horror against prelacy, with an antipathy to ceremonies and the liturgy, and with a violent affection for whatever was most opposite to these objects of aversion. The fanatical spirit let loose, confounded all regard to ease, safety, interest; and dissolved every moral and civil obligation.[42]

[42]* The great courage and conduct, displayed by many of the popular leaders, have commonly inclined men to do them, in one respect, more honour than they deserve, and to suppose, that, like able politicians, they employed pretences which they secretly despised, in order to serve their selfish purposes. It is, however, probable, if not certain, that they were, generally speaking, the dupes of their own zeal. Hypocrisy, quite pure and free from fanaticism, is perhaps, except among men fixed in a determined philosophical scepticism, then unknown, as rare as fanaticism entirely purged from all mixture of hypocrisy. So congenial to the human mind are religious sentiments, that it is impossible to counterfeit long these holy fervours, without feeling some share of the assumed warmth: and, on the other hand, so precarious and temporary, from the frailty of human nature, is the operation of these spiritual views, that the religious ecstasies, if constantly employed, must often be counterfeit, and must be warped by those more familiar motives of interest and ambition, which insensibly gain upon the mind. This indeed seems the key to most of the celebrated characters of that age. Equally full of fraud and of ardour, these pious patriots talked perpetually of seeking the Lord, yet still pursued their own purposes; and have left a memorable lesson to posterity, how delusive, how destructive, that principle is by which they were animated.

With regard to the people, we can entertain no doubt, that the controversy was, on their part, entirely theological. The generality of the nation could never have flown out into such fury, in order to obtain new privileges and acquire greater liberty than they and their ancestors had ever been acquainted with. Their fathers had been entirely satisfied with the government of Elizabeth: why should they have been thrown into such extreme rage against Charles, who, from the beginning of his reign, wished only to maintain such a government? And why not, at least, compound matters with him, when, by all his laws, it appeared, that he had agreed to depart from it?

Each party was now willing to throw on its antagonist the odium of commencing a civil war; but both of them prepared for an event which they deemed inevitable. To gain the people's favour and good opinion, was the chief point on both sides. Never was there a people less corrupted by vice, and more actuated by principle, than the English during that period: never were there individuals who possessed more capacity, more courage, more public spirit, more disinterested zeal. The infusion of one ingredient, in too large a proportion, had corrupted all these noble principles, and converted them into the most virulent poison. To determine his choice in the approaching contests, every man hearkened with avidity to the reasons proposed on both sides. The war of the pen preceded that of the sword, and daily sharpened the humours of the opposite parties.

. . . . . . . . . . .

That the king might despair of all composition, the parliament sent him the conditions, on which they were willing to come to an agreement. Their demands, contained in nineteen propositions, amounted to a total abolition of monarchical authority. They required, that no man should remain in the council, who was not agreeable to parliament; that no deed of the king's should have validity, unless it passed the council, and was attested under their hand; that all the officers of state and principal judges should be chosen with consent of parliament, and enjoy their offices for life; that none of the royal family should marry without consent of parliament or council; that the laws should be executed against catholics; that the votes of popish lords should be excluded; that the reformation

---

Especially, as he had put it entirely out of his power to retract that resolution. It is in vain, therefore, to dignify this civil war and the parliamentary authors of it, by supposing it to have any other considerable foundation than theological zeal, that great and noted source of animosity among men. The royalists also were very commonly zealots; but as they were, at the same time, maintaining the established constitution, in state as well as church, they had an object which was natural, and which might produce the greatest passion, even without any considerable mixture of theological fervour. (The former part of this note was, in the first editions, a part of the text.)

of the liturgy and church-government should have place, according to advice of parliament; that the ordinance, with regard to the militia, be submitted to; that the justice of parliament pass upon all delinquents; that a general pardon be granted, with such exceptions as should be advised by parliament; that the forts and castles be disposed of by consent of parliament; and that no peer be made but with consent of both houses.[43]

"Should I grant these demands," said the king in reply, "I may be waited on bareheaded; I may have my hand kissed; the title of Majesty may be continued to me; and *The king's authority, signified by both houses,* may still be the style of your commands; I may have swords and maces carried before me, and please myself with the sight of a crown and sceptre (though even these twigs would not long flourish, when the stock upon which they grew was dead): but as to true and real power, I should remain but the outside, but the picture, but the sign of a king."[44] War on any terms was esteemed, by the king and all his counsellors, preferable to so ignominious a peace. Charles accordingly resolved to support his authority by arms. "His towns," he said, "were taken from him, his ships, his arms, his money; but there still remained to him a good cause, and the hearts of his loyal subjects, which, with God's blessing, he doubted not, would recover all the rest." Collecting therefore some forces, he advanced southwards; and at Nottingham he erected his royal standard, the open signal of discord and civil war throughout the kingdom.

43 Rushworth, V, 722. May, Bk. II, p. 54.
44 Rushworth, V, 728. Warwick, p. 189.

# *From* Chapter LIX—Charles I

THE CHARACTER of this prince, as that of most men, if not of all men, was mixed; but his virtues predominated extremely above his vices, or, more properly speaking, his imperfections; for scarce any of his faults rose to that pitch as to merit the appellation of vices. To consider him in the most favorable light, it may be affirmed, that his dignity was free from pride, his humanity from weakness, his bravery from rashness, his temperance from austerity, his frugality from avarice; all these virtues in him maintained their proper bounds, and merited unreserved praise. To speak the most harshly of him, we may affirm, that many of his good qualities were attended with some latent frailty, which, though seemingly inconsiderable, was able, when seconded by the extreme malevolence of his fortune, to disappoint them of all their influence: his beneficent disposition was clouded by a manner not very gracious; his virtue was tinctured with superstition; his good sense was disfigured by a deference to persons of a capacity inferior to his own; and his moderate temper exempted him not from hasty and precipitate resolutions. He deserves the epithet of a good, rather than of a great man: and was more fitted to rule in a regular established government, than either to give way to the encroachments of a popular assembly, or finally to subdue their pretensions. He wanted suppleness and dexterity sufficient for the first measure; he was not endowed with the vigor requisite for the second. Had he been born an absolute prince, his humanity and good sense had rendered his reign happy and his memory precious; had the limitations on prerogative been, in his time, quite fixed and certain, his integrity had made him regard as sacred the boundaries of the constitution. Unhappily, his fate threw him into a period, when the precedents of many former reigns savoured strongly of arbitrary power, and the genius of the people ran violently towards liberty. And, if his political prudence was not sufficient to extricate him from so perilous a situation, he may be excused; since, even after the event, when it is commonly easy to correct all errors, one is at a loss to determine what conduct, in his circumstances, could have maintained the authority of the crown, and preserved the peace of the nation. Exposed; without revenue, without arms, to the assault of furious, implacable, and bigoted factions, it was never permitted him, but with the most fatal consequences, to commit the smallest mistake; a condition too rigorous to be imposed on the greatest human capacity.

Some historians have rashly questioned the good faith of this prince; but, for this reproach, the most malignant scrutiny of his conduct, which in every circumstance is now thoroughly known, affords not any reasonable foundation. On the contrary, if we consider the extreme difficulties, to which he was so frequently reduced, and compare the sincerity of his professions and declarations, we shall avow, that probity and honor ought justly to be numbered among his most shining qualities. In every treaty, those concessions which he thought he could not in conscience maintain, he never could, by any motive or persuasion, be induced to make. And though some violations of the petition of right may perhaps be imputed to him, these are more to be ascribed to the necessity of his situation, and to the lofty ideas of royal prerogative, which, from former established precedents, he had imbibed, than to any failure in the integrity of his principles.

This prince was of a comely presence; of a sweet, but melancholy aspect. His face was regular, handsome, and well complexioned; his body strong, healthy, and justly proportioned; and being of a middle stature, he was capable of enduring the greatest fatigues. He excelled in horsemanship and other exercises; and he possessed all the exterior, as well as many of the essential qualities, which form an accomplished prince.

The tragical death of Charles begat a question, whether the people, in any case, were entitled to judge and to punish their sovereign; and most men, regarding chiefly the atrocious usurpation of the pretended judges, and the merit of the virtuous prince who suffered, were inclined to condemn the republican principle, as highly seditious and extravagant: but there still were a few who, abstracting from the particular circumstances of this case, were able to consider the question in general, and were inclined to moderate, not contradict, the prevailing sentiment. Such might have been their reasoning. If ever, on any occasion, it were laudable to conceal truth from the populace, it must be confessed, that the doctrine of resistance affords such an example; and that all speculative reasoners ought to observe, with regard to this principle, the same cautious silence which the laws, in every species of government, have ever prescribed to themselves. Government is instituted in order to restrain the fury and injustice of the people; and being always founded on opinion, not on force, it is dangerous to weaken, by these speculations, the reverence which the multitude owe to authority, and to instruct them beforehand, that the case can ever happen when they may be freed from their duty of allegiance. Or should it be found impossible to restrain the license of human disquisitions, it must be acknowledged, that the doctrine of obedience ought alone to be *inculcated;* and that the exceptions, which are rare, ought seldom or never to be mentioned in popular reasonings and discourses. Nor is there any danger that mankind, by this prudent reserve, should universally degenerate into a state of abject servitude. When the exception really occurs, even though it be not previously expected and descanted on, it must, from its very nature, be so obvious and undisputed, as to remove all doubt, and overpower the restraint, however great, imposed by teaching the general doctrine of obedience. But between resisting a prince and dethroning him, there is a wide interval; and the abuses of power, which can warrant the latter violence, are greater and more enormous than those which will justify the former. History, however, supplies us with examples even of this kind; and the reality of the supposition, though, for the future, it ought ever to be little looked for, must, by all candid inquirers, be acknowledged in the past. But between dethroning a prince and punishing him, there is another very wide interval; and it were not strange, if even men of the most enlarged thought should question, whether human nature could ever, in any monarch, reach that height of depravity, as to warrant, in revolted subjects, this last act of extraordinary jurisdiction. That illusion, if it be an illusion, which teaches us to pay a sacred regard to the persons of princes, is so salutary, that, to dissipate it, by the formal trial and punishment of a sovereign, will have more pernicious effects upon the people, than the example of justice can be supposed to have a beneficial influence upon princes, by checking their career of tyranny. It is dangerous also, by these examples, to reduce princes to despair, or bring matters to such extremities against persons endowed with great power, as to leave them no resource, but in the most violent and most sanguinary counsels. This general position being established, it must, however, be observed, that no reader, almost of any party or principle, was ever shocked, when he read in ancient history, that the Roman senate voted Nero, their absolute sovereign, to be a public enemy, and, even without trial, condemned him to the severest and most ignominious punishment; a punishment from which the meanest Roman citizen was, by the laws, exempted. The crimes of that bloody tyrant are so enormous, that they break through all rules; and extort a confession, that such a dethroned prince is no longer superior to his people, and can no longer plead, in his own defence, laws which were established for conducting the ordinary course of administration. But, when we pass from the case of Nero, to that of Charles, the great disproportion, or rather total contrariety, of character immediately strikes us; and we stand astonished, that, among a civilized people, so much virtue could ever meet with so fatal a catastrophe. History, the great mistress of wisdom, furnishes examples of all kinds; and every prudential, as well as moral precept, may be authorized by those events which her enlarged mirror is able to present to us. From the memorable revolutions, which passed in England during this period, we may naturally deduce the same useful lesson which Charles himself, in his later years, inferred; that it is dangerous for princes, even from the appearance of necessity, to assume more authority than the laws have allowed them. But it must be confessed, that these events furnish us with another instruction, no less natural, and no less useful, concerning the madness of the people, the furies of fanaticism, and the danger of mercenary armies.

# REVIEW OF ROBERT HENRY'S
## *HISTORY OF GREAT BRITAIN*

[*Dr. Robert Henry, a Scottish clergyman, published in 1771 and 1773, respectively, Volumes I and II of what was to become a six-volume* History of Great Britain. *Henry, unable to find a publisher willing to purchase his work, published these volumes at his own expense, and in an effort to insure his financial and literary success, he asked for Hume's aid. Hume read an advance copy of Volume II; approving of it, he requested the opportunity to review it for the* Edinburgh Magazine and Review, *a periodical that had harshly treated an earlier work by Henry. Gilbert Stuart, editor of the* Review, *granted Hume's request, but he apparently had no intention of allowing a favorable review of the work to appear in his magazine. Eventually, through Stuart's chicanery, Hume's review was withheld and Stuart's own substituted. It is gratifying to note that this underhanded attempt to dissuade the public from Henry's work was unsuccessful.*

*The original proof sheets of this review, with Hume's own corrections, may be seen at the William Andrews Clark Memorial Library, Los Angeles. The text here, with the exception of two or three additional corrections of minor typographical errors, represents these proofs as Hume's own corrections leave them. For a fuller account of the intrigue in which this Review was involved, see Mossner, "Hume as Literary Patron: A Suppressed Review of Robert Henry's* History of Great Britain, *1773" (see Bibliography, p. liv).*]

*The History of Great Britain, from the first Invasion of it by the Romans under Julius Caesar. Written on a new Plan. By*

ROBERT HENRY, D.D. *one of the Ministers of Edinburgh. Vol. 2. 4to. London, Cadell, Edinburgh. £.1:1:0, in Boards.*

THOUGH THE second volume of Dr. Henry's history of Great Britain will not be published till the first or second week of January, as we are informed; yet, as many copies of it have been privately sold by the author, we cannot resist the inclination we have of communicating to the public the sentiments we entertain concerning that work in general; the perusing of performances of uncommon merit, and the recommending of them to the attention and particular favour of the world, being the most agreeable part of the office of Reviewers. We can venture, then, with the greatest sincerity, to recommend this volume to the perusal of every curious reader, who wishes to know the state of Great Britain in a period which has formerly been regarded as very obscure, viz. from the arrival of the Saxons in 449, to the landing of William Duke of Normandy in 1066. In those dark ages, this island produced few writers of history, and these few were only obscure monks of little learning and less taste, whose works cannot be read without disgust. It is, indeed, wonderful what an instructive, and even entertaining book, Dr. Henry has been able to compose from such unpromising materials! *Tantum series juncturaque pollet!*[1] When we see those barbarous ages delineated by so able a pen, we admire the *oddness* of their manners, customs, and opinions, and are transported, as it were, into a new world.

The first chapter contains the civil and military history of all the different nations inhabiting the island of Great Britain, from the arrival of the Saxons, A.D. 449, to the landing of William Duke of Normandy, A.D. 1066. It is evidently a most difficult task to form the civil and military transactions of so many nations into one perspicuous narration, through a period of more than six centuries. To accomplish this, Dr. Henry hath employed several contrivances with the greatest success. He hath divided this long period into five parts, each part constituting

---

[1] ["Such order and uniting is powerful!"]

the subject of one particular section. Thus, the first section contains the civil and military history of all the British nations, from the arrival of the Saxons, to the full establishment of the heptarchy, A.D. 600. The second, from thence to the accession of Egbert the first English monarch, A.D. 801. The third, to the death of Alfred the Great, A.D. 901. The fourth, to the death of Edward the Martyr, A.D. 978. And the fifth to the end of the period, A.D. 1066. In each of these sections, the civil and military transactions of the Anglo-Saxons are first related, and then those of the ancient Britons, Scots, and Picts, as long as they continued to form a distinct nation. In the second section, which contains the history of the heptarchy, the transactions in all the other states are regulated by the chronology of the west Saxon kingdom. By this delicate and well fancied method, the thread of the narration is preserved unbroken, and some degree of unity and order introduced into a portion of the history of Great Britain, which has perplexed the acuteness of our most philosophical and accomplished historians.

The second chapter contains the history of religion in each of the British nations, from the beginning, to the end of this period, and is also divided into five sections, with the same beautiful propriety and advantage. The first of these sections contains a very curious account of the priests, imaginary deities, sacrifices, and religious rites of the Saxons and Danes, while they continued to be pagans. In the second section, the conversion of the Anglo-Saxons to christianity is related, and a brief account is given of the instruments, the time, and manner of the establishment of that religion, in all the states of the heptarchy. In the other three sections, the ecclesiastical history of all the British nations is prosecuted to the end of this period. At the conclusion of each of these sections, is a brief delineation of the state of religion, and of the innovations which had been at that time introduced, of which the following instructive passage, at the end of the third section of this chapter, may serve as a proper specimen. "Ignorance and superstition increased greatly in the church of England, as well as in other parts of the Christian world, in the course of the eighth century. Pilgrimages to Rome became far more frequent, and were attended with worse effects than formerly;—the rage of retiring into monasteries became more violent in persons of all ranks, to the ruin of military discipline, and of every useful art;—the clergy became more knavish and rapacious, and the laity more abject and stupid, than in any former period. Of this the trade of relics, which can never be carried on but between knaves and fools, is a sufficient evidence. The number of holidays, and of childish and trifling ceremonies, which are equally pernicious to honest industry and rational religion, were very much increased in the course of this dark age. As the Britons, Scots, and Picts had little or no intercourse with Rome in this period, it is probable, that superstition had not made such rapid progress amongst them as amongst the English. But we know so little of the ecclesiastical history of these three nations in this century, that we can produce nothing of certainty and importance on that subject, unless the conversion of the Scots and Picts to the Roman rule in celebrating Easter, which happened in this century, can be called important."

The third chapter of this book will be esteemed by many readers the most curious, important, and interesting part of the whole work. It contains the history of the constitution, government, and laws of Great Britain, from the arrival of the Saxons to the Norman conquest. It is divided into three sections: The first contains a brief account of the several German nations which settled in Britain during this period; of the places of their original seats on the continent; of the situation and limits of their settlements in the island; of the political divisions of their territories that were made by them and by the other British nations. The observations on the state of population in the Anglo-Saxon times, at the end of this section, are exceedingly ingenious, and might have proceeded from the most experienced politician. The second section of this chapter contains a very particular description of the different ranks of the people; and of the courts of justice in the Anglo-Saxon times. The ranks of the people described in this section, are these five; Slaves, Frelazins, Ceorls, Thanes, and Clitones. The ranks of magistrates described are also five; viz. Borsholders, Hundredaries, Shere-geruves, Aldermen, and Cyrings. But the courts are only four, viz. the Decennary court, the Hundred court, the Shiregemote, and the Wittenagemote. Many of our readers will be agreeably delighted with the curious description of the great officers in the courts of the Anglo-Saxon and Welsh kings, at the end of this section. The subject of the third section of this chapter is, the history of laws in this period, particularly of the Anglo-Saxon and Welsh laws. This section is instructive and learned in the highest degree. It contains much original remark, and, in particular, a very distinct description of all the different Ordeals used in England in the period under observation.

The fourth chapter of this volume contains the history of learning. "It will be necessary, (says the author), to prevent confusion in this period, which is long as well as dark, to divide it into the several centuries of which it consisted, giving a concise account of the state of learning; of the most learned men; and of the chief seminaries of learning, in each of these centuries, in their natural order." This, we think, he hath executed in a very masterly manner; and produced a more satisfactory and entertaining account of the state of learning, in those dark ages, than could have been expected. Who, for example, could have expected so authentic and distinct an account of the sciences studied in England in the seventh century, as is contained in the following letter from Aldhelm, a student in the academy of Canterbury, to Hedda bishop of Winchester: —"I confess, Most Reverend Father, that I had resolved, if circumstances would permit, to spend the approaching Christmas in the company of my relations, and to enjoy, for some time, the felicity of your conversation. But, since I now find that it will be impossible for me to accomplish that design, for various reasons, which the bearer of this letter will communicate, I hope you will have the goodness to excuse my not waiting upon you as I intended. The truth is, that there is a necessity for spending a great deal of time in this seat of learning, especially for one who is inflamed with the love of reading, and is earnestly desirous, as I am, of being intimately acquainted with all the secrets of the Roman jurisprudence. Besides, there is another study in which I am engaged, which is still more tedious and perplexing,—to make myself master of all the rules of a hundred different kinds of verses, and of the musical modulations of words and syllables. This study is rendered more difficult, and almost inextricable, by the great scarcity of able teachers. But it would far exceed the bounds of a familiar letter to explain this matter fully, and lay open all the secrets of the art of metre, concerning letters, syllables, poetic feet and figures, verses, tones, time, &c. Add to this the doctrine of the seven divisions of poetry, with all their variations, and what number of feet every different kind of verse must consist of. The perfect knowledge of all this, and several other things of the like kind, cannot, I imagine, be acquired in a short space of time. But what shall I say of arithmetic, whose long and intricate calculations are sufficient to overwhelm the mind, and throw it into despair? For my own part, all the labour of my former studies, by which I had made myself a complete master of several sciences, was trifling, in comparison of what this cost me; so that I may say with St. Jerome, upon a similar occasion,—Before I entered upon that study, I thought myself a master; but then I found I was but a learner.—However, by the blessing of God, and assiduous reading, I have at length overcome the greatest difficulties, and found out the method of calculating suppositions, which are called the parts of a number. I believe it will be better to say nothing at all of astronomy, the zodiac, and its twelve signs revolving in the heavens, which require a long illustration, than to disgrace that noble art by too short and imperfect an account; especially as there are some parts of it, as astrology, and the perplexing calculation of horoscopes, which require the hand of a master to do them justice" (pp. 320, 321).

Aldhelm, Bishop of Shereburn, Venerable Beda, Alcuinus preceptor to Charlemagne, Alfred the Great, and John Scot of Air, appear, from the accounts here given of their genius and erudition, to have been the most illustrious luminaries of Britain, and even of Europe, in the times in which they flourished. How ardent a love of learning is expressed in the following

letter of Alcuinus to his royal friend and pupil Charlemagne:—
"The contemplation, O most excellent Prince! of that pure
and virtuous friendship with which you honour me, fills my
mind at all times with the most abundant comfort; and I cherish
in my heart, as its most precious treasure, the remembrance of
your goodness, and the image of that benign and gracious
countenance with which you entertain your friends. In my
retirement, it is the greatest joy of my life to hear of your
prosperity; and therefore I have sent this young gentleman to
bring me an exact account of your affairs, that I may have
reason to sing the loudest praises to my Lord Jesus Christ for
your felicity. But why do I say that I may have reason?—the
whole Christian world hath reason to praise Almighty God,
with one voice, that he hath raised up so pious, wise, and just
a prince, to govern and protect it in these most dangerous times;
a prince who makes it the whole joy of his heart, and business
of his life, to suppress every thing that is evil, and promote
every that is good; to advance the glory of God, and spread the
knowledge of the Christian religion into the most distant corners of the world.

"Persevere, O most dear and amiable prince, in your most
honourable course, in making the improvement of your subjects
in knowledge, virtue, and happiness, the great object of your
pursuit; for this shall redound to your glory and your felicity
in the great day of the Lord, and in the eternal society of his
saints. Such noble designs and glorious efforts, you may depend
upon it, shall not go unrewarded; for though the life of man is
short, the goodness of God is infinite, and he will recompense
our momentary toils with joys which shall never end. How
precious then is time! and how careful should we be, that we do
not lose by our indolence, those immortal felicities which we
may obtain by the active virtues of a good life!

"The employments of your Alcuinus in his retreat are suited
to his humble sphere; but they are neither inglorious nor un-
profitable. I spend my time in the halls of St. Martin, in teaching some of the noble youths under my care the intricacies of
grammar, and inspiring them with a taste for the learning of

the ancients; in describing to others the order and revolutions of those shining orbs which adorn the azure vault of heaven; and in explaining to others the mysteries of divine wisdom, which are contained in the holy scriptures; suiting my instructions to the views and capacities of my scholars, that I may train up many to be ornaments to the church of God, and to the court of your Imperial Majesty. In doing this I find a great want of several things, particularly of those excellent books in all arts and sciences which I enjoyed in my native country, through the expence and care of my great master Egbert. May it therefore please your Majesty, animated with the most ardent love of learning, to permit me to send some of our young gentlemen into England, to procure for us those books which we want, and transplant the flowers of Britain into France, that their fragrance may no longer be confined to York, but may perfume the palaces of Tours.

"I need not put your Majesty in mind, how earnestly we are exhorted in the holy scriptures to the pursuit of wisdom; than which nothing is more conducive to a pleasant, happy, and honourable life; nothing a greater preservative from vice; nothing more becoming or more necessary to those especially who have the administration of public affairs, and the government of empires. Learning and wisdom exalt the low, and give additional lustre to the honours of the great. *By wisdom kings reign, and princes decree justice.* Cease not then, O most Gracious King! to press the young nobility of your court to the eager pursuit of wisdom and learning in their youth, that they may attain to an honourable old age, and a blessed immortality. For my own part, I will never cease, according to my abilities, to sow the seeds of learning in the minds of your subjects in these parts; mindful of the saying of the wisest man, *In the morning sow thy seed, and in the evening with-hold not thine hand; for thou knowest not whether shall prosper, either this or that.* To do this hath been the most delightful employment of my whole life. In my youthful years, I sowed the seeds of learning in the flourishing seminaries of my native soil of Britain, and in my old age I am doing the same in France; praying to God, that they may spring up and flourish in both countries. I know also, O prince beloved of God, and praised by all good men! that you exert all your influence in promoting the interests of learning and religion; more noble in your actions than in your royal birth. May the Lord Jesus Christ preserve and prosper you in all your great designs, and at length bring you to the enjoyment of celestial glory." (p. 336, &c.)—The exclamation of our learned historian on this admirable letter, ought to be written on capitals of gold. "How few princes, cries he, enjoy the happiness of such a correspondence, or have the wisdom and virtue to encourage it?"

The fifth chapter of this volume contains the history of the arts, both necessary and ornamental. The necessary arts delineated in this chapter are such as are required for procuring food, as hunting, fishing, pasturage, husbandry, and gardening; for providing lodging, as architecture, masonry, glass-making, and the arts of working in wood and metals; for making garments, as the arts of spinning, weaving, dying, and embroidery; for defence against, and annoying of enemies, as the various arts of war and of fortifying, and attacking strong places. The state of all these arts is delineated in a more particular and satisfactory manner than could have been expected, from the few monuments of those times which are now remaining. The fine or ornamental arts, which are illustrated in this chapter, are those of sculpture, painting, poetry, and music, the two last of which appear to have been cultivated with much assiduity, and no contemptible success.

The history of commerce, shipping, and coin is the subject of the sixth chapter; a subject of infinite moment to a trading nation. Nor was there any part of this very valuable volume before us, that gave us greater pleasure in the perusal than the naval history of Alfred the great; but for this, we must refer our readers to the book itself, as it is much too long to be transcribed. The efforts of this admirable prince, to promote trade, to raise a naval power, and to make discoveries, both towards the north and south, are truly astonishing. The account which is given of the money and coins of the Anglo-Saxons in this chapter is at once clear, concise, and comprehensive; and the result of the whole is formed into the following table.

*Table of the names of the Anglo-Saxon denominations of money, and of real coins; with the weight of each of them in Troy grains, and value in the present money of Great Britain.*

| Names | Troy Grains | Present Value | | | |
|---|---|---|---|---|---|
| | | £. | s. | d. | q. |
| The pound.............. | 5400 | 2 | 16 | 3 | |
| The mark.............. | 3600 | 1 | 17 | 9 | |
| The mancus of gold....... | 56 | | 7 | 0 | 1 |
| The mancus of silver..... | 675 | | 7 | 0 | 1 |
| The ora................ | 450 | | 4 | 8 | 1 |
| The greater shilling....... | 112½ | | 1 | 2 | |
| The smaller shilling...... | 90 | | | 11 | 1 |
| The thrimsa............ | 67½ | | | 8 | 2 |
| The penny and sceata..... | 22½ | | | 2 | 3 |
| The halfling.............. | 11 | | | 1 | 1½ |
| The feorthling........... | 5½ | | | | 3 |
| The styca, a brass coin..... | | | | | 1½ |

The seventh and last chapter of this volume will afford singular satisfaction in the perusal, to a reader of taste and curiosity; but our limits will not now allow us so much as to name the many subjects which are introduced in delineating the manners, virtues, vices, remarkable customs, language, dress, diet, and diversions, of the people of Great Britain, and particularly of the Anglo-Saxons, in those remote ages. The following account of the extreme credulity of the Anglo-Saxons and Danes, may serve as a specimen.—"Both the Anglo-Saxons and Danes, and all the other nations of Europe in this dark period, were credulous to a degree that is quite astonishing. This is evident from every remaining monument of their history. What prodigious numbers of miracles do we meet with in every monkish chronicle; and how ridiculous are many of these miracles? The following one, which is related with much solemnity as a most unquestionable fact, by William of Malmsbury, the most sensible of our ancient historians, may serve as a specimen of these monkish miracles, though others still more ridiculous might be produced. This miracle Malmsbury relates in the following manner, in the very words, as he says, of one of the persons on whom it was wrought. "I Ethelbert, a sinner, will give a true relation of what happened to me on the day before Christmas, A.D. 1012, in a certain village where there was a church dedicated to St. Magnus the Martyr, that all men may know the danger of disobeying the commands of a priest. Fifteen young women, and eighteen young men, of which I was one, were dancing and singing in the church-yard, when one Robert, a priest, was performing mass in the church; who sent us a civil message, intreating us to desist from our diversion, because we disturbed his devotion by our noise. But we impiously disregarded his request; upon which the holy man, inflamed with anger, prayed to God and St. Magnus, that we might continue dancing and singing a whole year without intermission. His prayers were heard. A young man, the son of a priest, named John, took his sister, who was singing with us, by the hand, and her arm dropped from her body without one drop of blood following. But notwithstanding this disaster, she continued to dance and sing with us a whole year. During all that time we felt no inconveniency from rain, cold, heat, hunger, thirst, or weariness, and neither our shoes nor our clothes wore out. Whenever it began to rain, a magnificent house was erected over us by the power of the Almighty. By our continual dancing we wore the earth so much, that by degrees we sunk into it up to the knees, and at length up to the middle. When the year was ended, Bishop Hubert came to the place, dissolved the invisible ties by which our hands had been so long united, absolved us, and reconciled us to St. Magnus. The priest's daughter who had lost her arm, and two of the young women, died away immediately; but all the rest fell into a profound sleep, in which they continued three days and three nights; after which they arose, and went up and down the world, publishing this true and glorious miracle, and carrying the evidences of its truth along with them, in the continual shaking of their limbs."

The object of an antiquary has been commonly distinguished from that of an historian: For though the latter should enter into the province of the former, it is thought that it should only be *quanto basta,* that is, as far as is necessary and entertaining, without comprehending all the minute disquisitions, which give such supreme pleasure to the mere antiquary. Our learned and penetrating author has fully reconciled these two characters. His narration is as full as those remote times seem to demand; and at the same time, his inquiries of the antiquarian kind, which form four fifths of his work, omit nothing which can be an object, either of doubt or curiosity. The one as well as the other is delivered with great perspicuity and no less propriety, which are the true ornament of this kind of writing: All superfluous embellishments are avoided: And the reader will scarcely find in our language, except in the work of the *celebrated* Dr. Robertson, any performance that unites together so perfectly the great points of entertainment and instruction! It is happy for the inhabitants of this metropolis, which has naturally a great influence on the country, that the same persons, who can make such a figure in profane learning, are entrusted with the guidance of the people in their spiritual concerns, which are of such superior, and indeed of unspeakable importance! These illustrious examples, if any thing, must make the infidel abashed of his vain cavils, and put a stop to that torrent of vice, profaneness, and immorality, by which the age is so unhappily distinguished.

This City can justly boast of other signal Characters of the same kind; whom Learning and Piety, Taste and Devotion, Philosophy and Faith, joined to the severest Morals and most irreproachable Conduct, concur to embellish. One in particular, with the same hand, by which he turns over the sublime Pages of Homer and Virgil, Demosthenes and Cicero, is not ashamed to open with Reverence the sacred Volumes. And with the same Voice by which, from the Pulpit, he strikes Vice with Consternation, he deigns to dictate to his Pupils the most useful Lessons of Rhetoric, Poetry and polite Literature.

# OF THE POEMS OF OSSIAN

[*In 1760 James Macpherson (1736–1796) published in Edinburgh the* Fragments of Ancient Poetry, Collected in the Highlands of Scotland, and Translated from the Gaelic or Erse Language; *this he followed with* Fingal; an Ancient Epic Poem, in Six Books: Together with Several Other Poems, composed by Ossian, the Son of Fingal . . . *(1761), and* Temora; an Ancient Epic Poem, in Eight Books: Together with Several Other Poems, Composed by Ossian, the Son of Fingal . . . *(1763). Macpherson's claim was always that he was only a translator of these poems; that they had been composed fifteen or so centuries before by Ossian, a Gaelic Homer; and that the oral tradition that had maintained them was still very much alive. But almost from their very first appearance the poems were the subject of controversy—both with regard to authenticity as well as antiquity. In private, Hume was engaged in this controversy from the beginning. His belief in the authenticity and antiquity of the compositions underwent some variations, but was never, apparently, very strong. In any case, his final view and the reasons for it are cogently stated in the essay that follows, "Of the Poems of Ossian." This essay, probably written in the late spring of 1775, Hume did not publish; it is generally supposed that he suppressed it out of respect for his friend, the Rev. Hugh Blair, who was not only convinced of the poems' genuineness and great literary merit, but who had taken upon himself their public defense. The extent of Hume's interest in this affair and his attitude toward both Macpherson and the poems can be seen in the letter to the Rev. Hugh Blair printed below (p. 408). See also E. C. Mossner,* The Forgotten Hume, *pp. 82–102, and* The Life of David Hume, *pp. 414–420 (Bibliography, p. liv), for a more complete account of Hume and the Ossian controversy.*]

I THINK the fate of this production the most curious effect of prejudice, where superstition had no share, that ever was in the world. A tiresome, insipid performance; which, if it had been presented in its real form, as the work of a contemporary, an obscure Highlander, no man could ever have had the patience to have once perused, has, by passing for the poetry of a royal bard, who flourished fifteen centuries ago, been universally read, has been pretty generally admired, and has been translated, in prose and verse, into several languages of Europe. Even the style of the supposed English translation has been admired, though harsh and absurd in the highest degree; jumping perpetually from verse to prose, and from prose to verse; and running, most of it, in the light cadence and measure of Molly Mog.[1] Such is the Erse epic, which has been puffed with a zeal and enthusiasm that has drawn a ridicule on my countrymen.

But, to cut off at once the whole source of its reputation, I shall collect a few very obvious arguments against the notion of its great antiquity, with which so many people have been intoxicated, and which alone made it worthy of any attention.

(1.) The very manner in which it was presented to the public forms a strong presumption against its authenticity. The pretended translator goes on a mission to the Highlands to recover and collect a work, which, he affirmed, was dispersed, in fragments, among the natives. He returns, and gives a quarto

---

[1] ["Molly Mog, or: The Fair Maid of the Inn," by John Gay. The first eight lines are representative:

Says my uncle, I pray you discover
   What hath been the cause of your woes,
Why you pine, and you whine, like a lover?
   I have seen Molly Mog of the Rose.
O nephew! Your grief is but folly,
   In town you may find better prog;
Half a crown there will get you a Molly,
   A Molly much better than Mog.]

volume, and then another quarto, with the same unsupported assurance as if it were a translation of the Orlando Furioso, or Louisade,[2] or any poem the best known in Europe. It might have been expected, at least, that he would have told the public, and the subscribers to his mission, and the purchasers of his book, "This part I got from such a person, in such a place; that other part, from such another person. I was enabled to correct my first copy of such a passage by the recital of such another person; a fourth supplied such a defect in my first copy." By such a history of his gradual discoveries he would have given some face of probability to them. Any man of common sense, who was in earnest, must, in this case, have seen the peculiar necessity of that precaution: any man that had regard to his own character, would have anxiously followed that obvious and easy method. All the friends of the pretended translator exhorted and entreated him to give them and the public that satisfaction. No! those who could doubt his veracity were fools, whom it was not worth while to satisfy. The most incredible of all facts was to be taken on his word, whom nobody knew; and an experiment was to be made, I suppose in jest, how far the credulity of the public would give way to assurance and dogmatical affirmation.

(2.) But, to show the utter incredibility of the fact, let these following considerations be weighed, or, rather, simply reflected on; for it seems ridiculous to weigh them. Consider the size of these poems. What is given us is asserted to be only a part of a much greater collection; yet even these pieces amount to two quartos. And they were composed, you say, in the Highlands, about fifteen centuries ago; and have been faithfully transmitted, ever since, by oral tradition, through ages totally ignorant of letters, by the rudest, perhaps, of all the European nations; the most necessitous, the most turbulent, the most ferocious, and the most unsettled. Did ever any event happen that approached within a hundred degrees of this mighty wonder, even to the nations the most fortunate in their climate and situation? Can a ballad be shown that has passed, uncorrupted,

2 [Presumably the famous Portuguese epic *The Lusiads,* by Camoëns.]

by oral tradition, through three generations, among the Greeks, or Italians, or Phoenicians, or Egyptians, or even among the natives of such countries as Otaheite or Molacca, who seem exempted by nature from all attention but to amusement, to poetry, and music?

But the Celtic nations, it is said, had peculiar advantages for preserving their traditional poetry. The Irish, the Welsh, the Bretons, are all Celtic nations, much better entitled than the Highlanders, from their soil, and climate, and situation, to have leisure for these amusements. They, accordingly, present us not with complete epic and historical poems, (for they never had the assurance to go that length) but with very copious and circumstantial traditions, which are allowed, by all men of sense, to be scandalous and ridiculous impostures.

(3.) The style and genius of these pretended poems are another sufficient proof of the imposition. The Lapland and Runic odes, conveyed to us, besides their small compass, have a savage rudeness, and sometimes grandeur, suited to those ages. But this Erse poetry has an insipid correctness, and regularity, and uniformity, which betrays a man without genius, that has been acquainted with the productions of civilized nations, and had his imagination so limited to that tract, that it was impossible for him even to mimic the character which he pretended to assume.

The manners are still a more striking proof of their want of authenticity. We see nothing but the affected generosity and gallantry of chivalry, which are quite unknown, not only to all savage people, but to every nation not trained in these artificial modes of thinking. In Homer, for instance, and Virgil, and Ariosto, the heroes are represented as making a nocturnal incursion into the camp of the enemy. Homer and Virgil, who certainly were educated in much more civilized ages than those of Ossian, make no scruple of representing their heroes as committing undistinguished slaughter on the sleeping foe. But Orlando walks quietly through the camp of the Saracens, and scorns to kill even an infidel who cannot defend himself. Gaul and Oscar are knight-errants, still more romantic: they make a noise in the midst of the enemy's camp, that they may waken them, and thereby have a right to fight with them and to kill them. Nay, Fingal carries his ideas of chivalry still farther; much beyond what was ever dreamt of by Amadis de Gaul or Lancelot de Lake. When his territory is invaded, he scorns to repel the enemy with his whole force: he sends only an equal number against them, under an inferior captain: when these are repulsed, he sends a second detachment; and it is not till after a double defeat, that he deigns himself to descend from the hill, where he had remained, all the while, an idle spectator, and to attack the enemy. Fingal and Swaran combat each other all day, with the greatest fury. When darkness suspends the fight, they feast together with the greatest amity, and then renew the combat with the return of light. Are these the manners of barbarous nations, or even of people that have common sense? We may remark, that all this narrative is supposed to be given us by a contemporary poet. The facts, therefore, must be supposed entirely, or nearly, conformable to truth. The gallantry and extreme delicacy towards the women, which is found in these productions, is, if possible, still more contrary to the manners of barbarians. Among all rude nations, force and courage are the predominant virtues; and the inferiority of the females, in these particulars, renders them an object of contempt, not of deference and regard.

(4.) But I derive a new argument against the antiquity of these poems, from the general tenor of the narrative. Where manners are represented in them, probability, or even possibility, are totally disregarded: but in all other respects, the events are within the course of nature; no giants, no monsters, no magic, no incredible feats of strength or activity. Every transaction is conformable to familiar experience, and scarcely even deserves the name of wonderful. Did this ever happen in ancient and barbarous poetry? Why is this characteristic wanting, so essential to rude and ignorant ages? Ossian, you say, was singing the exploits of his contemporaries, and therefore could not falsify them in any great degree. But if this had been a restraint your pretended Ossian had never sung the exploits of his contemporaries; he had gone back a generation or two, which would have been sufficient to throw an entire obscurity on the events; and he would thereby have attained the marvellous, which is alone striking to barbarians. I desire it may be observed, that manners are the only circumstances which a rude people cannot falsify; because they have no notion of any manners beside their own: but it is easy for them to let loose their imagination, and violate the course of nature, in every other particular; and indeed they take no pleasure in any other kind of narrative. In Ossian, nature is violated, where alone she ought to have been preserved; is preserved where alone she ought to have been violated.

(5.) But there is another species of the marvellous, wanting in Ossian, which is inseparable from all nations, civilized as well as barbarous, but still more, if possible, from the barbarous, and that is religion; no religious sentiment in this Erse poetry. All those Celtic heroes are more complete atheists than ever were bred in the school of Epicurus. To account for this singularity, we are told that a few generations before Ossian, the people quarrelled with their Druidical priests, and having expelled them, never afterwards adopted any other species of religion. It is not quite unnatural, I own, for the people to quarrel with their priests,—as we did with ours at the Reformation; but we attached ourselves with fresh zeal to our new preachers and new system; and this passion increased in proportion to our hatred of the old. But I suppose the reason of this strange absurdity in our new Erse poetry, is, that the author, finding by the assumed age of his heores, that he must have given them the Druidical religion, and not trusting to his literature, (which seems indeed to be very slender) for making the representations consistent with antiquity, thought it safest to give them no religion at all; a circumstance so wonderfully unnatural, that it is sufficient alone, if men had eyes, to detect the imposition.

(6.) The state of the arts, as represented in those poems, is totally incompatible with the age assigned to them. We know, that the houses even of the Southern Britons, till conquered by the Romans, were nothing but huts erected in the woods; but a stately stone building is mentioned by Ossian, of which the walls remain, after it is consumed with fire. The melancholy circumstance of a fox is described, who looks out at the windows; an image, if I be not mistaken, borrowed from the Scriptures. The Caledonians, as well as the Irish, had no shipping but currachs, or wicker boats covered with hides: yet are they represented as passing, in great military expeditions, from the Hebrides to Denmark, Norway, and Sweden; a most glaring absurdity. They live entirely by hunting, yet muster armies, which make incursions to these countries as well as to Ireland: though it is certain from the experience of America, that the whole Highlands would scarce subsist a hundred persons by hunting. They are totally unacquainted with fishing; though that occupation first tempts all rude nations to venture on the sea. Ossian alludes to a wind or water-mill, a machine then unknown to the Greeks and Romans, according to the opinion of the best antiquaries. His barbarians, though ignorant of tillage, are well acquainted with the method of working all kinds of metals. The harp is the musical instrument of Ossian; but the bagpipe, from time immemorial, has been the instrument of the Highlanders. If ever the harp had been known among them, it never had given place to the other barbarous discord.

*Stridenti miserum stipula disperdere carmen.*[3]

(7.) All the historical facts of this poem are opposed by traditions, which, if all these tales be not equally contemptible, seem to merit much more attention. The Irish Scots are the undoubted ancestors of the present Highlanders, who are but a small colony of that ancient people. But the Irish traditions make Fingal, Ossian, Oscar, all Irishmen, and place them some centuries distant from the Erse heroes. They represent them as giants, and monsters, and enchanters, a sure mark of a considerable antiquity of these traditions. I ask the partisans of Erse poetry, since the names of these heroes have crept over to Ireland, and have become quite familiar to the natives of that

[3] ["To mangle a wretched tune on a grating straw" (Virgil, *Eclogues* III. 27).]

country, how it happens, that not a line of this poetry, in which they are all celebrated, which, it is pretended, alone preserves their memory with our Highlanders, and which is composed by one of these heroes themselves in the Irish language, ever found its way thither? The songs and traditions of the Senachies, the genuine poetry of the Irish, carry, in their rudeness and absurdity the inseparable attendants of barbarism, a very different aspect from the insipid correctness of Ossian; where the incidents, if you will pardon the antithesis, are the most unnatural, merely because they are natural. The same observation extends to the Welsh, another Celtic nation.

(8.) The fiction of these poems is, if possible, still more palpably detected, by the great numbers of other traditions, which, the author pretends, are still fresh in the Highlands, with regard to all the personages. The poems, composed in the age of Truthil and Cormac, ancestors of Ossian, are, he says, full of complaints against the roguery and tyranny of the Druids. He talks as familiarly of the poetry of that period as Lucian or Longinus would of the Greek poetry of the Socratic age. I suppose here is a new rich mine of poetry ready to break out upon us, if the author thinks it can turn to account. For probably he does not mind the danger of detection, which he has little reason to apprehend from his experience of the public credulity. But I shall venture to assert, without any reserve or further inquiry, that there is no Highlander who is not, in some degree, a man of letters, that ever so much as heard there was a Druid in the world. The margin of every page almost of this wonderful production is supported, as he pretends, by minute oral traditions with regard to the personages. To the poem of Dar-thula, there is prefixed a long account of the pedigree, marriages, and adventures of three brothers, Nathos, Althos, and Ardan, heroes that lived fifteen hundred years ago in Argyleshire, and whose memory, it seems, is still celebrated there, and in every part of the Highlands. How ridiculous to advance such a pretension to the learned, who know that there is no tradition of Alexander the great all over the East; that the Turks, who have heard of him from their communication with the Greeks, believe him

to have been the captain of Solomon's guard; that the Greek
and Roman story, the moment it departs from the historical
ages, becomes a heap of fiction and absurdity; that Cyrus himself, the conqueror of the East, became so much unknown,
even in little more than half a century, that Herodotus himself, born and bred in Asia, within the limits of the Persian
empire, could tell nothing of him, more than of Croesus, the
contemporary of Cyrus, and who reigned in the neighbourhood
of the historian, but the most ridiculous fables; and that the
grandfather of Hengist and Horsa, the first Saxon conquerors,
was conceived to be a divinity. I suppose it is sufficiently evident,
that without the help of books and history, the very name of
Julius Caesar would at present be totally unknown in Europe.
A gentleman, who travelled into Italy, told me, that in visiting
Frescati or Tusculum, his cicerone showed him the foundation
and ruins of Cicero's country house. He asked the fellow who
this Cicero might be, 'Un gradissimo gigante,' said he.

(9.) I ask, since the memory of Fingal and his ancestors and
descendants is still so fresh in the Highlands, how it happens,
that none of the compilers of the Scotch fabulous history ever
laid hold of them, and inserted them in the list of our ancient
monarchs, but we were obliged to have recourse to direct fiction
and lying to make out their genealogies? It is to be remarked,
that the Highlanders, who are now but an inferior part of the
nation, anciently composed the whole; so that no tradition of
theirs could be unknown to the court, the nobility, and the
whole kingdom. Where, then, have these wonderful traditions
skulked during so many centuries, that they have never come
to light till yesterday? And the very names of our ancient kings
are unknown; though it is pretended, that a very particular
narrative of their transactions was still preserved, and universally diffused among a numerous tribe, who are the original
stem of the nation. Father Innes, the only judicious writer that
ever touched our ancient history, finds in monastic records the
names, and little more than the names, of kings from Fergus,
whom we call Fergus the Second, who lived long after the supposed Fingal: and he thence begins the true history of the na-

tion. He had too good sense to give any attention to pretended traditions even of kings, much less would he have believed that the memory and adventures of every leader of banditti in every valley of the Highlands, could be circumstantially preserved by oral tradition through more than fifteen centuries.

(10.) I shall observe, that the character of the author, from all his publications, (for I shall mention nothing else,) gives us the greatest reason to suspect him of such a ludicrous imposition on the public. For to be sure it is only ludicrous; or at most a trial of wit, like that of the sophist, who gave us Phalaris' Epistles, or of him that counterfeited Cicero's Consolation, or supplied the fragments of Petronius. These literary amusements have been very common; and unless supported by too violent asseverations, or persisted in too long, never drew the opprobrious appellation of impostor on the author.

He writes an ancient history of Britain, which is plainly ludicrous. He gives us a long circumstantial history of the emigrations of the Belgae, Cimbri, and Sarmatae, so unsupported by any author of antiquity that nothing but a particular revelation could warrant it; and yet it is delivered with such seeming confidence, (for we must not think he was in earnest,) that the history of the Punic wars is not related with greater seriousness by Livy. He has even left palpable contradictions in his narrative, in order to try the faith of his reader. He tells us, for instance, that the present inhabitants of Germany have no more connexion with the Germans mentioned by Tacitus, than with the ancient inhabitants of Peloponnesus: the Saxons and Angles, in particular, were all Sarmatians, a quite different tribe from the Germans, in manners, laws, language, and customs. Yet a few pages after, when he pretends to deliver the origin of the Anglo-Saxon constitution, he professedly derives the whole account from Tacitus. All this was only an experiment to see how far the force of affirmation could impose on the credulity of the public: but it did not succeed; he was here in the open daylight of Greek and Roman erudition, not in the obscurity of his Erse poetry and traditions. Finding the style of his Ossian admired by some, he attempts a translation of Homer in the very same style. He begins and finishes, in six weeks, a work that was for ever to eclipse the translation of Pope, whom he does not even deign to mention in his preface; but this joke was still more unsuccessful: he made a shift, however, to bring the work to a second edition, where he says, that, notwithstanding all the envy of his malignant opponents, his name alone will preserve the work to a more equitable posterity!

In short, let him now take off the mask, and fairly and openly laugh at the credulity of the public, who could believe that long Erse epics had been secretly preserved in the Highlands of Scotland, from the age of Severus till his time.

The imposition is so gross, that he may well ask the world how they could ever possibly believe him to be in earnest?

But it may reasonably be expected that I should mention the external positive evidence, which is brought by Dr. Blair to support the authenticity of these poems. I own, that this evidence, considered in itself, is very respectable, and sufficient to support any fact, that both lies within the bounds of credibility, and has not become a matter of party. But will any man pretend to bring human testimony to prove, that above twenty thousand verses have been transmitted, by tradition and memory, during more than fifteen hundred years; that is, above fifty generations, according to the ordinary course of nature? verses, too, which have not, in their subject, any thing alluring or inviting to the people, no miracle, no wonders, no superstitions, no useful instruction; a people, too, who, during twelve centuries, at least, of that period, had no writing, no alphabet; and who, even in the other three centuries, made very little use of that imperfect alphabet for any purpose; a people who, from the miserable disadvantages of their soil and climate, were perpetually struggling with the greatest necessities of nature; who, from the imperfections of government, lived in a continual state of internal hostility; ever harassed with the incursions of neighbouring tribes, or meditating revenge and retaliation on their neighbours. Have such a people leisure to think of any poetry, except, perhaps, a miserable song or ballad, in praise of their own chieftain, or to the disparagement of his rivals?

I should be sorry to be suspected of saying any thing against the manners of the present Highlanders. I really believe that, besides their signal bravery, there is not any people in Europe, not even excepting the Swiss, who have more plain honesty and fidelity, are more capable of gratitude and attachment, than that race of men. Yet it was, no doubt, a great surprise to them to hear that, over and above their known good qualities, they were also possessed of an excellence which they never dreamt of, an elegant taste in poetry, and inherited from the most remote antiquity the finest compositions of that kind, far surpassing the popular traditional poems of any other language; no wonder they crowded to give testimony in favour of their authenticity. Most of them, no doubt, were sincere in the delusion; the same names that were to be found in their popular ballads were carefully preserved in the new publication; some incidents, too, were perhaps transferred from the one to the other; some sentiments also might be copied; and, on the whole, they were willing to believe, and still more willing to persuade others, that the whole was genuine. On such occasions, the greatest cloud of witnesses makes no manner of evidence. What Jansenist was there in Paris, which contains several thousands, that would not have given evidence for the miracles of Abbé Paris? The miracle is greater, but not the evidence, with regard to the authenticity of Ossian.

The late President Forbes was a great believer in the second sight; and I make no question but he could, on a month's warning, have overpowered you with evidence in its favour. But as finite added to finite never approaches a hair's breadth nearer to infinite; so a fact, incredible in itself, acquires not the smallest accession of probability by the accumulation of testimony.

The only real wonder in the whole affair is, that a person of so fine a taste as Dr. Blair, should be so great an admirer of these productions; and one of so clear and cool a judgment collect evidence of their authenticity.

# LETTERS

[*The very few letters reprinted here are meant to be samples of the many of Hume's letters that are concerned with various aspects of history. The first and fifth letters supplement, as noted, items reprinted above, whereas the second, third, and fourth letters reveal some of the issues in which Hume became involved as a result of the* History of England. *Noteworthy among these issues is one which has been given little notice in this volume, but which has been, nonetheless, widely discussed by scholars and readers of the* History—*the question of Hume's political bias. For decades, Hume's contention (in "My Own Life") that he had always revised the* History *to favor the Tory position was taken as the key to his opinion and intent, and he was invariably considered a Tory historian. In recent years, however, it has been seen that the question of Hume's and the* History's *politics is not as simple as this. Many of Hume's analyses and some of the revisions undeniably favor the Tory view, but there do not seem to be adequate grounds for inferring that Hume was of any strict party opinion. He tried rather, it appears, to be a critic of both parties. But, perhaps because of some Tory leanings, perhaps more because of his emphasis on the importance of custom in political matters, and because the Whigs in his day were the more powerful of the two parties (hence the most in need of checking), his work was more favorable to the Tories. A number of items relating to this problem are listed in the Bibliography.*

*The first and fifth letters are reproduced, by permission of the publisher, from J. Y. T. Greig,* The Letters of David Hume *(Oxford: Clarendon Press, 1932). The second letter is reproduced from "New Hume Letters to Lord Elibank, 1748–1776,"* Texas Studies in Literature and Language, *IV, 3, by permission of the co-editor, Ernest C. Mossner. The third and fourth letters are reproduced, by permission of the publisher, from* The New Letters of David Hume *(Oxford: Clarendon Press, 1954).*]

# Concerning "Of Miracles"

## To Rev. Hugh Blair, 1761[1] (*excerpt*, HL 188)

SIR,

I have perused the ingenious performance,[2] which you was so obliging as to put into my hands, with all the attention possible; tho not perhaps with all the seriousness and gravity which you have so frequently recommended to me. But the fault lies not in the piece, which is certainly very acute; but in the subject. I know you will say, it lies in neither, but in myself alone. If that be so, I am sorry to say that I believe it is incurable.

I could wish that your friend had not chosen to appear as a controversial writer, but had endeavoured to establish his principles in general, without any reference to a particular book or person; tho I own he does me a great deal of honour, in thinking that any thing I have wrote deserves his attention. For besides many inconveniences, which attend that kind of writing, I see it is almost impossible to preserve decency and good manners in it. This author, for instance, says sometimes obliging things of me much beyond what I can presume to deserve; and I thence conclude that in general he did not mean to insult me: yet I meet with some other passages more worthy of Warburton and his followers than of so ingenious an author.

But as I am not apt to lose my temper, and would still less incline to do so with a friend of yours, I shall calmly communicate to you some remarks on the argument, since you seem to desire it. I shall employ very few words; since a hint will suffice to a gentleman of this author's penetration.

*Sect. I.* I would desire the author to consider, whether the medium by which we reason concerning human testimony be different from that which leads us to draw any inferences con-

---

1 [The date is Greig's conjecture.]

2 [A manuscript of the *Dissertation on Miracles* by George Campbell (see Bibliography, p. liii).]

cerning other human actions; that is, our knowledge of human
nature from experience? Or why is it different? I suppose we
conclude an honest man will not lie to us, in the same manner
as we conclude that he will not cheat us. As to the youthful propensity to believe, which is corrected by experience; it seems
obvious, that children adopt blindfold all the opinions, principles, sentiments, and passions, of their elders, as well as credit
their testimony; nor is this more strange, than that a hammer
should make an impression on clay.

*Sect. II.* No man can have any other experience but his own.
The experience of others becomes his only by the credit which
he gives to their testimony; which proceeds from his own experience of human nature.

*Sect. III.* There is no contradiction in saying, that all the testimony which ever was really given for any miracle, or ever will
be given, is a subject of derision; and yet forming a fiction or
supposition of a testimony for a particular miracle, which
might not only merit attention, but amount to a full proof of it.
For instance, the absence of the sun during 48 hours; but reasonable men would only conclude from this fact, that the machine of the globe was disordered during the time.

Page 28. I find no difficulty to explain my meaning, and yet
shall not probably do it in any future edition. The proof against
a miracle, as it is founded on invariable experience, is of that
*species* or *kind* of proof, which is full and certain when taken
alone, because it implies no doubt, as is the case with all probabilities; but there are degrees of this species, and when a weaker
proof is opposed to a stronger, it is overcome.

Page 29. There is very little more delicacy in telling a man
he speaks nonsense by implication, than in saying so directly.

*Sect. IV.* Does a man of sense run after every silly tale of
witches or hobgoblins or fairies, and canvass particularly the
evidence? I never knew any one, that examined and deliberated
about nonsense who did not believe it before the end of his
inquiries.

*Sect. V.* I wonder the author does not perceive the reason why
Mr John Knox and Mr Alexander Henderson did not work as
many miracles as their brethren in other churches. Miracle-

working was a Popish trick, and discarded with the other parts
of that religion. Men must have new and opposite ways of establishing new and opposite follies. The same reason extends to
Mahomet. The Greek priests, who were in the neighbourhood
of Arabia, and many of them in it, were as great miracle-workers
as the Romish; and Mahomet would have been laughed at for
so stale and simple a device. To cast out devils, and cure the
blind, where every one almost can do as much, is not the way
to get any extraordinary ascendant over men. I never read of a
miracle in my life, that was not meant to establish some new
point of religion. There are no miracles wrought in Spain to
prove the Gospel, but St. Francis Xavier wrought a thousand
well attested ones for that purpose in the Indies. The miracles
in Spain, which are also fully and completely attested, are
wrought to prove the efficacy of a particular crucifix or relict,
which is always a new point, or, at least, not universally received.

*Sect. VI.* If a miracle proves a doctrine to be revealed from
God, and consequently true, a miracle can never be wrought
for a contrary doctrine. The facts are therefore as incompatible
as the doctrines.

I could wish your friend had not denominated me an infidel
writer, on account of ten or twelve pages which seem to him to
have that tendency: while I have wrote so many volumes on
history, literature, politics, trade, morals, which, in that particular at least, are entirely inoffensive. Is a man to be called a
drunkard, because he has been seen fuddled once in his life-
time?

# Concerning the *History of England*

To Patrick Murray, Lord Elibank,[3] June 8, 1756 *(excerpt)*

MY LORD

I regreated much yesterday, that I cou'd not attend your Lordship to the Country, when you did me the Honor to call on me. I am now engag'd in such a manner as will confine me during some time to the Town. My second Volume is printing at London[4]; & I receive a Sheet every Post and must return it corrected by the next Post. The Printer complains somewhat of this Delay, but wou'd be very much displeas'd, if I were not punctual.

Except this small Occupation, I am entirely idle at present; and Idleness, I own, has some Charms, after so much Application, as that which I subjected myself to. I am only sorry, that it should be attended with Confinement, and that I cannot enjoy it, as I coud wish, with Your Lordship. Some People tell me, that I will soon tire of doing nothing, & that I shoud think of some other Occupation. The History of the House of Tudor is recommended to me; and indeed I am fully convinc'd, that I shou'd have done much better had I wrote these Reigns previously to the History of the House of Stuart. For after having shown by a long Series of Facts the Nature of the English Government during that Period, it would have been easy to correct the Prejudices of those, who think that James the I & Charles the I ought to [be] judg'd by the same Standard which we woud apply to George the I & 2d. However, it has been remarked to me, that Tacitus went backwards, and wrote his Annals after his History; and that there is nothing absurd in a man's enlarging his Plan after this manner. I may hereafter think of this Scheme, if it happen, as is probable, that Idleness becomes a Burthen to me.

3 [1703–1778; a member of the Faculty of Advocates in Edinburgh, and a faithful Jacobite.]

4 [The volume, that is, dealing with the Commonwealth and the reigns of Charles II and James II.]

## To Gilbert Elliot of Minto,[5] March 12, 1763 (NHL 35)

DEAR SIR

In this new Edition,[6] I have corrected several Mistakes & Oversights, which had chiefly proceeded from the plaguy Prejudices of Whiggism, with which I was too much infected when I began this Work. I corrected some of these Mistakes in a former Edition; but being resolv'd to add to this Edition the Quotations & Authorities for the Reigns of James I & Charles I, I was oblig'd to run over again the most considerable Authors who had treated of these Reigns, and I happily discover'd some more Mistakes, which I have now corrected. As I began the History with these two Reigns, I now find that they, above all the rest, have been corrupted with Whig Rancour, and that I really deserv'd the Name of a party Writer, and boasted without any Foundation of my Impartiality: But if you now do me the Honour to give this part of my Work a second Perusal, I am perswaded, that you will no longer throw upon me this reproachful Epithet, and will acquit me of all Propensity to Whiggism. If you still continue to upbraid me, I shall be oblig'd to retaliate on you, and cry, *Whig, vous-même*.

In page 33, vol 5 you will find a full Justification of the Impositions laid on by James I, without Authority of Parliament; on p. 113, 114, 389, a justification of persecuting the Puritans; in p. 180 a justification of Charles I for levying Tonnage & Poundage with [without?] consent of parliament: In p. 100 I acquit James I of prevarication with which I had before rashly charged him. This last mistake, indeed was innocent, and I can easily account for it; I had read Buckingham's Narrative in Rushworth & Franklyn, the two opposite Collectors. I saw what I thought the same paper in the parliamentary History but I did not attend to a line at the bottom, in which it is said that the paper is taken from the Records more full than in the preceding Collection. When I read it lately, I found the Article here quoted.

[5] [1722–1777; a political figure of some importance and a close friend of Hume.]
[6] [The edition of 1762.]

So that this blunder proceeded not from any Spirit of Whiggery.

I now justify James II more explicitly in his Exercise of the dispensing Power, which was intimately interwove with Constitution & Monarchy—see vol 6 p. 393, 394, 395, 400. In volume 4 p. 322, 323, I mention a very remarkable Piece of Tyranny or of Exertion of arbitrary Power practised in that Period, and which came to my Knowledge since the first publication of that Volume.

There are many other Improvements & Alterations throughout the whole; and I am glad, that Millar has of himself made you an Offer of this Edition. Without flattering you, I must say, that there is no body, whom I more desire to see my Writings as correct as I can make them; and I was thinking to desire Mr Millar to make you this Offer.

To Catherine Macaulay, March 29, 1764 (*excerpt*, NHL 40)

MADAM,

The agreeable present[7] which you was so good as to make me, did not come to hand till a few days ago; it had been packed up with some of Lord Hertford's baggage, and was so long on the road: I should not otherwise have been so long wanting to express my thanks for the pleasure your performance has given me; and also for the obliging manner in which you mention me, even when you oppose my sentiments. I find, indeed, that you often do me the honor to keep me in your eye, during the course of your narration; and I flatter myself that we differ less in facts, than in our interpretation and construction of them. Perhaps also I have the misfortune to differ from you in some original principles, which it will not be easy to adjust between us. For as I look upon all kinds of subdivision of power, from the monarchy of France to the freest democracy of some Swiss

7 [This agreeable present" was a copy of the first volume of Catherine Macaulay's *History of England* (8 vols., 1763–1783). Her work is best classified as a Whig answer to Hume's *History*.]

Cantons, to be equally legal, if established by custom and authority; I cannot but think, that the mixed monarchy of England, such as it was left by Queen Elizabeth, was a lawful form of government, and carried obligations to obedience and allegiance; at least it must be acknowledged, that the princes and ministers who supported that form, tho' somewhat arbitrarily, could not incur much blame on that account; and that there is more reason to make an apology for their antagonists than for them. I grant, that the cause of liberty, which you, Madam, with the Pyms and Hampdens have adopted, is noble and generous; but most of the partisans of that cause, in the last century disgraced it, by their violence, and also by their cant, hypocrisy, and bigotry, which, more than the principles of civil liberty, seem to have been the motive of all their actions. Had those principles always appeared in the amiable light which they receive both from your person and writings, it would have been impossible to resist them; and however much inclined to indulgence towards the first James and Charles, I should have been the first to condemn those monarchs for not yielding to them.

# Concerning the Poems of Ossian

To Rev. Hugh Blair, September 15, 1763 (*excerpt*, HL 215)

DEAR SIR,

I live in a place where I have the pleasure of frequently hearing justice done to your Dissertation;[8] but never heard it mentioned in a company where some one person or other did not express his doubts with regard to the authenticity of the Poems, which are its subject; and I often hear them totally rejected with disdain and indignation, as a palpable and most impudent forgery. This opinion has indeed become very prevalent among

8 [Blair was author of the *Critical Dissertation on the Poems of Ossian,* (Edinburgh, 1763).]

the men of letters in London, and I can foresee, that in a few years the poems, if they continue to stand on their present footing, will be thrown aside, and will fall into final oblivion. It is in vain to say, that their beauty will support them, independent of their authenticity: No; that beauty is not so much to the general taste as to ensure you of this event; and if people be once disgusted with the idea of a forgery, they are thence apt to entertain a more disadvantageous notion of the excellency of the production itself. The absurd pride and caprice of Macpherson himself, who scorns, as he pretends, to satisfy any body, that doubts his veracity, has tended much to confirm this general scepticism: and I must own, for my own part, that, though I have had many particular reasons to believe these poems genuine, more than it is possible for any Englishman of letters to have, yet I am not entirely without my scruples on that head. You think that the internal proofs in favour of the poems are very convincing; so they are; but there are also internal reasons against them, particularly from the manners, notwithstanding all the art, with which you have endeavoured to throw a varnish on that circumstance: and the preservation of such long, and such connected poems by oral tradition alone, during a course of fourteen centuries, is so much out of the ordinary course of human affairs, that it requires the strongest reasons to make us believe it. My present purpose therefore is, to apply to you in the name of all the men of letters of this, and I may say of all other centuries, to establish this capital point, and to give us proof that these poems are, I do not say so ancient as the age of Severus, but that they were not forged within these five years by James Macpherson. These proofs must not be arguments, but testimonies. People's ears are fortified against the former; the latter may yet find their way, before the poems are consigned to total oblivion. Now the testimonies may, in my opinion, be of two kinds. Macpherson pretends that there is an ancient manuscript of part of Fingal in the family, I think, of Clanronald. Get that fact ascertained by more than one person of credit; let these persons be acquainted with the Galic; let them compare the original and the translation; and let them testify the fidelity of the latter.

But the chief point in which it will be necessary for you to exert yourself, will be to get positive testimony from many different hands, that such poems are vulgarly recited in the Highlands, and have there been long the entertainment of the people. This testimony must be as particular as it is positive: it will not be sufficient, that a Highland gentleman or clergyman say or write to you that he has heard such poems: nobody questions, that there are traditional poems in that part of the country where the names of Ossian and Fingal, and Oscar and Gaul, are mentioned in every stanza. The only doubt is whether these poems have any farther resemblance to the poems published by Macpherson. I was told by Burke, a very ingenious Irish gentleman, the author of a tract on the Sublime and Beautiful, that on the first publication of Macpherson's book, all the Irish cried out, "we know all these poems, we have always heard them from our infancy." But when he asked more particular questions, he could never learn, that any one had ever heard, or could repeat the original of any one paragraph of the pretended translation. This generality then, must be carefully guarded against, as being of no authority.

Your connexions among your brethren of the clergy, may here be of great use to you. You may easily learn the names of all ministers of that country, who understand the language of it. You may write to them, expressing the doubts that have arisen, and desiring them to send for such of the bards as remain, and make them rehearse their ancient poems. Let the clergymen have the translation in their hands, and let them write back to you, and inform you, that they heard such a one (naming him) living in such a place, rehearse the original of such a passage, from such a page to such a page of the English translation, which appeared exact and faithful. If you give to the public a sufficient number of such testimonies, you may prevail. But I venture to foretell to you, that nothing less will serve the purpose; nothing less will so much as command the attention of the public.

Becket tells me, that he is to give us a new edition of your Dissertation, accompanied with some remarks on Temora; here is a favourable opportunity for you to execute this purpose. You have a just and laudable zeal for the credit of these poems; they are, if genuine, one of the greatest curiosities in all respects, that ever was discovered in the commonwealth of letters; and the child is, in a manner, become yours by adoption, as Macpherson has totally abandoned all care of it. These motives call upon you to exert yourself; and I think it were suitable to your candour, and most satisfactory also to the reader, to publish all the answers to all the letters you write, even though some of these answers should make somewhat against your own opinion in this affair. We shall always be the more assured that no arguments are strained beyond their proper force, and no contrary arguments suppressed, where such an entire communication is made to us. Becket joins me heartily in this application, and he owns to me, that the believers in the authenticity of the poems diminish every day among the men of sense and reflection. Nothing less than what I propose, can throw the balance on the other side. I depart from hence in about three weeks, and should be glad to hear your resolution before that time.[9]

9 [Blair did agree to undertake the task Hume sets, as may be seen from Hume's letter to him on October 6, 1763 (HL 217).]

# APPENDIX A

## Posthumous Editions of *The History of England*

OVER THE course of several years, Professor T. E. Jessop has compiled a list of the posthumous editions and translations of Hume's *The History of England*. This list is not only intrinsically interesting; it also shows, in the most forcible way possible, just how popular the *History* was, and how influential it must have been. For this reason the editors asked Professor Jessop to allow them to include part of his list in this volume, and he has very graciously consented.

Included here are entries in three categories: (I) Posthumous Editions in Great Britain and Ireland; (II) Editions (all posthumous) in the United States; and (III) Abridged Editions in Great Britain, Ireland, and the United States. Two additional sections prepared by Professor Jessop, Continental Editions in English, and Translations, have been omitted. The latest version of these will be available in his forthcoming *Bibliography of David Hume and of Scottish Philosophy*, to be published by the International Archives of the History of Ideas.

In the following list, the number of separate imprints listed in each section is given in parentheses after the relevant heading; the total number of imprints here noted is more than 150, and the omitted lists bring the grand total to about 175. Professor Jessop has placed an asterisk after the date of items he has not personally seen, and square brackets around data not found imprinted in the editions.

### I. *Posthumous Editions in Great Britain and Ireland (76)*

1782, London (Cadell), 8 vols. 8vo; reprinted 1786, 1789, 1790–1791, 1791, 1792, 1793, 1796–1797.

1788, Dublin (White), 8 vols. 8vo.

1792, Edinburgh, 8 vols. 8vo.

[1793–1794], London (Cooke), 12 vols. 16mo.

1793–1795, London (Parsons), 22 vols., including continuations by Tobias Smollett and J. Barlow.

1796, Montrose, 5 vols. 8vo.

1802, London (Cadell & Davies), 8 vols. 8vo; reprinted 1807, 1812, 1818.

1803, London (Wallis), 10 vols. 8vo.

1803–1804, Edinburgh, 8 vols. small 8vo.

1803–1805*, London, 16 vols. 8vo, including Smollett.

1805, Edinburgh (Lockington, Allen & Co.), 8 vols. 8vo.

1806, London (Bowyer), 10 vols. folio.

1808–1810, London (Scholey), 10 vols. 8vo; reprinted 1818.

1810, Edinburgh (Hill & Doig), 8 vols. 8vo.

1810–1811, London, 10 vols. 12mo.

1811, London, 15 vols. 12mo, including Smollett.

1812*, London, 12 vols.

1814*, London, 20 vols., including Smollett.

1816, London, 8 vols. 8vo, bowdlerized "for family use" by the Rev. G. B. Mitchell.

1817, Edinburgh (Bell & Bradfute), 2 vols. large 8vo.

1818, Edinburgh (Laing, Guthrie, &c.), 16 vols. 8vo, including Smollett.

1819, London (Wilson), 10 vols. 12mo, including Smollett.

1820, London (Taylor, Christie, &c.,&c.), 2 vols. 8vo.

1822, London (Baynes, &c.), 8 vols. 8vo.

1823, London (Cadell, Davies, &c.,&c.), 8 vols. 8vo.

1823, London (Cowie), 2 vols. large 8vo.

1823, London (Kelly), 3 vols. 4to, including a continuation to George IV by Hewson Clark; reprinted [1832], 4 vols.

1823–1824*, London, 4 vols. 8vo, including Smollett.

1824, London, 16 vols. 12mo, including Smollett.

1824, London (Jones), 1 vol. large 8vo; reprinted 1825, 1828, 1832.

1824–1825, London (Dolby), 6 vols. 8vo.

1825, London (Cowie), 13 vols. 8vo, including Smollett.

1826, Oxford, 8 vols. 8vo; reprinted 1827*.

1828, London (Tegg), 20 vols. 12mo, including Smollett and continued by Jones.

1832*, London (Dinnis) and New York (Leavitt), 1 vol. large 8vo, including Smollett.

1833*, London (Robinson), 1 vol. 8 vo.

1834–1836, London (Valpy), 21 vols. small 8vo, including Smollett and continued by T. S. Hughes.

1835*, London, 4 vols. 12mo.

1836, London (Westley and Davies), 1 vol. 4to, including Smollett.

1838, London (Rickerby), 16 vols. 12mo, including Smollett and continued by Hy. Stebbing.

1848, London (Longman, &c.), 10 vols., including Smollett.

[1848], London (Virtue), 3 vols. 4to, including Smollett and continued by Ed. Farr; reprinted [1859], 4 vols., further continued by E. H. Nolan to the 23rd year of Victoria; reprinted [1873–1877], 4 vols., continued to the 36th year of Victoria.

1848*, London (Bohn), 1 vol. large 8vo, including Smollett; reprinted 1860.

[1848], London (Kelly), 3 vols., 4to, including Smollett and continued by J. C. Campbell.

1852–1854, London and New York (Tallis), 4 vols. 4to, including Smollett and continued by Thomas Gaspey.

1853, [London] (Valpy's Standard Cabinet Edition), 7 vols. small 8vo.

1854–1855, London (Bell), 18 vols. 8vo, including Smollett and continued by Hughes.

1864*, 8 vols. 8vo, including Smollett, large-type library edition.

1864, London (Longmans, Hatchard, &c.), 5 vols. 8vo.

[1868-1871], London (London Printing & Publishing Co.), 4 vols. large 8vo, including continuation by Wm. C. Stafford.

[1874], Glasgow (Semple), 3vols. 4to, including Smollett and continuation by Jones and Wilson to 1874.

## II. *Editions in the United States (48)*

[1875], London (Ward, Lock), 3 vols. 8vo; reprinted 1880 and 1894 (latter by Routledge).

[1882], London (Warne), 6 vols. 8vo; reprinted 1884.

1891, London (Ward, Lock), "The Imeprial History of England," with continuation by Wm. C. Stafford and Hy. W. Dulcken, 3 vols. 8vo.

1795–1796, Philadelphia (Campbell), 6 vols. large 8vo.

1810, Baltimore (Coale & Thomas), 7 vols. 8vo.

1810, Philadelphia (Leavis & Weaver), 7 vols. 8vo.

1810, New York (Inskeep & Bradford), 7 vols. 8vo.

1810*, Boston, 7 vols. 8vo.

1816, Albany (Packard), 4 vols. 8vo.

1821*, Philadelphia (Parker), 1 vol. 8vo.

1828, Philadelphia (Littell), 4 vols. 8vo.

1828, Philadelphia (Bennett & Walton), 4 vols. 8vo.

1832*, Philadelphia (M'Carty & Davis), 2 vols. 8vo; reprinted 1835, 1840, and 1859* (last by Lippincott).

1832*, New York (Leavitt) and London (Dinnis), 1 vol. large 8vo, including Smollett.

1849–1850, Boston (Phillips, Sampson), 6 vols. 8vo; reprinted 1852, 1854, 1854–1856.

1850, New York (Harper), 6 vols. 8vo; reprinted 1851–1852, 1852–1853, 1854*, 1864, 1879.

1852–1854, New York and London (Tallis), 4 vols. 4to, including Smollett and continued by Thomas Gaspey.

1854, Boston (Little, Brown & Co.), 6 vols. 8vo; reprinted 1863*, 1866, 1872*.

1856*, Philadelphia (Polock), 2 vols. large 8vo.

1860, Boston (Crosby, Nichols, Lee & Co.), 6 vols. 8vo; reprinted 1861.

1872*, New York (Putnam), 3 vols.

1873, Philadelphia (Claxton, Remsen & Haffelfinger), 6 vols. 12mo; reprinted 1876.

[*ca.* 1876], New York (Workington), 6 vols. 8vo; reprinted 1880.

[1885*], New York (Alden), 6 vols. 8vo.

1886*, Boston (Estes & Lauriat), 3 vols. 12mo; reprinted 1887* in 6 vols. 12mo.

[1887], New York (American News Co.), 6 vols. 12mo.

1895*, New York (Merril & Baker), 6 vols. 8vo.

### UNDATED EDITIONS NOT PRECISELY ASSIGNABLE

*ca.* 1875, Philadelphia (Porter & Coates), 5 vols. small 8vo; reprinted in 6 vols.

———, Philadelphia (H. T. Coates & Co.), 5 vols. 8vo.

*ca.* 1875*, Philadelphia (Polock), 4 vols. 8vo, including Smollett and continued by J. R. Miller.

*ca.* 1875*, Philadelphia (Lippincott), 6 vols. 8vo.

*ca.* 1875*, New York (Scribner), 3 vols. 12mo.

———, Boston (Aldine Publishing Co.), 6 vols. large 8vo.

———*, New York (Harper), 6 vols. 12mo.

## III. *Abridged Editions*

(a) American, abridged by John Robinson, 1 vol. 8vo.

1824, New York (Wilder & Campbell).

1826, New York ("for subscribers").

1826, Buffalo, New York.

1827*, Hartford (D. F. Robinson & Co.).

1826*, New York (Robinson, Pratt & Co.); reprinted 1827*, 1839, 1843*.

1828*, Exeter, New Hampshire (Williams), 2 vols.

(b) *The Student's Hume*

1858–1910, London (Methuen), 1 vol. 8vo, 22 printings (95,000 copies), last in 1910. Also issued in three parts, 1884–1894 (14,000 copies). The number of copies here given is less than the actual number printed because there is a gap in the publisher's records between 1873 and 1884.

1859, New York (Harper); reprinted 1860, 1863, 1864, 1865, 1868, 1869*, 1877, 1880*, 1892.

# APPENDIX B

## Index of Authors Cited by Hume
## in This Volume

FOR THE interest and convenience of the reader, we have here listed alphabetically, and amplified, the references made by Hume in the footnotes to the selections reprinted here. Two lists, one of classical, the other of medieval and modern authors, have been made. Where a work in a language other than English is cited, only an English title has been given if the work is readily available in translation. Where no English translation of the work is easily available, the original title is given, then followed in brackets, where it seems necessary, by the editors' translation of the title. In some cases we have not been able to identify the work cited, and in others it is not possible to determine which of an author's works is referred to. Where the latter is the case our conjecture is prefaced by "probably."

### I. *Classical Works*

Aeschines. *Orations.*
Appian. *Roman Civil Wars.*
Aristotle. *Politics.*
Arrian. *Expedition of Alexander.*
Athenaeus. *Banquet of the Learned.*
Caesar, Julius. *The Gallic War.*
Cato. *On the Countryside.*
Cicero. *Epistles.*
———. *Orations.*
Columella. *On the Countryside.*
Demosthenes. *Orations.*
Diodorus Siculus. *World History.*

Diogenes Laertius. *Lives.*

Dion Cassius. *Roman History.*

Dionysius of Halicarnassus. *Roman Antiquities.*

Herodian. *History of the Roman Empire.*

Herodotus. *History.*

Hirtius. *The Spanish Wars.*

Isocrates. *Areopagitica.*

Justin. *History.*

Juvenal. *Satires.*

Lampridius, Aelius. *Life of Heliogabalus.*

Livy. *Roman Histories.*

Lucian. *De mercede conductis potentium familiaribus.*

Lucretius. *Of the Nature of Things.*

Lysias. *Orations.*

Mela, Pomponius. *On Geography.*

Ovid. *Love Poems.*

Plato. *Apology.*

Plautus. *Stichus.*

Pliny the Elder. *Natural History.*

Plutarch. *Concerning Those Whose Punishment Is Delayed
     by the Deity.*

———. *Lives.*

———. *Moralia.*

———. *Symposium.*

Polybius. *History.*

Quintus Curtius Rufus. *History of Alexander.*

Seneca. *Letters on Morals.*

———. *Of Anger.*

———. *On Peace of the Soul.*

Sextus Empiricus. *Outlines of Pyrrhonism.*

Strabo. *Geography.*

Suetonius. *The Lives of the Caesars.*

Tacitus. *Annals.*

———. *Germany and Its Tribes.*

———. *The Histories.*

———. *The Life of Julius Agricola.*

Terence. *Phormio.*

Thucydides. *History of the Pelopennesian War.*

Varro. *Agricultural Topics.*

Xenophon. *Anabasis.*

——. *Memorabilia of Socrates.*

——. *The Polity of the Athenians.*

——. *Ways and Means.*

## II. *Medieval and Modern Works*

Anderson, James. *Collections Relating to the History of Mary Queen of Scotland.*

Bacon, Sir Francis. *Novum Organum.*

Bede. *The Ecclesiastical History of the English Nation.*

Blackstone, Sir William. *Commentaries on the Laws of England.*

Boderie, Antoine La Fèvre de la. *Ambassades . . . 1606 jusqu'en 1611 . . . [Dispatches . . . 1606 to 1611 . . .].*

Brussel, Nicolas. *Nouvel Examen de l'usage général des fiefs en France pendant le XIe, le XIIe, le XIIIe, et le XIVe siècle . . . [New Examination of Fiefs in France, 11th to 14th Centuries].*

Buchanan, George. *Rerum Scoticarum Historia [History of Scotland].*

Burnet, Gilbert. *Memoirs of . . . James and William, Dukes of Hamilton.*

Camden, William. *Annales rerum Anglicarum et Hibernicarum regnante Elizabetha [Annals of English and Irish Affairs in the Reign of Elizabeth].*

Cange, Charles du. *Glossarium mediae . . . latinitatis.*

Carte, Thomas. *Life of James, Duke of Ormonde.*

Coke, Sir Edward. *Institutes.*

Collier, Jeremy. *An Ecclesiastical History of Great Britain . . . to the End of the Reign of Charles II.*

Cotton, Bartholomew de. *Historia Anglicana [History of England].*

Crawford, David. *Memoirs of the Affairs of Scotland.*

Davies, Sir John. *The Question concerning Impositions, Tonnage, Poundage, Prizage, Customs, etc.*

Diaconus, Paulus. *History of the Lombards.*

D'Ewes, Sir Simonds. *Journals of all the Parliaments during the Reign of Queen Elizabeth,* ed. Paul Bowes.

Digby, Everard. *Papers.*

Digges, Sir Dudley. *The Compleat Ambassador.*

Dugdale, Sir William. *A Short View of the Late Troubles in England* . . . .

Fontenelle, Bernard le Bouvier de. *Histoire des Oracles.*

Fortescue, Sir John. *The Difference Between Absolute and Limited Monarchy.*

Franklyn or Frankland, Thomas. *The Annals of King James I and King Charles I.*

Fuller, Thomas. *The Church History of Britain.*

Gale, Thomas. *Historiae Anglicanae Scriptores Quinque ex vetustis Codicubus MSS.* [*Five Writings of English History from Ancient Manuscripts*].

Gildas. *The Fall of Britain.*

Goodall, Walter. *Examination of the Letters Said to be Written by Mary Queen of Scots to James, Earl of Bothwell.*

Grafton, Richard. *A Chronicle at large and meere Historye of the Affayres of Englande.*

Guthry, Henry. *Memoirs of Scottish Affairs, Civil and Ecclesiastical, from the year 1637 to the death of Charles I.*

Hall, Edward. *The Union of the Noble and Illustre Families of Lancastre and York.*

Haynes, Samuel. *Collection of State Papers relating to Affairs in the Reigns of Henry VIII, Edward VI, Mary, and Elizabeth, from 1542 to 1570. Transcribed from the Original Letters and other Authentick Memorials left by W. Cecil, Lord Burghley* . . . . These papers were continued to 1596 by William Murdin.

Hemmingford, Walter de. *Chronicle of English Affairs.*

Holinshed, Raphael. *Chronicles.*

Hyde, Edward, first Earl of Clarendon. *True Historical Narrative of the Rebellion and Civil Wars in England,* generally called the *History of the Rebellion.*

James I. *Collected Works,* ed. Bishop Montague.

Jebb, Samuel. *De Vita et rebus gestis Mariae Scotorum Reginae quae scriptis tradere auctores sedecim* [*Concerning the Life and Deeds of Mary Queen of Scots . . .*].

Johnston, Robert. *Historia rerum Brittanicarum . . . ab anno 1572 ad annum 1628* [*History of British Affairs . . . 1572 to 1628*].

Keith, Robert. *The History of the Affairs of the Church and State of Scotland from the beginning of the Reformation in the reign of King James V to the Retreat of Queen Mary into England Anno 1568.*

Kennet, White. *Compleat History of England.*

Leslie, John. *Negociations,* in Anderson, Vol. III.

Madox, Thomas. *The History and Antiquities of the Exchequer of the Kings of England.*

Malmesbury, William. *Deeds of the English Kings.*

May, Thomas. Probably his *History of the Parliament of England which began on 3 Nov. 1640, with a short and necessary view of some precedent years,* known as *History of the Long Parliament.*

Melville, Sir James. *Memoirs.*

Milton, John. *Prose Works,* ed. John Toland.

Monstrelet, Engrerrand de. *Chronique.*

Montesquieu, Charles Louis de Secondat, Baron de. *L'Esprit des Loix.*

———. *Lettres Persanes.*

Montgeron, Louis-Basile Carré de. *La Vérité des miracles opérés par l'intercession de M. de Paris.*

Nalson, John. *Impartial Collection of the Great Affairs of State . . . 1639 to the murder of King Charles I.*

Paris, Matthew. *Chronica Majora.*

Raleigh, Sir Walter. *History of the World.*

Rushworth, John. *Historical Collections.*

Rymer, Thomas. *Foedera.*

Sanderson, Sir William. *A Complete History of the Life and Reign of King Charles I.*

Spenser, Edmund. *A View of the State of Ireland.*

Spottswood, John. *History of the Church and State of Scotland from the Year of Our Lord 203 to the End of the Reign of King James VI, 1625.*

Stowe, John. Either his *Annals* or his *Chronicles of England.*

Swift, Jonathan. *Gulliver's Travels.*

Trivet, Nicolas. *Annales sex Regum Angliae* . . . [*Annals of Six English kings (1136–1307)* . . .].

Tytler, William. *Enquiry Historical and Critical into the Evidence against Mary Queen of Scots.*

Walker, Clement. *The History of Independency, with the Rise, Growth, and Practices of that Powerful and Restless Faction.*

Walsingham, Thomas. Probably his *Historia Anglicana.*

Warwick, Sir Philip. *Memoirs of the Reigne of King Charles I. . . .*

Wellwood, James. Probably his *Memoirs of the most Material Transactions in England for the last Hundred Years preceding the Revolution in 1688.*

Wentworth, Thomas, first Earl of Strafford. *Letters and Dispatches,* ed. William Knowler.

Whitlocke, Bulstrode. *Memorials of the English Affairs from the beginning of the Reign of Charles I to the happy Restoration of Charles II.*

Winwood, Sir Ralph. *Memorials of Affairs of State in the Reigns of Queen Elizabeth and King James I.*

Wood, Anthony à. *Athenae Oxoniensis.*

Wykes, Thomas de. *Chronicle* (in Thomas Gale, *Historiae Anglicanae.* . .).

### WORKS CITED BY TITLE WHOSE AUTHOR OR EDITOR HAVE NOT BEEN PRECISELY IDENTIFIED

*Cabala . . . Mysteries of State and Government; In Letters of Illustrious Persons and Great Ministers of State.* . . .

*Discourse of the Manner, etc.*

*History of the Gunpowder Treason* [perhaps the work of this title by J. Williams, Bishop of Chichester, which is to be found in *The Harleian Miscellany,* or that of the same title which is included in G. Smeeton's *Tracts*].

*Journals of the House of Commons* or *Journals of the House Lords.*

*The Parliamentary or Constitutional History of England,* by "Several Hands."

*State Trials.*

# INDEX *

* Proper names contained in Appendixes A and B have not been included in the Index.